MEMOIRS
OF A TIBETAN LAMA

LOBSANG GYATSO

translated and edited by GARETH SPARHAM

Snow Lion Publications
Ithaca, New York

Snow Lion Publications
P.O. Box 6483
Ithaca, New York 14851 USA
607-273-8519

ISBN 1-55939-097-2

Library of Congress Cataloging-in-Publication Data

Blo-bzaṅ-rgya-mtsho, Phu-khaṅ Dge-bśes
Memoirs of a Tibetan Lama / Lobsang Gyatso;
translated and edited by Gareth Sparham.
p.   cm.
ISBN 1-55939-097-2 (alk. paper)
1. Blo-bzaṅ-rgya-mtsho, Phu-khaṅ Dge-bśes. 2. Lamas--China--
Tibet--Biography. 3. Refugees, Religious--China--Tibet--Biography.
4. 'Bras-spuṅs (Monastery). 5. Institute of Buddhist Dialectics
(Dharmsāla, India). I. Sparham, Gareth. II. Title.
BQ942.L597A3 1998   294.3'923'092--dc21
[B] 98-25832 CIP

Printed in Canada on recycled paper.

TABLE OF CONTENTS

ACKNOWLEDGMENTS

This book would not have been written without the help of many people. At the Institute of Buddhist Dialectics, Lobsang Yeshey spent many long hours, both before and after his great uncle Lobsang Gyatso's murder, listening to tapes with me and explaining obscure references and incomprehensible words in the Kongjo-rawa dialect. The present Director, Geshey Damcho Gyaltsen, in his gentle and un-assuming manner kindly allowed a number of valuable pictures to leave the school's collection for reproduction and has offered every necessary support. I owe a particular debt of gratitude to the Assistant Director Kalsang Damdul who anticipated my every need and more, and extended to me a true hand of friendship during the difficult period after Genla's death. I would also like to thank the office staff at the Institute for stepping in to help solve computer and printer problems.

I would like to thank Snow Lion Publications for accepting this work for publication and for their generous editorial assistance. In particular I must acknowledge the contribution of Chris Hatchell, whose detailed editing has greatly improved this book.

Finally, I would like to thank the Dalai Lama for his quiet, moral support and Nga-hua Yeo for being a benefactor to me as a monk and giving me the time to complete this work.

INTRODUCTION

Memoirs of a Tibetan Lama, published here for the first time, is a Tibetan *namthar*—a life story as Buddhist teaching—written in the candid style of a tell-all autobiography by the famous Tibetan Buddhist teacher Lobsang Gyatso (1928-1997). Inevitably the life of Lobsang Gyatso will be seen through the lens of his death. He was born in Kham, eastern Tibet, about seventy years ago. Called Drang-te (Beggar's Rubbish) as a boy, Nag-po-pa (Fleabag) or Choo-churwa (after his village in Kham) by his classmates, and Gen-la (a mix of comrade and teacher) by his students and friends, he was killed in the Institute of Buddhist Dialectics in Dharamsala, India, next door to the Dalai Lama, in February 1997 along with two of his students.

Lobsang Gyatso (Ocean of Fine Thoughts, his monastic name) was recording these memoirs at the time of his death. A master raconteur with an eye for human foibles and a wicked sense of humor, he steps out of his remembrances as a roly-poly delinquent with a fierce sense of justice, a love of pork and beer, a dangerous temper, and a love of guns and knives. These memoirs take the reader up to Lobsang Gyatso's first years in India, ending in about 1963. Narrated in an unusually realistic style, his account of his early life as herder and *ben-chung* (young monk or lout) in the semi-nomadic community in eastern Tibet where he grew up, his journey to Lhasa, and his life as a monk in Drepung (at that time the largest monastery in the world) recreate what was special in old Tibet—the Shangrila of western imagination— but with an openness and realism that is sometimes disturbing. He describes a country and a people as they really were, and he describes himself honestly as an ordinary man, with all his failings, caught between the pull of the world and the tranquility of spiritual life.

Lobsang Gyatso left his homeland in Kham to study in central Tibet at about the age of seventeen, entering Phukhang house, in the Loseling section of Drepung Monastery in 1945. He was at first little more than a debt collector for the house guru, but finally was taken in hand by the saintly Gen Yaro who for seven years led him through the traditional monastic curriculum. He became well known in Drepung as a capable debater and he spent long periods, during study sessions, in the caves above Drepung in retreat. Later he would say that whatever personal and intellectual honesty he had stemmed from his spiritual training during this period. In 1954 Lobsang Gyatso became the Phukhang house guru and demonstrated a talent for administration and financial matters; in 1956 he became the house grainkeeper, a position he held until he fled as a refugee to India in 1959.

In 1974 the Dalai Lama and Lobsang Gyatso founded the Institute of Buddhist Dialectics in Dharamsala. After some difficult early years it established itself as one of the success stories of the Tibetan exile community. The founding of the Institute of Buddhist Dialectics is the work for which Lobsang Gyatso will be best remembered. Unencumbered by past history and unfettered by formal ties, it evolved under the guidance of Lobsang Gyatso into a diverse institution defined only by the wish to properly educate Tibetan youth in exile.

That Lobsang Gyatso was a deeply spiritual man is obvious from these memoirs. His descriptions of his Red Uncle (his first guru), and the gratitude he feels to Gen Yaro (the guru who began to develop his prodigious intellectual talents) evoke memories of famous gurus of the past. And his love for his home monastery Dondup-ling in Kham, and for Drepung Loseling in Lhasa, is unmistakable. But Lobsang Gyatso writes obliquely. He details his own shortcomings and sillinesses rather than openly describing the excellence of his gurus, and he is confident that his description of the grubbiness and even horrors in the monasteries will gently lead the reader to find for him or herself the noble sense of community that was there as well.

Of particular interest is Lobsang Gyatso's detailed description of the Tibetan economy before the Chinese occupation. His eyewitness account of Tibet's market-oriented economy, based on the monasteries as banks, will do much to put to rest once and for all the self-serving myth of Tibet as a feudal land where peasants toiled and the rich lived off the fruits of their labor.

Lobsang Gyatso's memoirs take their place alongside the other records of pre-1959 Tibetan society, the best known of which is the Dalai Lama's *My Land and My People.* But Lobsang Gyatso's memoirs are unique for a narrative style strongly influenced by realism, and for the perspective he brings to his description: that of an ordinary Tibetan. His willingness to embrace controversial issues head on and his tragic death at the hands of sectarian fanatics will ensure his memoirs a lasting place in Tibetan literature.

Lobsang Gyatso's memoirs are characterized by the same humor and fearlessness that he showed in his life. More than anything else, he valued authentic spiritual endeavor, free from hypocrisy and unfettered by mere conformity to rules and ritual, and he was supremely confident that what was authentically good in Tibet and Tibetans, embodied in the Dalai Lama, would prevail. His outspokenness and love of Buddhism and his country are summed up in his memorable critique of his fellow Tibetans: "too much faith in Buddhism and an inflated notion of their own country."

Memoirs of a Tibetan Lama, spoken in Tibetan into a tape-recorder over the last two and a half years of Lobsang Gyatso's life, are rendered here into English by his close friend and student Gareth Sparham.

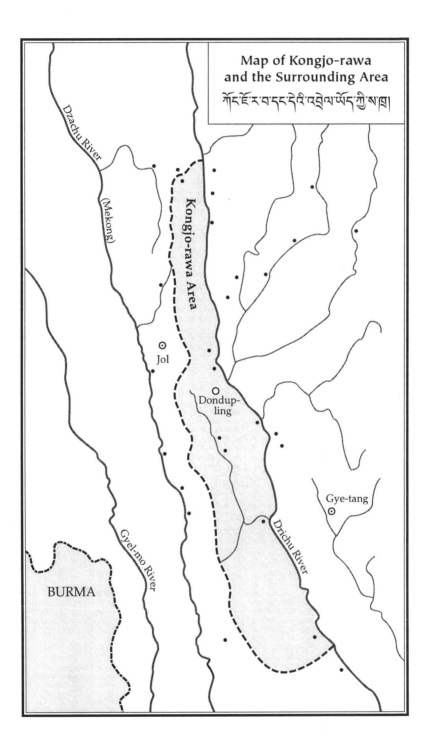

Map of Kongjo-rawa
and the Surrounding Area
ཀོང་ཇོ་ར་བ་དང་དེའི་འབྲེལ་ཡོད་ཀྱི་ས་ཁྲ།

Dzachu River

(Mekong)

Kongjo-rawa Area

Jol

Dondup-
ling

Gye-tang

Gyel-mo River

Drichu River

BURMA

1

FROM THE VALLEY
OF A TANG PRINCESS

My name is Lobsang Gyatso and there is nothing particularly spectacular in my life. What you have with me, I'm afraid, is just an ordinary fellow spinning around in the world of life and death. As of now I am in charge of the Institute of Buddhist Dialectics here in Dharamsala, North India, and I am head teacher here. There are things in my life which are worth recording, no doubt, even which need to be said, but with me everything that has happened is confined to this ordinary world.

I was born in the northern part of Kongjo-rawa, in the four rivers and six mountains region of Kham, not far from the Burmese and Chinese borders. One of the four great rivers of Kham is the Drichu (called the Yangtse when it gets to China), and Kongjo-rawa is the name for the western bank of this river for about two hundred kilometers or so just before it enters China. We share the lower part of Kongjo-rawa with the Jang people. They are not actually Tibetans, though they are Tibetan Buddhists like us, and they live in the southern part of the valley closer to the Chinese border. The valley cut by the Drichu is so deep along this part of its course that the other side of the river, a region called Zanam, is almost completely cut off from us.

Kongjo-rawa is never more than seventy kilometers wide even at its widest. For its entire length it is hemmed in at the back by high mountains, and only a few passes leave the region, heading over to the region of Jolwa. Like Kongjo-rawa, Jolwa also lies alongside a valley carved by one of the four great rivers—the Mekong. The northern parts of the two valleys of Jolwa and Kongjo-rawa are referred to together as Jol-kong-ra. Sometimes the region is called Jol-kong-gye, referring to Jolwa, northern Kongjo-rawa, and Gye-tang, which is to the south, on the other side of the Drichu River.

Kongjo means "Tang princess." The old kings of the Tang dynasty were known as *kongs*, and their daughters were called *kongjos*. During the seventh century, at the time when the great Tibetan king Songtsen Gampo was invading China, the Tang king had to give one of his daughters to Songtsen Gampo to keep him from taking over his capital. The *kongjo* whom the Tang king sent became one of Songtsen Gampo's wives, and was the one who brought the famous Buddha statue which is the central figure in the temple in Lhasa. Songtsen Gampo sent one of his ministers, a fellow called Gal-dung-dzin, to collect his *kongjo*. It would have been a long trip, and on the way back, I suppose the two fell for each other.

The *rawa* in "Kongjo-rawa" means "garden" or "pleasure stop." While journeying back to the king in central Tibet, the couple passed through my part of Kham, and stayed for a while having an affair. So that is how it got its name, "The Pleasure Garden of the Tang Princess." Some others explain that *kongjo* is actually the local pronunciation of *pongjo*, which means "the one who abandoned her child." While traveling from China to Tibet with Gal-dung-dzin, the princess got pregnant, and unable to find an easy place to cross the Yangtse, the caravan stopped in Kongjo-rawa, where the princess gave birth. Knowing that she could not take the baby with her to central Tibet, she put it in a basket fashioned of reeds and let it float back to China. Kongjo-rawa therefore got the name "The Pleasure Garden of the Princess Who Abandoned Her Baby."

I was born there in 1928, in a village named Choo-chur, which means "bitter water" in Tibetan. The bitter taste of the local water came from its high soda content. If you used this water when you cooked, you would not need to put any baking soda in your dumplings or bread to make them rise. The village was quite famous for this and people from neighboring villages would make a special trip to get some of our water to use for their cooking.

The village was inhabited by perhaps ten or twelve families when I was a boy, so it was not big by any standards. It is located at the base of a rock formation that looks like an elephant, and the great monastery of Dondup-ling was located high above. When you approached

Kongjo-rawa, the lie of the land made it look exactly like the monastery was on the crown of an elephant's head, with my village down and off a bit to the left, situated at the elephant's left foot.

My family name is Ye-drong Nya-me Nam-pa. We got the name because of where we lived in the village. The two houses of my extended family are about ten meters apart from each other, and are set off from the rest of the village a little way up the hill. *Ye-drong* means "the villagers a little way up." Because one of the houses was further up the hill than the other, it was known in the village as Nya-me Nam-pa, "one a bit higher up," while the lower one was known as Wo-ma Nam-pa. I belong to Ye-drong Nya-me Nam-pa; it is the house where I was born and where my family still lives.

My family was *sa-ma-drok*, which means "not farmers but not nomads." My family owned fields and had permanent houses, but our lives were also partially nomadic. In the late spring we would take our flocks up to the high grazing lands. Most families in Kongjo-rawa lived like this. In other villages, families made their living by doing business, using their animals to transport goods for trade. In others, families simply worked their fields. Sometimes, but not often, farmers engaged in trade by transporting goods on pack animals that belonged to others. Other families made their living by plying a trade; there were iron workers—lots of them—and there were the petty traders who lived by small business alone.

There was a lot of business in my region. The bigger traders would bring up tea, brown sugar, and soy noodles from China, sell what they could in Kongjo-rawa, and then take the rest up to central Tibet. They would then pick up the many different grades of woolen goods and take them on to India. In India they would buy cloth to sell on their return to central Tibet, and when they came back home to our region they would bring loads of woolen goods. Traders who did not have the capital to do such big business would just head down to the Chinese border and then come back and sell their wares in Jol, or in the regions just on the borders of Kongjo-rawa.

Our family had particularly good fruit trees, and we had fields sufficient for two households. So by local standards, though we are by no means considered very rich, we are certainly not considered poor. We are not a noble family by any stretch of the imagination and are not a family with a glorious history, but over the previous generation or two some of our family did make a name for themselves in the region with their magical powers, and got quite rich performing rituals to identify and punish thieves. My maternal grandfather knew how to make a figure of a person representing an unknown thief, and he would put a piece of thread around its neck. He would slowly tighten the thread until it started to cut into the figure, and then he would ask his client, "Do you want to kill him or not?" If the client said yes, he would tighten the thread so much that the head would be sliced off, and for sure somewhere in the district the thief would fall into a terrible sickness from which he or she would soon die. I grew up hearing a lot about my recent ancestors, these local religious figures who had been skilled in a mixture of Bön magic and Buddhist learning, and I knew there had been quite a rivalry between my ancestors and two other local magicians.

I was born into this family in 1928, probably in the tenth or eleventh Tibetan month, just before new year that falls in very early spring. My mother had nine children in all, but only three of us survived infancy. My older sister, Tsering Chern-dzom, was eight when I was born and my younger sister was born two years after me. My older sister was the local beauty and the villagers used to say that when the village went up to a festival all the men would go to see her, not the performance. She knew that everybody was looking at her too, and she always had a sense of pride. She had an incredibly sharp tongue and was not to be crossed lightly, but she was a fine worker and when the house and fields came into her charge she took over with confidence and skill.

I was very sickly when I was born and my mother used to tell me how close I had come to death when I was a week old, and then again a month after that. I was on the verge of certain death, she said, when they called in a Dondup-ling monk named Barshing Dulwa, a distant relative of ours who was famous throughout the district. He gave me a *chin-ten*, a blessed pill, and then I got well. My mother often said that had I not been given that pill I would have died for sure.

The fact that I was so sickly and that so many other children in my family had died in infancy explains the name I was given as a child. I was called Drang-te. *Drang* means "beggar" or "destitute," and *te* means "something that has been retrieved." So my name, a horrible one so that no malicious spirit or person would have any interest in me, meant something that a destitute had thrown out and that had then been picked up by someone else. That was the name they hung on me—"the fellow scavenged from the beggar's rubbish."

ALTHOUGH OUR FAMILY had a lot of animals and its holdings were quite large, it was in a state of decline. My father had a stroke early on, leaving him with one side of his body partly paralyzed, and he went around with one hand clutched tightly to his body. My mother, bless her, was a rather simple woman, and with no grown-up children to do the work the herds and fields had not been properly looked after. Eventually my sister took charge and later, when I was only about seven or eight, I was sent out to tend to the sheep and goats since there was nobody else available. I can hear them now, telling me carefully that there were eighteen sheep and goats, and telling me what I had to do to take care of them. They gave me good food and sweets to take with me and made me a new pair of slipper shoes.

Since I was so young I could not go off to tend the animals on my own, so I was teamed up with a neighbor's slightly older son who was looking after a large flock. Although sometimes he was friendly to me, sometimes he was very nasty and would make me feel stupid, so I gradually came to hate him. My family would give him treats too, but he would lie to my mother and she believed everything he said. One time he took my new shoes, which I had taken off and laid aside while I was running in the fields. He insisted that I had lost them, and I did not see them for weeks until one day he turned up wearing them. Of course, I could not say anything to him because he was bigger than me and he was in charge. If I had told my parents they would not have believed me, and I would have just come in for a scolding, but I thought that one day when I grew up I would teach him a lesson. I carried that grudge around with me for a long time even though I had to go out herding with him nearly every day.

I remember one time when the two of us were out with our flocks; we were close to a beautiful retreat house built nearby the home of the village headman. It was a very peaceful place that had been made for a member of the family who had been to central Tibet and become a geshey. There were fruit trees nearby and we were sitting underneath them, helping ourselves to the villager's apricots and peaches without a care in the world, blissfully unaware that our flocks had all got into the neighbor's field, which was just about ready for harvest. Suddenly a tall monk who was the caretaker of the retreat house came running across the adjacent field in a towering rage, driving our goats and sheep in front of him. We ran off as fast as we could, both heading along one of the level paths away from the retreat house. As he began to gain on us we split up, my companion heading up the hill and me running down as fast as I could. The monk at first came after me and came within an inch of catching me, but my companion tripped on a thorn bush and the monk went after him. He caught up with him and beat the daylight out of him.

I kept on running and crossed a small stream and hid under a thorn bush. After a time I could hear the sound of footsteps; I peered out from under the bush and saw the tall monk start off in the general direction of my house. I started to worry that the monk would tell my family and that I would get a beating from him and from my family too, so I leapt up and ran home as fast as I could without returning to the goats and sheep. When I arrived and found that the monk had not been there, I decided I had better make up a good lie to explain why I was home so early in the afternoon—it could not have been much more than two or three o'clock. My sister with the sharp tongue was very hard to fool, but my mother believed me right away when I said I felt terrible and that I had started to vomit. She was very gentle with me and said to the others that I was very sick. Inside I was terrified of being found out, but my mother made me the object of her attention and bundled me up in bed. She even brought me a special rice porridge.

Towards dark I said that I was feeling better and that I would go out to see about the flock. I had gone a short way when I met Namgyal, my companion, coming home alone with the animals. I could see he was in a foul temper and he asked me where I had gone. "What could I do?" I said. "The monk was going to beat me so I ran home." When I asked him how he had fared he said he had been beaten to a pulp. The monk had taken a stick and beaten him so hard that there were black and blue marks all over him, which he showed to me. He shoved me about a bit, but that was one occasion when I came off better than him.

THE TRUTH IS that Namgyal was not really a very good fellow. One time while we were playing he picked up some fresh dung on the end of a stick and came running after me, trying to smear me with it. I ran off as fast as I could and he came chasing after me. I went off quite a long distance to escape from him, and when I got back to where we had left our food for the day he said that the crows had taken all mine, even though it was obvious that he had eaten it.

I had to go out with Namgyal until I was nearly eleven. Then as I gradually got older we started to go out separately. One day I had taken the animals out by myself and had gone quite a distance to a place close to a cliff face. I was playing there by myself, letting the flocks graze, when suddenly out of nowhere a single big boulder came crashing down and landed just a short way off from me. There was nobody about and nothing further up the cliff. It was as if it had just fallen straight out of the sky. I felt scared and immediately drove the sheep and goats further down the mountain. Later I met up with a local woodcutter who warned me not to go near the cliff because a leopard had just given birth to a litter and was keeping them there. I kept thinking about that big boulder that had fallen from nowhere. If it had not fallen to scare me I wouldn't have known there was a danger and would have just kept on playing—the leopard would have killed me for sure. I felt certain that a god or goddess had been looking down on me and had protected me. A few days later I went over near the cliff with some friends and we could see the leopard with her kittens, just as the woodsman had said.

I remember another day when I was out by myself with the flocks. I had taken them up behind the village along a stream that ran through a dense piece of forest. Suddenly I saw a man with a huge stomach— it looked like he had a cow's stomach, really. The rest of him was as thin as a stick man sketched out of charcoal. I ran off to call another boy who was looking after his herd close by and told him what I had seen. We both ran back to the spot where I had seen the strange apparition, but there was nothing there. I felt so strange—I knew that I had seen something, but now I was there with my friend and there was nothing there at all.

When I was about the same age I had become friends with one of the yak and dzomo herders in the village. He was a fellow with a limp who had taken a liking to me and sometimes gave me treats: fruit or pieces of meat or little pieces of brown sugar. One time he told me that I should keep my ears open and come immediately if I heard him clap his hands. The next day when I took the flocks out, quite early on I heard him clapping so I went down with another village boy to see what was going on.

When we arrived, we found the herder getting ready to force-feed his cattle to strengthen them before taking them to the spring feeding grounds. The cattle in our parts get very emaciated during the long winter months, so in the spring the herders feed them pork to strengthen them. It works very well—you mix the meat, mainly the fat, together with grain or ground barley and you open their mouths and push it in. The cattle quickly regain their strength, and then when you take them up to graze they do very well.

This herder was in charge of all the cattle belonging to one of the main administrators of the monastery, so to feed them all he had to cook up a great pile of pork. He had stolen quite a bit of pork in addition to what was allotted for the cattle, and though some of it was a little old, some of it was still very tasty. As he cooked, he would give us some tasty bits, eat some himself, talk about this and that, and then go back to work again. There were three or four of us there and we spent the best part of the day enjoying ourselves, totally unconcerned with the fact that our untended flocks were wandering far afield.

By the end of the day there was only a kilo or so of the pork left. When I finally went out to see what had happened to the animals, I saw the whole flock running in a panic out of the woods and down the side of the hill. When I counted them there were three missing, but what could I do? Nothing but tell a lie, right? I decided it would have to be a good one to conceal a whole day spent eating pork, especially since I had not touched any of the bread given to me for my lunch. "I fell terribly sick," I said as I came lurching in, and my mother immediately began to worry about me. Mothers are like that, are they not? They have such a feeling for their kids that they always take their side. "But why didn't you come home immediately if you were so sick?" she asked. To cover my tracks I said I was so sick that I didn't feel I could make it home. My mother tucked me up in bed, brought me hot water and told me not to worry. But of course I was worrying inside because I knew that three of the flock were missing. To make matters worse, my sister and her husband were getting ready to go out searching for the missing sheep and I said that I had taken the flock in the opposite direction to the one I had come from so that they would not meet up with the herder and find out what had really happened. They went out in the wrong direction hunting high and low for the missing animals, but of course they came back much later without having found even a trace of them.

A few days after that, the remains of the three carcasses turned up in the forest. There were just some traces of the hair and hide remaining; a leopard had eaten all the rest of them up. After a month or so the family heard the whole story of the pork-eating incident, which was making the rounds in the village. Everybody was laughing about it, and by the time my family heard about it, the time for a beating was long past. As they discussed the incident they were alternatively stern and joking, and my sister asked me why I had not at least been truthful about the direction I had taken the flocks—they might at least have

been able to salvage some of the carcasses. I told her straight. "Sister,"
I said, "you are always on my case and you scold me for the smallest
mistake. If I had told you honestly that three of the flock had been
eaten by a leopard while I was enjoying myself eating pork, you would
have eaten *me* alive on the spot." Everyone had a laugh at that and my
sister just had to let it pass because she knew what I said was true.
Dear old mother, she looked at me shaking her head. "You should not
lie, you know that," she said. "It was wrong to tell a lie, you naughty
boy." And that is how the whole incident passed off, turning into an
often repeated family joke. The villagers enjoyed talking about the
incident too. If truth be told, I was a naughty fellow and was known
for it. Often when people met me they would say, "You are the young
fellow who spent the whole day pigging out on pork instead of following your flock, aren't you?" Then they would give me a slap on
the back and go off chuckling.

THERE WERE A LOT of wild animals and birds in our region. There were
flocks of two or three hundred blackbirds, and you could see hundreds of the white stork with red legs that we called the "whitebird."
In the winter when the deep snow fell on the high regions the
whitebirds would descend into the valleys to feed. In the evenings
there would sometimes be so many of them that they would cover the
fields in a white blanket, just like the snow in the higher regions covered the mountain tops. Nobody would ever lift a finger to hurt them.
In summer, the birds would disappear up into the high regions and
you would not see them again until next winter. It was the same with
the wild animals: they would come down into the fields when the
snows were heavy in the high regions, but when the snows melted
they would disappear again into the woods.

Although there was so much wildlife, none of those who lived in
the valley were supposed to hunt, and by and large none did. It was
considered low. People from outside the valley would come in to hunt,
but if you caught one of these poachers you would immediately confiscate everything he had and send him away. On the other hand, wood
was not held in any special respect. There was so much of it and it was
only used for cooking and house-building, so there was not really any
need to have special customs to protect it. After all, there was no lum-
ber industry to talk of, nobody was cutting down the trees and selling
them, so whoever needed wood from the forests would just take what
they needed. There was one forest though, on one mountain which

was sacred, and cutting trees there was not allowed. Still, there was a carelessness even then about the trees and forests—even back then our people were at fault in the way we went up and indiscriminately cut any trees we wanted without any thought for their place in the environment. We thought clearly about the animals and birds, protecting them quite well, but we didn't think much about the trees.

Though no one hunted, the villagers were happy if someone was able to kill a marauding leopard or wolf. These animals went after the flocks, so if someone killed one it would be considered excellent. I remember there were some devious beggars in our parts who would get hold of a leopard pelt and go through the villages begging. They would pretend that they had killed the animal, thereby protecting the flocks of the villagers, and would ask for bounty money from each villager. We called this *zig-long*, which means "leopard-begging."

IN OUR PART OF THE WORLD, it was the custom to use some of the local land as common property. Families who had no fields of their own could make their entire living on the common lands by grazing livestock, sheep, and goats. At festival time, when each family gave a part of their harvest for the rituals and celebrations, the families who used the common lands would pay the community back by contributing an extra share of their harvest. Families who had their own fields would give some of their harvest, but it would only be a little bit. Orchard owners would be expected to give some of their fruit, but since there were no orchards on common lands, the amount of fruit at the festivals was less than the amount of the other offerings. This system, called *sa-bab-kyi-thun-kyen* (requirements in accord with what is taken from the land), was a kind of land tax, though not what one thinks of as land tax nowadays.

There was a natural order to things. Three families were responsible for collecting this tax, and every three years the responsibility would pass on to other families, who would take up the work without question. The amount that each person gave to the communal pot was always offered with happiness; no one felt, "This is a tax that I have to give though I do not want to give it." When the monastery had to raise materials to carry out rituals that ensured the well-being of the region, the same sort of procedure was followed, but again there was no feeling on the part of the villagers that it was a tax. It was an offering to the monastery by those who owned fields and livestock, and the herders, field owners and orchard owners each contributed their share.

LIVING AT HOME WITH US when I was still a little boy was my maternal grandfather, who we called Anyi. He was a very old man and had suffered a series of strokes that had left him more and more paralyzed. He lived until he was about eighty-two, I think, and for the last year of his life he could not even get up. But boy could that old man eat! Whatever you served him, he would have it down immediately and he was never sick. He was almost blind, so he would just lie there, but he knew exactly what was going on, and took a very active interest in things. He had a soft spot for me and was always saying, "Come over by me," or asking where I was, or what I was doing.

One day, I was already a monk by then, my grandfather called us three children together—my elder sister Tsering, me, and my younger sister Bhuti. He had us sit down and began to talk seriously to us. Now, my uncle, which is to say his son, was an important figure in our local monastery, Dondup-ling. "He is well off," Anyi said about my uncle, "so we do not need to consider him here. When I die, he will take care of you and be in charge of you." He then turned to my sister and said, "The house and the authority over the house and what is in it are all in your hands, Tsering Chern-dzom, and I want you to remember that if you put yourself to the task you will be successful at it. It is me who set you up here, set the whole thing right for you." He always had a lot to say about that and never let people forget it. Then he said to me that as a monk I had a responsibility to go up to the monastery in Lhasa, which was a very expensive proposition. Therefore he said he was going to give me most of his belongings as an inheritance, in order to be able to help meet some of those expenses. When he was younger he had four very good dzomos and a bull that went with them, and he ran off each of their names for me there and then. They were no doubt excellent in their day but of course they had died long before, and since he had his strokes he had not had any cattle. Very warmly he said to me, "I want you to have those five animals—I want you to take care of them and then when you are ready to go up to Lhasa I want you to sell them and use the money to help to pay your way. That is your inheritance, my boy." He also gave me a big walnut tree that belonged to him. "You can either use the walnuts for food or sell them each year," he said, "but I am giving you the tree as well."

Old folks, when they are very old, seem to see more and more clearly those things that happened when they were young, so here he was giving away to me as my inheritance things that were nowhere except in his mind. And there I was saying thank you, and my sisters knowing what was going on. Both of them were nearly splitting apart trying to contain themselves. He was very warm and kind about it: "This, my boy, is your inheritance—those four dzomos and that bull!" And there I was saying "Thank you grandpa, thank you," knowing I was not getting a thing. "Be very careful with those dzomos, my boy. They will fetch you a good price when you sell them and it will help you when you go up to Lhasa." I can hear him now, and my older sister enjoying every minute of it. As for my younger sister, he said to her that he would advise her not to marry out into another family, that she would be better off to stay at home. He said that he was giving her a field as her inheritance; I think there was maybe another walnut tree in it for her too, if I remember rightly—I am a bit unclear now because it was a long time ago.

When he was finished what could we do except say, "Thank you grandpa, we will do just as you have said." There was nothing else to be said, right? When we went outside my sister was enjoying herself as much as I have seen her saying, "Now you take good care of those dzomos, you hear me, that is your inheritance. You be sure to milk them well and keep them well fed now, you hear me?" And there I was, with nothing to show for the experience except the cows of his youth that he loved so much in his mind.

THE DIFFERENT REGIONS on the Sino-Tibetan border were given a considerable amount of autonomy, a policy that can be traced back to the time of the Tibetan dharma-king Ti-re-pa-chen. He devised a system of regional autonomy for Gye-tang, Jolwa, and Kongjo-rawa, allowing them to mobilize their defenses immediately if there were any encroachments on the borders of the Tibetan kingdom. The protection of the borders of Tibet, therefore, was a particular duty he laid on these regions. If the border regions were unable to deal with a threat they were expected to inform the central Tibetan dharma-king in Lhasa, who would then respond by sending reinforcements. I cannot say that this description is based in actual historical fact, but I do know that this was what was said about the origins of our form of highly autonomous administration. What it led to in practice was a number of small principalities, almost little kingdoms. We were grouped under the central Tibetan authority, but we had great autonomy. It was a state of affairs that continued until the early part of the present century when the power of China, for the first time, became too strong for the Tibetans to stand, and we began to have to bow in the direction of their wishes. Until that time, our laws were local laws that were administered by locally originating bodies of authority. After our defeat by the Chinese, we had to pay a war indemnity which continued down to my own days.

In 1909, when the Chinese first started coming in, they set up a settlement of about a hundred soldiers in the center of the Kongjo-rawa region. They were going and coming every day, bringing in all sorts of things. There was much talk about the soldiers, and fearing their intentions, an armed party from the monastery wiped out the lot of them, barring two who were able to get back to China and report what had happened. You can imagine the size of the force they sent to avenge the atrocity. All the monks ran away into the hills and the Chinese were about to raze the monastery, insisting that the monks who had done the killing be handed over to them. Anyi, my maternal grandfather, was an important intermediary in this dispute, and had a Chinese incense burner that he had been given as a gift by the general who led the forces that finally subdued our district.

A representative left by the Chinese occupying authorities became the most powerful figure in the region. He had the final say in a lot of matters, and made an administrative base in Zhayi, a pretty little place about three hours' walk away from Choo-chur. When there was a meeting of the different people of the district he used to call on my grandfather, who served him as a sort of minister. He had quite a high status from this.

My maternal grandfather was an unusual man. He was not from our part of Tibet, but from a place some way off. He came from a large extended family but due to some circumstance or other he had killed a man, or was involved with someone else who had killed someone. He had to flee his home district, and he sought refuge with Tra-tang Rinpoche, an incarnate lama of Dondup-ling. Tra-tang Rinpoche sent him into our family as a *ma-pa*, a husband for a woman who is in charge of the family's property. At that point our family was quite wealthy. With him also married into it, smart as he was and always finding occasions to succeed, the family became quite rich and made a name for itself.

My grandfather was truly an intelligent man of the world. Our traditional chief or head villager would often consult him about the best course of action in some situation or other that had arisen. In general our chief was held in very great esteem. He represented the interests of the region and was expected to take care of negotiations concerning the law. If in the course of such consideration a difficult issue in law came up he would not make a decision himself but would customarily call on the elders of the village and discuss the matter with them. Since this was the way administration of the region was carried on, there was little strife; everything was transparent and everyone could see that what was being carried on was in the common interest.

My grandfather was an extremely forthright man who always spoke his mind. He eventually became a secretary to our chief, so people who wanted disputes settled had to approach him first to arrange the appointment. He no doubt took a hefty fee to arrange appointments for the more wealthy, but they say he went out of his way to help the less fortunate for little or no personal benefit. There are a lot of stories about Anyi, some of them quite funny. Once there was a poor family in our village and Anyi went up to their house and gave the parents the advice not to let the kids have any soup. We Tibetans have all sorts of soup, sometimes with noodles, sometimes with different grains. In our part of the world we had a corn soup which was very tasty. "Don't let your kids near it," Anyi told them. "It makes their stomachs expand—they will get pot bellies, and then they will get bigger and bigger appetites and you will go destitute trying to feed them." He had all sorts of unusual ideas.

As he got very old and his death was obviously approaching, he used to tell us that there would be no need to do any funeral rituals at Dondup-ling after he died because he had already taken care of them himself! He said he had made three or four very large offerings to all the monks, so certainly there was no need for any more rituals than that. He said that when he died we should simply burn him. "I have already made all the offerings that people have to make when somebody dies. Just take care of my things," he said, "they are no longer a concern of mine. I have had my funeral and am ready and prepared."

Anyi died at the age of eighty-two. One day he sent a message to me to come down from the grazing lands. It was after the first harvest of the year, when we had already put the second crop in the ground. I went to be with him, and knew he must have been aware of his imminent death. He told me to go out and gather some early yellow apricots, which grew in abundance down a ways from the house. They were all ripe. I picked some and brought them back for my grandfather. Then he said to me that everything at home was fine, that there was nothing further to do, and that I should return to the grazing lands. He told me to be sure to come back to him three days later, and to be sure to arrive before lunch. He stressed this and I said that I would come. He was preparing for his death.

I headed down the mountain three days later as he had told me to, intending to get there before lunch. But I was still a young boy, remember, and I caught sight of a big hornets' nest with all of the hornets streaming in and out of it. Of course I stopped to watch, and it was not long before I was throwing stones at it and seeing if any of them would come flying after me to attack me. If they did, and bit you, it felt like you had been run through by a spear. So much time passed like that that I was late arriving down at the house.

My grandfather had sent up a message to his beloved son, my Red Uncle, and had asked him to come down from the monastery. In my family my uncle was known as Ashang-me, or "Red Uncle," because of his red monk's clothes. Ashang-me was very skilled in the prayers and rituals said at the time of death. He led my grandfather in the Medicine Buddha prayer, and in the other prayers. My grandfather began asking about me as his breath got weaker, "Is he here yet? Is he here yet?" He kept waiting for me, but I did not get there until after lunch, and by then he had already passed away.

When I walked in, the lower room was empty and untidy, quite unlike it usually was. My sister had been so upset they had taken her out of the house, so she had not tidied up. My mother had been taken off somewhere too, so the place was empty. I was about to go up to the room where my grandfather had been staying when a fellow came and said not to go upstairs, to stop and have a cup of tea. Then my uncle said to come. He asked me where I had been, and I said I had been busy with a friend. Then he told me that grandfather had died, and I suddenly felt a great chill come over me and I felt as though my grandfather was there in front of me. My Red Uncle said to me, "Do not be upset, boy. We were together and we said the Medicine Buddha prayer. He was a very old man and he was ready and prepared to die. We said the prayers and he passed away peacefully. It was a shame that you did not get to be with him, but that is the way things are, do not get worried over it."

Then my Ashi (we called an elder sister *ashi* in my part of Tibet, they say *achala* usually) came in with some of the other villagers. She was weeping enough to drown us all and it was not long before she made me start crying too. Finally, my Red Uncle told me to go back up to the grazing lands. He said that I should come down on a particular day a

bit later and then we would do all the necessary rituals at that more auspicious time. I went back to the grazing lands and came down a few
days later and did the last rites for my grandfather with my Red Uncle.

Many years later when I was in the monastery in Lhasa and had
learned something of Buddhism and psychology, I remembered with
a chuckle how my grandfather had so lovingly given me those dzomos
which were nowhere but in his mind. I wondered if it was just the
onset of senility or if it was an illusory appearance, a hallucination he
had of something that he had enjoyed so much. Something totally
nonexistent seemed so vibrantly to exist for him. I forgot about the
walnut tree he gave me for a long time, but many years later when I
was in India as a refugee, I met a nephew of mine called Phuntsog. He
kept saying to me that life had been hard but bearable thanks to me.
This was in a few of the letters that came through to me as well, that
thanks to me things had been bearable. At first I did not take any notice of it, but then when my nephew said it again I asked him what he
was talking about. "There are thirteen or fourteen of us in the family,"
he answered, "and amongst us there are none that are particularly
gifted. Still we have all done rather well and there are none of us who
have fallen on terrible and hard times. We all say that it is the blessing
of you, our Red Uncle." That is what I am called now, many years
later, just like we used to call my guru "Red Uncle" when I was young.

Phuntsog said that early on the Chinese authorities had outlawed
private property and all the lands and trees were owned by the commune. During those years there was not a single walnut that came on
the trees that was not eaten by the parrots. The parrots in our part of
the world are very numerous and they are very destructive. When the
change to partial privatization came, because we had a lot of trees
before, the commune said that our family could pick one tree which
we could have as private property. They said that we should talk
amongst ourselves and decide which one. This put the family in quite
a quandary because my tree had borne no fruit for years. The parrots
ate it all year after year. My nephew told me, "We thought that if we
were not to choose your tree then it would be inauspicious. We decided to ask for ownership of that tree even though it looked like we
would get no walnuts from it. When we told the commune they said
that we were being fools and that we should choose a better one, but
we told them the history of it and they said they understood and gave
it to us. Well, from that time on we have been having a steady crop of
walnuts off that tree. The parrots come and circle around it," he said,

"but they pass it by and leave the nuts for us." Then my nephew, who is a bit of a drinker and cares more about appearances than realities, said, "I traded my dzomo for this good-looking one and there was quite an altercation in the family about it. Then, suddenly the dzomo began to have calf after calf and started giving incredible amounts of milk. We all say it is the blessing of the Triple Gem and our Red Uncle." I myself thought about this and thought it was strange. I said, "It is not me, of course, but I have tried to work for His Holiness the Dalai Lama and perhaps this is something. And of course the blessing of the Buddha, Dharma, and Sangha can help us, so make your heartfelt prayers to them."

I REMEMBER WANTING to be a monk even while I was a little boy. There must have been some trace of the life left somewhere in my mind, because when I was very little another young fellow and I decided to leave home to become monks. This was even before I had started to look after the flock, so we could not have been more than five or six. We had wandered up a kilometer or two towards the monastery when a monk coming down met us and asked where we were going. "We are going to become monks," we said. "Ah yes, but becoming a monk is very hard and you have a long way to go. Aren't you too young?" he asked. My friend and I looked at each other and decided that maybe we were a little young, so the monk kindly took us all the way back home where everyone was surprised to learn what we had been doing.

Then, when I was about twelve or thirteen, I remember my mother told me clearly that a neighbor was making inquiries about me as a prospective groom for his oldest daughter, who was going to inherit the control of the family property. "You are going to be a husband in the not too distant future," she said. "They are already starting to talk about it." She made very clear to me what was going to happen; this was quite unlike her usual way of talking about things and it upset me. I knew I did not want to get married and I became determined to become a monk as soon as possible to escape the married life. I started to think seriously about how I could arrange it.

It was about this time that my Red Uncle, my guru-to-be, took over as disciplinarian of the monastery. In our district, he was famous as a capable and strict elder. I knew that it was considered good for a disciplinarian if a lot of new monks were inducted into the monastery during his tenure, so I decided to approach him directly with my request. He was at our home visiting when I broached the subject, just after night had fallen when we were all readying for the evening meal. "I want to be a monk," I said. "Even if you cannot accept me into the order right now I want your promise that you will accept me later. I want it to be confirmed that I am destined to become a monk, that I have been listed as one of those who is to be inducted." I told him to promise me that I would become a monk or I would run away. My Red Uncle said nothing to me in response.

That evening the family talked about it a lot, the pros and the cons and whether or not I would be capable of the life. I became anxious as the evening wore on and got quite agitated about it. My guru was put in a bind. With the conversation about my future marriage already underway it would not be easy to explain that I had decided to become a monk, but if he did not accept me, there was the real possibility that I would run away from home. He turned to me eventually and told me, "Being a monk is not just a game, you know. There is all the studying you have to do, all the playing and fun you cannot take part in. There is the discipline. Are you sure that you can handle that sort of life?" "I can," I said. "I know I can." "Well then," he said, "we will see. There is no way that a decision like that can be made so quickly, but we will see about it." I thanked him and we left it at that.

The rest of the family was totally against it. It was not just that there was no one else to do the work and that arrangements for my future marriage had already been started, it was also the sort of person I was. One of the things that I was well known for when I was little was my liking for liquor. All the villagers brewed barley beer and distilled a little spirit on the side, and I used to put my hand under the spout where the distilled spirit dripped out and lick it up. I loved it and often I would drink so much that by nighttime I was quite tipsy and I would lie there in the evening drunk. "You like beer and liquor too much to become a monk," they said. "How would a fellow like you, who everybody knows is naughty, who is so proud of himself, and who has such a liking for liquor ever be able to be a monk?" "I can do it. I know I can do it," I kept replying. And so the conversation went back and forth until they started saying, "If you were able to be a good monk we would all be happy, but becoming a monk and not being able to be a good monk is no good." I kept saying, "I know I can be a good monk, I want to be a good monk."

After a while, my Red Uncle came to visit again and said that since it was obvious I could not be prevented from becoming a monk, and because I wanted to, it would be best to let it go ahead. He said the time was auspicious since he was disciplinarian and with that they all agreed. My guru turned to me and asked me straight, "Do you want to be a monk?" "Yes," I said. And that was it. It was decided that I would become a monk, and soon after three other village lads and I became new novice monks inducted into the monastery by my Red Uncle. I do not remember exactly how old I was when it happened, but I do know I was a monk for about six years before I left for central Tibet at the age of seventeen. So I must have been eleven or twelve.

As a monk I had to go up to the monastery when there were rituals to perform or when there were festivals, but at other times I would just stay home and do the same chores as before. The one difference was that as a monk I was not allowed by custom to work as a goat and sheep herder anymore. I turned that work over to my younger sister, and I remember that when I did so there were forty-seven in the flock, nearly a threefold increase since when I first took over—not a bad record. I was not to have nearly as much success with the yaks and dzomos that I began to look after from that time, though. In our part of the world the altitude was too low for the female counterpart of the yak, the *dri,* and too high for the cows that you find in places like India. The herds were mainly made up of dzomos, which were crosses between yaks and cows. They make excellent cattle, are quick to respond to human commands, and give plenty of rich and creamy milk. When I took over as herder we had about seventeen or eighteen head, including a yak or two and one or two small cows. When I left for Drepung about six years later I think there were only a total of twenty-six head, hardly a spectacular increase.

During the breaks between residence periods at the monastery I would come home and look after our family's herd of dzomos. During the times when the monks were expected to be in residence I would do a little memorization and be called on to recite what I had learned. I never really learned much of anything else, studywise, while I was there. In the late spring I would take the herd up to the higher pastures to graze, living up there in the grazing lands in a tent like a nomad. In the winter I would bring them down near our home in Choochur and keep them supplied with grass. There was always a lot of work involved with this, so any additional study was impossible. My guru was very careful with me. He would never let me stay overnight in the monastery when I came to visit him during periods when monks were not expected to be in residence. Towards evening he would always send me home and tell me to do my chores properly.

There were four families from our village who went up with their herds to the grazing lands: my own immediate family, the herders working for the village headman, and two families below us. Sometimes we would pitch our tents together and graze our herds in the same places, and sometimes we would go off separately and graze in different parts of the highlands. One of the four herds belonged to my paternal grandfather's family and the youngster in charge of that herd was my cousin, a boy called Kalsang Phuntsog. We often pitched our tents together.

As I started to get older and bigger I began to feel more and more confident about throwing my weight about. All through the years I had harbored that grudge against the older boy—the fellow called Namgyal—who had tormented me when I was young and stolen my food and shoes. I kept thinking how I could get back at him. It is gross really, the sign of a horrible person, to keep bearing a grudge like that and not let it pass. Finally I decided it was time to get back at him, so I asked another monk friend of mine to go and get him to come over to a deserted place. I remember him coming without a care in the world. I guess he thought we were going to play or something. He was a year or two older than me but I was pretty tough. I brought up the things he had done to me when I was little but he did not see how serious I was and tried to be friendly, saying that was in the past and gone. I said, "The nasty things you did to me might be in the past and gone but the nasty things I am going to do to you for it are right here and now!" I grabbed his long hair—he was not a monk so he had long hair—and I was able to pin him down on the ground where I beat him terribly. I gave him a real thrashing. That was me, the monk, in those days—not a very pretty sight I am afraid, but that was the reality of it. I said to him as he was pinned down there bleeding, "This is for what you did to me before! I have paid you back now for what you earlier did to me!" With that my friend and I swaggered off back to the monastery.

I really beat that boy up badly. In general, the monks, particularly young monks, were even more feared than the young laymen. There was a lot of fighting amongst us young men and the young monks were known to be particularly dangerous in a fight. So while it was not such a special occurrence that I had been fighting, when word of the beating I had given Namgyal got back to my family, they were disgusted with me and scolded me for hours, saying how bad it was to bear a grudge for so long, especially as a monk. I was unrepentant though, and kept saying he deserved it because of what he had done to me as a small child. That was the sort of personality I had and everybody knew it.

I USED TO SPEND a lot of time on the grazing lands with my cousin Kalsang Phuntsog who was a few years older than me. He was a lazy fellow and would always want me to look after his herd while he took naps. Then I would be running around the meadow looking after both of our animals while he would be lying there snoring. He had frightened me once by asking me to make sure no demon came by to attack him in his sleep. Since he was older and more self-assured than me I never had the confidence to stand up to him and tell him to do his own work. One time, after we had brought our herds down close to the village for the winter, the two of us were taking them to graze in a small gully. The moment we got there he said, "Watch out for my cattle will you," and went to sleep immediately. I felt so frustrated and I thought it was time to teach him a lesson.

Kalsang was such a deep sleeper that I was able to tie both of his feet and his left hand to big pieces of firewood. I carefully tied his long hair to another big piece of wood and then I loaded up his right hand with a big wad of fresh dzomo dung. He slept on soundly, like a baby. Then I put a burning piece of tinder gently on the end of his nose and scampered as quickly as I could up into the branches of a tall tree. As the tinder, a dense mountain moss, slowly burned down he began to feel the heat on his nose and started to twitch. Finally the burning ember got right to his nose and his right hand came around and plastered his face with the dzomo dung. By then he was wide awake but he could not move properly because of the way I had tied him down. He was sputtering with a face full of dung and I was up hidden in the tree nearly killing myself laughing and scared to death in case I gave my hiding place away. Finally he succeeded in getting himself free and went running all over the place in a rage trying to find me. He had picked up some rocks and if he had seen me in the tree would have pelted me with them for sure. When he ran off a bit in one direction looking for me I jumped down from the tree. Thinking that if he got me he would thrash me, I headed straight for home as fast as my legs would take me.

DURING THE SUMMER MONTHS, as I said, we had to take the herd up to the grazing lands. I was the boss of our little operation but I did not know how to milk the dzomos properly. If you do not give them a good milking every day, they will dry up and stop giving any milk at all, so I had a helper who the family hired to do that part of the work. He was much older than I was, and the family was worried that he would take advantage of me. One of the other herders, a neighbor of ours, was a fellow with a great big goiter. They asked him to keep an eye on me and tell them how I was doing, and I must have been pretty good, because he sent down word that though I was very young I still made a very good boss. The helper always asked me for a handout or some sort of treat that I would not give him, and he sent down word that I was a hard boss who kept tabs on everything and was not an easy fellow to get things off at all. So I suppose that even while I was deficient in one way I had a streak of responsibility in another.

In those early days as a young monk, I was still a pretty bad character, a delinquent really, naughty at the best of times. When I think back on it I was capable of sinking to some pretty deep depths. Nobody would let me get my hands on a gun because they knew I was too volatile. I loved guns and I loved the long sword that people from my part of Tibet used to carry, and I always wanted to get my hands on them. When I was going up to the grazing lands one spring, my brother-in-law sneaked me a beautiful long barreled muzzle-loader. One day I saw a big black bird sitting up in the branches of a tree and took it into my head to kill it. I was not a bad shot and slowly took aim at it. Instead of just sitting still, however, it kept bobbing back and forth so that now it was in my sights and now it had disappeared behind a branch. I was totally intent on what I was doing and did not notice that my sister had come up from the village. She came up right behind me and flew into a rage. She started beating me and shouting at me, "Aren't you a monk? What do you think you are, wearing the clothes of a monk and trying to kill the animals?" She went on and on and there was nothing I could do but sit there taking it, because she was not a woman to try to talk back to when she was in a rage. I went down to the house and that evening she tore into her husband and tore into me again. "What do you think you are doing, giving him a gun? You know the sort of person he is, and today I caught him trying to kill a bird just for the fun of it." She went on for hours. Then my mother found out about it, and she said to me that if I ever hunted and killed anything that she would die from it too. Usually she did not know how to say anything effectively but somehow she found the words that night.

MONKS WHO HAD NOT been up to a big monastery in central Tibet were called *ben-chungs*. Nobody really cared if the *ben-chungs* got into fights so long as it was not within the confines of the monastery. If a monk who had returned from central Tibet got into a fight, however, it was a big issue and there would be all sorts of repercussions. Our fighting ground, just beyond the monastery walls, was a spot marked by a goat's horn. One time I had picked a fight with a monk who was a little bigger than me and we had gone with a group of my buddies to the fighting ground. I guess he was a bit apprehensive because although he was bigger than I was, I had a few friends on my side. We started pushing each other, a shove here and shove back there, not really doing anything serious. Then I took out my key—the big heavy sort that we carried attached to a cord at our belts—and took a swing at him. It landed right on his temple and ruptured a vein and the blood came pouring out of him in a stream, getting all over him and me as well. Everyone was scared so the fight stopped right there. He was not able to get in any blows on me, so in that sense I won.

I washed off the blood as best I could and went back to my guru's room, not knowing that a bit of blood remained on my ear. Talk of a fight had already been going around the monastery and my Red Uncle must have heard of it, but he was unsure if it was me or not. When he saw the blood on my ear he caught hold of me and said he would show me what happens for fighting. He had a rope and a good-sized stick on hand at all times, and he had tied me up to a beam and was just getting ready to lay into me when a friend of his walked in. He asked what had happened and when my guru said I had been fighting the monk said, "You must not beat him, he should be given melted butter! He beat the fellow cold—the other fellow did not lay a finger on him. He is the talk of the village. The most important thing when you fight is not to lose, everyone knows that, and he beat the fellow for sure!" My guru sort of smiled and let me go. But a bit later he took out the rope and stick, as he often would, and shook them at me. "I should have given you a beating and you know it," he said. "But you watch out, I have these ready and if I hear of you fighting again I will give you the beating of your life!" The truth was that he would often threaten me, but he would never really beat me severely. In those days I was in fights all the time. I had a reputation as a fighter. But I do not think there is any need to talk more about that, it was a long time ago.

MY GURU HAD A PART FRIEND, part servant who we called Gelong, which means "Venerable One." This name was something of a joke, and was sometimes used for monks who had never been to central Tibet to do their three years in one of the big monasteries. Older monks who had not made the trip to central Tibet were treated in a patronizing manner by the others because everyone felt that a monk should make the journey. These monks could never sit with the monks who had made the trip, but had to sit at the head of the *ben-chungs*, the newly ordained novices. They could never move out of this no-man's land, or take up any of the offices such as grainkeeper, chant-leader, or any of the other positions of authority. There was no monastic work available to them, and there was this name for them, "Venerable One," but with a sort of sarcastic upward tone at the end of the word.

A monk who made the trip to central Tibet had to stay for three prayer festivals, that is, he had to stay for about three years. Before leaving Lhasa to return home, that monk had to make a considerable offering to the monastic university in which he had stayed. When he returned home he was referred to by a special name, *ben-ser* (man of the cloth), instead of by the patronizing name "Venerable One" or the title *ben-chung*. A returning monk would also make a customary offering to his home monastery and then he was truly a *ben-ser* and would enjoy considerable status in the community. All the monastic offices were open to him, depending on his ability, and he would have considerable power and influence in the community.

Every monk was expected to go. Only those with a real physical deformity or real deficiencies in their faculties were excused. Such people would have to ask for permission not to go and would have to humble themselves considerably. It was a great loss of face.

Anyway, the Venerable One used to come over to my guru's apartment to cook or sew, and whenever he was there he would tell my guru about all the bad things I had been up to. I came to feel a strong dislike for him because he was always stirring up trouble between me and my guru, who would shout at me and scold me for the things that he found out about. I got sick of him coming over and causing trouble all the time.

Dondup-ling Monastery was a big halfway station for the salt and tea trade between China and Tibet. Tibetan salt caravans would come down to our region and the labrangs of the lamas, the office holders of the monasteries, and individual monks would all buy the salt and then store it until caravans arrived from the Chinese border, bringing tea, brown sugar, and soy noodles. There were a lot of these caravans. Tibetans who lived right on the Chinese border would bring the goods up and then the buying and selling would go on in the monastery, with the different people in the monastery acting as middlemen. Monks were permitted to trade, but not beyond the specific borders of their region, in our case down to Jol and as far as Gye-tang. What this meant was that monks who were not so interested in learning or the spiritual life could get rich in business, and indeed there were a lot of that sort in the monastery.

The Tibetan traders carried their salt in sacks that were closed up at the top with strong sticks, maybe four inches or so in length, quite rounded and smooth. We kids used to play with the sticks from the used sacks. One day the Venerable One was upstairs talking away with my guru and I decided to put a bunch of these sticks on the stairs leading down from his room to teach him a lesson. I placed four or five of them on a high step and then went into my room and pretended to be studying. Finally the Venerable One got up to leave. As he was concluding what he had to say to my guru, he began heading down the stairs. He never finished the conversation. He stepped on those sticks and as they rolled out from underneath him his legs went up and he went bouncing down the stairs, landing dazed at the bottom and unable, for the moment, to get up. I ran down to him pretending to be very concerned and at first he did not see the sticks and did not know that it was me that had put them there. My guru came running out of his room too, and when he saw that the Venerable One was not really hurt, but had just badly bruised his pride, he could not stop laughing. When they saw the sticks both of them quickly understood what had happened, but my guru could not stop seeing the humorous side in it.

Next door to my guru lived an old monk with a crooked leg who had a student with a crooked leg too. Another old monk was always coming over to talk with him and we could not get any sleep. He would talk away until late in the night, driving me and the young monk with the crooked leg crazy. We decided to teach the old monk a lesson and stop him from coming over by putting some sticks on the stairs. Unfortunately the old monk with the crooked leg came down the stairs first, and even though they were not very high stairs he went crashing down. He was unconscious for the best part of twenty minutes, and though we both knew it was very serious we could not stop laughing. My guru came and he suspected what had happened, but of course I denied it to the death. We could hardly have confessed to that one could we? I guess I was just a born delinquent.

OUR MONASTERY WAS SUPPOSED to receive a yearly tribute of barley grain, called the *phug-dray*, from the Lapo region down on the Chinese border. One year the tribute did not arrive as expected, and my guru was put at the head of a force of about one hundred *mami-trabas*—

"soldier-monks"—to go down and inquire about the cause of the delay. While he was away I stayed in the monastery to look after his things, and as you can imagine it was not a time when I engaged in a lot of study or other monklike activity.

Every year there was a big ceremony to expel all the bad forces from the monastery that had collected during the year. It consisted of a long ritual that ended with the abbot throwing sacrificial cakes called *tormas* into a huge bonfire that was built outside the monastic compound. Before throwing the cakes into the fire, the abbot, preceded by four young monks carrying incense and blowing on long Tibetan horns, would circumambulate the entire monastery. All the monks from the community would take part in the procession and it would usually be watched by many of the villagers as well. That year the cake-throwing ceremony took place while my guru was away trying to collect the unpaid tribute, and it happened that a close friend of mine was chosen to be one of the *trer-dzin-pa*, the group of four young monks preceding the abbot. Those monks wanted to be dressed in their finest clothes because they were at the very front of the line. My friend, who knew that my guru had a lot of good monk's robes, came running in one day to ask me if he could borrow some. I was adamant that he could not. "You can have all the food you want," I said, "but I cannot go near my guru's clothes or other expensive belongings." Even though he was a very close friend and it was an important occasion I would not budge on that issue. Later when my guru got back from the expedition he heard about this and was very pleased that I had such a sense of responsibility when it came to his belongings.

On another occasion my guru sent me off to collect some interest on a loan he had made. In our part of the world grain and money were often lent for interest. In the monastery the main business was the lending of seed grain. The monasteries were the beneficiaries of donations from the farmers, so over time the monastery would build up a store of grain. This grain served as capital, and the monastery's grainkeepers lent it. There were three or four grainkeepers in the monastery at any one time. At the harvest time the grain would be repaid with interest and the extra grain would be used by the grainkeeper for the different general assemblies and rituals when all the monks had to be fed. Besides the monastery, there were also a number of wealthy families who would lend out their capital at interest in this way.

When I arrived at the house of the people to whom my guru had lent grain, I could see that they were totally destitute. They said quite openly that they had nothing to give, so I was in a quandary. I wanted to collect the payment, but it was obvious they did not have it. Finally they said that if I wanted to I could take their pig in place of the interest. I could tell that the man didn't think I would take him up on his offer because it would be so hard to get the pig back to the monastery. But I accepted him at his word and put the pig in a sack, tied it up, and somehow or other lifted it onto my back. It was squealing and kicking but I staggered off under the load. After a while the pig got tired, resigned itself to the inevitable, and stopped squealing and kicking. Sometimes I dragged it, sometimes I carried it in front of me, and sometimes I carried it on my back, but I got it back to the monastery, which must have been an eight-kilometer walk.

When I arrived, my guru asked me what I was carrying and when I told him I had taken their pig he was angry and deeply embarrassed, yet somehow happy at the same time. "Nobody takes the pig of a destitute family when they do not have the money to pay," he said. "If this gets out, I will be despised by the whole district!" But I could tell that he was also pleased that I had wanted to do the work for him, and that I treated my work for him so seriously that I was determined not to fail. He would say, with a certain defensive pride, that for all my faults I was a fellow who would get every penny of what belonged to his guru. He did a great deal for me, I realize now, and I could not have asked for a better preparation for the complex life I was to live in the big monastery in central Tibet. He never taught me anything of the Buddhist literary tradition but he prepared me well for my future.

WHEN I WAS IN DONDUP-LING MONASTERY in Kongjo-rawa, I never thought about who my guru really was. To me he was always simply Ashang-me, my Red Uncle. The fact that most people referred to him as Choo-chur De-pa, the "Boss of Choo-chur," and the fact that he was quite famous and would be called to teach by important families and by the labrangs—the establishments that come up around incarnate lamas—this was of no importance to me. I was simply striving to be popular, and to establish myself as the best fighter amongst the *benchungs*. In many ways I think Ashang-me was probably the most important person in the monastery, but I didn't even realize it at the time.

Ashang-me was quite rich, but he never dressed me in special clothes, even when I finally set out for central Tibet. It was the custom for novice monks to wear lay clothes when they were traveling up to the monastery in central Tibet, but he made me wear a white chuba that was really cheap. Some of the people I met even asked me, "Aren't you the nephew of the Boss of Choo-chur? How come he didn't give you something a better than that to wear?" Since I was a naturally vain sort of young man, my lack of fancy clothes irritated me immensely. My guru, however, not only gave me ordinary material, he made me sew my own clothes as well. I would often ask the other older monks for a loan to be able to buy better clothes so I could look more fashionable around the monastery, but they never loaned me money. I realize now that they would never have interfered with my guru's way of bringing me up. And though I felt irritated at the time, in fact the training served me well when I got to Lhasa, because I was able to stitch my own clothes and save much needed money. Somehow or other the upbringing I received from my guru in Dondup-ling enabled me to avoid the life of the vain Lhasa fighting-monk, which I suppose my guru could see was going to be a real temptation for me once I got there.

IT WAS THE CUSTOM that a monk from our home monastery could not leave for central Tibet until he had completed a certain amount of memorization. There was a special textbook, quite thick, which contained basic academic topics and all the prayers and recitations for the various assemblies and rituals. Although it was a rule that the monk could not go until it was all memorized, if he had passed five or so years as a member of the monastery then it was felt that it was absolutely necessary for the monk go up to central Tibet, even if it necessitated waiving the memorization rule.

Just before his departure for the journey, a young monk would offer a special meal to the four most important officeholders of his home monastery. The four persons were called "those in the calling of the high offices" or "those in high office worthy of offerings," and were the abbot, the disciplinarian, the leader of the chant, and a monk who had already held the office of disciplinarian. One of the things that had to be done during the course of this ceremonial meal was an accounting between the guru and student. Before the high guests arrived, the guru would review the student's finances. By custom a monk would have given whatever money he had received to his guru, so this was the time when that money was accounted for. The guru would tell the student that this was the amount of money that he had kept for him, this is the amount of it that he had spent on food for him, and this is the amount left over that he would be giving him now for his journey to Lhasa. The student would then look at the accounting and if he was happy with it would say, "I have not been cheated at all and

I have studied with you to such-and-such a grade." This accounting would then be set forth to the four officeholders. If the relation between the student and the teacher was, as with me, a close blood-relation between an uncle and nephew, the accounting would not have to actually be done. Both would just say they were happy with what had transpired and that would be acceptable.

One of reasons for this accounting was that when a monk returned from Lhasa he would no longer be under the teacher he had lived with while he was young; he would be a member of the monastery in his own right. Therefore this ceremony made sure that there was no outstanding animosity between people who would later be equal members of the community. Also, you must remember that when a young monk came into the monastery he would be put totally under the charge of his teacher. The teacher did not have to pay anything to the student and could work him as hard as he wanted and the student had to do everything he was told. Because all of the young monk's money had to be handed to the teacher, this accounting was a way to make sure that the students were not abused, and also to make sure that there was some consideration of the need to make preparations for their trip to Lhasa. The departing monk would be given a special dispensation from keeping the rules of his home monastery (such as attending particular assemblies and so forth) for the time after the ceremonial meal until he left his homeland. He would have set aside temporarily being a member of his home monastery.

In the months before I left for central Tibet, my guru's lecturing about the need for discipline became more and more intense. Every time we would sit down to eat he would tell me about what I could not do when I got to Lhasa, or what I had to do at such-and-such a time. I could not do anything right. He would start in on a lecture about the need to do this, or the need not to do that, and I would get sick of listening to it. I started to go to other people's rooms to eat and would even sleep in other people's rooms to keep away from him because whenever I met him he would immediately start up again about discipline. It was a trying time for me, but my guru was worried both for me and for the embarrassment he would feel personally if I got there and then made a spectacle of myself, or was expelled for some sort of crime or misdemeanor.

As the time for me to leave drew close, I was invited out by all the villagers. Most of my time before leaving was taken up with doing the rounds. Some of the villagers asked me to come for the whole day and offered me good food and gave me presents of special *chari* (the apple-shaped tea blocks which are a specialty of Kongjo-rawa) or silver coins. While I ate they would offer advice and encouragement. Other households would have me over for the main meal of the day. They encouraged me and showed their admiration for me as well. But the advice of every one of them came to the same thing, "Boy, you are not cut out to spend a long time in central Tibet. Do your three years there and then come straight back. Your Red Uncle is a fine man and you have an excellent career in front of you working for him and looking after his affairs. On no account should you stay on. You are not cut out for it, so come straight back." Every one of them said that I was a delinquent, too quick tempered, too fond of food, and too lazy to study. But for myself, I felt I could study if I wanted to. It was not that I was so excited about a life of study, but I felt that I was capable of it, that I could make the grade and stay on if it came to that.

It was during this period that I was invited out by a man who was thought to be the most learned of all in the region. He was a very tall fellow, a distant relative who lived all by himself in a hovel a bit off from the rest of the village, and he spent his days saying his prayers and doing recitations of Dug-karmo (the Goddess Protectress Who Holds the White Umbrella). He was just about destitute, poor fellow. As I approached his place I could hear the sound of a chicken squawking loudly, and it sickened me when I realized what he was doing. In preparation for my visit he was killing the bird for me to eat. I felt ashamed for the old man. He was doing something terrible on my behalf and I thought I should say that I could not eat the meat since it had been killed especially for me. But he was the volatile sort, and was held in awe by the village so I was too shy to say to his face what I was thinking in my heart.

I went inside his little hovel and he seated himself in the place of honor, put me down beside him, and proceeded to serve up his dinner of freshly killed chicken. On the table he also set down a couple of silver coins and a *chari* or two as gifts. Then, as we got under way, he launched into a long diatribe directed against my Red Uncle. He told me that my guru had disgraced himself three times. "First," he said, "when he was young the family was very rich. He went up to the monastery in central Tibet on a bridge of gold and still did not study. When he came back he was dressed up like a peacock but he had not become a learned monk." That was the first disgraceful thing my guru had done. "Then," he said, "he disgraced himself again by coming back here to Kongjo-rawa and only attaining the position of disciplinarian. He should at least have become the leader of the chant." Now this was my guru he was talking about, the man I admired most in my heart, and I began to boil thinking about the awful food and the terrible things he was saying. "The third disgrace," he was unstoppable, "is the sort of things he is involved in right now...." I had heard talk that he did not like my guru and as he went on and on I began to think that this was the root of his diatribe. I decided that I would make a stiffly dignified exit—just walk out of there without accepting any of his gifts. But then he turned on me. "There is not a reason in the world I should give you a penny as a gift," he said. "You have plenty of money. Choo-chur has plenty of rich people but there is nobody here to teach Buddhism. Now you are going up to central Tibet and you should study and learn about Buddhism and come back here and teach the people." He said the whole purpose of making the journey to central Tibet was to study and learn Buddhism, and that if I came back to Choo-chur a learned Buddhist monk he would personally prostrate himself before me if he had not died in the meantime. "If you cannot become really learned in the Buddhist scriptures," he said, "at least learn about the basic Buddhist practice of going for refuge to the Three Jewels." And then he looked at me and said, "If you ever come back to Choo-chur without at least learning about going for refuge I will cover your face with spit!" I was aghast. I wanted to insult him but I could do nothing but sit there listening to him as he went on for more than an hour. When I left I was not nearly brave enough to refuse his gifts. What he had said about me I did not mind but what he had said about my guru was nearly unbearable and I left his place feeling deeply upset.

It is now nearly fifty years since that old man gave me his parting advice. Some years ago here in exile in India, long after that old man had left the Pleasure Garden of the Tang Princess for other realms, I wrote a book on going for refuge. I wrote it because of what he had said and sometimes I think about going back and finding him still alive. I know it can never be, but I think, were it to happen, that he would not spit in my face and he might even smile.

A SHORT TIME BEFORE LEAVING for central Tibet, Aku-me, my red uncle on my father's side, told me to watch my dreams carefully and tell him what occurred. About two months before I was scheduled to leave I had a very vivid dream. I was up in the forest above the village underneath a big walnut tree. The nuts had ripened and fallen and I was collecting them and putting them in my upper garment. Suddenly a totally naked black woman riding saddleless on a big black mule appeared in the dream and told me to follow her. I started to go after her and then, after a short time woke up. I was unsettled by the dream because I thought it might be a portent that I was going to have some trouble with my monk's vows. As for my guru, he knew nothing about dreams and did not invite people to tell him about them. But Aku-me was very pleased indeed. "Excellent!" he said. "That was Palden Lhamo, the Glorious Goddess, the protectress of Drepung, and it is a definite sign that you will be entering into Drepung." I still had my doubts and thought the dream was probably inauspicious, but he had been to Drepung and I think he was set on me going to Drepung too. Later I had a second dream. I was in the same place near Choochur when I saw a tall, extremely handsome man dressed up in a white Tibetan chuba with long sleeves. He was pointing out a path to me and telling me to go in that direction. As I started to walk that way I woke up. When I told Aku-me about this dream he was even more pleased. "Excellent!" he said. "That was Nechung, the protector of Drepung." He was pointing to the south, the direction of Lhasa from Choo-chur. "It is a dream that means you will be entering Drepung when you get to Lhasa." And it was not just him, all the elder monks in my part of Dondup-ling Monastery were old Drepung monks, and they all wanted me to go there and not to either Sera or Ganden—the other two big monasteries in central Tibet.

WHEN THE TIME TO LEAVE finally arrived, my guru told me that I should go to visit my family the next day and tell them that I would be leaving in two days. "Have your final talk with them," he said, "but tell them you will be coming the next day as well just to drop by and say a final good-bye. Then, without them knowing about it, leave the following day for Lhasa. That will avoid all the troubles that could come with leaving." So the next day I went down and had my final words with them. I told my older sister Tsering Chern-dzom that she should not be nasty with my mother. "Sister," I told her, "you have a sharp tongue and you sometimes hurt people with it. Our father died when we were very little and you have had to take charge, but you should be gentle with our mother." My sister listened to me silently with tears in her eyes and I could see that she was a little bit hurt by what I had said. Then I turned to a man who lived in our house. He had been afflicted by leprosy and had been turned out of his own home. He went around on his knees, propelling himself by his hands. Our family had taken him in and he did chores around the house during the day in exchange for a place to sleep and some food. He also did his own work at night and had been able to build up a small savings. So I turned to him and said to my sister that she should not be hard on him either. "He has to go around like an animal," I said, "but never forget that he is human like we are. He has fallen on very hard times and he, of all of us, is the one we should be kindest to. I want you to promise that you will not shout at him ever, and that you will be gentle with him." I actually asked her and my brother-in-law to promise to me that they would do that and they did so. For their part they asked me to make a solemn promise that I would come back in three years, that I would not stay in Lhasa. I said that I could not make that promise but I said that I would definitely come back.

Then I left them, saying I would drop by briefly the next day. When I got back to the monastery my guru asked me what I had said and what they had said to me. I told him everything in detail, and when I told him about my advice to my sister he was very pleased. He said how excellent to ask others to be kind, and he told all sorts of people what I had said. "The boy told them to be gentle and kind," he said. "The boy gave them excellent advice." He was really pleased, though I am not quite sure why, perhaps because he felt he had seen some trace of a noble person in me. "This boy is a born delinquent, it's true," he said, "but he has a spark of something in his heart, and I think there is still a chance that he may turn into something to bring credit to us all."

Early on the morning of my departure I got up and went to all the holy statues in the monastery and prayed to the monastery's protectors. Then my guru walked with me as far as the walls of the monastery. It was before dawn and we were alone there for a few minutes. Until that time he had never been gentle with me. In the days before I left he had lectured me about discipline, and his criticism of me had been incessant. When we reached the walls of the monastery, however, he stopped and changed. He turned to me and took me by the hand. "I will come with you no further," he said. "Up until now I have been your mentor, and you should not have any doubts about what I have done for you. I have not made you learn any rituals, not only because you yourself did not seem to show any aptitude for them, but because I did not want you to get called out all the time by families in

Lhasa who need rituals performed. I want you to be able to study when you are there. That is also why I did not teach you to write. I know how to read and write very well but I knew that if I taught you, when you got to Lhasa people would find out and you would always be called on to do office duties. I did not teach you for that reason and you should know that. Now you go up to Lhasa and study. For as long as you want to study there you need have no worries. I have plenty of money and I will support you and I will pay for you to take your final exams if you get that far. But if you are not cut out for studying, after your three years are up come home. I will be waiting for you here. I trust you completely and I will give you control over all my things. I have two guns, a rifle with a six-shot cartridge and a handgun, and I promise you that the moment you get back I will give them to you personally. If you come back you can become disciplinarian or even the leader of the chant. What I do not want you to do is to stay in central Tibet not studying. Most of all I will be happy if you study there." I was deeply moved by what he said, and both of us shed tears at our parting. I promised him that I would do as he had said—that I would study, and I said that if I did not take to the study I would come back immediately after my three years were up. With that, early in the morning I took leave of my guru, my Red Uncle, and set out.

The path to central Tibet joined up with the path to the monastery just above Kongjo-rawa, and we had wanted to get clear of the village before anyone could see us. I was traveling with another monk from the same monastery—Phuntsog, the boy with whom I had run away to become a monk when I was little. We came in sight of the houses below us just as light was coming up and the villagers were making their daily offering of incense to the gods. Just where the path down to the village branched off from the main path, the village headman was waiting for us. He had seen us coming and greeted us with a small bag of ground dried fruit and brown sugar. "When you get high up near the top of the passes," he said, "you will sometimes feel like you are losing all of your energy. This will keep you going." Then he gave us an offering scarf and told us to hurry on our way. "Quick," he said, "the village is stirring and you two *ben-chungs* had best be on your way." We started then to walk quickly but my sister's eldest boy who was about six caught sight of us from the door of my house. He started to shout, "They are going, they are going!" and he began running up the hill towards us in the early morning light. He was naked and running as fast as his little feet would take him. But we could not turn back even though it is inauspicious to leave a place where the people are crying and calling after you—it is a sign that you will never return. The little boy kept running after us, kept calling out to us, and from below the people from my house kept calling after him to come back. I was crying and crying and felt as though my heart was going to break but we kept going. And now, fifty years later, as I recall this I think that it is true that it is not auspicious if people cry when you leave home. I have not ever seen the Pleasure Garden of the Tang Princess since that day, and my friend Phuntsog, killed in the uprising against the Chinese in Lhasa in 1959, was never to return.

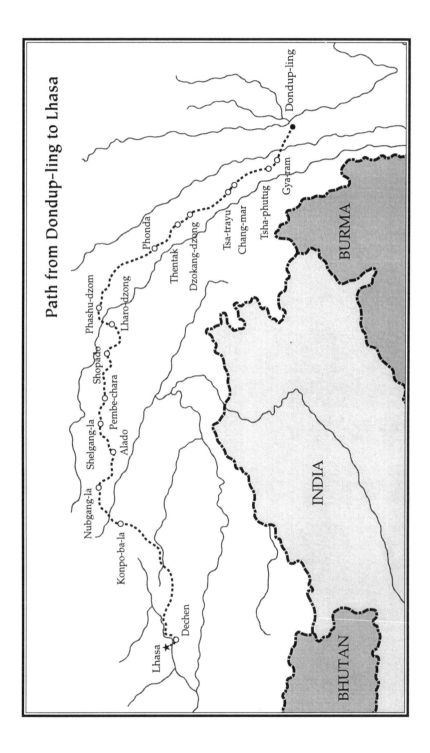

Path from Dondup-ling to Lhasa

2

TO THE LAND OF THE GODS

I was only seventeen when I went up to Drepung, so my guru paid the traders to load my things on their mules and pack cattle, and I had both my arms free to walk easily. I had a long sword at my waist and a short dagger and a little bit of ready food. The owner of the caravan would head off early each day to scout for a good place to water and feed the animals that evening. The packmen were the ones who worked for the owner, loading and unloading the animals, and I would be expected to help them a bit. Apart from that I was free.

There were established traditions for long trips to central Tibet. Those who were a little older, say between twenty and twenty-five, might simply attach themselves to a trader and carry their own food and bundle, making their way to Lhasa under their own power. Others would hire themselves out as packmen for the trip and not only get food on the way but also end up with some money at the end. The majority of the monks heading up to Lhasa, though, would be between fifteen and twenty and thus not sufficiently mature to either carry their own loads or to work as packmen. They would pay a fee to the owner of a packtrain and then attach to it, being fed and looked after on the trip. The fee paid for food and drink for two months and a day. The money would be given to the boss, and then the young monk would simply be another member of the caravan for the length of the trip, eating and drinking whatever was given to the rest of the travelers and workers. The young monk would have a personal pack into which he would put the particular little things that he would need on the trip, a few treats, a little tea, gifts, and so forth. He was allowed to put that on one of the pack animals, and did not need to carry it himself.

For the first few days of the journey I did not have trouble, but then my feet and calves began to give me excruciating pain. There was nothing I could do except keep up. I hobbled on, stopped, ran to catch up, and then stopped again trying to ease the pain. After four or five days I got used to it and then I could go swiftly wherever I wanted. There were about twenty pack animals in the caravan and two packmen, one an older fellow and one a youngster. The younger of the two was given the job of watching out for me. I had to help him with the animals, though of course I did not have the strength to lift the loads up onto the animals.

It was a very happy time for a young man. You had this long sword tied on your belt, and there was a special place for a dagger and a place for your amulet box. There was another place where you hung your tea bowl and you also carried a little bit of cash, but not much. The money that you would need when you got to Lhasa was always deposited with the caravan owner, and he would give it to you when you arrived. The owners kept their money in town to avoid robbery on the road.

Each evening when the traders made camp, we monks would have to go and collect branches of evergreen for the morning smoke offering to the gods, and we would also be expected to make prayers. The packs would be off-loaded and we would immediately sit near them in a makeshift camp, making the tea offering, reciting the prayer to the Goddess Protectress Who Holds the White Umbrella, and reciting the *Heart Sutra*. There was considerable importance given to the smoke offering, and the packmen would be careful to tell us well in advance if the place we would be camping for the night did not have any evergreen trees close by. Then we would load up boughs on our backs as we went along to make sure we would have the material for the offering. These were the customary duties of the monks on the long caravans traveling through Tibet; Phuntsog and I took them seriously and wanted to do them as well as we could.

About a month into the trip we arrived at Tsa-go-ching-tang, a huge plain. The packmen's tradition was to drink melted butter as soon as they hit that huge open space. They must have melted down about four kilos and were totally amazed when I was able to drink not just one, but two whole cups of it. Phuntsog was only able to drink half a cup and mixed the rest in with the barley flour that he was carrying. I must have been famished from the walking because I enjoyed that butter immensely. The packmen said I was a fool to drink so much, and that I would be sick for sure, but it did not cause me any trouble in the least. After crossing the plain we had to cross a pass which brought us to a village where the traders would always stay for a day or so to rest. They bought a yak between them and divided it up for food. The older of the packmen refused to give me any, however. He said that after eating so much melted butter I would be sick for sure if I ate meat on top of it.

Before I left, my family and friends had warned me not to fight with the packmen. This older packman, not only did not give me my share of the butchered yak, but he did not even give my part to the others so that they could have some. I began to boil thinking about the injustice. Then a day later when we woke up in the morning somebody had got bad diarrhea and in his hurry to relieve himself had messed on one of the pegs that were used to tether the pack animals for the night. The old packman immediately started in on me, saying that I had been told not to eat so much butter, and that now I had diarrhea and was soiling the pegs. I could not stand it. "I was a nomad herder for a long time," I said, "and I am used to drinking melted butter. There is nothing wrong with my stomach at all. It is you who are shitting all over the place because you have guzzled down a double helping of the yak meat!" When I said that, he flew into a rage. He had been treating me like a little kid since we had set out and now he was not going to put up with me. "What, aren't you supposed to be a monk, little boy? Yet here you are spoiling for a fight with me." I went for him but others in the group held me back. After a day or so the old packman got so sick that he could not stand up. He had to be carried on the top of a pack animal for a few days and even though he was so sick I should have looked after him, I was so angry I did not do a thing for him.

Our caravan arrived at Tsa-drayur on the banks of the Chinese Ngu-chu River. The apricot trees were just ripening and wherever one looked there was a beautiful appearance. I had been told again and again about the dangers of eating the apricots in Tsa-drayur; that eating them would cause a flu called *tse-pa*. But they looked so appetizing I could not help myself. I ate a few and put perhaps six of them in the fold, we call it the *amba*, of my chuba without letting anybody know about it. We started off soon after and had to cross a very high pass.

As we got up high and the final ascent to the pass loomed before us, I began to think of the wonderful food I had back home. My homeland came before me clearly and I began to hear again, as if for the first time, the words of advice I was given before I set out. I thought of the burning words of the old man who said he would spit in my face if I returned home without knowledge of the dharma, and thought that I must try as hard as I could to study once I arrived in Lhasa. I got to thinking that he had offended me and my guru but that he had given his true heartfelt advice. As I trudged high up towards the pass, alone with my thoughts, this recollection had a great effect deep within me. How embarrassed I would be if I returned without learning anything.

THERE IS A GOOD STORY that I learned from the monks in my part of the world which is related to the journey to Lhasa. Back at the end of the seventeenth century the great Fifth Dalai Lama built the monastery at Gye-tang. Some time later, his political minister Sangyay Gyatso traveled to our part of Kham to find out what was happening there. He traveled incognito with another poor traveler so that he would have a better opportunity to find out what was really going on. After he had made his inspection of Gye-tang he had to cross the Drichu in our region, and to do so he had to use a boat called a *wa*. When he got on board, the man operating the *wa* asked for his fee but Sangyay Gyatso had no money. The boatman raised his hand to strike him for coming on board without the money to pay for the trip, and Sangyay Gyatso took off his hat and bowed his head in supplication, asking not to be beaten.

Now, it was well known that Sangyay Gyatso had a very distinctive flat head. When the boatman saw the fellow's flat head, he said, "I will let you off without having to pay the fee because you have a flat head that is the same as Sangyay Gyatso's." He did not think he actually was Sangyay Gyatso, of course. Later in Lhasa, Sangyay Gyatso wrote a letter that the monks from our part of Tibet were to be excused from all taxes and tolls levied on the road up to central Tibet, and were not to be given any punishments or troubles. He said that, were someone from one of the lama's labrangs to travel with those monks, they too would be exempt from the taxes. Actually no monk traveling to the great central Tibetan monasteries was ever asked to pay the tolls or taxes, but the traders and so forth were expected to, and did so without question.

ONE DAY THE BOSS rode off a day or so in advance of our caravan, which had linked up with another trader's pack animals. One of the packman with those animals was a nasty fellow who immediately started to pick on me and Phuntsog. We did not mind helping with the chores around the camp, but he sent us out to collect wood, and then as soon as we got back told us to go and get water. We did that without saying anything, but then when we got back with the water he immediately told me to go and look after the animals, which were out grazing on a plain strewn with small rocks. I said nothing but I did not get up to do what he said either. Right away he flared up. "I told you to go out and look after the pack animals, didn't I? Well are you going or not?" I had noticed that there were plenty of rocks out closer to where the animals were, so I held my tongue until I got closer to them. I was worried that if it did come to a fight he might get the better of me, but with the rocks close at hand I told him straight, "You are the one getting paid here, not me, so you are the one who is supposed to be doing the work." He was up in a shot and started to walk towards me saying, "You *ben-chungs* are always quick to talk back." I immediately picked up a good-sized stone and got ready to fight him and he was not going to back off, that was clear. The younger packman with our animals got hold of him and at the same time Phuntsog came and told me that I should not get into a fight. He knew I was very hot-tempered so he said to me, "You know how much you used to fight back in the monastery, and you know how close you came to killing that one fellow, so you must not get into another fight—who knows what you will do." He was clearheaded enough to see that even if I was able to knock the packman out right away with a blow from a rock, it was still a long way from Lhasa and he would be sure to pick a time for his revenge.

One morning, some time later, we woke up and got ready to break camp only to find that one of the pack animals was missing. The animals had wandered off while grazing, and one of them had gone so far that the packmen could not locate him. Two of the packmen came up to me and said I had to throw a *mo*—do a divination—to find where it had gone. I said that my divinations were totally unreliable and that it would be silly for me to do it, but they insisted. What the divination foretold was that the animal had gone off in an easterly direction and was behind some big bushes. They said that was stupid, there was no way it would have gone in that direction. Then the caravan moved off, leaving the two packmen behind to search for the animal. Later in the day we saw them coming along with the lost animal towards the place where we had camped. They were full of admiration for me because they said they had searched all the other directions before going to the east. When they finally went were I had suggested they found the animal behind a clump of trees, just as I had said.

Most of us goat and yak herders knew this little three-stone divination trick. You would throw three small stones into the air after offering up a prayer. It the stones landed placed like the three stones of a cooking fire it meant that there was no worry from leopards and other wild animals. If they fell in a straight line it meant that there was danger lurking about. I had noticed that sometimes the divination was right and quite often was wrong. What I had done was think of a direction and when the throw came out like the three stones of a cooking fire decided the animals would not be there. When the stones came out straight I said it was that direction. Regardless, from that divination I went up a bit in the packmen's estimation.

In fact they had to treat me well because my Red Uncle was the main investor in the caravan. The boss of the caravan, who was quite beholden to my Red Uncle, had told both of the workers to look after me and to treat me well. My standing increased even further when one evening a very imposing fellow riding a very big pack animal stopped by to camp with us in the middle of a huge plain. He kept glancing in my direction as if trying to decide exactly who I was, and I had a faint recollection of having met him somewhere earlier. My Red Uncle had told me before I set out that there was a friend of his called Chandzo Rabti who he had not seen for three years. He told me to look out for him in Lhasa because he would help me in whatever way I asked. Finally the trader called out to me and told me to come close. "Who is your guru?" he asked, and when I told him it was my uncle he became extremely pleased, saying that my uncle was his guru too, and had started him out in the beginning with a loan to get his donkey transport business underway. He said his business was thriving and that soon we would both be in Lhasa. "Be sure to come to me anytime you need anything," he said, and with that he gave me three coins each of the three-sang weight. "We will be seeing each other in Lhasa," he said. He had already left early in the morning by the time I got up, but once the packmen thought that I was the nephew of a big trader, they began to talk about me and treat me with much more respect. Chandzo Rabti was not really that close. He was the manager of a lama's estates in Karnda, the birthplace of my maternal grandfather, a valley about four days' hard walk along the path to central Tibet from Kongjo-rawa. But he had quite a reputation in Lhasa as a big trader so it rubbed off on me. They would say to me, as we walked along, that I would have no trouble in Lhasa since I was related to Chandzo Rabti.

BACK IN MY HOMELAND my Red Guru took snuff and he used to grind up enough for a year's supply and store it. I would steal it from him and when he caught me taking it he would be very angry and say that I should not get into the vile habit. When I was at home my brother-in-law would grind up a supply and give it to me and I thought I looked sophisticated as I snuffed it up. But I never did it in front of my Red Guru. My brother-in-law, as I set out to Lhasa, gave me some cans as a gift. He said that when I returned, I would have a lot of say over what happened in the house, but that I should remember that the way of the householder and the way of the monk were different. If householders drank a little and if they took snuff, that went with the territory, he said, so I should not come back from the monastery acting pious and trying to stop him from doing it. "Quite the opposite," he said. "You should remember that I supplied you as a youngster and should bring me some back." I used a little of the snuff until I was a month or so from Lhasa, but when I thought of the bad habits of my homeland and my hopes for being a good monk, I made a decision to stop and gave my remaining tins to the packmen. But then after I had been in Lhasa a few months I was with some monks who were taking snuff, and I began again. After that I became quite addicted and was not able to break the habit for a long while.

One of the packmen was carrying a *ri-pi-ja-ko*—that is what we called a repeating rifle with a revolving cartridge. I really liked the look of that gun and asked if I could carry it for a while. The packman was glad to get rid of the weight, so for a while I was able to swagger along with it on my back, even though there had been warnings all around that I should not be allowed near any of the guns. At one point our party was passing by an upland meadow where there were a lot of big rabbits hopping around and I immediately wanted to shoot one of them. The rifle was a nice gun but I had never seen a revolving cartridge before, so I did not know how to use it. I asked the others how to shoot it and they were in the middle of showing me how to load it and aim it when the boss came along and began to get really angry.

He shouted at the others that he had told them not to let me have any of their guns, and he asked me what I thought I was doing as a monk, setting out to kill. So that was the end of that episode, and they took the gun away from me for good.

Finally we were within a day's quick ride of Lhasa, at a place called Itu-rong where there were good grazing lands—about two days out for the pack animals. One of the bosses told me to go ahead to find a grazing place for the animals near Lhasa so that they could be put to pasture after the loads had been taken off. The boss assigned me to go with the packman from the other caravan with whom I had nearly gotten into a fight. We set off, both of us feeling a mutual dislike for each other. When we stopped for lunch at a house, my companion immediately started drinking beer. When I said that I would have tea the owners said that there was none available. He kept on saying to me that I should join him for a drink, that there was no harm in it at all, that all the monks drank when they were in Lhasa. I kept refusing, saying I did not drink, that I could not because I was a monk. After a while, the lady of the house got up and went into the kitchen and brought me some tea and some very good tsampa and butter. There had been tea all along. She was very solicitous and said how fine I was not to drink, that monks should not drink no matter how much people tell them to. I then realized that the packman had been trying to make a fool of me. I do not know what he would have had to say if I had succumbed, but I am sure it would not have been very flattering.

We left that house and went on, spending the night at Dechen, just outside Lhasa. By this time the rest of the caravan had caught up with us and the next morning we were held up at the river crossing, where there were many caravans being taken across on the rafts. We did not get across until very late. Darkness was already falling by the time we arrived on the outskirts of Lhasa and I never realized I was in the city until I asked someone. As I hurried along I could see some buildings but only their outlines. By the time I got to Banak-shol where there was a house that the traders used, it was totally dark. There was no way I could go directly to the central cathedral to pay my respects to the main Buddha statue there; it was too late, and I was totally exhausted, so I stayed the night in that house.

That night I remember very clearly I had a dream. I was in a two-room cottage with a veranda running along the outside. I was alone in the house, but on the veranda were many women, some of them very beautiful. I thought that it was a very dangerous place, that I would have to be very careful about my monk's vows. I had a sense of fear and shrinking. I tried to hide myself in the back corner of the back room, but every now and then the women on the porch would look in through the windows and we would see each other. Then someone in the dream said that I should move to another room. The room was small and dark, the plaster was falling from the walls and there was a dank smell. It was a fearsome place and I felt that there might be scorpions around. But when I shrank into the corner of this room, I felt that the beautiful women would not be able to catch sight of me. Then I woke up. The dream troubled me. I thought that it was an omen that I might have a difficult time in Lhasa keeping to the basic monk's training and I told myself that I must be careful to try to keep my vows.

It was very early when I woke from the dream, but that was good. The traders had an excellent custom. They would arrive in the city late at night, like I had done, and then very early the next morning, even before drinking a cup of tea, they would make their way to the Jokhang to see the main statue of the Buddha. So it was very early in the morning that I found myself in the Jokhang, presenting myself before the Buddha and the images in all the other chapels to receive their blessings. I had done the most important thing on my first full day in Lhasa, even before the sun was up.

DREPUNG AND SERA MONASTERIES each had a subcollege house that accepted monks specifically from my part of Tibet. These were Lawa house at Sera and Phukhang house at Drepung. When a caravan from my part of the world arrived in Lhasa, the trader in charge was responsible for letting both of these houses know that new young monks had arrived. There would also be people in Lhasa itself on the lookout for new arrivals, aware that young monks were expected from the monasteries that sent their monks to those particular houses. When new monks arrived, the two house gurus would get together and with great care and secrecy draw lots. The students' names were written on pieces of paper and put into a cup. Each of the gurus would draw a name in turn. If there were two monks, it was simple—one would go to Drepung and the other to Sera. If there were three then a blank piece of paper would be put in the cup, and a note would be made of the discrepancy; the next single monk to arrive would immediately go to the monastery that had come up short. At the end of each year there would also be an informal accounting, and if more had gone to one monastery than the other it would be rectified the next year. There was great care given to the drawing of lots as it concerned newcomers from Dondup-ling because there had been a big problem at the Phukhang house of Ganden earlier. Dondup-ling monks no longer went there because of that trouble, so great care was taken to make sure that everything was clear at Sera and Drepung. Even if two young monks with the same mother and father came to Lhasa, the lots would be drawn and one could go to Drepung and the other to Sera. There was no room for argument.

After the decision, the house guru would take the new student back to the house. The student would be provided with a special place to sit and then would be given a very nice meal, served with great care and delicacy. After the meal, arrangements would be made to find a guru for him. If the new student had a teacher who was expecting him, then there would be no trouble and he would be put in touch with his new guru. He would probably have a letter with him to make sure that the arrangements for this went smoothly. It was also open to a new monk to mention the name of someone he knew in the house of whom he would like to be a student. It was not definite that he would be accepted, but his wishes would certainly be taken into account. It was one of the responsibilities of the house guru to arrange gurus for incoming monks, and he would go around discussing the matter with people, asking them to be the guru, until the arrangements were complete.

There were thirteen feeder monasteries for Phukhang house in Drepung: Dondup-ling, Kenda-gon (in Makham), Ngang-zang-gon (on the other side of the river from us), Gye-tang Tsarong-gon's Rongba house, and Jol-gon (in Jolwa) were the main ones. There were a number of smaller monasteries too, but often they would not even supply one monk a year. Dondup-ling on occasion would supply as many as fifteen monks, and other big monasteries would send at least five or six a year. There were probably between forty and fifty new entrants to Phukhang each year from the different feeder monasteries.

This was the pattern for most of the different houses. Of course there would be differences from monastery to monastery, but in essence the relationship between Phukhang and Dondup-ling mirrored the situation throughout the different parts of Tibet. Some monks from the nearby regions of central Tibet, however, were admitted to the big monasteries through a policy called *nyen-kur* (local admissions). The houses that admitted these monks, the large houses of central and west central Tibet, were not as strict about entrance standards or rules as the houses that admitted particular monks from particular feeder monasteries. The expectations for these new monks were not so exacting. My own house of Phukhang was extremely sensitive about monks coming from our part of Tibet. If a monk's lot fell to Drepung but it was found out that he went to Sera, immediately monks would go over there to sort it out. You could not just go into any house you wanted if you were from our part of the world. But after you had been at the monastery for four or five years, if it really was not where you wanted to stay, then you could resign from that house; this would be quite acceptable, and after that you could go where you wanted.

MY RED UNCLE had made arrangements for Chandzo Rabti to look after me, so immediately after breakfast on my first day in Lhasa I went to see him. During my talk with the Chandzo, he had said that I did not need to worry because there were two lamas from my own monastery in Drepung—Ludrub Rinpoche and Tra-tang Rinpoche—and that Gachag Rinpoche had his household, his labrang, in Sera, so whichever way the lot fell I would be okay. I said to him, however, that I did not want to stay in a labrang, that I wanted to be an ordinary monk and study the scriptures. He said not to worry about it, if that was what I wanted, he would put me with a guru called Lobsang Gyaltsen if I went to Drepung or the Yargang guru from Kazur if I ended up in Sera.

Because there was this uncertainty about whether I would be entering a labrang or entering a monastery as an ordinary monk, I ended up staying the next night in the labrang of Ludrub Rinpoche. I arrived still dressed in the clothes of my journey—long pants and a chuba. In the kitchen of Rinpoche's house was a fellow who had arrived a month or so before me, and he told me to go on up into the chapel where Rinpoche was making a ritual with a number of other monks. I prepared a scarf, and an offering of three coins and a ball of tea. I had last seen Ludrub Rinpoche in Kongjo-rawa while he was still young, and I thought that he would still look the same. When I went in and made my prostration I felt unsure about who the Rinpoche was because at the head of the row was a tallish man in ordinary clothes, while at the end of the row was a short, well-dressed fellow. I did not recognize either of them so I began to shuffle my way backwards out of the room in acute embarrassment. Then the monk at the head of the row said in a loud voice, "Hey young fellow, you do not know who I am, do you? I am Ludrub, it is to me you have to give that scarf. How come you do not recognize me?" I explained how I had last met him when he was young and thought that he would still be short. Rinpoche laughed and introduced me to everyone present, praised my Red Uncle and said that everyone had high hopes of me too. Whenever I came to visit him after that he would always say, "Here is the fellow who does not know who I am." I was an idiot when I first arrived, totally at a loss.

I BEGAN TO MAKE my first forays into Lhasa town. At first I only dared to walk a little distance, carefully noting all the houses so I would not get lost and would be able to make my way back safely. Then each time I would walk just a bit further afield. On one of my little forays I bumped into a distant relative of mine called Samdup. We went for a walk around town and I suppose we must have gone most of the way around the Barkor when he set me down on a cushion and went off into a store to talk about something with the owner. After a long time he came out and was surprised to find me still there. "Hey, you have to go draw lots. Do you know the way there or should I take you?" Now, I had not the slightest idea of the way to get there (it was going to take place in the house I had stayed in the first night) but I felt I would look stupid if I said that, so I said that of course I knew the way, and I set off with a pretend confidence, not knowing where in the world I was going. In a few moments I was lost but I kept walking with a purposeful stride, becoming ever more mindful of some advice my Red Uncle had given me about not walking around by myself in the streets of Lhasa, particularly in the side streets where there were muggers and thugs ready to take advantage of any fool who happened to wander by. I kept going up one street and down the next, recogniz- ing one sign on a house and thinking that I had finally located myself, only to get totally lost and disoriented again. Finally I took to walking in the large crowds going around the Jokhang with the thought that there would be safety in numbers. As I was walking, three monks from Sera caught up with me on the Barkhor; these monks had been de- puted to witness the drawing of lots and had heard that I had arrived. One of them was originally from Yargang—a place in Kongjo-rawa a few days walk from my village. They had set out to find me, no doubt knowing that new monks often got lost, and approached me directly. "We have come from Sera to witness the drawing of lots. Do you want to go now to do it?" I said yes, and we set off together. After we had gone a short distance I began to have doubts about them. What if they were the muggers I had been warned about, dressed up in disguise?

Suddenly I turned to the three monks and said, "No, I am not going to go after all, I have to go back to the Barkor." I took off in the opposite direction and they began to follow me, which only increased my suspicion. I began to walk even faster, and as they kept following me my suspicions were confirmed.

I quickly hid from them in the crowds going around the Barkor. I recognized a street sign, but there were two or three roads leading off in different directions and I could not be sure which way to go. I started off down one street. Soon the three monks appeared again. Immediately the older of them began to talk in my own dialect. "I am from Lawa house at Sera," he said to me. "My native valley is Yargang and I am from Kazur-gang family. The teacher in charge of our house instructed me to come to witness the drawing of your lots. You don't need to be afraid of me." As he was speaking in my own dialect I felt reassured and I began to remember before leaving that I had been told that if my lot fell to Sera there was a monk from Kazur-gang family there who I should get in touch with. We were slightly related and people had said that I would do well to ask him to be my teacher if I were to end up in Sera. So I opened up to him and admitted that I was totally lost and going around in circles. "We could see that," he said, "but we could see that you were having doubts about us too so we were not sure what to do. But don't worry. Come along with us and we will get the drawing of lots straightened out." Then he gave me some cake offerings blessed in one of the Sera chapels and told me to turn in the direction of Sera when the lots were drawn and pray to be able to go there.

I made the prayer, though to be honest, deep inside I did not want to go to Sera. My guru had been to Drepung and Tra-tang Rinpoche from Dondup-ling was a Drepung lama and his *chandzo* had said that if my lot fell to Drepung he would help me. So I was hoping that it would be Drepung, but at the same time I was open to fate, knowing that I would go wherever my karma would take me.

As we were all heading back to draw the lots, they were chuckling at what had happened and were talking and laughing amongst themselves about how I had thought they were thieves. But by then it was late so we hurried along. When we arrived, two Drepung monks—Gendun, the house guru of Phukhang house and his helper—were already there to witness the falling of lots, so it was immediately done. My lot fell to Drepung and Phuntsog's fell to Sera. I had to go off with Gendun immediately.

Night was already falling as I first entered Phukhang house. The monks were in the assembly chanting the worship of their protectress goddess Palden Lhamo, and I immediately made my three prostrations and forged the lasting spiritual bond between myself and my new spiritual house, as was the custom. I was then taken to the anteroom of the large kitchen, offered tea and tsampa, and treated with great dignity. I was beginning to think that I was going to like living in this house. Many monks stopped to say hello to me. "Who are you? Ah, I see, you are the nephew of the Boss of Choo-chur. Ah!" I think that most of them knew who I was, but still it was a very pleasant formality, and after I had said who I was to quite a number of them I felt that I was known.

Finally the cooks called me into the large kitchen to find a place to sleep for the night. One of the cooks was from my region, and he told me that I should sleep there in the kitchen until I was assigned a permanent room. I looked around for a place, and at the back in a recess there was a bed built up out of bricks, a very rude structure, the sort of thing that a beggar in India might make. I went to sit there and the cook brought me a cup of tea. After I had finished it he quietly said that it was auspicious that I had chosen that seat, but it was a place that was reserved for the storekeeper or any of the monks who had served a term as the general house guru. Others were strictly forbidden to sit there. "Come and sleep over here," he said. I was devastated. I thought that I was finished. Here I had just arrived in Drepung with the warnings of my guru and family that the discipline was going to be very strict, and on the very first night I had done something forbidden. I had a sinking feeling that I was going to make a complete mess of it and that I would become a disgrace to all who knew me. The cook kept saying that it was a good omen, and that there was no trouble in it, but I felt doomed. As I look back, I think it must have been a good omen because later I was to become a successful house guru.

The next day, the house guru, Gendun, told me that there was an expectation that I would be joining the household of Ludrub Rinpoche. But I stuck to my wish to be enrolled as an ordinary monk. I was originally slated to have Lobsang Gyaltsen as my room guru, but maybe because I had a name as a relative of Chandzo Rabti, Gendun said that he would personally take me as a student. People in the house were put out by this, especially the oldest student of Gendun, but I had no real say in the matter and I had to follow along with what was decided.

Gendun took me to my new room, and later that night when I had lit a candle and was getting ready to sleep I was struck by the fact that it was the exact same room I had seen in my dream about the women. The plaster was falling off the walls, the window was in exactly the same place, it was dark and hidden in the back, and it was damp. It made me feel differently about my dream and I began to think that the women must have been the women of the Glorious Goddess herself. I had some faith in the Glorious Goddess from when I was a child, particularly since she was the protectress of Phukhang house.

It was a terrible room, so bad that nowadays if someone were given such a room they would cause trouble, but there were many living in such squalid quarters so there was nothing to say about it, and it became my room for the first two or three years of my life at Drepung.

HAVING BEEN FURNISHED with a guru and a room I headed down to Lhasa to do the accounts with the trader who had been the boss on my caravan. He had brought in a big load of tea my Red Uncle had given me to take as gifts to some of his friends—he had asked me to give one man a two tea-ball string, another a five tea-ball string, and so on. After I distributed the tea there was still quite a bit left, and the caravan boss had earlier agreed to buy what was left from me.

I had begun to worry about the trader during my journey from Kongjo-rawa. There was a custom that monks heading to Lhasa would give a feast for all the packmen and the boss, and since I was always the sort of person who wanted to show off to others, I had taken a lot of care to prepare for this feast so people would speak well of me. I had brought a lot of special things for it, and not long after setting out I had told the boss that I was ready and asked him when I could offer the *thabja*—the feast. He kept saying there was no hurry, there was lots of time since Lhasa was a long way off. As we were going along sometimes the packmen would joke with me saying that I had better not forget about offering the *thabja*. But whenever I told the boss I was ready he would put me off. In the end he never let me offer the feast, and I couldn't figure out why.

When I met with the trader in Lhasa, it didn't take long for him to rob me. There were four or five hundred balls of tea left from the original load, and he should have given me four and a half sangs apiece for them, but he only gave me three. Then he charged me for an offering called the *gruma*, which I had never made, and to top it all off he charged me in full for the *thabja* even though he had not given the packmen anything. I was furious and went off immediately to inform Chandzo Rabti. I told him what had happened and he said he would take the fellow to court over it. I asked him to do it for me and I was so angered over the whole affair I felt I might burst. But after a while the Chandzo began to back off from his promise. "We are from different parts of Kham," he said, "and this could lead to problems." The trader was from Kongjo-rawa, you see, but Chandzo Rabti was from Karnda and he had to be careful about it becoming an issue of local pride. "That trader is rich and powerful and it could be difficult," he said, "What you had better do is write a clear letter home letting your uncle know exactly what happened and see if he can clear it up from that end. Just accept the loss." I was boiling. The amount of money involved was considerable. I lost hundreds of sangs on the tea, and having to pay for the feasts and so forth meant the money that my guru had banked with him was lost to me in the accounting. Just five silver sangs in those days was an amount to reckon with. You only had to pay fifteen sangs for fifty weights of butter. This trader who robbed me used to be a monk in our monastery and had then given up the robes and gone into business. Later his business went downhill and he ended up very poor.

AFTER A FEW DAYS I went to Dampag a few kilometers down from Drepung to get my robes made. New incoming monks had to make their robes out of *yaday,* a sort of wool that was not the best quality. Gendun told me to accompany a fellow called Adrag who was going down to buy some material and would show me the way. I had the money for my robes safely tucked away in the fold of my traveling chuba. As we were going down Adrag said, "I hope you have got your money stowed away properly there, you do not want to lose it." "Oh yes," I said, "it is safe inside an inner pocket of my upper vest." I felt inside to check that it was there, pushing it firmly down to make sure it was not bouncing out. Then a bit later he said again, "Be careful, now, with your money." This made me a bit nervous so again I reached inside to check and again firmly pushed it down. Unfortunately there was a small hole in the pocket of my vest that I had not known was there and with my nervous pushing, the money must have fallen through the hole. When we finally got to Dampag I found I had lost a lot of it; probably a total of a hundred sangs had fallen out. I lost the present day equivalent of maybe three thousand rupees. I thought my heart was going to burst. There was no way to get it back. There were people traveling up and down the road and it would be gone by now. I had already lost so much money from the trader and now, of my little remaining, I had lost even more. Adrag told me that I would just have to go back to Drepung—there was no reason for me to go looking at the material because I had no money.

I went back by myself, heartbroken, thinking how poor I had become, how I had been taken by the trader, how my savings were gone, how hard it was going to be, and how much my new guru would scold me for my carelessness. So I lied to him. I said that the previous night I had a terrible dream and that I was so distracted by it and the lack of sleep that I had lost my money. My guru, and in this he was a good guru, did not scold me but tried to comfort me. He said that I should not think overly about it, and though it was a hindrance I should try to think that it was over and about how to do well in the future.

All told, I lost just about every penny of my ready money, except for a small reserve, and the only money left was the money that my uncle had banked with others. I did not have enough ready money left to even think about making a good set of monk's robes—it was going to have to be the very cheapest of the cheap. I had imagined that as the nephew of the famous Boss of Choo-chur I would not just dress in any old monk's clothes, but in something more suiting my rank. But with my loss, my whole plan of cutting a fine figure in the monastery came to an end. I settled into the thought that I was going to be dressed like one of the plebs, and was going to be a pleb because that was all my meager money supply would allow. I certainly did not want to borrow and right from the start get into debt.

Reduced to these straits, my worldly side began to weaken and my spiritual side manifested itself more strongly. I began to regret how I had lived in the monastery at home, never studying anything at all, only reciting just as much as my guru insisted and never doing anything more. I began to see how the adversity that I was facing was in fact the best thing that could have happened to me, how the loss of the money that I was planning to use to be a monk like I had been at home was in fact not going to be a loss to me, but the cause of far greater gain. I had carried my Dondup-ling lifestyle with me to Lhasa, but now I had banged my nose three times, and banged it hard, and that old lifestyle was getting dented. Being totally taken by the trader had bruised my ego, and then I had been so ignorant as to sit on the bed reserved for those who were at a high level, and now finally I had lost all my money for clothes. I felt deflated but somehow with the inner tears of my loss was a growing determination to study, to study hard and make a name for myself as a monk and scholar. I again remembered the old man's threat to spit in my face, and what he had said acquired a depth of meaning in my consciousness, against the backdrop of my first unhappy days in Lhasa, such that I began to feel he had a special wisdom.

MY GURU, GENDUN, had pushed to get me as his student and word of this had got around. Understandably, the oldest student of Gendun was not very well disposed to me, and from the start he would glare at me and would tell me nothing about the various customs which one had to know about to stay on the right side of the college rules. One evening, begrudgingly, he told me that I had to go to the *damcha*—the assembly when the debaters get together and all put their questions to a selected few. By the time I got there it had already started and I felt shy about going in late, so I hid myself at the back of the compound. After a while a fighting monk walked slowly from the darkness. He had the last part of his upper garment tightly pulled around his neck like a scarf, instead of draped over his shoulder, and he passed by me in what I considered a threatening manner. He slowly went outside to urinate and I felt so scared of him I plucked up the courage to go inside and sit down. I found myself seated next to a young monk from my same part of Kongjo-rawa and it was not long before we got lost in conversation, me telling him about the latest news from home and him telling me all about life in the monastery. Now, although house gurus would tend to be a bit lenient with new arrivals who might not be keeping all the rules perfectly, the monitors called *parsha-rawas* were not at all. As we got more and more into conversation and our voices began to rise with excitement, we totally failed to notice one of the *parsha-rawas* coming towards us. Without a word of warning he gave me a tremendous slap across the cheek and asked what we thought we were doing. "What about the guru whose name you give when you are asked whose student you are? What about your elder classmates and roommates? Is there nobody who tells you what you can and cannot do in this place?" I was totally flattened by this, pounded, as we say, as thin as the fine membrane around a muskdeer's gland.

Coming on top of what had been happening since I arrived, I was overwhelmed with the thought that there was no way I was going to be able to make it, and that I might as well resign myself to the thought that I would not be able to stay at Drepung even for a few years but would have to leave for home in the next short while. In that deeply upset state I went back to my room after the assembly was over and, somehow or other, was able to motivate myself to study a little.

My guru should have appointed somebody to teach me but did not do so. Luckily there was a boy from my own monastery who was ahead of me and it was from him that I learned the first debates. After teaching me for a while he asked me one day to go to the general house study-guru to ask permission for him to do his recitation in his room instead of going outside onto the open veranda. It was a college custom that a younger student could go to ask permission for an older student to do his recitation inside, but not vice versa. So I went off to ask. In the monastery back in Kongjo-rawa when a monk went to ask for permission there was a particular way of asking. We would say, "Can he stay inside or can't he?" We did not phrase the request in a way such that it was an exact unequivocal request for him to stay inside. So in a blissful ignorance of the way to do it at Drepung, and without being told by anyone exactly what I should or should not do, I entered the guru's room. He was a good man at heart but was extremely direct and brutal on the surface, so when I addressed him in the language of my part of Kham he looked at me ferociously and said in a loud voice, "What did you say?" I said the same thing again, "Can he stay inside or can't he?" And after the second request in an even more infuriated voice he said again, "What did you say?" I asked a third time in the same way and he exploded. "What do you mean, asking me if he can or cannot stay inside? Are you asking me if he can stay inside? Don't you know how to ask properly? Do you dare to come in here without the proper care and respect?" With that he gave me three or four tremendous wallops with the heavy thong that he hung his keys from. He did not really hurt me, and I do not know to this day if he really was as infuriated as he seemed, but he kept saying "Can he or can't he...," as though he was beside himself with anger. When I got back to the young guru who was teaching me the debate and told him what had happened, he was terribly sorry and apologized again and again for not having told me the proper way to address the request. But the damage had been done and my confidence was totally gone.

Back in Dondup-ling I was one of the worst of the monks, egotistical and arrogant. From these early experiences in Drepung, however, I became very deferential and retiring, quite the opposite of my earlier self. Back at home everybody had said I would never be able to last at Drepung because of my arrogance, that I would come up against the discipline and get into trouble. But now here I was, after just a few weeks, totally deflated and deferential. I thought of what they had said with a bittersweet taste.

WHEN A NEWCOMER arrived he had to make an offering called the newcomer's tea. It was not particularly necessary for him to give a big or small tea, but at the least he had to supply two rounds of tea to the two hundred or so members of the house. If the person was poor that would be the best he could do. A richer person would give better tea, make a big show of it and hand out money offerings which would then entitle him to the name of *chon-dze*—"a facilitator of the dharma." A person who wanted to be a *chon-dze* also had to offer a fine *mi-tag* noodle soup, and make the money offering twice to the whole college. Those who were not rich enough to give the money offering twice, but who could offer the noodle soup, were not *chon-dzes*, but their offering did exempt them from the roster for house duties. Monks who were not able to make these offerings while they were in Lhasa would have to make an offering in their home monastery as big, or bigger, than the one expected of them in Lhasa. When the monk got back to his part of Tibet he would say that he had not been able to offer the *mi-tag* noodle soup and then there would be a specific amount that he would offer to the monks of his home monastery which would serve as the equivalent. In essence, the newcomer's tea was obligatory but the *mi-tag* noodle soup might, on occasion, be left out.

If a new monk did not have the funds to offer the *mi-tag* soup he went into a pool of people who had to do duties around the house. Since I had lost nearly all my money I was not going to be able to make the offering and word of this got back to Chandzo Rabti, who called me down to the labrang office. He asked me why I was not giving the *mi-tag* and I said that I did not have enough money to give it. "Well you can borrow the money for it, can't you?" he said. "Going into debt I am not going to do," I said, and after some more conversation I eventually went back to the college. Then again a few days later I was told to go and see the Chandzo. There were two big loads of butter sitting on the floor when I got there and the Chandzo told me to pick them up. They were so heavy I could not pick up even one of them without staggering, never mind both at the same time. The Chandzo asked me, "Can you carry things like that? That is what you have to do if you go into the work pool." I just looked at him. "So you can see, then, that the offering of the *mi-tag* is very important—it is something that you have to do. Do not worry, I will help you with what you need." I sheepishly thanked him and then went back to the college.

I went to the college administration and arranged the dates and so forth and made it definite. Then one day I went down to the Chandzo and he gave me a load of butter to carry back to the monastery. It was not quite the size of the earlier ones but it was still big enough—it must have weighed forty kilos or so. I staggered out with it and it was incredibly difficult. It took me half the day to get to Drepung from the center of Lhasa. The rope around the leather skin that contained the butter cut into my back and I thought that there was no way I was going to be able to do this sort of work, and that it was definite, whether or not I went into debt, that I would offer the *mi-tag*. Luckily a huge monk from the same part of the college was making his way back to Drepung at the same time, and I asked him to help me the last part of the way because the cuts in my back from the ropes were so painful. "No trouble," he said, and took the load the last of the way up.

After that I was certain about offering the *mi-tag* and went to see my guru to tell him that I had definitely decided to do so. The total cost of a good tea and *mi-tag* would come to about twenty dotse; I had about fifteen or sixteen dotse left, nothing more, but with Chandzo Rabti's butter and his offer to help, I told my guru that I wanted to do it properly, that I was not going to just give an offering that came in under the mark. "Excellent," he said, "and now you have the backing of Chandzo Rabti, so I will sanction it and advance you any extra money you need."

I was slated to offer my *mi-tag* in the tenth month when two different monks took over as house gurus. I was scheduled to offer it in the evening and I woke up very early in the morning of that day feeling extremely anxious. I immediately went to the kitchen to see how the preparations were going. A proper offering was not just a thick *mi-tag* soup, but was supplemented with a *paktsa mar-gol*—a barley flour dish with a melted butter crown. For that you needed lots of melted butter as well as the fruit and cheese and so forth that went in the barley flour. One of the cooks saw how nervous I was and played a joke on me by holding up a ladle of watery soup and saying that this was what I was going to be serving because I was so short of ingredients, and wasn't I ashamed to be confronting the house with such slop? I was crushed, and believing everything he had said I rushed off to my guru's room to tell him that I was going to back out of the *mi-tag* because my soup was not good enough to offer. He sat up immediately and said, "What, the soup is no good?" and we both rushed off to the kitchen. The cook said that he had just been joking and that in fact the soup was excellent. "I could see how worried you were when you walked in this morning so I thought I would put the wind up you," the cook said. "Don't worry, the food is going to be fine; it is all taken care of." My guru had a great laugh at this, and by midmorning many of the older monks had heard the story. They were laughing and pretending to scold me. "You cannot back out of a meal, even if it does not come up to your expectations—you still have to serve it," they said. "You really are the dictator aren't you—putting down your foot in the kitchen when the soup is not up to your standard." My guru said that he would have to watch out for me from now on or I would bankrupt him. "What were you going to do with all the soup that was not up to your lordship's standard?" he asked laughing. "You have already spent all your money and a good bit of mine on the ingredients. What exactly was it that you had in mind, throwing it all out for the dogs?" He chuckled away to himself. It made the rounds, this story, and even after the event had passed off successfully and the meal had been enjoyed by all, the old monks would ask me if I was the one who was going to cancel the soup because it was not up to the standard.

When I finally did the accounts with the Chandzo for the feast I came up about six dotses short. The entire cost, over twenty dotses, must have been the equivalent of twenty thousand Indian rupees in today's money, but the Chandzo said that I should not worry about it, that I would not have to starve or wear rags. He said that when he had started out in business he had nothing but a single mule and my Red Uncle had staked him and helped him immensely. Now my uncle was not in need of anything but I was. So whatever help he could send my way, he said, it was more than a pleasure to do it. He said that he had gone over the accounts carefully in order to acquaint me with the procedure, but that I should not consider myself in debt to him for the outstanding six dotse that he gave me to pay back the advance I had taken from my guru Gendun. I thanked him profusely. Then he said that if I ever ran into trouble I should be sure to come immediately and ask him and that he would take care of it. It turned out that I never received any more money from the Chandzo. I often would think that I must go down and ask him for something but when the time came and he would ask me how I was doing and if I needed anything I would always feel shy and say that I was making out alright. But his openness and his willingness to be there if I got into trouble was a great comfort. You know how it is, even if the person actually comes up with nothing it is still very nice to have someone say that they are ready to help. He never ever put money in my hand, probably knowing that I would spend it immediately and that I would use it to look good around the college.

WHEN A NEW MONK first arrived in Lhasa everybody would tell him how important it was to study, what a special opportunity it was and so forth, and how important it was to follow the conduct becoming of a monk. At the monastery, as he went about in his early days, many people would make a special effort to impress on him how important it was to study, to be modest, and to make good use of the time. But that is not to say that everyone did study. There was a certain amount of memorization to be done, and some of the new monks ended up doing a bit of that, but not really studying. After a few months, the monks who were not studying at all would start to wander about, making sure that they cut a fine figure as they did so. There were all sorts, some just hanging around waiting for their three years to end.

The house gurus appreciated the efforts of the studious monks, and their status in the monastery went up. Still, there was no set of rules in the monastery saying that those who stayed there had to study. It was up to the student himself. If one adhered to the three basic trainings (a basic morality, some contemplation, and some intellectual activity) one could stay. So it was a very liberal environment, an accommodating one. If one wanted to study one did, but from the outside there was not a strict discipline that required it. There were many monks in Drepung, but I would venture that no more than three thousand of them were involved in the study of Buddhism. There were definitely some who did not study and did not do anything else, who were not particularly noble people, and if they came to the notice of the monastery authorities they would be asked to leave.

In some houses, though not in my own, there were monks who were traders. They were businessmen and that was their job. There were not many of them but there were some in the monastery. And there were also meditators, people for whom the quiet contemplation of truths in their own rooms and on their own time was the main thing. There were different sorts and they were all allowed the freedom to do as they wanted, within the general rules and regulations of the monastery and colleges.

Financing the stay was always a problem. Many monks went back home simply because they could not afford to stay. Others went back because the discipline in the monastery was something they could not take. There were always letters from home urging one to return and one would always remember the ample food and freedom of one's native place. It was not easy to study, and there was a tremendous pull on the new monk to just give up and head back to the familiar territory of his birthplace. There were also monks who would find employment in one of the different labrangs, or who would find some other sort of work and thereby be able to live relatively well, but at the expense of time which otherwise would have been given over to study.

AFTER A GURU had been arranged for a new arrival, the young monk would give all of his money to him and it would be properly entered into an account at that time. Then the monk's food and clothes and the cost of the necessary ceremonies would be met by his guru from this money. If a monk was poor, his clothes and food would all have to be supplied by his guru. When this poor monk received money from donors during the assemblies, it was then expected that he would hand it over to his guru, who would use it to meet these expenses.

Monks got up at dawn and went to the Drepung general assembly, which lasted for as long as two hours. The gesheys and older monks were required to attend, though there was a schedule so that all of them did not have to go at once. A required number of new monks always had to be in attendance. The tea that these new monks got in this assembly was just black tea because all the butter would have already been poured out into the cups of the gesheys at the heads of the rows. The black tea was given out three times and the monks mixed it with their tsampa. When there was a money offering in the Drepung general assembly you did not have to go and sit for the tea in order to receive it. You could stand outside in the courtyard, though sometimes you had to wait for up to an hour. After the general assembly was over, Loseling and Gomang colleges (the two biggest of the Drepung colleges) had their own morning assemblies. During debating periods this would take place right after the general assembly in the debate ground. Attendance at this assembly was mandatory for all new monks who had not completed three years of residence in the monastery, but of the older monks only the leader of the chant and a few monks with strong voices attended. It did not last long and was over in about forty-five minutes. Tea was not served though there might be other offerings. The house assembly and morning prayer was after this and lasted for about two hours. If a monk had not been to an earlier assembly he would have to go to this if he wanted to get any tea.

After the house assembly there was a break of about two hours before the daily debate. This was the period when one went to one's guru for teachings, or if one did not have a teacher, when one studied oneself. The daily debate went from about one in the afternoon until about four and was the longest of the debating periods. After this, if there was a sponsor for an evening tea, it would be signaled by a clapping of hands and would be the occasion for the evening meal. For this tea the ingredients were supposed to be put in a churn and mixed well, but the kitchen workers rarely took care to ensure this happened.

Then there was a break before evening pre-debate prayers. During this time, again one went for teaching from a guru or one would study by oneself. The prayers started in the early evening with all of us reciting the twenty-one praises to the goddess Tara. That prayer was said twenty-one times and then there were a number of other praises, all with long chants, so the evening prayer went on for a long time. When the chant was slow and drawn out, the monks who were studying recited their memorized texts in a very soft voice, did the mantra of Tsong-khapa, or just sat there thinking and contemplating the part of the scriptural tradition they were studying, in order to better utilize their time. New monks had to attend the evening prayer, whether they wanted to study or not, but older monks who were serious about study missed the evening prayer and came out when debate started. Others would teach during these long recitations. Without letting others know what they were doing, they would quietly teach a particular part of the scriptural tradition to a student or friend they were sitting next to. Immediately after the end of the evening prayer, very new monks returned to their house and, under the watchful eye of the house guru and the *parsha-rawa*, they had to recite what they had memorized in a loud voice, outside their rooms. They had to keep at it until the house guru told them they could stop. Other monks went to debate, which lasted until ten or eleven. Debaters did not have to recite for the house guru, but they would usually do at least a short recitation after they returned from the debate.

The disciplinarians made sure that all monks were present for the first hour of debate; after that they did not take much notice, so only the ones who wanted to debate would stay on, some until as late as twelve o'clock. Those who debated late into the night experienced a special feeling in the debate courtyard. Even in the middle of winter one did not feel the cold, and in the warmth of summer, debating amongst the trees, there was a wonderful cool feeling.

GENERALLY SPEAKING, the first months were the hardest for a monk. As he got older he would be more capable of looking after his affairs, more capable of budgeting properly, and also would be more looked up to. But it was the guru who was his surrogate parent, and it was the guru who was summoned by the general disciplinarian or the general governing body if the student got into serious trouble. Say the student stole something. The guru would not have to answer for it as an accomplice, but he would be upbraided and asked why he had not properly looked after his student; how could the student have been involved in thievery without his knowing? On the other hand, if the guru gave terrible food to the student or dressed him in rags, or if he abused him with beatings, then the guru would be called up to answer the charges. The truth is that being a guru was a very important role in the monastery, but the job was not that easy. Sometimes the guru would sustain a real financial loss looking after a student, though it could also happen that the student would be a source of greater wealth for a guru, or that the guru would be well looked after by his students.

In Phukhang house a new student had to stay with his guru for his first five years. During that time he was not allowed to set up on his own or cook in his own kitchen. After that he could find himself new rooms, cook by himself, and also could begin to take in students of his own. Hence a monk had to stay with his guru, to eat with him, and apart from the little bit of money he was able to hide away for his own private use, he had to give the guru everything he had. I think all the houses were run on basically this same system.

A guru's expenses for a monk's food were taken care of at a monthly accounting. The amount of money that the student had brought in from the prayer assemblies, and the amount of money that the guru had paid out in food and so forth were totaled up at this time. At the end of the year there would be an accounting as well. If the student lived a frugal life and was careful not to waste money or food, he could make it through his time at the monastery and at the end of his stay have enough left over to buy material for a reasonable set of new robes to go home in. But there would be plenty of monks who bought special food they could not afford, with too much meat or whatever, or who felt they had to have the latest fashion in material or robes, and they would find that the amount of money they received from the donations in the assemblies was not enough to cover their needs.

The guru one was assigned on entering the monastery was not necessarily the most important person in one's studies. The disciplinarian in the big assemblies and the house gurus were the main ones checking on this. They made sure a monk was in the assemblies or in the debating sessions that he was expected to attend. Some houses were not so strict in this, but Trehor, Gowo, and Phukhang were incredibly strict about attendance, and the house gurus were always about with their lists, checking that everyone was there. The monks in these houses were themselves careful to turn up where they were expected, so the disciplinarians were usually better disposed towards them. If some infraction occurred, the disciplinarians were more likely to treat the offending monk from one of these houses more lightly. The disciplinarians would quickly bring the guru looking after the monk into the discussion when the student had some sort of fault. "Didn't your guru tell you about this? Haven't you been told exactly how and when this is supposed to be done?" If the fault was serious, the disciplinarian would confront the student and his guru together and give the both of them a tongue-lashing.

IT WAS HARD FOR ME because I always had a big appetite. I always wanted to eat but never quite had enough to spend on food. That is not to say that I was short of money. My Red Uncle had been intelligent about the way he had set up my finances, taking care of every possible eventuality. So even though I had lost large amounts, the offerings that I had to make to Loseling and to Drepung had been safely routed through Ludrub labrang. In addition he had given me two sets of money to carry on my person. One he told me to put on my belt where it was easy to get to. "If the packmen ask for a loan you can give them a little bit of this," he said. The other set of money he told me to keep in a hidden pocket under my arm. "Do not show this even to your guru," he said. "Just keep it safe so you will have something to buy food with when you are hungry." I kept that money, quite a bit really, never letting my guru know that I had it, and I used that to assuage my hunger and thirst. Since nobody on the way into Lhasa had asked me for a loan, I had most of that money left too. I kept it secret, so I was never one of the really destitute monks.

Still, I was always hungry—greedy I suppose is the word. No matter how much I ate I always felt hungry and always felt like eating something. Sometimes it was quite painful, this feeling of hunger, and I was always on the lookout for food. One time my guru had gone out and I was dying for something to eat. My guru had left out some low quality mustard oil, the sort of oil that you needed to cook at quite a high temperature before using, and I decided to mix some of this with tsampa and eat it. I got it down alright and since I had not used much of the oil my guru did not notice it. But having tried it once I knew it was there and I got to eating more and more of it until one day he asked why the oil was disappearing so fast. I confessed that I had been putting it in tsampa, in the place of butter, and he was shocked. "You cannot eat that oil!" he said. "It is not like apricot or walnut oil, it will kill your stomach." He was quite concerned and said we would have to go to the doctor right away. But when I said I had been eating it for quite a while, with only the occasional diarrhea, he allowed himself to believe that I was alright. It seems that two young monks from Pombara house had cooked themselves up some barley flour with a melted butter crown using mustard oil in place of the butter, and had died a most painful death from it. The story had made the rounds and my guru was very worried that the same would happen to me.

In these early months I was not very enamored with college life. I hated feeling hungry and kept thinking of how it was at home. I thought to myself that it was unlikely I would stay in Drepung after my allotted time of three years was over, but even so I kept studying the scriptures. I did not have a good teacher, but the young monk from my part of Kham who had helped me learn the opening debates was very fine and humble and he helped me as much as he was able. My own guru was not even the head of our little part of the house even though he was the house guru. The real head of our part of the house had gone to Kongpo to do some business and was not there. So there was not really anyone who took an interest in my affairs or who looked after me in an attentive way. The elder student, as I said, took an active dislike to me. I was very shy then, too. I had never been taken to any of the common rooms of the college and was too shy to go there by myself. What with the hunger, the feeling of abandonment, and the loneliness it was an unhappy time.

There was one boy from Dondup-ling living down the hall and I would often go over to his room to seek out his friendship. His guru had gone off to the winter debate called the Jamyang Gun-cho. My friend lived next to an excellent monk and scholar called Tsering

Chophel who had gone to the Jamyang Gun-cho as well. At that time for some reason or other my own guru was also not around. One day my friend showed up with a piece of pork that he had stolen from the room of Tsering Chophel. He did not have any cooking facilities in his room and he knew that my guru did. I said that even though my guru was away I could not let him cook there because many people came by and if my guru came to know I was using his things he would not be happy about it. Some time later my friend came by with another bit of pork. This time it was cooked pork that you could eat with tsampa and he gave me some. I asked him where he got it from because it was unusual, and he said that he had to go into Lhasa quite often to see the *chandzo* of a labrang and it was from there that he got it. It seemed plausible enough so I chose to believe him. Later he brought a very nice piece of woolen cloth called a *phu-rug*—a piece of cloth better than a *yaday*—and said he was going to make an upper jacket with it. Then, a few days before the participants in the debate were expected back, he brought a bundle of things and asked me to keep them in my room. I did not feel comfortable about having his things in my room, but there was a little annex to it where I said he was welcome to put them if he really wanted to.

When Tsering Chophel got back he found his room pretty much cleaned out. My friend had been going there everyday, eating what he found and taking his belongings. The day after he got back there was an assembly and my friend walked into it carrying Tsering Chophel's tea bowl. When he was seen doing this, people knew he was the thief. Quite a few of Tsering Chophel's belongings were found in his room. Then, since we were known to be friends, suspicion fell on me too. My guru confronted me and asked me if I had been involved. "Did you steal from Tsering Chophel?" he asked me, and I said no. "Did you eat any of his meat?" "Yes," I said, "I did eat some." "And did you go together with him to get it?" "No I did not," I said. "He came with it and when I asked him where he got it he said that it had been given to him in Lhasa." I told him that I had not eaten much of it. "Have you received anything else from him?" he asked, and I told him about the bundle that he had brought and left in the annex. Then my guru said to me straight, "That boy is a thief and I think that you were in on it with him." I said that even though Tsering Chophel's room was close by I did not know about it.

A day or so later the boy's guru and Tsering Chophel came to see me. They said that it was a very dangerous situation. The boy was a thief and the next day there was going to be a general Drepung assembly where he would be formally accused and then expelled from the monastery. In fact they both liked me, but to test me they said that I would probably be summoned before the assembly as well. Although they were joking, I cannot even begin to tell you how scared I was. The thought of facing my Red Uncle having been expelled for stealing, even if I had not done so, was unbearable. I could not settle down and as night fell I was totally beside myself. They found out about how scared I was and immediately sent for me. "We were only frightening you," they told me. "We know you did not do it and we have decided not to take the matter to the central authority of Drepung because if we did you would also probably get into trouble. Your friend is leaving the monastery at the new year so we have decided to let the whole thing blow over. Study hard and do not worry." I was so scared that I did not trust them. I thought that the authorities would come at any moment, no matter how much they reassured me. They said to me that I should be careful about my friends, that I should not eat with just anybody, and that I should be particularly careful about avoiding the gangs of troublesome monks if I was going to be successful with my studies. Tsering Chophel told me, "Go with the well-behaved monks, not forgetting that there are all sorts of people here in the monastery. He robbed me but since you were associated with him you got stained. And be careful also when you go into Lhasa as well. Do not go around with people with bad reputations—even going to certain monks' quarters is an act you should be mindful of." He gave me excellent advice and it connected with me, went deep into my heart. How terrible I thought, not to have been in the monastery for even a year and to have such a story get out and be known back in my part of Tibet, just because of choosing my acquaintances carelessly.

It was on account of this, and the other early experiences, that my sense of confidence, my arrogance, disappeared. It was there within me but only faint like a dream after this. It was as if I had the stuffing knocked out of me. Later, looking back on those early experiences which so scared me, which left me so apprehensive of making a mistake, so uneasy about entering into relationships, which left me feeling shy and humble, I saw them as most fortunate indeed. Hardships that turn into friends, that is what they are called. At the time they are experienced they are most distressing, but they stamp out arrogance and youthful delinquency and give a young man the break which sets him on a better path.

In those early days at Drepung I did not get much opportunity to study. I felt very sad when I contemplated this because when I had first arrived I had the opportunity to go into Ludrub labrang. Even though I would not have had the opportunity to study there, I would have been earning my keep; I would not have just been spending money and having trouble with food, living quarters, and acquaintances. I started to think that maybe I did not have the forehead, as we say in our part of the world, for studying the dharma. I did not have the merit. I could not go over to the labrang now because I had said I wanted to study, but my guru had not arranged for anybody to teach me scripture—he was only interested in using me as a debt collector.

ONE OF THE DUTIES of the house guru was lending out house money at interest and it became one of my jobs to go with him to collect what was owed. At first he took me with him to show me where to go and how to do it and then later he would send me off alone. I was always having to go off to collect this money, and my study periods, not long anyway, shrunk even further. Things went on this way, with a bit of study now and then, but mainly I was collecting debts for my guru.

I remember being sent out to Nyimo-ganga, across a big river that came down from Tilung-phug. The people I had to go to get the money from had a roof over their heads but not much to eat. It made me feel terrible to be collecting a debt from people who were so poor. I had set out in the morning with a proper meal's worth of good tsampa, and here I was faced with the task of asking for money from people who were eating far worse tsampa than mine, and hardly enough of it. How could I force them to pay? When they, trying to be respectful to a monk, gave me some of their blackish tsampa and tea I said that I could not possibly take it off them. I spoke openly with them, gave them some of my own tsampa and said that if my guru ever came they should tell him that I gave them a really hard time trying to collect the money, not to tell him that I had been friendly and given them some of my own food.

There was another person who owed our house money who lived in a dirty hut. When I arrived, there were six or seven people huddled in there trying to keep warm. The place was so horrid that I didn't even want to go inside, but it was far from the monastery and I had to stay the night. All they could give me to sleep on was a *phu-kug*, a thick Tibetan grain sack, and a few other bags and a black covering. In the evening they made a soup of the nettles that we Tibetans say carry the blessing of Milarepa. It was revolting to look at but once you ate some it was not bad. We ate huddled around their little stove and then I had a fitful sleep, freezing like all the rest of them. We got up early in the morning and I told them that I could not ask them for the grain that they owed. I knew I was going to get an earful from my guru, but there was just no way I could get the grain back. I told them too, if my guru came, not to tell him that I had let them off.

That summer my guru told me to go back to Nyimo-ganga, to the first house where I had failed to collect the debt. When I had gone before, the river bed had been pretty dry; none of the overflow rivulets had water in them and I had been able to go across just by hiking up my monk's robes. This time I was in over my knees even as I was crossing the rivulets. The people in the house caught sight of me and shouted for me to go back, but I figured they were just pretending it was too dangerous because they did not want to face me asking for the repayment. In fact I should have realized that it was too dangerous, because if the water was up over my knees in the rivulets it was definitely going to be very deep in the main channel. I made it across some of the rivulets and then followed the path of a rock channel which was used to divert the water to different fields. Then I started out across the main floodway. It was all churned up, carrying sand and small pebbles, but by then I was too far across to turn back and I had to keep going. The water was up well above my waist and was going at a terrific speed. I hit a pool at the same time as a wave came through and I experienced terror as I started to be swept away. Luckily I found a big, strategically placed stone and was able to save myself. My mind was racing and I began to think of the stupidity of it all—how hard it had been to make the trip to Lhasa from my part of the country. I thought of my house, and of my hopes for study in Lhasa, and how I only ended up as the unpaid servant of a man who wanted me to go out collecting his debts. I felt enraged at my guru.

The people I was trying to reach were all looking at me anxiously from their house, and I began to back up, a careful step at a time, until I reached slightly higher ground. By then all thought of crossing the river to collect the debt had gone. The people were waving to me to go back; there were by then a line of people who had left their work in the fields and were all watching my progress anxiously. I was exhausted, but still had a big stretch of river to go back across. My fear and fatigue made it difficult, but I hiked up my robes, put my food on my head and with fervent prayers to the Glorious Goddess somehow made it across to the shore. I could see the people slowly returning to their work when they were sure I was safe. By this time it was quite late and I stopped for a rest at a different house that had earlier borrowed seed-grain from the monastery, but which was now seeing better times. They said that it was wrong to send out a new young monk who had no understanding of the district in such a way. I was not able to eat any of the food that I had brought with me because I was still in a state of shock. They gave me some tea, which I eventually drank, and then slowly slowly I made my way back home. I arrived probably well after twelve o'clock at night and fell asleep, exhausted.

When I woke the next morning, instead of getting up as I would usually do and going along to see my guru and have breakfast, I just stayed in bed. I could not stop myself from thinking that the whole situation was hopeless. I had come up to study but was totally alone in the world and was just being worked like a donkey. I was so depressed I stayed in bed until finally my guru came looking for me. When he asked me what was wrong I said to him that I wanted to give up and go home. I told him I had come to study but he kept sending me out again and again to collect the debts. I was no more than a donkey, I said, without anybody who loved me, so there was no reason to stay. I felt humiliated and I had decided I could put up with it no more. My guru said he had not realized that the work he was giving me was so hard on me. "Do not worry," he said, "I will not send you out again and things will go better for you. Do not give up hope." Then he sent me to another monk for breakfast (he must have told him about my state of mind) and this old monk encouraged me, saying that I should not go home but should stay for my three years. He said that Gendun had not realized how hard the work was for me and that I would not be expected to do it again.

ONCE INTO ITS RHYTHM there was a certainty to the monastic year. The new year fell in early spring. The time from the beginning of the third Tibetan month until the full moon of the sixth was called "crowned by debates," and contained three debate periods. The first debate period lasted fifteen days, and the monks were given two breaks called "wood-collecting days." It had once been the custom of the monasteries for the monks to go out to collect wood on these days, but now it was just the name for the weekly holiday. On the evenings before these breaks there was a formal debate in the house that could easily go on until two or even until five in the morning. Younger monks who had nothing to debate about simply sat there while the more learned ones debated on into the night. The house guru would sometimes call out one or more of the new monks from the debate to recite a particular passage that should have been memorized, to make sure that they were studying hard. He could not, however, call out an older monk, only the very new arrivals.

The morning after an all-night formal debate, you could sleep in and miss the general assembly tea. There were no prayers scheduled in the house for that day and you could make tea in your own room. The monks would also prepare a better meal and have a special time. This meant that of the fifteen days, there were two days when you had a good meal. On the wood-collecting day you could also go outside the boundaries of the monasteries to wash and take it easy, arriving back in the monastery in the evening after a pleasant day off. New students did not have to sit for their evening recitation on that day, so they always carried around in their minds that it was so many days until the next wood-collecting day, though the day was not on a calendar and could be put off for a while or brought up a few days earlier. The second debate lasted twenty days (this was during the fourth Tibetan month) and there were three wood-collecting days. The final debate lasted for a month, and had four wood-collecting days.

After the period called "crowned by debates," a long summer retreat took place that lasted from the full moon of the sixth month to the new moon of the eighth. Most Loseling monks, particularly the studious ones, would go to live in caves during this period. At Sera this custom was not so widespread. Drepung Gomang monks would find themselves a room to live in around the monastic complex and study there. At Ganden, individual monks had particular households who sponsored their study breaks. The monks would go off to those different households to do their study and they would receive alms from the sponsors. If the monk was diligent, the sponsors would send them back from the break with food and coins, and when it came time to become a geshey the sponsors would often meet their expenses.

The summer break (called the "rains retreat" in India) was a time when monks had to remain in one place, so from that point of view our retreat in the caves was not right because we would always have to wander about to find wood to make our tea. The general Drepung governing body sometimes banned monks from going up into the mountain caves for the long study retreats because of this. But it had become a tradition in many of the houses of Loseling, so the general governing body usually did not insist on having its way in this matter. The monks who went up to the caves did not take the summer rains retreat vows to keep within strict boundaries. They treated their study as even more important, at this point, than keeping the formal *vinaya* rules of the summer rains retreat, and missed the latter in order to do the former more fully.

During the winter, when the weather got too cold, the monks returned to the monastery, though some would stay on even until the end of the eighth month, missing the first month of autumn debate. A few hardy souls would return to study in the caves as early as the study break in the third Tibetan month, and by the ten-day break in the fourth month many were studying there.

After the end of the summer retreat a long uninterrupted debate period of two months would begin, with only a fifteen-day break. During this time the new monks would arrive, often bringing letters that had been sent from one's homeland. If you had letters to send back, it was during these times that you would write and send them. So it was not a time for deep study. There were relatives and people from home to talk to and traders to contact before they left Lhasa to return to Kham.

The study year ended with a winter debate called the Jamyang Gun-cho. It took place in a special debate ground not far from Lhasa where all three monasteries had buildings. The monks stayed there for about six weeks studying and debating the topics in Dharmakirti's *Commentary on Valid Cognition.* They returned to their home monasteries just before new year and then came together again to participate in a number of prayer festivals, the most important being the Monlam Chen-mo, which began in Lhasa on the fifth day of the new year and lasted until nearly the end of the first month.

DURING MY FIRST SUMMER RETREAT my guru, Gendun, was attending a series of teachings and we younger monks were sent to the caves to attend to our memorization and study. One day about halfway through the study period, I came down to get some things from my room and I had to find my guru to get the key from him. I found him in the assembly hall just as the lama was beginning the teaching. The lama had on the yellow hat of Tsong-khapa and was putting a text to the top of his head in reverence. I had never seen anything like that before in my life and was filled with wonder. I must learn from this man, I thought, I must have the opportunity to listen to him teach. I asked who the solemn and imposing lama was and learned he was the Khyab-chi Shudrub Rinpoche, from Litang. I went back to the caves full of enthusiasm and was able to memorize nearly the whole of the root text on Perfect Wisdom at that time.

Towards the end of this first summer retreat I fell sick. There was some sort of epidemic going around the three monasteries in those days and I must have caught it. I was in bed for the best part of two months, with no one to look after me. It was not the custom to take solicitous care of the sick as it is nowadays. One day I was visited by the *gendag*, a special monitor who made sure that monks were attending to their memorization. He had been wondering where I was, he said, because before I had been working so hard but then had been absent. When he saw me there sick without anyone looking after me he said it was not right. "I wonder if your teacher is looking after you as he should be," he said. "I will have a few words with him."

SOME OF THE MONKS were quite wealthy and lived well; some were as poor as mice. But there was a certain honor given to the very poor who still attempted to study. The teachers took a particular pleasure in the presence of such people and it was not long before they were given gifts and help. The house gurus in particular would treat them kindly, holding them up as examples to others, saying that they put their study even before their food. Even the abbots would get to know about a poor monk who was trying and would send down a little gift and inquire to make sure he was supported. So poverty in a monk was never the cause of his being looked down on; it was always a cause of being given greater respect in the monastery. This was one of the unique features of monastic life.

If a monk kept strongly to his studies he would often find himself very poor in worldly terms. In this sense it was built into the course of religious study that a monk would find that he would have to put his spiritual life ahead of even his own well-being, and to that extent would have to find a deeper faith to go ahead. But it was also built in that the monk who indeed found such a faith and inspiration within himself was never a peripheral figure in the monastery, but was rather the very central and most sustaining force within it. If a monk gave up even having enough to eat in order to be able to pursue the spiritual life, as he went further and further the respect accorded to him would grow and grow until his commitment and struggle became the cause of attaining the very greatest status in the monastery.

THE MONASTIC YEAR
AT DREPUNG LOSELING IN 1945

Days and months listed below are according to the Tibetan lunar calendar, which begins in late winter or very early spring.

1/1 - 1/4	New year celebration (*Losar*)
1/5 - 1/25	Big prayer festival (*Monlam chen-mo*)
1/26 - 1/30	Five-day study break (*Cho-tsham*)
2/1 - 2/15	Monastery debate (*Tratsang chodra*)
2/16 - 2/20	Five-day study break
2/21 - 2/30	Small prayer festival (*Tshogcho*). The last day of this was called *tshogcho sertreng suwang*, when all the valuables of the main temple were taken out in procession and big dances were held in front of the Potala.
3/1 - 3/30	Study break and the great spring debate session *(Che-cho chen-mo).*
4/1 - 4/10	Ten-day study break
4/11 - 4/30	Fourth month long debate
5/1 - 5/15	Fifteen-day study break
5/16 - 6/15	Summer month-long debate
6/15 - 8/1	Summer retreat in caves (*Cho-tsham chen mo*)
8/1 - 9/1	Autumn month-long debate (*Tong-cho chen-mo*)
9/1 - 9/15	Fifteen-day study break
9/16 - 9/30	Debate
10/1 - 10/15	Fifteen-day study break
10/16 - 10/30	Debate
11/1 - 11/15	Study break
11/16 - 12/15	Winter debate of all three monasteries (*Jung gunchoe*)
12/22 – 12/30	Seven-day prayer festival for all monks of Drepung (*Jamzhung chen-mo*). After this ended, it was the new year's holiday.

3

DREPUNG MONASTERY

Young monks arrive in Lhasa from their home monasteries in late fall, in the eighth Tibetan month. The first thing they do after settling in is to begin studying *Du-dra* (Collected Topics). Some studied this for one year, some for one and a half years and some for two years. There was no specific time for this early part of the course. Halfway through this course of study, after the end of the prayer festival, the student had to take an oral examination. After this was successfully completed he could go on to the Perfect Wisdom class that began in the second month, after the end of the Monlam Chen-mo prayer festival. Because of this, since new monks from Kham arrived in Lhasa in late summer, it was possible that some students would begin to study Perfect Wisdom after just half a year of Collected Topics. The Perfect Wisdom course was a six year one. The course was divided up into parts—there was a tradition of what was studied during each year and there were particular topics which had to be dealt with. The teaching would be structured to convey the essentials of particular topics. In the first two years there were less topics but the amount of debate about them was more. In the third and fourth years there were more topics but it was not absolutely necessary for every topic to be fully covered if there was not enough time. It would often be that some of the crucial topics were taught over again to make sure that the essence of the topic was indeed conveyed to the student. If a student, for whatever reason, missed some topics of an earlier year, there was no provision for repeating them. One just missed that part and picked up with a gap.

The first year of Perfect Wisdom was known by the topic of the Three Bodies of the Buddha, and the year following that the new monk would be introduced to Definitive and Interpretative Statements. Students would prepare for this by memorizing Tsong-khapa's *Speech of Gold*. When a monk was doing this topic it was not absolutely necessary that he get taught Tsong-khapa's book, but if one had the time and fortune to do so, it would be considered a full and excellent teaching. Similarly, when one was doing the topic of Bodhichitta, which gave its name to the third year, it was not necessary that the relevant sections of Tsong-khapa's *Great Exposition of the Path* be consulted, but if they were included, it would be considered full and excellent. The basic text used was the monastic *yik-cha*, or textbook, through which the essence of the topic would be conveyed. Going beyond that was better, but not necessary.

What one's guru was trying to get across was the essential point of a topic. The full text, the different chapters in it, the sentences and what each meant or did not mean were not the focus. The simple transmission of a part of a text through having heard it read aloud was not considered particularly helpful or important either. Once the essentials of a topic were explained, the different ramifications of the point of that topic had to be explored through debate.

The community of learned monks did not rate so highly the person who was able to set out in full the divisions of an argument or the exact way that a particular author went through it. The scholar-monk most highly regarded was the one who had grasped the deeper implications of a topic and could explore those implications in a structured debate without feeling lost when moving away from the specifics of a particular presentation. There were scholars in the community of monks who were great at book learning, who would be able to skate all over the surface of a number of sacred texts and who had the ability to recite from memory large pieces of them. But if they could not, in a debate, leave the surface of the text to explore with confidence some of the deeper ramifications of a particular argument, they were not rated amongst the finest. They were called "uncle parrots" for their ability to recall what they had heard without having plumbed the meaning of it.

The finest of all, beyond even the ranks of competition, was the rare monk who was blessed both with the ability to recall from memory passages from sacred texts and to move with ease through the depths of arguments that teased out the implications and deeper meanings.

If one had to be sacrificed, though, it was considered better to lack the ability to quote from memory passages of the sacred texts. The monk who could bring out the essential meaning quickly and keep it in focus for the other participants to consider, coming at it from a number of angles, was the object of great admiration. The point is, of course, that he was talking about something real, and reality has a pull of its own. People naturally prick up their ears when they hear a debate or conversation that is coursing in reality, in the way things are from one's own experience or intuition. Such a person is always admired even if in the end he is defeated with a number of carefully constructed arguments. Even the fact that the particular position that such a person has attempted to defend is demonstrated to be untenable in the final analysis is not considered so important if, in his attempt to defend it, he demonstrated an ability to penetrate to the essence and to retain it in his mind and allow exploration of it. Those who are capable of debate, who are intellectually gifted, will not reject such a person as an interesting and valuable interlocutor even though he may well lose in debate again and again.

Monks who insisted on a close reading of what a text literally said and who were scared to venture afield into the realm of thoughts that followed naturally from an apprehension of the essence of a topic were not only not valued particularly highly but could even be hauled up by the older monks. The abbot might tell them to stop being so literal-minded and to look deeper for the meaning. Conversely, even if a debater was off a bit from what a sacred text said, still, if his debate was based on some contact with a reality which was authentic, then he would be admired, even praised for his honest attempt to find meaning. Even if he was in opposition to an accepted position of the monastic textbook, his straightforward and honest intellect would be praised. Who cared if a person was not following the party line if his position was one which opened up a view of reality? Since that was what we were drawn to, we naturally felt admiration when it became opened to us.

It was because of this search for meaning that the more important topics might be taught to a student not just once but two or three times, while there were other topics which should have been learned, but which were skipped over and not taught in any depth at all. Those less important parts might be taught in a day. One might be in a class where the teacher read quickly through fifteen or twenty pages of a text when it was not a crucial part, and then at another time one would not get through a page even in an hour and a half. At another time one would be stuck on two lines for a day or more. The lines might occasion a whole series of investigations such that when the class next met, the teacher would be stuck right there and another whole class would be spent dealing with the ramifications, going through the argument with the responses and the counter-responses, the lines of ideas which led to dead ends or which led to greater and clearer vistas of the vast and profound. The teachers would be happy on account of such occurrences, not irritated that they were not able to go quickly on.

That is how the teaching proceeded and the student's knowledge increased. The yearly oral examinations went on, but they were not strict affairs. During the year there were also interclass debate sessions when the next higher year debated with the class below it. At such times only the more gifted of the class would debate. For the rest, particularly those who had not been studying much, it was not much more than a show, and they watched from the outside without entering into the contest. The only strict oral examinations were those that the new monks had to take in front of their house guru when they first came into the monastery. After that, at higher level, it was not strict, and how much one wanted to push oneself was a personal matter. If one had nothing to recite, nothing to be examined on orally, then nobody would come and tell you that you had to do an oral examination. If you wanted to be examined you could be examined on the amount you knew; if you did not have anything that was alright as well. Your teacher or the abbot might give the general advice that it was important to study, or might even belittle or abuse you for wasting precious time, but such advice was just that—there was never any talk of being expelled from the monastery if you did not study. If you took the advice to heart you studied; if you did not, that was your own choice.

There were quite a number of older monks who hardly ever went to teachings; they were totally out of that part of the monastery life. But again there were some amongst those who would, after a time, begin to attend classes again and begin to study more and more. On the other hand there were those who had spent their whole lives in study only to become slowly slowly more caught up in some sort of more ordinary activity, such that the time they gave to study became less and less. Over us all there was no fearful monastic authority insisting that this or that had to be done on threat of expulsion or whatever. When a monk who had studied hard began to descend into the ordinary worldly activities of the monastery, nothing was there to stop him, though he knew that in the silence of the halls, behind his back, the other monks were remarking on how sad it was, what a waste that so-and-so had fallen to spend his time in less meaningful activity.

There were also monks in the monastery who were not gifted at study but who lived a sincere life saying their prayers, doing their recitations, and attending the assemblies with faith and devotion. They were much valued and praised for their practice and it would be said of them in conversation that though they were not gifted intellectually they were admirable, sincere in their spiritual practices, and ornaments to the community. There was another sort of monk who would be found in the classes studying but then would not be there for a few days. He would have accepted an invitation to perform a ritual in the town, for the laity. Such a person was looked down on somewhat because it was considered that he liked the ease of city life, liked being treated as someone special, and liked the good food and offerings that would come his way from having done the ritual. That is not to put them down, though. It was hard to be hungry when there was a way to get a good meal. When you were hungry, when you had been studying hard, and all you had to do was accept an invitation to do a ritual to get a good meal, then it was understandable that you would do it, but it was not something that engendered respect. The problem was that after having a taste it was hard to keep from returning to it. Once you went to do one lay ritual it tended to escalate until there was nothing else that you were doing besides that.

A SPECIAL MILESTONE was reached when a class got to the topic of Definitive and Interpretative Scripture. All of the students from the different houses who were in that class would pool their money and buy good food and have a good time during the debate period. The disciplinarian and sub-disciplinarian would turn a blind eye during these few days and let the monks enjoy themselves because they wanted the monks who studied hard to know that enjoyment was not divorced from the life they had chosen to lead. When monks were that far into Perfect Wisdom they were no longer just dabbling and had a certain status that allowed them to ask for this special dispensation from the strict discipline of the monastery.

After a year or so of Collected Topics and six years of doing as much Perfect Wisdom as one was able, one went on to the study of the Middle Way. There were only two years to this course, but when a monk had advanced this far, everyone knew he was serious. The monks of that class would offer a meal to the general authority of the monastery, and having done so they would be allowed to carry on their shoulder the distinctive yellow hat of our order and they could wear it in the assemblies. Prior to this they were not allowed to wear their hats. Now when they went to the general assembly they no longer needed to line up outside, but with much dignity, with their hats on their shoulders, they could pass the younger monks and enter directly into the assembly and take their seats. Those who had not advanced to that stage in their monastic career had to stay outside where they recited the mantra of Tsong-khapa. The great doors into the main assembly hall would be opened wide as the older, hat-bearing monks entered. Then, after they had all entered, the doors would be closed and the newer monks, still reciting the Tsong-khapa mantra, would rush up the steps to crowd in against the door which would soon be flung open and they would all rush in. Once inside, the hat-bearing monks did not have to get up to answer the call for tea-pourers; they had passed beyond that stage. This was the case both in the general and college assemblies—those with hats did not have to pour tea.

After two years in the Middle Way class, those in Drepung Loseling passed on to five years in the study of Vinaya (Discipline). After that, they passed into the first or highest class—the fifth of the five classes. This was when one studied Abhidharma and revised the earlier work one had done, and then could finally become a geshey. There was an exception made for incarnate lamas, but it would usually take an ordinary monk twenty or even twenty-five years of study before he would be allowed to be able to enter into the ranks of the gesheys.

MY STUDIES BEGAN with the first topic in the Collected Topics, on colors, and then about five or six months after that, we moved on to the "Little Cause and Effect" chapter on the topic of karma. In the sixth month of their first full year, students have to pass an oral examination in this topic, so it is thought to be especially important. My own teacher, the young monk who helped me when he saw my guru Gendun was not teaching me, was not a particularly learned person, and was only three years above me, but he was a truly humble and spiritual being. To prepare me for this oral examination he explained to me the line from Dharmakirti's *Commentary on Valid Cognition* that says that no result will come about unless and until all the component parts of a necessary causal complex are present. I felt a great confidence in the truth of this statement and the doctrine that lay behind it. Even while I had been in my home monastery I had great faith in cause and effect because there was a teacher there who used to tell me stories from the sutras about karma. He was a riveting storyteller and his words had a great effect on me. My belief was strengthened even more by my study of cause and effect during my first year at Drepung, and as my faith grew so did my intention to remain in the monastery studying until the end of the course. Even during my first twelve months at Drepung when life was so hard, when I was only able to study very little, I still carried within me this growing intention to stick at it, even though I always felt pulled in two directions.

My attachment to my home in Kongjo-rawa was very strong. I had an imprint so deep in my mind that even though I was moved deeply by the advice of my gurus and friends, my thoughts would keep returning to my homeland. Sometimes it was so strong I could not stop it. But just when it was nearly unbearable, the other part of me would surface and I would be filled with a desire to study even if it meant never seeing my family or homeland again. That is what happens in a mind that has become habituated to places or people—even when it is filled with faith and enthusiasm, it can be suddenly overwhelmed with the desire to see something from the past. The need can totally overpower you.

SOON AFTER I RECOVERED from my sickness, the monks began preparing to leave for the Jamyang Gun-cho winter debate. I had missed the first one since my guru Gendun had made no arrangements for me to attend, and when I asked him if I could go to this one, he said it would be stupid because I had not been studying. I got quite upset and said the reason I had not been studying was because he had not arranged for me to have a teacher. I threatened to quit, saying I was going home immediately after the next prayer festival, and I told him that since I was learning nothing I wanted to go to the debate at least to get the blessing from the place. This was a silly reason but it was enough to get my guru to let me go.

When I arrived at the winter debate I was completely lost. My guru had not arranged for me to meet a teacher, so I was alone again. Luckily there were instructors for people in my situation. There were overseers who found out which monks were without teachers and we drew lots to decide where we should go. My lot fell to Gen Yaro, perhaps the most famous teacher at the gathering. There were about ten or twelve other students already with him, and he taught logic. I entered the class with another monk, but neither of us could understand any of the teaching. I think someone must have told Gen Yaro because after a few days he said that we should come separately and we did. Even with his help I still couldn't do the rudimentary memorization, nor was I capable of understanding even the most basic things, so Gen Yaro said to me that I should not go to any of the debating sessions or to the recitations. He told me just to go to the prayer and during the rest of the time to make prostrations. I followed his instructions, and was very happy to do so.

For the whole time that the debate was going on I prostrated fervently. After a short while, I starting receiving personal instruction from Gen Yaro again and I began to get the hang of it. I started going to the debates. I improved so quickly that by the end of that winter debate I was better than the new monks who had come to the debates the year earlier. I was pleased with myself and my teacher was also very pleasantly surprised that I was so good after such an inauspicious start.

For the first time I began to feel that it was possible for me to study and be successful at it. About a month of the debate had passed by this time. During the two weeks left the debate slackened off as we began to memorize the things that we would have to know when we arrived back at our colleges. We met in groups where we would do recitations and have more general discussions. One day Gen Yaro told me to go out and lead the discussion. When I first got to the class I had been so stupid that the other students had been talking about me, but now Gen Yaro wanted to use me as an example for the others. Most of the other monks participated in the session I was leading, but three of the best students from before did not join in. Gen Yaro berated them: "Just a month ago you were saying how stupid he was, how he could not understand anything. It was you who were way out in front, but you have been lazy while Lobsang Gyatso here has been working as hard as he can. Now it is you who are lagging behind and he has overtaken you!" I got quite puffed up over all this success and towards the very end of the winter debate I began to be unable to understand as well as I had earlier.

At the end of the Jamyang Gun-cho there was the main debate when everybody had to get up and show their skills. I did quite well. Some of the others were limited to just reciting aloud bits of memorization but I was able to utilize some of the more basic principles of pervasion and logic to demonstrate a more comprehensive understanding of the topics. My memorization also went off excellently so the whole event was, for me, a great success.

When I got back to Drepung, Gendun said that I had done well and that I should give up my plan to go back home after the new year's prayer festivals. There was an extra thirteenth month in the calendar that year (you get an extra month now and then because ours is a lunar calendar) and during that month Gendun said I should start learning Perfect Wisdom and he taught me some basics. One day when I was in his room he started debating with me on some logic and I was quite good in my answers. He was obviously pleased and said to me that I was intelligent and showing promise, but that I was getting too conceited and arrogant. He told me that as one studied one should never allow arrogance or conceit to come in. Actually I was not so conceited, but Gendun's other main student was jealous of me because he was not catching on as quickly, and he had told Gendun that I was becoming very conceited and arrogant. So Gendun really laid into me and said I was getting unbearable. It was true that I was a bit full of myself in the sense that I thought I was from a good background and had an ample share of talent, but I did not feel I had done anything to make people consider me arrogant. But what could I do? He filled up a valley with his scolding and I had to listen to all of it.

ON THE FIFTH DAY of the new year many of the monks go to see the famous Sera *ton-je,* a huge figure of the Buddha that is put on display. I was still considering going home after the prayer festivals so I thought it would be a good idea to get the blessing of the *ton-je* before leaving. I asked my guru if I could go, and having received permission I set off with a few other monks. Until we passed beyond the fence of the monastery grounds we wore our clothes properly, but once we got outside the fence we all changed our clothes into the fighting monks' style, hiking up our lower garments and slinging our upper garments in a rakish way above our shoulders. All the fighting monks wore a red rope bracelet on their upper arm, around the muscle, and we got out ours to wear. I do not know why, but I had quite an idea of myself as a fighting monk, it held out quite an aura to me.

When we got to Sera I stayed with the monk Phuntsog, my traveling companion from my trip to Lhasa. After a day or so we got talking and he asked me why I was wearing my clothes like a fighting monk. "You went to the winter debate," he said. "You have been studying. It

is not right to go around like that. You should be thinking of studying
as hard as you can." He gave me a long lecture on how it was wrong
to go around as a fighting monk and about how important it was to
study. Because of that I put my lower robe down properly and for the
rest of the time I dressed and acted like a proper monk.

While I was there the Sera monks from Kongjo-rawa all got together
and said I had to sit *damcha*, to be the main respondent in a debate. I
refused. They said I had to do it—wasn't I the young monk who was
the star of the general winter debate? They came after me in a group,
and sort of as a joke, but also to show off their learning at my expense,
they lifted me up bodily and took me to the debate ground. They had
a low throne there but I could not sit on it; I felt totally inadequate to
be on a throne. Then one of them started debating and asked me the
definition of a valid reason. I said, "Something that *is* the three modes."
Now, in Sera Monastery they say, "something that meets the requirements of the three modes," so when I gave my different answer they
were totally perplexed. Since they were new they had never heard of
such a definition and were dumbfounded. After a little while one of
the older monks came to say that I had done well. He said that it was
an auspicious beginning to things and said that I did not need to sit to
answer anymore. He praised me very much.

I began to think that I would have to learn Buddhism well, otherwise there was a real danger that I would lose face. I had been carried
bodily into the debate ground and even though I had been able to
acquit myself with credit, it was really just luck on my part. If it happened to me again then I would be stuck out there on my own unable
to answer and everyone would take me for a fool. I remembered what
my Red Uncle had said to me time and again about the importance of
studying, and I thought about how many other people had told me the
same. For the first time I really began to get a strong urge to study, and
to study hard and long enough to be able to acquit myself with dignity and to feel pride in the presence of my mentors and countrymen.

I WENT DOWN TO LHASA to attend the prayer festival and continued
with my memorization and study of the scriptures. Many people urged
me to keep on with my study and gave me advice about its importance and not giving up. Many monks were very solicitous and kind
to me. On the fifteenth day of the prayer festival I was wandering
about and came across some booksellers. I picked up a little book—I
think it must have been a book about the practices of Bodhisattvas—

and bought it. A bit later, when I was going through it, I came across a passage that grabbed my attention. It said, "One's native place is the prison of the demon Mara and one's parents are the snare that he uses to get one inside." How strange, I thought, to say of one's mother and father, who are the very kindest of all people, that they are the snare of Mara. It does not seem quite right. Then some time later, when I was back in the monastery and the debate sessions were underway again, I asked Gen Yaro what the verse meant. He had become my teacher and was gentle as he gave me a complete explanation. "It is like this," he said. "If one does not stick to one's attempt to train in the higher spiritual life but leaves the monastery and returns to one's native place, it is as though one is being dragged back by a demon, in the form of attachment to one's parents, to a life that, without higher understandings, is but a prison. There one has to attend to all the work around the house and in the fields and one has to become involved with all the hates and needs of the house-owner. What is this," he asked, "but a prison? There are so many things that have to be done to run a house properly; there are so many things that are never quite right, that require attention and take one away from one's higher training. One's love becomes restricted to a family circle and those outside are no longer important, taking away one's possibility for higher spiritual life. As for the way in which one's parents are the demon's snare, it is because they are always sending you letters to come home—they are always saying they miss you so much, telling you that you have studied enough and that you should come back home. It is in no way saying that one's parents are not the kindest of all; it is not denying that one has a great responsibility towards them. But their letters and concerns slowly build up to cause you to leave the spiritual life and go home, like a snare around the neck of a person being led off to jail."

Then he said that in my case only my mother was left at home, my father having already passed away, and she, bless her, was a simple soul and unable to lead me along a spiritual path. It was my older sister who continually wrote to say that I should come back. "It is those letters," he said, "like that one you got from your sister a short while back, and that you showed to me, telling you to come home. There it is! The demon's snare dragging you back to your homeland where you will become nonvirtuous and suffer in the jail of cyclic existence." Gen Yaro then leaned over towards me and asked me why I had such a feeling of homesickness. "Think about it deeply," he said, "and then come and tell me what you have found. And think about the meaning of the two lines: is your native place a jail? Are letters from your relations the snares of Mara or not? If you think about this you will feel in your heart the meaning of these two lines."

So I thought about it. "Just what is it exactly that is so attractive in my homeland that exerts such a pull?" I asked myself. "If I leave here and decide to live in my monastery back home what will happen? The first five years I will have my head stuck in memorizing the monastery's different rituals and chants and prayers. My world will revolve around that. Then there are the different responsibilities that get apportioned out. I will have to do those. And on top of this I will have responsibilities to my ancestral lands and family members which I cannot escape. If the country was attacked, as a monk of Dondup-ling I would have a responsibility to mount a defence and would have to carry arms." I began to feel strongly that there was no way to be a monk, as a monk was expected to be, unless I stayed in Drepung, and that if I went back to my homeland any possibility of being a decent monk would be lost forever. This opportunity provided to me by my life—that I could truly be a fine monk—there was no doubt, I felt, if I went back home it would be irrevocably wasted. "Apart from not wanting to be separated from my kinfolk, what else is operating within me?" I asked myself. The advice of that old man who killed the chicken began to ring in my ears, as it had once before on the journey up to Lhasa, and with it came the thought of him coming up to me and spitting in my face out of disgust. It began to sound like precious advice, and I thought that I simply had to continue studying—there was no other proper path for me to follow.

After five or six days I was with Gen Yaro again and he asked me what I had been thinking. "I have been thinking," I said, "that if I go home there is nothing there for me. So I do not want to go home, but I see the hardship involved in staying and that is a little bit frightening." My teacher was pleased and encouraged me with the story of Milarepa, reading from his biography. "Look how he struggled, living just on the first leaves of the nettle bush and making such an effort that in a single lifetime he reached the stage of enlightenment itself. Compare your food with his—your situation is not that bad at all. I am not saying you will get enlightened, but I am saying that if you keep trying you will gain a great result. Your Red Uncle is urging you to keep at your studies and not return. He has studied and knows about virtue and nonvirtue in the deeper sense of the words, something that the other members of your family do not know, so you should pay heed to his advice should you not? The advice of those who are ignorant of virtue and nonvirtue should not have more influence over you than the advice of those who know what virtue and nonvirtue entail." I then told him what the old man had said to me before I left and he said I was lucky to get such advice—it was precious oral instruction itself. "As for your ability to learn," he said, "do not worry about it. You will do all right. It will be difficult but you will be able to bear it. If you really get into any problem with money and food, come and tell me and I will try to help you as much as I can."

WHEN I GOT TO THE important section in the first year of Perfect Wisdom where it says that things are neither one nor many, I went to Pangon Rinpoche and asked him to teach me. He accepted and during that time my interest in the ultimate meaning was sparked and I began to reflect on emptiness. Of course I had not even heard the profound middle-way philosophy at this time (that would come more than five years later), but the idea that something is real only insofar as it is given reality because of looking the way it does made a strong impact on me. I would sit reflecting and meditating on the truth of it.

One day Gen Yaro told me that if I wanted to complete the whole course of study and become a geshey then I should begin showing respect to those who wore the tattered clothes of the fully ordained monk. In Loseling we had the custom that only monks who had studied Vinaya (Discipline) could wear those clothes, and they were the only ones who could wear the *chab-ben*—the square of brocade, at the top of which is a small container for water for the monk to wash his mouth out after a meal. I took his advice to heart, and if I was sitting down and a monk wearing those tattered clothes came by I would immediately stand up and bow with respect.

NOT LONG AFTER I ARRIVED in Drepung, the young Fourteenth Dalai Lama was being introduced into the three great monasteries and there were huge preparations taking place. At this same time a problem came up between Sera Monastery and the central government, and this ended in a fight. Those who know modern Tibetan history will know all about this fight, and I will talk about it in more detail later. It happened during the small prayer festival that takes place in Lhasa at the end of the second month.

Following the Thirteenth Dalai Lama's death, Reting Rinpoche, the great reincarnate lama of Sera Jay college, had been appointed as regent of Tibet. But in 1941, after seven years in office, Reting quit mysteriously and Dalung-drak (also called Taktra Rinpoche) rose to power.

Some say that Dalung-drak was only meant to be a temporary regent, and that he and Reting Rinpoche had made a secret deal that Reting would reassume his power after three years. Regardless, the Reting household was still one of the most powerful and influential in all of Tibet, and its members were still in many of the high offices of government. As Dalung-drak's power grew, so did the conflict between his household and that of Reting. This conflict led to the arrest of Reting Rinpoche in 1947.

The Sera Jay monks were outraged by the arrest, mediation with the government failed, and the monks soon rose up in revolt. A battle followed, ending in the defeat of Sera; many monks died, and the government troops occupied Sera Jay college. During this troubled time we Drepung monks were forbidden to go down to Lhasa and were confined to the monastery. All of us were very unhappy because we felt that an attack on the monks of Sera was an attack on us and our interests as well. Since Dalung-drak was at the head of it all we had a very bad feeling about him; we were all depressed and would talk badly about him. One day Gen Yaro had heard that I had been criticizing Dalung-drak, and told me that it was wrong. He reminded me of the example of Songtsen Gampo, the religious king who was in fact an emanation of Avalokiteshvara, the god of compassion. Songtsen Gampo's work for the good of the people was beyond an ordinary person's comprehension, and sometimes what he did was hard to understand. My guru told me stories about him and also reminded me of the story of a monk at the time of the Buddha who saw everything the Buddha did as hypocritical. For seven years the works of the Buddha himself seemed to this monk to be just the deceitful actions of a devious person. "Practice the mind training that sees all of the actions of Dalung-drak as emanating from within a pure realm, without fault," he said, "and do not criticize him." So from then on I did not voice my dislike openly, but in my heart I did not like Dalung-drak at all.

It was a depressing time. After the defeat of Sera and I went down to see Chandzo Rabti and found him very dejected. He said that Dalung-drak had not been crooked, that the monks of Sera just would not listen. "It was a terrible shame that the war happened," he said. "So many monks have been ruined, their religious lives destroyed. It was Sera today," he said, "but it could just as easily be Drepung tomorrow. It seems to me that you should get out of the monastery as soon as you can, and we will both go home together. I cannot say that I am going to be able to look after you as I had promised your uncle earlier. We should just leave. I will buy you the clothes you need for the journey back and if you want to stay in Karnda Monastery, fine, or if you want to go back and stay in Dondup-ling I can arrange that too. One way or the other you should not stay in Lhasa."

When he said this I remember I was happy, thinking that it was certain that I was going home. Chandzo Rabti had even said that I could go home on a horse if I wanted. When I went back to the monastery and told Gen Yaro he told me that he doubted such an extreme step was necessary and said I should first go to ask for a divination from Pangon Rinpoche. "There are thousands of monks in Drepung," he said, "and all of them are not despairing and leaving for home. Go see the Rinpoche."

I went off to see Pangon Rinpoche, and my guru had obviously talked to him before I got there. When I asked for permission to go he said no. I did not know how to argue, so I lied and said I was having bad dreams. "So am I," said Rinpoche, "and so what? A dream is just a dream and means nothing." Then I said, "I am having terrible trouble with my teeth and am too poor nowadays to fix them." He said I was being idiotic. "If you are having trouble with your teeth the last place on earth to be is your homeland since there are no doctors or medicine there. Better to be in Lhasa where there are people who could do something about it." I tried every avenue to get him to agree, but no matter what reason I gave he said it was stupid and there was no need to go home. I began to think that it was wrong to keep pressing so hard when a holy being like the Rinpoche was so set against my going home. I wondered what profit he saw in my staying in Drepung.

A few days afterwards I began to have some doubt about whether I should really leave. When I talked to the Rinpoche again I said that I was still very worried, because even if I did stay I would have a lot of trouble later when I became the house guru because I was not going to have enough money to do the job. Rinpoche pulled out a great big wad of money and said he had plenty, and if that was what I was worried about I should put it out of my mind because he would bankroll me through without any problem. He made signs that I could take any money that I wanted. So I left in two minds, unsure if I should go or not. Pangon Rinpoche was closely associated with Chandzo Rabti, and during this period he sent word to the Chandzo, saying not to lead me astray by telling me it was time to go home. The next time I visited Chandzo Rabti he said to me that he had been wrong to be so negative. "I was depressed about the situation at that time," he said, "and I spoke out of turn." He told me that the Rinpoche had been speaking to him and that he should not have told me to prepare to leave. He advised me to stay and study, and said that although he was leaving town, he would leave money for me so that I would be taken care of.

Chandzo Rabti wanted to buy me a nice set of robes before he left, so he took me to the bazaar where they sell expensive woolen cloth. As a young monk I was not allowed to wear expensive wool, so even though he wanted to give me this gift, I could not accept it. But when finally we found a lower quality *yaday*, the coarser woolen cloth the poorer monks wore, the Chandzo was not happy about the quality and said there was no way he was buying that sort of rubbish. "If you want to buy it go ahead and do so," he said, "but I am not having anything to do with it." So in the end he didn't buy me anything. Then he said, as I was leaving for Drepung, "Be sure to come before I leave. I will be going soon and I have some things for you."

I felt humiliated at the way he had treated me and my pride led me to decide not to visit him again. Had I done so it would obviously have been to get a gift, and I felt that if the Chandzo really wanted to give me something he would do so whether I went or not. This was a stupid attitude on my part because he wanted to help me, but by not going when he was expecting my visit, I made him angry. He did not call me, and irritated by my silly behavior he left Lhasa without setting aside anything at all.

I always ended up poorer than expected. Because I was the nephew of the Boss of Choo-chur, a relative of Chandzo Rabti, and was known to Tra-tang labrang, everyone thought I had plenty of money. Everyone was sure I had many people looking after me, but in fact the money I brought from home and the money my Red Uncle sent to me was the only money I had.

I had a particular idea of karma—that each person should use what comes to them, but should not try to use the possessions of others. A person should not go around asking others for a share of their possessions, the things that they had come into because of the deeds that they had done in their earlier lives. My own merit gave me the right to what came my way, but it did not seem to me that I should try also to make use of other's merits. So I appreciated it if someone gave me something, but I would never ask for anything. I would write letters home telling my Red Uncle that a certain amount had arrived and thanking him, but I would not write letters asking for money, or saying that I had such and such a need. Before I left home, my Red Uncle had told me not to allow myself to become very poor—I was going to Lhasa to study, he said, and I had to stay in decent health to do that. He said that if the money he sent did not suffice for any reason, I should go to the Chandzo and take money off him and he would pay him back. "Do not use things without awareness," he said, "but do not sink into poverty either. Look after your health." So there was money with a number of people in Lhasa but I never asked for it, and since from their side they did not make an effort to give I became quite poor.

My study guru told me the stories of the holy beings and how poor they had been, how much they had to struggle—how Sonam Dragpa, the famous teacher of Loseling, had not even proper clothes to wear when he studied, how Jamyang Shepa, the famous teacher of Gomang, had to eat the dry leftover offering cakes, and how Trehor Chupon Rinpoche had nothing but a cracked earthen pot to cook in, and how he lived on soup. Of course, he also told me again and again how Milarepa had lived in cave eating nothing but nettles which had made his skin turn green, but how, by such hard work he achieved the state of enlightenment in one life. These stories made me feel that living as a poor person was the correct way to be, and the stories gave me a great inspiration, a capacity to go on.

Sometimes, with the same low quality tsampa day after day, I wondered if I could go on. But at other times this would turn to enthusiasm, and remembering Gen Yaro's advice I would feel happy and confident, even without food, thinking of my good fortune.

My understanding of karma also meant that I did not feel comfortable asking others to do work that I considered to be my own. In the monastery it is common for the senior monks to give some of their work to the younger students, but I have never felt comfortable with that custom. I try to do what I am supposed to do myself. I cook my own food, I do not ask for loans, and I do not try to cash in on others' good fortune. Even in India, where at times I have faced real hardship, I have not done so. As head of a school I have sought loans sometimes for the good of the school and students, but never for a personal project. Sometimes I have seen something attractive—a radio or tape-recorder—that a friend might have in his room. It comes to my mind that it would be nice to have something like that, but I hold back from asking. That is not to say I do not feel the tug, but I never ask, and if the person offers I always say no. If someone really has decided to give me something and has it there for me I will take it, otherwise not, because I made a sort of promise to myself back in those earlier years not to go beyond what my karma delivers to me. This is the kind of restraint that I learned in my first years in Drepung.

I STUDIED AND DEBATED HARD that year, becoming one of the best in my class. Then the Jamyang Gun-cho came around again. This was the cutoff point. Those who had decided to go home would not go to the debate and would start making preparations for departure after the Monlam Chen-mo prayer festival. I had told my teacher that I was going to stay, so even though I felt a tremendous pull to go home, I did not make any obvious preparations. Among those who had come up in the same year as me from my homeland, only one or two stayed on. All the other new monks in Phukhang house returned home.

After that winter debate, I went to my third prayer festival. I saw my friend Phuntsog from Sera, but the discipline was too strict for us to talk. Finally, on the last day of the *tsog-cho*—the smaller prayer festival that took place on the last ten days of the second month—there were not many sponsors and the discipline was more relaxed. We got together at a ceremony called the *su-wang*, and watched as all the valuables of the main temple were taken in procession around the Potala. We watched the big dances held in front of the Potala for the nobles, and Phuntsog told me that he had decided not to go home and was pleased that I had decided to stay and study as well. On this final day of the mini prayer-festival my guru had given me some extra money and some bread, so during the dances Phuntsog and I retired to a quiet place where we could talk at length. He spoke to me seriously. "We are next-door neighbors," he said. "I know your home and you know mine. We both know what is waiting for us there and we both know it is nothing but the waste of a precious opportunity. I have decided, come what may, that I am not going back and I want you to make a solemn oath to me, here and now, that you too will not return." This conversation hit me deep inside. Though Phuntsog was more gifted than I, still in years I was older than him and I should have been the one giving the advice. At Sera he had the great good fortune to find excellent house and scripture gurus. He had learned much while I was still basically ignorant. It upset me. I said that I could not make an oath but I would do everything in my power to remain and study, and I said that if I did decide to go home I would not go before coming to talk it over with him.

It was not just ordinary homesickness that made me hesitate about swearing an oath; our situations at home were different. There were many children in his family but I was the only boy in mine, and I felt more strongly the sense of responsibility that comes with that. I thought about the goats and yaks with no one to herd them, the work around the house that was my responsibility. But Phuntsog said to me that I should put all of this behind me and stop thinking about home. It was perfect advice at just the right moment.

We went back to the closing ceremonies of the *tsog-cho* and then I returned to Drepung. Later, when I went to see my guru, I spoke quite openly with him. I told him that I was in two minds. A part of me strongly wanted to stay but there was still this other part of me tugging me back home. I told him the advice Phuntsog had given to me and said that it had affected me deeply, but that in all honesty there was still a little part of me that wanted to leave and I did not know if I could hold out against it. "You can," he said. "I have no doubt that you can hold out against that need to return. You have a precious friend in Phuntsog, a man who is a real friend. Those who lead you astray are bad friends and those who lead you along a wholesome path are good ones. So rejoice in your good fortune and decide, regardless of the difficulty, that you will stay. I will look after you."

Following that crisis the thought to return home did not bother me for nearly two years. I decided that if I had some success at study I would keep at it, but if I found I was not suited to it only then would I return to Kongjo-rawa. I wrote a letter to my Red Uncle and told him my intentions.

IN THE SIXTH TIBETAN MONTH, in late summer, there is a special morning assembly of all the monks of Drepung called the *ridra* assembly. Tea is given to the whole community in the great hall of Drepung, and during the tea some of the monks have to stand up and debate in front of the whole assembly. This debate has a special name—*tsog-lang chung-wa* or "minor debate." Each monk first has to do a recitation in front of the entire assembly, then one of the monks puts questions and one gives answers. Lots are drawn to decide which of the monks have to debate on which of the various subjects. I was in my first year of studying Perfect Wisdom, and when I drew my lot it said that I would have to stand up and debate the topic of revelation and interpretation. A monk from Gomang at the same stage in his career would be debating against me.

My house was very pleased because it was considered a most auspicious event when one of the house members rose up to debate in the great hall, but I was terrified by the thought of having to stand up in the presence of nearly ten thousand monks. There was a particular line of chant that I would have to master, and while reciting it I would have to match my steps with the chant in a manner that would allow me to cover the entire distance up and down the spaces between the long rows of monks. Since it was a huge hall this was no easy matter, getting the recitation to end at exactly the same time as one finished walking up and down the rows. I spent many hours measuring the exact places where I would have to end up at the different times of the recitation in order to do it properly. As I applied myself to the preparation I found my little store of confidence evaporating, so I went to Gen Yaro and told him I did not think I was going to be able to do it— the recitation alone was as long as the Praise of Dependent Arising prayer, and my debate topic was the most difficult of all. But Gen Yaro was a truly extraordinary being and he said to me that debating in the great hall was a rare opportunity and that I should simply go there and try my best. So, armed with his confidence and advice I kept preparing for the big event.

That year, when the time arrived for the *ridra* assembly an even larger number of monks than usual were assembled for the tea. The monk from Gomang took the position of the elder and I the position of the junior so I did not have to put questions to him, I only had to do the recitation and then give answers. There was a tradition in Drepung (whether based on fact or not I do not know) that if a monk paused on the huge flagstones that marked the head of each row as he did the recitation and prayed to the goddess Saraswati as he rounded from the end of one row to the head of another, she herself would appear. I can report that Saraswati did not make herself known to me, nor for that matter did any of the other fabulous animals or mysterious personages that were said to make an appearance to the faithful. I did not see a thing. But I remember clearly that the recitation went well. The debate, however, quickly veered into whether Maitreya was a Buddha or not. Since Gomang traditionally held that he was a Buddha while my college, Loseling, held that he was not, there could be no certain resolution of this debate. My debating partner cited many scriptures to buttress his argument and I dealt with them as well as I could, but still I was left with the feeling that I did not acquit myself with great distinction.

After the assembly there was a celebration in my house. My guru had made preparations for it and had set up in his room a small throne, a large cushion, a carpet, and a monk's mat on top of the symbols of immovability, ready for my return from the assembly. The preparations were the same as those made for the arrival of a high lama and the moment I returned from the assembly I was served tea and my guru gave me a scarf. Many others, mainly the new monks, came and gave me scarfs as well. One of the most senior of all of the gesheys—probably second or third in seniority amongst all the gesheys in Drepung, a very old, bearded, tremendously imposing man called Ngaram Tenpa, sent his student to give me a scarf and a very generous gift, the equivalent of three or four hundred rupees in present day India. The student gave me this message from Geshey-la: "I think you did very well in the assembly. I do not know who you are, but from your accent I think that probably you are from Phukhang house. It has been many years now since I have had the pleasure of seeing a member of Phukhang house rise up to debate in the assembly, and I found your recitation very much a pleasure to listen to, the rise and fall of your voice perfectly appropriate. Besides, it is most auspicious, I feel, because the day is most excellent astrologically, there were many large benefactors today, the assembly was very full. I do not know who you are, beyond that you are from Phukhang, but I express my happiness to you and urge you to continue on with your study until the very end."

From then on Ngaram Tenpa was very solicitous about my career. Our house often gave him special offerings of tea, and if I was the one who took them to him, he would show himself to be particularly pleased.

AFTER MY MINOR DEBATE in the assembly passed off with success I went up to the caves for the study break. During this time I would sometimes come down from the caves to buy butter from the bowls of the senior gesheys. The gesheys sat at the head of the rows in the assemblies and were first in the line when the tea was served. Since the butter quickly rises to the top of Tibetan tea, the senior gesheys had large amounts of excess butter in their bowls so they would collect it and sell it in amounts of two or three kilos. This was not as expensive as fresh butter but was still good butter and was not dirty. When I went to buy some they would often say they were very happy that I was going up for the study session, and would add in, on top of my purchase, a kilo or perhaps a half kilo of the leftover butter as a gift. One time I came down to buy leftover butter from Geshey Drimay. He was one of those very calm gesheys—one with long intestines, as we say—nobody could rush him. "Sit down for a while," he said, as he pottered about in his room doing one thing or another. After a little time he prepared for me some tsampa with ground cheese and butter. It was not fresh butter but I can remember the excellent taste of that bowl of tsampa he gave me even today. It is here, that ball of tsampa, clearly before my eyes right now. Today I doubt we would even eat leftover butter in tsampa, but there is a special taste to food when you are really hungry, and that tsampa was incredible. Then he said how pleased he was that I was studying hard, and that he had been in the assembly and seen my minor debate go well. "Keep at it," he said, giving me yet another dollop of butter as a gift, "I am happy to see you study." There were quite a few gesheys like that.

MY STUDIES PROGRESSED to the part of Perfect Wisdom where it says that those with sharp intellects do not believe in spiritual attainment until they see it is really possible. Their belief in the possibility comes from contemplating the fact that there is no true existence anywhere. While I was studying this I began to feel more confidence and even began to feel that I might be able to understand emptiness itself—a rather vainglorious hope. I would spend long periods when I thought that I was meditating on emptiness, though I have no idea what it was exactly that had come into my mind. One thing is for sure, the wondrous clear path of emptiness was not what I was thinking about, so I must have been just sitting there in a sort of black hole with a sense of vacuity believing that somehow that was it, the real thing, the most profound ultimate truth.

Because emptiness was not appearing to me with the clarity that I wanted I thought that it was because of the obscuration in my mind. People said that to be successful in study one had to acquire merits, and that a good way to do so was to recite the praises of the goddess Tara and to say Tsong-khapa mantras. Gen Yaro also said that, so I began from then on, for some years, to recite Tara and Tsong-khapa mantras all through the night, not undressing but just sitting there cross-legged reciting, falling off to sleep and then reciting again each time I woke until morning. I found that I was not physically able to do it for more than ten or fifteen days a month. During the other days I would take off my robes and lie down in my bedclothes in the normal way. I think that my understanding began to bloom at that time. I became more of a renunciate, a monk unconcerned with the sort of clothes, shoes, or food I got. Sometimes I would eat tsampa with just cold water and sometimes I had only torn clothes to wear, but I had no thought for anything but the course of study. I would not take time out to go to prayers, I would not get involved in unimportant little jobs, and would try to spend every waking moment studying.

I came to have a great belief in the Svatantrika school of Buddhist philosophy, a belief I carried with me until some time later in India. It was not that I had really plumbed the depths of it, of course, but I had some idea of what the words were trying to convey, and it affected me. I would meditate with blind faith that there is no true existence anywhere.

One of the last topics in the first year of Perfect Wisdom is called Wheel of the Dharma. While studying it, the tradition was that higher classes debated with lower classes and vice versa. Classes lower than mine were not included in this debate. The older class was seated to one side and the lower class to the other. When the debate got underway it happened that the only member of our class capable of giving any answer was me. I do not remember much about it now, but I remember that they were debating and I was answering and that after the event people came up to me and said I had answered well.

In those days the debating courtyard was a ground strewn with rough and sometimes sharp gravel. I had shoes but they never fit me properly, so I would go to the debate barefoot. One of the people in my class was an incarnate lama, a student of the abbot Tsangpa Khen Rinpoche, and one time he asked his student about this classmate of his who spoke in the dialect of Sera Lawa house and wandered into the debate barefoot. "He must be from Phukhang," he said, "and he seems to be very poor because he has no shoes and his clothes are tattered. He is a thoughtful young man, he gives good and reasoned answers, he shows great promise." At that time I was also given the nickname Nag-po-pa (Blackman, or Fleabag). Some said the name was after an earlier member of our house, Geshey Nag-po-pa, who had distinguished himself as a scholar. Others said it was because my clothes and my face were so dirty, and because I never washed and was smelly.

During this period Gen Yaro would spend at least one study period a week explaining how a monk leads a sincere spiritual life. If he taught us from the scholastic texts five days a week he would teach us directly from his experience about spiritual life on the sixth day: the correct way to read a spiritual text, the motivation one should have, the type of attitude to cultivate, as well as all the ordinary spiritual practices of Tibetan Buddhism. He taught us how to prostrate, how to behave in the assemblies, and he made clear with a simple faith the spiritual life that unfolds, stage by stage, for a monk. My guru had much practical spiritual advice and even when he would be teaching from the scholastic texts he would again and again relate what was being taught to our conduct and attitude. There were five or six of us studying with Gen Yaro at that time, but I was the only one with the good fortune to study with him right to the end.

When I got up in the morning I would immediately do the daily preparation practice starting with cultivating the proper motivation for the day's work ahead. When I went to the bathroom in the morning I would recite the ancient Buddhist verse that says everything created is like a morning star, a lamp, an illusion, a water bubble, a dream, a cloud, and a flash of lightning. I would snap my fingers at the end of this verse, reminding myself that nothing lasts more than an instant in the vast eternity of time. This verse goes back to the time of the historical Buddha who recited it after his meals. When going to the bathroom there was another mind training which allowed one to transform even excretion into a positive act of giving. I would recite to myself the verse which says, "By the power of this giving, may all living beings never be separated from the self-originated Buddhas, the earlier victorious ones, and may every living being be freed by this." "There are many living beings that utilize excrement," Gen Yaro used to say, "and one should not forget them, or feel they are gross or unimportant." He told us to try to train the mind even when excreting, to cultivate a noble thought and consider it a gift to those living creatures. I continued with this daily mind training up until my flight to India. Since arriving in India, though, sometimes I remember to do it and sometimes I forget.

I DID NOT EVEN take time out to brush the floor of my room I was so intent on study. I neglected even to wash my clothes. Just outside the fence of Drepung there was a hill called Digo where I sometimes went for a walk. There was water there and sometimes it struck me that it was wrong not to keep clean, so I would wash my body and clothes. During the summer picnic period the whole of Drepung would go down to the river to wash.

The strange thing is that the terrible smells you get from people who do not wash in India did not seem to be there in Tibet. Maybe it was because the climate was so much drier and colder. Here nowadays, if you went for two weeks without a bath wearing the same clothes you would stink unbearably and no one would come near you. Also, washing more often seems to be helpful to physical well-being here in India, so my habits in this regard have undergone a big change. But this fixation on having a shower again and again does not seem to be of particular value. A shower twice a week strikes me as a middle way. I really do not know how to explain why we did not stink unbearably in Tibet, because there really was not a lot of opportunity to wash.

IN THE EIGHTH OR NINTH MONTH of my first year of Perfect Wisdom, a letter arrived from my Red Uncle carried by a trader. When I went to get it I was very surprised that it contained almost no money—there were just a few three-sang coins. Since I had written to my guru to say that I was planning to stay and study, and since he knew that it was not possible for me to study unless I was supported by him, I was very confused when the trader said that there was nothing else. I went back to the college in a state of anxiety thinking that even though some people could live on the handouts from the monastery, there was no way a fellow with my appetite could do so. I began to suspect that somebody had been talking to my uncle behind my back, poisoning him against me.

In fact he was testing me. He was still not sure that I was really studying, so he had told the trader to check before giving me any money to see if I was sincerely studying or if I was just hanging around Lhasa. If I was wasting time, I was to be brought back home and under no circumstances to be given any money. After a few days of checking, the trader called me down from Drepung and gave me a big bag of money. There must have been eighty or ninety of the three-sang coins, a good amount of money in those days. He told me that my Red Uncle had told him to check on me before giving it to me, but that he had found I was studying. He said that he was personally happy to see this, and that it was what my uncle wanted more than anything else. "If you need anything," he said "just tell me, because your uncle told me to meet any need you have, if you are studying, and that he would pay me back."

I told Gendun that I had received a big pile of money, but I did not feel I had to give it all to him. He was not a person with any advice to offer, but Gen Yaro would have advice and I wanted to listen to it. I told him what had happened and Gen Yaro said that I now had the chance to continue with my study and I should be happy about it and continue to study as hard as possible. "Stop thinking about going home," he said, "and study hard." I determined to do so from the bottom of my heart.

IN PREPARATION for the study of the interpretation of texts with divergent meanings, students began memorizing Tsong-khapa's *Speech of Gold.* I started in on this during the period when the traders arrive in Lhasa from Kham. I was with my guru in the caves to the east of Drepung, he in a little cave lower down and I tucked into a open cave with a slanting roof, hardly more than a crevice in the rock. I was memorizing at a rate of probably three or four pages a day. Then one day, when I had gone down to get some tea, a goat got made off with eight or nine pages of my text. When I got back and realized what had happened I could see the goat with the remains of the pages still in its mouth, but it was too late to retrieve them. I told my guru and he said that I should expect obstacles when studying the *Speech of Gold* because it is a very profound book.

I was able to borrow the leaves that had been destroyed and my memorization was progressing well when one day there was a loud noise outside my cave that sounded like a fall of loose earth or a rush of hail. I thought it was a prankster up above so I did not let myself get scared, but kept at my task. A bit later the noise came again, this time louder than the first and then, after that, again still louder. I wanted to see what was happening but decided not to break my memorization. A few days later I scouted around to see if I could determine what had happened, but found nothing. I went to ask my guru about it, and again he said that there would be obstacles that I would face, so I should not let myself get upset but should recite the Buddhist refuge formula again and again. He asked me if it had started me worrying. I said it had not. "That is a good sign," he told me, "so know there are obstacles but know that you can overcome them too."

After I had been up in the cave for eight or nine days I got a message that the traders from my homeland had arrived. As I headed down to Drepung, for some reason I was filled with foreboding. That night I had bad omens in my dreams. I arrived at Ludrub Rinpoche's residence but was told that my letters were in the possession of a man called Gangphag, a wonderfully radiant monk, tall and peaceful, who had moved permanently into Lhasa to become the *chandzo* of a rinpoche. Ludrub Rinpoche's people told me to collect my mail from him, so I went off to Lhasa, feeling confused.

Gangphag was a man of great beauty to behold, and just being in his presence caused a feeling of peace. When I arrived at his residence he said to me, "Ah! You have come. Sit down for a little while and take it easy." He gave me tea, went about some work he had to do and then served me a meal. He was a man with very long intestines. Eventually he sat down across from me and said that he did not have my letters, that they actually were at Ludrub Rinpoche's residence, but they contained some unhappy news. The Rinpoche had felt that I should be told by someone I felt close to. The letter was not clear, he said, but my mother had fallen very sick and there was bad news. "Do not let it upset you," he said. "This is the nature of this ongoing stream of life, that once we are born we fall sick and die. One is to bear with this reality, to feel compassion for those caught within it." I knew then that my mother had died.

I felt a peace that my mother's death had happened while I was in Lhasa. If I had heard the news on the road home I would not have been able to pray for her and make offerings on her behalf in the central temple, and I would not have been able to approach the lamas to pray for her well-being. And even if I had been at home during the time of her death what could I have done for her? There in Lhasa I could make offerings before the three main statues—the one in the central temple, in the Ramoche temple, and in the Potala—and ask the lamas to dedicate the prayers for her benefit.

Even when I returned to Ludrub Rinpoche's residence they did not immediately give me the letters. Finally the Rinpoche's *chandzo* said that my mother had passed away. When I said, "I am glad," my response took him aback somewhat. "What do you mean, you are glad?" he asked. "My mother was a very old lady," I said, "and her dying while I am here studying in Lhasa makes it possible for me to make offerings in the very holiest of places and to approach the most spiritual of beings to pray for her. If I was at home all I could do is be with her as she died, and this is not a particularly beneficial act in the absence of the rituals and prayers. She was an old lady, and the time of her death was not far off in any case, so I do not feel I should push against that inexorable tide in human life." "What a fine way to think," he said, "an excellent way to approach this sad event." Ludrub Rinpoche then gave me the letters where the death of my mother was spelled out clearly, and he said he was making offerings for her well-being and told me to do so as well, that money had been sent from home for this. I took the money from Rinpoche—it was a large amount—and for two or three days I did not go back to the monastery as I made all the offerings and had all the prayers properly performed. After I had finished, the death of my mother hit me strongly. She was gone now; one of the people in Kongjo-rawa who I had wanted to visit so much was no longer there.

BEFORE RETURNING to my cave I went back to Ludrub Rinpoche and he told me that he was very pleased that I was studying. There had been some discordance between us when I first came to Lhasa because I had been expected to live in his household, but had entered Drepung instead. At that time Ludrub Rinpoche had suggested to my Red Uncle that I not do the offerings required for entry into Drepung, but rather, along with a section of the new monks coming up from Kongjo-rawa, go straight into the higher tantric college, by-passing the colleges of Sera and Drepung. The chants in Dondup-ling were a mix of chants from the upper and lower tantric colleges and from Namgyal Monastery in the Potala, but they had no real sanction from a higher spiritual institution. Rinpoche had therefore thought it would be wise for some Dondup-ling monks to enter the upper tantric college to learn their rituals and chants in order to set the home monastery's ritual activity on a more certain basis.

The time when I would have entered the tantric college, if I had acted according to Ludrub Rinpoche's plan, was just as Perfect Wisdom study began. At that time I had received a letter from my Red Uncle saying that although Ludrub Rinpoche wanted a number of monks to enter the tantric college, I should not feel I had to do so if I was really able to study, and that I should find a delicate way to put it to him that I wanted to remain at Drepung. My house guru in Drepung was also of the same opinion, so when the time came I went down to ask the Rinpoche for his permission to keep studying. He was rather displeased. He said that of the monks coming up from Dondup-ling there were none performing very well, whether in study or in the tantric colleges, and he intimated that he would be washing his hands of the whole matter if it went on in this way. "As for you," he said, "you are probably living in a dream world to think you can stick at the study. It is highly unlikely it will lead to anything except a vain attempt to be an important person." However, if I went to the tantric college, he said, I would have a special status when I returned home, so I should really consider the matter and follow his advice. I respectfully asked his permission again, and said that I would come down to him, year by year, and if my study was collapsing I would follow his wishes and enter the tantric college. He just about sneered at me, "You youngsters from Dondup-ling are not acquitting yourselves well at all, do you hear me?" Still, the Rinpoche valued study highly and would never stand in the way of someone who was really studying, so I could only apologize and say I would honestly try as hard as I could, and that if I failed in the attempt I would come down and enter the tantric college later.

That was what had passed between us a year or so earlier. So right after the death of my mother, when he told me that he was very pleased that I was studying it was a very encouraging comment. My ability to see my mother's death with detachment had impressed him. "Your study has begun to work its way into your heart, which is where it must be," he said. "I am very pleased that you are studying and on top of the money that has arrived from your home for the rites of your mother, I am including a small offering for you so that you will dedicate the merit of your wholesome work to me. I am not sure," he said, "whether I should be receiving death offerings or giving them." I did not know what the Rinpoche meant by this last gesture and wondered if it was a joke.

I then returned to my cave above Drepung and began my memorization anew. I went to see Gen Yaro and told him everything that had happened in detail. "These are the expected obstacles on your spiritual path," he said, "but I feel now they are finished. Go back to your work and try to memorize as much as you can."

After four or five days I got a message from Ludrub Rinpoche asking me to come. I went immediately and he showed me a terrible rash that was afflicting the insides of both of his thighs and asked me to swear to him that I would continue to study until the end. I did so, and he then said to me quietly but with great strength that I should try with all my heart to study the dharma. "Do not come and see me again," he said, "just remain at your books. It may be the case that this will be the last time we meet together, but I want you to stay at your study; do not feel you must come down to show your concern."

I returned to my cave yet again and told Gen Yaro all that had transpired. He said that Rinpoche had earlier given me a death offering and that probably was a sign he knew his own death was imminent. It was very likely that he would die in a few days. As he reflected on this Gen Yaro became lost in thought. Ludrub Rinpoche was a man of great spiritual depth and learning, and that he was to pass from us filled him with a sense of sorrow. He sent me back to my cave and told me to continue work. About three days later I got the message that Rinpoche had passed away. I went down to the labrang in Lhasa and the reality of Ludrub Rinpoche's death made me deeply cold inside even while my heart felt like it was on fire. For two or three months I carried within me a feeling of great loss and emptiness.

Rinpoche's main assistant was so affected by his death that he was on the verge of distraction. He asked me to take responsibility for moving the body to the different places where it had to be taken, and for arranging the different rites. A geshey from Gangshing, a village in Kongjo-rawa, and a number of other older monks took responsibility for the Rinpoche's funeral rites. I was one of those who carried the body on a ceremonial seat to the cremation ground. We made a procession to a small mountain monastery near Drepung and laid it on a pyre, where it was given over into the flames. After the cremation, the Rinpoche's house gave the monk's robe in which the Rinpoche had been dressed for his journey to those of us who had done the last rites. This was a gesture of thanks which we greatly appreciated because though the robe was not particularly expensive, it had been next to the body of our lama and we therefore held it in the very highest esteem. After some discussion the older monks decided to let me take the garment, which was fragrant with the perfume of Rinpoche's perfect morality. I kept it for a year or so until a friend of mine who was returning to Kongjo-rawa asked me if he could take it home as a sacred object for the people to pay homage to. That is what I remember about the passing away of Ludrub Rinpoche while I was in Lhasa. I have talked about this only to give an honest idea of how important a homeland rinpoche like Ludrub Rinpoche was to us. We considered him to be in a completely different sphere of existence from our ordinary selves.

I returned to my cave to try to continue my memorization, but by the end of the year I was not able to memorize more than about fifteen pages of the *Speech of Gold*.

I REMEMBER THAT YEAR at the general winter debate I began to study the opening lines of Dharmakirti's *Commentary on Valid Cognition*. Gen Yaro gave us a long and detailed explanation of the opening lines where the author says he entertains no illusions about the people who will be interested in his work. "Ordinary people are dominated by ordinary needs," it begins (that was me, I thought) "and do not have the intel-lectual capacity to understand profound texts." (Again me, I thought.) "They do not have the staying power to get to the meaning," (me again) "and they are stained with the dirt of jealousy." I did not feel jealous, but I still ended up with three of the four stains. It was a tremendous teaching that affected me deeply and inspired me to redouble my ef-forts. These words by Dharmakirti put across to me with great clarity that if I did not take personal responsibility for my attitudes, values, and behavior no one else could help me—not Dharmakirti or even my spiritual friends and gurus.

It is strange how much effect just a single verse of a religious text can have if it is the right time. That verse and the long commentary by my guru affected me as personal religious advice, and I feel its effect even today. At other times, if you are not in the right frame of mind, a whole text can be explained and you can understand it intellectually, but it has no power as spiritual advice—your inner life is left unmoved and the writer's intentions just pass you by. When I heard Dharmakirti's works, I saw clearly how ordinary work robs us of the opportunity for turning to a spiritual life and developing our higher talents. I saw vividly the pettiness that comes with the round of household chores, monastic rituals, and the comfortable life of the businessman monk.

Nowadays, when I hear the Dalai Lama give a discourse, the clar-ity of the points he makes, the correctness of what he advises, strikes me so vividly, but my inner world, now hard, is not transformed as it was then. I feel a great sense of personal dissatisfaction when I see that, even taught so well, still Buddhism does not transform my atti-tudes deep inside and make me the better person the Dalai Lama would have me become. Either I go to listen to the Dalai Lama too much, or I do not go enough, or my own spiritual standards have degenerated from what they were in those years. One way or the other, it leaves me with a feeling of loss.

DURING THE NEXT Jamyang Gun-cho we studied the next topic in the *Commentary on Valid Cognition*—about reasoning from results to causes: that a result directly perceived presupposes its own causal complex. I began to think deeply about the doctrine of karma and I began to see how our suffering is the result of an unwholesome inner causal com-plex. I saw how difficult it would be to change that unwholesome inner world of mine and its selfishness and pettiness. But I felt the truth of the doctrine of karma even stronger than before, and I stopped talking down to others from above the reality of my own station, and misleading people for personal gain. It struck me that spiritual life was rooted in the belief in karma, that if a person did not look into it and consider it deeply, the way to peace was impossible to gain, because without some feeling for cause and effect no one could maintain the discipline of the monks and nuns, or even keep the laws of a country.

One day I had gone down to Lhasa to buy some provisions and was returning with two large packets of tea that somebody else had asked me to pick up for them. On my way back I came to the large open space called Chang-tang Lam-ka, where the roads to Sera and Drepung part. A little beyond that is a bridge we knew as "Halfway Bridge" because you were about halfway at that point. It took an hour's walk to reach this bridge from downtown Lhasa, and it was about an hour from there to Drepung. I sat down for a rest and when I went through my money I found I was left with more than I should have. I began to worry that I had not paid the full amount to the trader. I checked again and when I still came up extra I went all the way back to Lhasa and told the trader to check his sums because I had a feeling he had shortchanged himself. He checked but came up with the same figures. "But I have extra," I said. He checked again and said, "Monk, we are businesspeople. When we add up figures we make sure we never shortchange ourselves, of that you may be sure. Exactly where your extra comes from I do not know, but I can assure you that you did not cheat us." There was a woman there who said it was good of me to come all the way back. "Usually when a deal is done no one will change it, so I appreciate your attempt to be honest," she said. "But go back to Drepung now otherwise you will be late. You are going to have to be careful in the future or else you are going to lose out again and again on your business dealings." They were very pleased and gave me a gift of a ball of tea, a few pieces of fruit, and a little bit of money as well and told me to study hard. They said it was a pleasure to behold an attempt to be honest, even if it was based on a mistake.

I got home very late that night and now, as I look back on it, it seems to me a sign that my mind had been affected by the teachings on cause and effect, because to go so far back into Lhasa for just seven or eight coins was, in a certain sense, an odd thing to do. But I feel pleased that I did it because those were days of great poverty for me, and it would have been easy to simply pass over it. To treat the possessions of those more wealthy than myself as important even when I was poor seems to me a good state of mind, because it is always easy to rationalize unwholesome acts based on the reason that one's own state in life is not as good as one would like it to be. Nowadays I know more than I did then, I have studied for many years, so I feel that the extent of my personal honesty should be even greater than it was in those years. But I wonder. Still, I look back and am pleased to think my study of karma affected my inner world and my behavior, and was not simply an intellectual exercise.

Earlier that same year, if my memory serves me well, during one of the early general assemblies not long after the *ridra* assembly, I had just come down from studying in the mountains and was dying for a good meal. We newer monks never got any butter in our tea; by the time it came to us at the ends of the rows it was nothing but black tea with salt. It came into my mind to steal some of the butter from the tea offered to the assembly.

In the assemblies it was the custom for a few of us younger monks to jump up when a bell was sounded and rush out to the kitchen to bring back the large kettles of hot butter-tea. We were called "line runners." All the runners had to go to the head of the line first and serve the elder monks. That meant there was a short time when there was a big crush of tea servers up at the head of the line. I was up there, with a full pot of hot butter-tea in my hand, and after a few minutes of serving, I ran out of the hall as though my pot had been emptied. I waited outside, watching the progress of the pouring, and when it came to where I was seated I immediately went back into the assembly hall and poured from my full pot right into my bowl, and into the bowls of the two monks to my left and right. Having emptied the pot I then went back to the kitchen where I was suddenly struck with a tremendous feeling of dread.

This little trick was not really considered to be stealing at Drepung, it was more of a misdemeanor that would warrant a sharp blow across the shoulders, but my Red Uncle had said to me again and again that I should never do it, and I could hear his words as clearly as if he were there speaking to me directly. So it was with a great feeling of dread that I re-entered the hall. The three bowls which had butter on top seemed to me to be like blazing suns amongst all the other bowls full of black tea, advertising my wrongdoing. The monk who had the specific duty of checking the rows did not notice. Had he done so he would have shouted out for all in the assembly to hear: "You thieves, stealing the butter!" and we would have been beaten on the spot. I began to feel more and more regret for what I had done and stayed huddled under my gown. "In this assembly of monks," I thought, "there are definitely Bodhisattvas, and yet I have stolen from them." The fellows to my left and right had already added in tsampa to their bowls and were very pleased to be getting a hearty breakfast of tsampa and butter. "Drink up," they said. "What is wrong?" I told them I had a bad headache, and did not feel like drinking it. Beckoning across to the person sitting opposite me I asked if he wanted to change his black tea for my butter. "No problem at all," he said licking his lips. I mixed some tsampa with the black tea, and ate thinking of the purposelessness of traveling all the way from my homeland and working hard at study only to end up stealing butter. I made a silent commitment to myself that until I died, and in any other life that I may find myself, I would never steal anything again. I prayed from the bottom of my heart that this would come to be. This helped to lighten somewhat the feeling I had. My friends had by this time finished their delicious meal and kept nudging me to find out what was wrong.

I went back to my room still feeling depressed, and soon after I told my study guru about what I had done. His basic message was that my Red Uncle had given me good advice, and that it was good that it had come through loud and clear at that moment. But as I was telling him the whole saga, stage by stage, he could not help breaking out into laughter again and again, and clicking his tongue and saying "What an embarrassment, what an embarrassment." He asked me why I decided to steal the butter, in the first place. "I was starved," I said. "I had been up in the mountains and I was dying for a real bowl of tsampa." It could all be traced to my need for a good feed.

This incident left me with that commitment that I have carried in my heart, and the realization that those without good fortune will always do the sort of things I did in my youth. Over the years I have learned more and more, and now I think that if I were to consciously do wrong the Buddhas and Bodhisattvas who fill space in all directions would feel a sadness in their hearts that I could not bear to behold.

4

CAVES OF INCREASING GOODNESS

There were a number of caves around Drepung. Some were up above the monastery to the east and some were to the west. Way off in the east, there were big cave complexes called Tema-mo and Phug-shag. Near Gonpa Ritro, high up on Tema-mo's mountain, there were some excellent caves. There was a big one there that a group of us used as a communal eating area, and a slanting one above it that I used as my personal cave. Inside the caves was a fine, absolutely dry sand; they were not damp like the caves nowadays in the foothills of India. We would each put down fresh grass on the sand in a little cave, and our bedding on top of that. Outside there were just thorn bushes, no big trees, and during the day we would go out in the mountain grass and recite and study. It was indeed a beautiful retreat, peaceful and perfectly suited to study and meditation. In the morning and evening we did recitations and memorization. Sometimes Gen Yaro would come up and he would give teachings. It was a happy time.

In the fourth month, during the ten-day break, monks would do a retreat in the caves and would return again in the fifth month for fifteen days. In the sixth month the long retreat would begin. A group of five or six of us would find ourselves caves relatively close to Drepung for the shorter study periods, but on this long retreat we went off to the more distant caves in the east. We had a large cave which served as a kitchen and storeroom, and each of us had our own smaller cave for our recitation and reflection. When I think back on it now I remember it with a sense of incredible pleasure, as though it were almost a paradise. But young monks, never satisfied, would begin thinking wistfully about the pot boiling back home whenever a strong pang of hunger came in their stomachs. That always happens, does it not, once you begin to get hungry?

As new monks, we rarely got the good balls and rectangular bricks of tightly pressed tea that come from India and China. We usually made a drink called "the beverage of Tsong-khapa" from a small red-leaved bush that grew in the sand. If you boiled the root you got water of a deep red color and if you mixed a little of your precious real tea with it and added butter it was drinkable. It seemed tasty at the time, if a bit without body since it was nothing but the root of the plant. If you then got some real ball or brick tea, and made a full cup with that, it tasted incredibly fine. If you drink real tea daily it can never taste as good as it does when you have been in the mountains and not had a cup for weeks.

Once a week we all got together to make ourselves a slightly better meal, and would spend the afternoon enjoying it. Even hermits and yogis must eat enough each day to keep alive—not special food, but food which is healthy and simple. You know you have really dedicated your life to the study of the dharma when you give up special food and eat just enough to be able to live and study.

When we stayed in the caves close to Drepung we would go down to the assemblies given by benefactors to receive the offerings. When we stayed at Tema-mo and Phug-shag, however, it was too far to return. If there was something of great importance the monastery would send someone up to get us; otherwise we remained there without break.

Waking in the morning, one first would start a round of memorization that lasted until about eight o'clock. When five or six of us were at the caves together we took turns making morning tea, so at eight whoever was the cook clapped his hands loudly to announce that breakfast was ready. We ate together, quickly and without talking much, sometimes downing our tea and tsampa outside, or, if the weather was not good, in the larger cave. We would then return to our memorization and studies until about twelve-thirty, when we would eat together and take it easy for a time, chatting and playing jokes until about three o'clock in the afternoon. At three we would have a cup of tea and then spend the afternoon outside on our individual rock perches reciting what we had attempted to memorize so far, seeing if our ability to recall was perfect or not. Sometimes we would stay there reciting, patching up parts that we had started to forget, making a seamless flow, until ten or even eleven o'clock at night, even until the early hours of the morning. We would stay at it until we could do it no more.

GEN YARO EXPLAINED to us how poor retreat monks make water-bowl offerings. He said we should use our drinking bowl, carefully cleaning our bowls and offering water after morning tea, throwing that water away just before lunch. I had the notion that this sort of offering was not good enough and I had begun saving my money to buy a proper set of seven bowls. I was very frugal with the offerings I received in the assemblies, and saved up a nice little sum, always keeping it with me to make sure it was safe.

When I was in the caves just to the east of the monastery, I would sometimes be visited by a goat herder who would come up from Dampag, a village just beneath Drepung. Once we had talked for a long time, and when I heard the call for tea I said that I was going, and left him there alone. When I returned he had gone and I thought nothing about it.

A few days later I realized that my money was missing. My first thought was that one of the other monks was playing a joke on me. Earlier I had snuck into one of my friend's caves and hidden two of his balls of tea for a week, so I thought he had found out a way to pay me back for my nasty little joke. I watched him carefully for a day or two, but there was nothing in his demeanor to suggest that he had taken my money. I even hinted to him that I had lost some money, but there was nothing in his bearing to suggest he was hiding it. Finally I asked him directly, and he said he would never play those sorts of jokes with money. "You have definitely been robbed by that goat herder," he said. "He used to come up here everyday and for the last while we have seen nothing of him." So all that money I had so carefully hoarded up, precious little coin by precious little coin, was wiped out in moment and there was nothing I could do about it. Thinking that at the end of the day a thief may very well run off with all of one's wealth certainly lowered one's desire to build up a hoard of money.

On another occasion I was returning from Drepung and some monks told me that a mountain leopard had been resting in my cave. After staying there for a long time it had stretched and walked away amongst the thorn bushes. Some said it did not matter, and others said they would be scared if it had happened to them. Later this same leopard came in the night and sat itself outside my guru's cave some distance away. When my guru had moved about to let the leopard know he was in there, it had growled, so the next morning my guru went back down to the monastery, taking this as a bit too much danger for his liking. I stayed in retreat and the leopard returned again; it sat on the rocks above my cave and then left. After this I decided I had to go see the oracle of the goddess Tema-mo. On hearing what I had to say, the oracle went into a trance and then communicated that the animal was a protector leopard who was there because I was going through a period of danger from thieves. The oracle said that the leopard would only come when I was away, so I should continue my study as before. "But what about my guru?" I asked. "I do not know," was the answer.

I also asked some of the older monks. They said that the mountain was the sacred dwelling of the goddess Tema-mo and that she had a special relationship with those who studied there. Sometimes retreat monks had to listen to what Tema-mo might be trying to say. "She could certainly send a leopard to ward off thieves," they said, "or she could send a leopard to rear up and scare you if you were playing about instead of studying." So all agreed it was an emanation of Tema-mo.

Another year we lived in the caves at Phug-shag. I had a nice-sized cave there. To get into it you had to bend nearly double, but once inside you could stand upright. Off in the distance Drepung was visible, shining out. When it rained a beautiful fringe of water dripped down across the low roof in front my cave. Our guru lived a little lower down than me in a bigger cave where we all came together for meals. Nearby were a number of small caves traditionally used by the monks at Phukhang house from Kongjo-rawa, some with walls built up in front and with windows. Above these was a very big cave and some smaller ones traditionally used by Nyakri house.

This part of the mountain was called Phug-shag, after a spirit of that name who inhabited it. Some said that he was the customary owner of this part of the mountain, and that he was a warrior god in the larger retinue of the goddess Tema-mo. He was extremely pleased that we were using his mountain for our study, and when everyone was hard at work a wonderfully fragrant smell of fresh beer would waft by on the breeze, a sign that the god was enjoying what we were doing. Perhaps once every two or three days you would smell it, a delightful smell just wafting by faintly on the breeze.

Once some monks had died in these caves; during very rainy weather, the stones above shifted and crushed them to death. Shortly before their death a man had appeared out of nowhere and urged them strongly to go down to the monastery, saying it was not a good time to stay. It seems they did not heed Phug-shag's warning and during the night their caves collapsed, burying them alive.

One year it rained heavily while we were in Phug-shag studying during the long summer retreat. In the middle of the night I heard the repeated thudding sound of a rock. The next morning I saw that a very big boulder—it would have taken twenty-five strong men to lift it—had fallen down from the rocky part of the mountain where the god himself lived. It had rolled down the mountainside and lodged just in front of a cave that was big enough to sit in but not big enough to live in. I went and told Gen Yaro who said that he had heard the thudding too, and had thought it was an earthquake. The rock had headed directly towards the cave where our study guru and a few monks were sleeping, and it would probably have killed them all had it just come crashing straight down. But it had lodged up against an outcrop of rock. The strange part was that the place it should have landed, as one looked up the trajectory, was right above the big cave, but there were drag marks from that place to a place about eight or nine arm spans off to the side. It was as if it had been dragged to a place where it would not cause harm if it fell in the future. Gen Yaro said he was not able to just shrug off a danger like this and that he would have to consult the Phug-shag Oracle.

The oracle lived in a house surrounded by poplar trees at the foot of the mountain. We all went down; through the oracle the god said he could not protect us from everything when it was raining so hard, but that we had seen how he was working as hard as he could. He said that since the rain looked like it was going to continue he could not promise that he would protect us, and that we should think about going back early to Drepung. He was happy that we were studying but it was for us to decide.

It was only three or four more days until the end of the retreat period and the monks below us were staying on. For myself, I thought how my guru was always going off to gather branches, and was always doing *chöd*, the meditation where you imagine cutting yourself up and then contemplate emptiness while blowing on a thigh-bone trumpet and shaking a small drum. I remembered how the leopard had come up and been displeased. So I had this thought inside that the goddess Tema-mo was displeased with him. One day I went down alone and asked through the oracle if I was doing alright. The god said that I should rest easy, that he was very pleased with my study and that no bad would come to me. "You have smelled the beautiful fragrance of beer," he said. "That is when I come to check on you and make sure it is going well and all is safe. You should know that." And it was true, I had smelled the wonderful smell that only a meditator in a cave can smell. As I think of it now, I suspect that smell still sometimes wafts over that part of the mountain. If one day we Tibetans regain our freedom I will go back there and sit again, reciting with faith in my heart, until I smell again that intoxicating smell on the breeze and Phug-shag comes by. I can see it now, as I often see it in my mind's eye, the beauty of that place, and I often think what it would be like to go back there in my old age to do meditation again. What a beautiful and perfect place it would be; no doors on your home, just thorn bushes in front to keep the goats out.

DURING RETREAT in the caves I did a meditation called "giving-and-taking." I had attended a long guided explanation of the Guru Puja which the Dalai Lama had given in the Norbulinka, and he had explained giving-and-taking meditation where the text says, "May all the merit and good that I have go out to others and may all their shortcomings and problems come into me." Gen Yaro, who had practiced the graduated-path system deeply, urged me to do giving-and-taking meditation and I got excellent advice from him on how to do it. Sitting in my cave I watched my breath going in and out. As it came in I imagined all the problems of others coming in and landing on my selfishness, which sank down into the vast accommodating earth leaving me patient and capable. Sometimes I imagined my selfishness in the form of an owl or a dangerous snake and imagined chasing it away. As my breath went out I imagined it carrying all my happiness, knowledge, and merit to all living beings, covering them all. At other times I imagined that as my breath went out it reached all the Buddhas and Bodhisattvas and made offerings to them, and that as it came back it brought with it all the capacities and knowledge of those holy beings, with all the love and compassion that is in their hearts. Sometimes my recitation and memorization would naturally turn into watching my breathing and linking it up with the idea of giving and taking. Sometimes the meditation would have great depth and intensity. I would sense a great vacuity inside and a great lightness as I let my breath go forth carrying my own good fortune, and I would sometimes feel a tremendous weight as the shortcomings of others came upon me. It left me with a special feeling of pliability and softness in my mind. "If a meditator keeps on this path," I would think, "indeed, Bodhichitta, the thought of enlightenment will rise up of its own power."

I tried to persevere, but the precious thought of enlightenment did not rise up in me. At other times the meditation just receded and I forgot about doing it. I would turn my mind to it but it did not click in that special way, and I would forget about it. But as I think back on it now, during some of those giving-and-taking meditation sessions something special happened, an indication of a level of meditation, because right down to today, even while I have a very hard edge to my personality, a pigheadedness that makes me totally impossible to influence, and so many responsibilities and the control over many people that should lead to anxiety, still I can feel detached and carefree. These moments of well-being and deep peace and the ability to just step away and not feel overwhelmed even by the most complicated responsibilities seem to me to be a splendorous wave from that giving-and-taking meditation I did so many years ago in the caves above Drepung. That meditation left me without a strong feeling of partiality to one group or another; it has left me without animosity, and has let me find a patience when some seem nasty and spiteful. I feel that my mindstream was ennobled and purified by the meditation.

I ARRIVED IN DREPUNG just as a raging debate over the practice of *chöd* was dying down. A charismatic teacher of *chöd* called Geshey Donden was the strongest proponent of that form of meditation and had made the practice widespread. He stressed this teaching so much, and attracted so many disciples, that the number of people attending the assemblies and debates in the monasteries dwindled to a very small number. One party in the monasteries said this was not right while another said it was. Denma Tonpon Rinpoche, a strong opponent, insisted there was no scriptural corroboration for the practice of *chöd* and came out totally and unequivocally against it. This led to a polarization and considerable friction. Denma Tonpon Rinpoche had Reting Rinpoche on his side, while behind Geshey Donden were a number of aristocrats who were themselves deeply involved in the practice. The government was in a quandary over what policy to follow in this matter and finally called Geshey Donden and Tonpon Rinpoche together to debate the issue, but then cancelled it at the last minute. An edict was issued that said Tonpon Rinpoche's criticisms were valid, and that the dwindling number of monks studying and attending assemblies in the monasteries was regretted, but that Tonpon Rinpoche had been intemperate in the level of criticism he had directed at the practitioners of *chöd*. The edict also criticized Geshey Donden for giving the *chöd* empowerment to so many monks and causing so many to stay away from the assemblies and debates. Thus they found fault and good in both parties to the debate and brought it to an amicable conclusion.

By the time I arrived at Drepung, Tonpon Rinpoche's view had largely carried the day. There were many monks I met who would say of another monk, "He is no good, he does the *chöd* practice." Those refraining from the practice were more in accord with government policy, while those doing *chöd* were in an opposition though primarily a religious, not a political one. But Geshey Donden was still at Drepung and my room guru Gendun, for one, was a fervent practitioner of *chöd*. Implicit in his advice to me was that I should take the *chöd* empowerment and begin to practice.

One time Gendun said that Geshey Donden was in the Ratsa-ritro and that he was going up to get the empowerment and teaching, and that I should come along too. Foolishly I did not go. The general criticism of the practitioners of *chöd* was probably well placed—that they were doing so much of it that it was harming their studies. But that did not mean that the actual practice itself was not a valuable and excellent one when properly fit into a spiritual life. There can be no doubt that Gen Donden was a highly realized being. So I missed out on that precious opportunity. My refusal to practice *chöd* was not from thinking about it deeply and understanding a shortcoming in *chöd* practice, it was rather just a prejudice that I had allowed to creep up inside me, nourished by a faint distaste for the picture of the beggars I had seen doing the practice beside the road. Nobody said to me it would be a bad thing to do. It was just a dislike I felt for it, based on a careless way of thinking. Gen Yaro had nothing to say on the matter. Gendun was sometimes critical and would say that just dry book-learning would not make a true spiritual person; a practice like *chöd* was needed to deepen one's practice. But his words were not sharp and did not constitute a forceful attempt to make me do it. From my side, I just did not like the idea. I suppose I had a more researched understanding of scriptural Buddhism, which did not allow a strong place for a practice like *chöd*.

WHILE IN THE PHUG-SHAG CAVES doing retreat I would find a rocky outcrop to perch on and do my recitation. Below were green fields of *janma* trees, where monks came to picnic, pitching different sized tents, playing at dice and other games, and enjoying themselves. Their shouts would reach up to me, and although they were far off, the thick, creamy butter on the tops of their tea cups was right there in front of my eyes; the smells of the meat they were eating along with their bowls of tsampa came to me as if I were sitting right next to them. I could not see the paradise called nirvana that is said to come from studying and living alone in a cave in the mountains, but I could certainly see the happiness that those monks were having down there on their picnic. "If there is no nirvana," I would think, "then I am making a big mistake by living on black tea and coarse tsampa."

Then I would feel a surge of confidence and inspiration. Although I did not understand the intricacies of the path to enlightenment in those years, I was filled with the faith that if the great masters could do it, then by following in their steps I could do it too. "I can attain enlightenment and turn the wheel of the dharma," I thought. "In life after life I have experienced the pleasures of paradises that make the pleasures of a picnic insignificant but nothing is left of those experiences now. Those monks enjoying themselves down there perhaps got money for their picnic by being devious in their villages, with their minds dominated by the thought of experiencing a bit of pleasure. Perhaps they have not met the guru who ripens their interest in the dharma. Seven thousand of the monks in Drepung are not studying so I am fortunate to have entered this path."

When I went down to see Gen Yaro I told him what I had been thinking and he encouraged me and told me about the deep existential problems that exist even in the happy times of our lives. Without his guidance in those early years, I would not have been able to go on. Thinking back to my study periods on the mountains above Drepung I am filled with wonder at how much peace there was, what a feeling of spiritual purpose. The mountain was called Ge-phel, "Mountain of Increasing Goodness," by the local people, and indeed it was that. I feel inspired even today when I think about it; of all that I was able to do in my early years at Drepung, my mountain retreats stand out as most precious of all.

I FIRST STARTED TO MEMORIZE Tsong-khapa's *Speech of Gold* in my first year of Perfect Wisdom, but stopped when I had to deal with the death of my mother. I returned to the text again in my third year. In the third Tibetan month I devoted my study break to memorizing it, and again during the fifth month when my study gurus were called away to do prayers for the laity. During that time I stayed in my room in Drepung and memorized a large amount, beginning at six o'clock each morning. There were days when I memorized as many as five pages. When I had memorized about forty-five pages and was beginning to feel confident about my ability to finally learn the *Speech of Gold*, I fell sick.

This was at the very end of the study period; my study gurus had returned from the prayers and the debate period was scheduled to begin on the following day. I had decided to make a melted-butter tsampa dish with cheese—a dish similar to the scrumptious tsampa with a melted-butter crown, called *paktsa mar-gol*. I melted the butter and poured it on the tsampa along with a bit of oil. The sickness began to creep up on me soon after I had finished eating it. For three years an epidemic had been going around the monasteries and now, three years after my first sickness, it was my turn again. I felt ice-cold inside, began shivering uncontrollably with a high fever, and fell so sick I finally collapsed and could not get up. Gen Yaro came to see me but left soon after with all my gurus to attend a teaching by Trichang Rinpoche. The person who nursed me during this terrible sickness, treating me with a kindness I can never repay, was a young student not even from my part of Tibet. We had no real bond between us, but he looked after me with incredible care.

Slowly my illness got worse. The fever was terrible and I fell into deeper and deeper sleeps. Realizing that I was descending into a sleep from which I might never awake, I rubbed chili on the end of my nose to try to keep myself alert. My nurse would hit me on the cheek to bring me back to myself and would make me get up and keep walking; sometimes he made my eyes burn with chili to keep me from slipping away into a final sleep. During this time I felt great peace inside. I noticed what was happening and it dawned on me that I was keeping my nurse from his study and I felt bad about that, but no bitterness. I got weaker until I fell into a coma-like state where I could no longer see, or hear conversation. My gurus came back from the teaching, and after seeing and talking to me they must have decided that I was finished because they made preparations for my death. By now I was totally inside my own world; I felt no discomfort and thought I was alone and that all the people who were helping me had left. Even though I was surrounded by people, I was oblivious to all of them.

Then Gen Yaro came to my bedside, lifted me up, and said the mantras of Shakyamuni Buddha and Mahakala, the wrathful form of the Compassionate Buddha. I remember recognizing that it was my guru, but it seemed as though he was far off in the distance. It came in my mind that I must be very sick and I began to think that there was a terrible smell on my body.

A power in the mind of Gen Yaro came across to me when he repeated those mantras; they revived me a little, and though I was not able to say them aloud I started repeating the mantra of Shakyamuni over and over within. I could hear my guru saying that I should pray that my terrible sickness would purify all of the karmic obscurations to my practice so that I would be able to recover and continue for the benefit of all. "Pray for all your hindrances to be gone," he said. "Pray that all the unwholesomeness you have done from time without beginning are purified by this sickness, that by experiencing this illness all the sicknesses experienced by all the holy beings of Tibet will be ended." I could hear Gen Yaro as he gave me this advice, but when I tried to get up and see him I found that I was blind.

I dreamed repeatedly that I was walking back and forth in a field with a river in it. It was a tremendously clear dream, totally real. Two paths opened up in front of me. I tried to go down the path on the right but a huge man blocked me and I turned back. It was from that time, that part of the dream, I believe, that I finally began to slowly come back to health.

I also dreamed about Toden Lhatruk, the man in charge of taking away the dead body when someone died in Drepung. He was taking corpses off to the cemetery, and he came to me, put me on his back, and carried me off. He threw me on a pile of corpses, but all the bodies were good-looking, sleek and with fragrant smells. The corpses filled up an entire ocean, and the bodies were in flames, making an ocean of fire.

Finally somebody went to Kanjur Rinpoche in Lhasa and asked him to do a divination. He said that it was necessary to perform the *cha-sum* ritual, and agreed to do it. The butter lamps of the ceremony appeared to me (far away though they were on Kanjur Rinpoche's altar in Lhasa) as lights glimmering in the distance, and I thought I saw huge people with one, two, and three heads. From then I began to improve markedly and I began to see and hear again.

As I got better I began to walk in my sleep. I would get up in the middle of the night and walk around without knowing what I was doing. When this happened, I could not hear anyone talking to me, and I was very hard to restrain. My friends tied large ladles on the windows so that they would make a clatter and wake people up if I began to walk out of a window. One time I sleepwalked right outside and was at a ladder that led downstairs. As I started walking down they grabbed me and tried to shake me into awareness, but I slipped off again into a deep, coma-like sleep and they had to carry me bodily back to bed. For many days nothing in the outside world could get through to me.

When I was a little better, my friends told me that my eyes had been shut tightly for days; I had been aware of nothing, and they could not even make me sit upright, I would just fall back to sleep. They said that I had been unable to keep food down and that everyone thought that I was certain to die. Everybody was amazed when I started getting better, and they said I was like a spirit who had returned from the land of the dead. When Gen Yaro saw that I had gotten better he was very happy. "You have burned up a lot of obscuration and bad karma," he said. "Now you will be able to study well." I told him about my dreams and he said that the ocean of burning corpses was a good sign that a lot of bad karma was purified. I also told him how I had heard him reciting the mantra from far away and how I had not been able to see him. My guru said that in fact he had taken my head in his hands and said the mantras right in my ear.

This disease was called *tse-pa*, and was a sleeping sickness that caused very high fever, often ending in death. In all, I was sick for about two months. After my illness another student fell sick but I nursed him for a long time and he was able to pull through. Then a third student fell sick, and though I nursed him he quickly got worse. He would toss about uncontrollably in the night, throwing off all his bedclothes. No matter how often you put them back on him, he could not bear it and would throw them off again and lie there naked. I remained with him, but people said it was a hopeless case, that he could never pull through. His eyes went red and his nose began to flatten back into his face as the signs of death began to appear. His breath became labored and I was told that I should put the special pills of death into his mouth when he breathed a long breath. I had never done this before and was uncertain about the exact moment to give him the pills. I hesitated, and the poor monk thrust out his limbs and expired. I put the pills in his mouth even though his breath had stopped, and then put him into a sitting position, crossed his legs, and sat him in a dignified posture.

I called for Toden Lhatruk, the person who took away dead bodies, and when he arrived he asked me if the monk had died in the posture in which he was sitting. I said no, that I had seated him in that more decent looking posture after he had expired. Toden Lhatruk said that this was going to be a problem. One of his jobs was to report any suspicious circumstances surrounding a death, and I had broken a strict law of the monastery which stipulated that nobody was allowed to touch a dead body until it had been inspected. He told me that he would have to go to the central monastic authorities and report that the corpse had been tampered with. I waited nervously as he inspected the body very carefully, from head to toe. "You are obviously a new monk," he said when he was done, "and you do not know the rules. I am not going to make a problem, but you should be aware of the seriousness of the matter." I was relieved, because had the central monastic authority been called in, I could have been in real trouble.

This may seem like a strange rule, but the death of a young monk was taken seriously by the central authority because it had to ensure the security of all the monks. The position at the time of death would be an important factor in deciding if a monk had died from starvation, from a room guru's total lack of concern, from abuse, or if he had actually been murdered. Only after Toden Lhatruk declared himself satisfied could the corpse be bound up and taken to the cemetery. As was the custom, the clothes the dead person was dressed in fell to Toden Lhatruk as his share of the deceased's property.

AFTER I HAD PASSED four or five prayer festivals in Lhasa the letters from my Red Uncle telling me to come home stopped. My sister had not tired of telling him that he should tell me to come back, but he began to ignore what she was saying and let me study in peace. My sister got to know that he was not passing on her messages and decided to try another route. She got somebody else to write that she had made an incense offering to our local spirits of the earth (there were three of them, called the "Three Laypersons") asking them to do whatever was necessary to get me to return. She wrote that she had prostrated herself in front of the Three Laypersons asking them to fulfill her request. Those gods were my birth gods, and I had a strong relationship with them. Just before the letter from my sister arrived telling me what she had done I remember feeling a bit uncomfortable and I remember I also had a few strange dreams, but otherwise the gods did not hurt me; they did not do anything to help me, but they also did not cause me any mischief or harm.

She worded her letter to me very strongly. "I was the one," she said, "who held your hand and taught you how to walk, who sat you up in a chair and taught you how to sit. I looked after you during the time you were a small child. Now, when both our mother and father have died and I am here looking after all the family affairs by myself, you show no concern for your family at all. You stay far away in Lhasa and show no signs of returning. I think you should be ashamed of yourself for having so little concern for your family."

The advice of my guru about impermanence and the problems of home life had their effect, and my homesickness had all but disappeared by this time, but when I read her letter I felt a stab in the heart. I was flooded with concern. Later, though, when I reread it, I saw that the reason she wanted me back was just to help with the household work. There was lots of talk about the closeness of family, how we were one, but the real message was, "Hurry back home, will you, there is a pile of work to do here and I want you to do it." My sister, I thought, placed great importance on those few she took as family, but felt irrelevance, even dislike, for those outside that narrow circle. It was a mind governed by notions of some people being close and the rest being outside. I just read her letter and put it aside. I remembered the words that one's home is a prison and one's family Mara's snare. My closest relative—my dear sister—was tugging at me to get me back, but to what? Nothing but samsara, nothing but an unending prison. After this I never had a strong wish to return home.

A letter from my Red Uncle arrived a bit later than my sister's letter. He suspected what my sister was doing. "It is possible that your sister is causing trouble trying to make you return," he wrote. "Take no notice of her, all she wants is an extra servant around the house, and you should stay at your study if it is going well and just ignore her." He sent a large amount of money with the letter and said he was happy that I was studying and to try to stay at it.

I had to reply to my sister, of course, but was unsure how to do so, so I went to talk to Gen Yaro. He said that I must write, but that I should be very careful, so I went to a letter writer and wrote that I was not forgetful of my family and our close relationship, that I held it dear, but that I was trying to study and even hoped to become a geshey. After taking the geshey degree, I said, I would return, but until that time it would not be possible to do so. I said that I was not in the monastery to have a good time, quite the opposite; life was hard, the food was terrible, and I was living on coarse black-pea tsampa and black tea. I said that my room was dark and the mud floor was bumpy and uneven, that from the point of view of the day-to-day life I was having a terrible time but that I wanted to persevere at it in order to become a geshey. I said they probably thought I was having a fine time in Lhasa, being my own master, eating and living well, but they were wrong. I told them to ask others about the life I was living. I asked them to send me money if they could afford to, but said that I would not be writing again and again to ask for it, it was for them to decide whether it was something they wanted to do. I sent off this letter, which represented a final severing of the cord that bound me to home. From then on I got letters from home with money, but never again one urging me to return.

The trader who took my letter back told them that it was no use trying to make me return home, that I was totally set on studying and would not do so. He said that the arrogance that I was known for at home was gone, that whereas everyone used to say that I was too arrogant and proud to succeed in the monastery, I had changed and was the most self-effacing of the monks, slinking around almost as though I was invisible. Because of this I did not get on bad terms with my family, our relationship remained as it was before, except that the insistence that I return home stopped. My Red Uncle got word of what I had written to my sister and a later wrote me a letter saying that I had written well, and I had said what needed to be said.

IN OUR HOMELAND during the eighth or ninth Tibetan month there was a particular set of rituals associated with fall that took place once the yearly harvest had been gathered. People asked high lamas what rituals should be done and then invited the monks to perform them. Sometimes the villagers would invite as many as twenty monks for a day or more of prayers, and thirty or forty villagers as well would come and have a good meal. The feasting would go on for two or even three days. To supply food for these special meals at least two dzomos that had passed beyond their best milking years would be slaughtered, and pigs as well. It was not absolutely necessary to slaughter them at that time, dried pork would be available, but it was often done and had become a custom.

I thought much about how my people slaughtered these animals because they felt they had to make prayers, and it was something I did not like. It seemed wrong to be slaughtering animals to make Buddhist prayers. I asked Gen Yaro about it and he said there were prayer rituals to the Victorious Goddess, to Tara, and to the Medicine Buddha that needed big offerings, but that required the food be strictly vegetarian. He said I should write to my people and suggest they make those rituals in the fall, rather than the rituals which required them to slaughter animals.

I wrote home to say they should make rituals based on these other deities and should avoid rituals which required feeding the monks large amounts of meat. I said that it was for my sake, that I was going to experience problems if the slaughter of the animals went on (this was a pious fiction, of course, but one that I thought might influence them). I told them that they could buy dried pork and use that in the food they offer in order to be able to serve meat, but that they should avoid the yearly slaughter.

When word of what I had written got back to my Red Guru he was very pleased. He called the family together and said, "The boy is thinking about what is virtuous. He is urging us to stop the slaughter of animals, and indeed we will do what he is urging. "From now on," he said, "we should only serve pure food and not consider it necessary to go each year and ask the lamas what rituals are necessary in the fall." He told them to do the vegetarian rituals that I had suggested.

My Red Guru said that if the family felt it was necessary, they could do the long and complicated Torgyak ritual of throwing out the offering cake. Otherwise the family would do the long and expensive offerings to the Victorious Goddess, to Tara, or to the Medicine Buddha. He said that the slaughter would be a hindrance to my life, and also would not be good for the family. He wrote to me saying that he was very glad I had sent the letter, that he had himself thought about my idea earlier, but that he had not been able to institute a family custom of sponsoring better prayers. He said that they would be doing what I had advised, and was happy at my life and aspirations.

From then on the family's affairs went very much better, and my family was more clearly set on the path of virtue. My family members tell me that even down to today the prayers the family makes are usually the sort I recommended, that they avoid the slaughter of animals.

5

PHUKHANG HOUSE

After my first year at Drepung I went to the general winter debate—
the Jamyang Gun-cho—eight years in a row, attending every year until
I became house guru in 1955. When you arrived at the winter debate
you spent the first two days gathering wood. The debate would then
begin and if the wood did not last you would have to go collecting
again, sometimes two more times. In the old days there was plenty of
wood close by, but by the time I attended you had to go a very long
distance, a two-day journey, traveling both ways over a high mountain pass. We young monks left at two in the morning and did not
arrive at the place where there was wood until seven. A senior monk
remained camped in one place, preparing tea while the rest of us went
far off in all directions. There was a custom that you could only cook
where a senior monk lit the fire, so it was often a very long time until
you got a cup of tea.

My self-image always caused me to push myself. If I went off to
collect wood or dried dung I would never return until I had an unusually large load. But on one wood-gathering expedition during my
second winter debate I could not find any. I went off a great distance,
descending a mountain into another valley far from where the senior
monk was brewing tea. When I only found half a sack there, I set off in
another direction which took me even farther away. It was one o'clock
in the afternoon before I gave up, still without enough for a full sack.
I had been walking for nearly twelve hours with nothing to eat or
drink, and I was beginning to feel faint. Carrying my heavy sack, I

involuntarily began thinking that this was the last time I was going to do this, that after the upcoming prayer festival I would go home and leave this dog's life for good.

Some monks finally came up to help me, and after I had something to eat and drink I began to revive, but by then the other monks were getting ready to start the long journey back to the debate grounds. The senior monk asked why I had been away so long, and I told him how far I had gone. "You are still a new monk and do not know how to pace yourself," he said. "You will learn and it will get easier for you." The others had large loads of wood and dried dung, but for all my effort I only had a half-sack of dried dung. I felt like an exhausted fool.

It was the tradition for the young monks to enter the debate grounds in a single file with their wood. The strongest would lead the line and stride into camp with a huge load. I liked to picture myself at the head with a gigantic load but this time I straggled in far to the rear, totally defeated. I had such a little load that the other monks gave me a bit of their wood so that I would not lose face. An elderly monk asked me why I had nothing spectacular to show for my efforts this time and my companions told him what had happened. "You should not feel bad about that," the old monk said kindly. "To come back with a little is fine if you tried your best and you should not feel upset."

During the prayer festival that followed at the beginning of the new year after this winter debate I remember that I was seated next to a younger monk from my part of Kham, a joker who never rose to the serious side of monastic life. I was serious about study by this time and I counseled him to try to study hard. I gave him advice as best I could, but he was not interested.

Amongst the new monks the most senior were the *parsha-rawas*, the minor disciplinarians. There were two of these disciplinarians, and they were responsible for keeping new monks in order when the house guru was busy with other responsibilities. It was a position that might lead to being elected house guru after one or two years. At this time, one of the *parsha-rawas* was a monk called Tsondru who was smart, but full of himself and his status. He never gave me any trouble because he was well disposed to monks who were trying to study, but he knew that this young monk was not serious, and he had decided to give him a good thrashing.

One evening during the prayer festival all of us young monks were in a line doing recitation. The joker monk—his name was Tangdo Shuwa—was seated near me a little down the line. We were all bent over reciting as the *parsha-rawa* came down the line looking for Tangdo Shuwa. He had a piece of stick for meting out punishment which *parsha-rawas* did not have the right to carry. Since it was already dark and a wind was stirring up the dust, Tsondru mistook me for Tangdo Shuwa and began to beat me. As he gave me a terrible thrashing he shouted out all the bad things that I had supposedly done: "You have been fooling around! You are not studying, you are a disgrace to Phukhang house, and you are not decent enough to be allowed amongst the monks!" He went on and on, each time with a blow more vicious than the last. As he was beating me I was frantically running through my mind, wondering what I could possibly have done to deserve it. The only thing I could think of was a piece of dried bread I had eaten in secret during a break in the afternoon part of the prayer festival when monks were supposed to fast. Otherwise, I could not think of anything that could have upset him. Then the swirling dust settled down and he saw who I was. As soon as he realized his mistake he immediately stopped and left. Gen Yaro had told me that wrongdoings are purified by enduring hardship and it was in a person's best interest to cultivate patience, so I did not feel any bitterness for the beating. I just thought that a karmic obscuration had been removed. But Tangdo Shuwa, the intended object of the beating, thought the whole incident was terribly funny and could not stop laughing at my expense. He knew that he was the one the *parsha-rawa* was after, but he had buried himself deep in his cloak. I felt embarrassed because I had been telling him to be well behaved, and yet I had ended up with a severe beating. The monk with the good advice had been thrashed, the monk he had been advising had got off free.

During the prayer festival the discipline was very strict. After the recitation ended, monks had to go straight to their rooms without talking to each other, so I did not say anything to anyone about what had happened that evening. But the older monks were furious and said that Tsondru always tried to be so strict, but he had made a mistake himself this time, and they were going to raise the issue in the house meeting. The next day when I was giving Gendun the offerings I had received in the prayer festival, he asked me what had happened. He too said that he would lodge a complaint, but I told him I did not feel hurt and I thought that the *parsha-rawa* had made an honest mistake. The common guru of the house also came by to ask me what had happened. He said it would have to be raised up in the house assembly, that Tsondru was devious and arrogant and it would serve everybody well if he were upbraided publicly. I replied that I would rather let it pass. "I do not feel any bitterness, so I would rather just absorb any loss instead of making it escalate. I would prefer you do not bring it up," I said, "but if you do, just say that I see the beating as the result of my own shortcoming and that I do not want anyone else blamed for it." The common guru was pleased. "If it is not an issue with you," he said "then I will not pursue it."

Both my room guru and the common guru did, however, bring up the beating during the house assembly. They both mentioned that I wanted to drop the incident, but there were other issues to do with Tsondru, and he came in for censure. A few days later Tsondru took me aside and said he had made a mistake. "I consider you a friend," he told me, "and I was wrong to beat you. I ask you to forgive me for what I did." He also insisted that I take a ball of leftover tea-butter. I said it was absolutely unnecessary, that mistakes were always made and that I did not hold it against him, but he insisted so I came out of it with a ball of butter.

There was always bullying in the monastery, with those at a higher level causing trouble for the younger ones, but I always took bullying as my own fault and it never left me with bitterness or hatred. I am lucky to have the ability to think this way even today. You will always meet with abusive people in higher positions. It goes with life, and it is in your own interest to feel patience instead of bearing a grudge.

MY ILLNESS the previous year had prevented me from studying Definitive and Interpretative Statements as well as I had hoped, but one did not redo a particular topic, one just forged ahead. After the prayer festival I went on to the third year of Perfect Wisdom—the Bodhichitta year. It was during this year that I had something go wrong with my energy winds and the pressure in my eyes made my eyeballs swell up badly. Later on I learned it was glaucoma. I was told that the best cure was drinking melted butter, so I took the ball of butter Tsondru had given me, boiled it up and drank it. It definitely helped.

In the fall of my Bodhichitta year my studies were interrupted again. This time I had to go to the winter debate grounds to help build new rooms. This was not something one chose to do, one simply had to do it, even though it was a hindrance to study. I am a fellow with a huge appetite, but I am also someone who can work very hard. During the time we were out at the winter debate grounds building, everyone was surprised at how hard I worked.

THE FOURTH YEAR of the study of Perfect Wisdom is called Twenty Members of the Community. During this year I was finally chosen for the *tsog-lang che-wa* or "major debate." The major debate was a far more exacting test of knowledge than the minor debate that I had completed some years before. A pair of monks called the major debater and assistant debater was chosen from a number of competing candidates. The major debater and the assistant sat together to answer any questions during the series of debates that took place over a period of months that were the necessary prerequisite and led to a final grand debate at the general *ridra* assembly. The major debater had to do the recitation and direct a debate at that final assembly, while the assistant sat with him to field questions and supply answers, but did not have to do a recitation or put any questions.

There was a rush to do the major debate. All the better students of each house wanted to do it. The final decision on major debate candidates was made at the beginning of the new year by a senior monk called the *lama shung-len-pa* , and the final *ridra* assembly debate took place about six months later.

During the fifteen day, twenty day and month-long debate periods in the period called "Crowned by Debates" there were wood-collecting breaks. Each night before a wood-collecting day there was an assembly debate in each house. Senior monks listed for the geshey examination to take place during the next new year's prayer festival were first called to sit at the head of these debate sessions. If they were not available, then those younger monks who had won the competition to do the major debate would be invited to sit there. If even they were not available, the house would decide which of their own monks would sit at the head of the assembled monks to answer questions.

Listed gesheys let the different house gurus know a few days before a debate session that they were coming. If two gesheys said that they were coming at the same time to the same house they worked it out between themselves who would come first and who would come later. Younger monks doing the major debate, on the other hand, asked permission from their own house guru to sit for a debate in another house. They said that they were going to such-and-such a house on such-and-such a day and asked their house guru for permission to do so. Their house guru gave permission on condition that no geshey suddenly decided to sit there. If a geshey did decide to go, the younger monk listed for the major debate was denied permission even if he had been slotted for that date. Three days before a debate the gesheys made their final decision. If there were no gesheys, then the major debaters' house gurus would make it definite with the other house gurus and the monks listed for the major debate would sit in the other houses as arranged. There were twenty-three houses in total and monks listed to do the major debate made the rounds of them, going to different houses on the nights before wood-gathering holidays up until the assembly in the sixth month.

Besides sitting in front of the assemblies of the twenty-three different houses, the Loseling monks listed for the major debate also had to debate in the Loseling general assembly. All the learned monks, the *lama shung-len-pa*, and the Loseling abbot attended to ensure that the debate was conducted at a high standard. There was a Loseling tradition that a monk listed for the major debate from the highest class—Abhidharma—debated only with others from his own class. Otherwise, each higher class debated with monks from the class below, so in my case, since I was in the Twenty Members of the Community class, I debated with those in the class above me doing Chapter Four of Perfect Wisdom. After the circuit of debates was finished the monks listed for the major debate presented themselves to the *lama shung-len-pa* for guidance on the final *ridra* assembly and were told the exact time that the debate was scheduled to take place.

When I first went to seek permission to do the major debate from the *lama shung-len-pa* many other monks were there with offerings asking for the opportunity to do the debate as well. The *lama shung-len-pa* said to me that I did not need to make any money offering, that if I passed an oral examination to ensure I could do a recitation he would put me forward as one of the candidates for that year. I thanked him for his kind gesture because those *shung-len-pa* lamas usually received a large amount in money offerings.

There were four of us at the oral examination, amongst whom I and a monk from Para house acquitted ourselves well. The *lama shung-len-pa* said it was up to us to decide who would be main debater and who the assistant. Still, he directed the question in the first instance to me, as a favor, so I had first refusal. I chose the position of assistant because after a monk from Para house had successfully completed a major debate he was exempted from a number of otherwise time-consuming house duties and expensive ritual offerings to the house. Since this was not the case at Phukhang house, where the major debate was highly esteemed but did not carry with it any exemptions from duties or offerings, I accepted the role of assistant and he took the role of main debater.

We were both able to acquit ourselves well in the series of house debates and at the Loseling debate, in particular, neither of us were left in the dark and we both responded clearly and to the points the debaters were making. The assembly of elder monks was pleased.

After completing the circuit of debates we presented ourselves to the *lama shung-len-pa* for guidance on the *ridra* assembly. At our meeting he told us that he was pleased with our standard of debating up to that point. He also said that if we did as well in the final assembly we would not have to make the offerings normally made to him.

So then the *ridra* assembly came around, the time of the great assembly debate when one would rise up. As the main participant, my partner had to make some substantial offerings. He had to offer a number of good meals to those monks who had supported him, and he had to give a very good meal to the *lama shung-len-pa* as well. For myself, I had no work to do at that time except eat.

In the final debate my partner from Para house did his recitation and made large offerings. The monk representing Gomang was quite famous so many Loseling monks flocked to debate with him, but since we were unknowns not many came from Gomang to debate with us. Still, people said we performed well, and when we went to thank the *lama shung-len-pa* and give him our offerings he told us he was pleased and that if the job fell to him next year he would list us for the major debate again.

PHUKHANG HOUSE had a special text some twenty or thirty pages long written by Phukhang Nag-po-pa on the more complex subdivision of Members of the Community into forty-eight. After I had been chosen for the major debate a few monks joked with me that there would be a big test to see if Phukhang's unique little book could stand up to scrutiny during the series of debates. Thinking there would be a lot of debate on this and wanting to defend the honor of my house I memorized the whole text and prepared myself fully. Unfortunately, after all that preparation there was not one person who debated on anything even remotely connected with it during the whole cycle of debates! I prepared the whole thing for nothing. Well, not quite, because right down to this day I have that section of Perfect Wisdom right at my fingertips.

During the interhouse debate sessions my arrogance sometimes got the better of me and I would tell others that they did not know what they were talking about. Gen Yaro was sometimes at those debates and when we returned to our rooms he would not berate me but would say firmly that was not the way to act. He said that there were learned monks at the debates and to be so arrogant was inappropriate. Gen Yaro was a humble and self-effacing man and he did not like arrogance. He often told me to check on my motivation because otherwise the purpose of debating would be lost.

One time earlier during my Bodhichitta year, word got out that the class above mine, where Gen Lam-rim-pa and the class captain were good debaters, would be meeting head to head with my class. The debate was hot and furious and went excellently. I came back to my room very excited and pleased with myself and sure that Gen Yaro would be happy as well. But instead he sat withdrawn into himself and did not say anything at all. Finally he said I was a disgrace to watch, so puffed up and driven by pride. "There are holy beings at debates," he said, "people making a sincere effort at spiritual life. You seem to have lost all track of why monks go to debate." He told me to remember that the aim of debate was to pacify the mind and to be calm and at peace.

EACH DAY AFTER HOUSE PRAYERS and debate ended, the free debates would begin, continuing until eleven or twelve, even into the early hours of the morning. During the main debating season the weather was quite warm and staying out to debate was very pleasant. All three of the great monasteries had night debate, but Loseling had a particularly fine tradition in this respect. New monks had to stay close to the disciplinarian. Then, as the night wore on, debaters from higher classes would begin to drift in closer to the younger ones who were left. The disciplinarian would have left by this time and older monks would come and ask the younger monks difficult questions. We would spend hours wriggling this way and that, unable to answer. When we tried to get up and leave they would grab hold of us and keep us there until we gave a satisfactory answer. One time this had gone on for over an hour, the older monks making a total fool of me, when I had sensed that my guru Gen Yaro had come to listen. After they finally let me go my head was spinning. During the whole night I could not sleep as I replayed the debate over and over in my mind. I felt the embarrassment of not having risen to the occasion with the right answer. The next morning I went to see Gen Yaro expecting him to scold me, but instead he told me that he thought the debate had been excellent. "Your older spiritual friends, they sure stopped you last night, did they not? That is a benefit indeed, far better than the transitory pleasure of besting an opponent in debate. To be unable to answer makes you think and gets rid of arrogance. A feeling of humility and admiration for others, a wonder at how much there is to know—these will overcome this arrogance you have," he said. "It is a good lesson." This insistence on the deeper purpose of debate and his intense dislike of arrogance were special blessings of Gen Yaro.

THE FIFTH YEAR of Perfect Wisdom is called "Concentrations and Absorptions." During my careful study of the Members of the Community I had dealt at length with concentrations and absorptions so I felt, as did quite a lot of others in my class, that it was not necessary to study this topic intensely. We thought we were armed for the interclass debates. Others warned us that there were lots of gaps in our knowledge, but I was arrogant about my capacity to answer and marched into the first of the interclass debates and made a total ass of myself. "Phukhang Nag-po-pa," they taunted, "enlighten us about this, please," and I did not even know enough to identify the topic, let alone give an intelligent answer. The abbot was enjoying my discomfort immensely and I felt like a total fool. After the debate my classmates asked me why I had not answered. "You made a fool of us," they told me. "You let down the class." What could I say? That I thought I knew it even though I had not studied? I went to my room. Gen Yaro was silent at first, but finally he said that not being able to give answers was no terrible thing if it served to overcome afflictive emotion. "It will be a good experience in the long run," he said.

Though not unbearably conceited, I was arrogant about my ability to answer. When I left a debate my thoughts would run on uncontrollably: "I should have answered like this instead of like that. I would have won if I said that...." I could not stop the continual need to come out on top—a sure sign of conceit. After this debate, though, I was unsure if I could debate at all.

From then on, when I headed out to an important debate I always asked myself why I was going, I checked my motivation and reminded myself that the purpose was to stop the nasty parts of my personality from operating, that I should not try to debate just for the sake of looking good and letting my pride bloom. Gen Yaro always stressed the silliness of being top of a class just in order to get puffed up about yourself. This incident was an excellent illustration for me of how a person who gets conceited finds that their path through life gets more and more difficult.

MY NEXT YEAR was Perfect Wisdom, Chapter Four. I studied hard and debated well until the interclass debates, even blocking Gen Lam-rim-pa with my questions and answers. But then those in power in Phukhang house felt it was necessary to make one hundred thousand Tsong-khapa statues. And once that had been decided, the long ritual prayers that went with the blessing of the statues had to be done too. There was no way out except to take up the task with joy and enthusiasm. I and some others felt we had to volunteer to make the hundred thousand Tsong-khapas and do the associated rituals too to demonstrate our wish to put the well-being of the house even before our own personal goals.

The work started off slowly but once we got into the rhythm we were churning them out so fast you would not believe it. I had a partner, Apay, and the pair of us went at it like a whirlwind: I made the balls of clay, Apay stuffed them into the mold, and a third monk cut off the extra from the mold while other monks got them out and lined them up in the sun. We felt very proud about our work; we started before six in the morning and only stopped briefly for the low quality house food that was the only payment we got for doing the work.

We made more than one hundred and twenty thousand in total, and I remember vividly to this day the terrible food the house storekeeper gave us while we were working. He did give us tsampa in the morning, but beyond that we got only watery soup with blobs of tsampa in it and soggy servings of tasteless, stringy vegetables. That storekeeper was a tightfisted one; he parted with his tea like he parted with his most prized possession. It makes me laugh, because we were livid about the food at the time but had accepted responsibility for the statues and could not get out of it. That lousy soup with those infinitesimal blobs of tsampa was so bad I can see it before me now.

After the statues were made they had to be painted and the faces had to be done. We had an excellent monk from Gomang to paint them, but he insisted I remain with him as his helper. He brought it up in the house assembly and said that it was absolutely necessary that I stay with him or else he would not do the work, so I was caught again and had to remain until the painting was finished. It all took a very long time and it meant that I was denied an opportunity to study the fourth chapter of Perfect Wisdom deeply. I got back to the classes when they were studying the Signs of Irreversibility topic. I was, however, able to go to the Jamyang Gun-cho as usual, and though I was not able to sit for the debates as I had during earlier years I still studied well. I did the Exclusion Theory of Knowledge topic from the *Commentary on Valid Cognition* and I also did prostrations. I had made this a habit during the winter debate because of that first time when Gen Yaro had told me to go out and do them. Each time recitation period finished I would go to do prostrations, and would even miss some of the debate sessions in order to keep up with them.

A MONK WHO WAS seriously studying was certain to be appointed house guru at a certain stage of his career. There was a lottery amongst those who accepted nomination for the position and a decision was made a full year in advance. Before being appointed house guru, a monk would serve at least one term as a *parsha-rawa* (minor disciplinarian). When I was twenty-five I was appointed *parsha-rawa*. This was a difficult year for me. While my class was studying the middle way refutation of the mind-only system, I was running here and there preparing for the upcoming year, when I was expected to be house guru. With my new responsibilities, I soon found that I was no longer putting enough time into study. I sometimes found myself totally lost in a debate and without any idea of the context or subject being discussed. I was still one of the better students in my class and was good at debating about subjects that I had studied, but I had large gaps in my knowledge. I wanted to keep studying and did to some extent. I admired learning deeply, and I had no wish to involve myself in worldly life that would take me away from spiritual endeavor.

I always had a vision of myself as a geshey going home to my birthplace. Down a ways, across a stream not far from our house in Kongjorawa, was a plot of land. There were trees growing there and in the middle of them was a small house. I hoped to move there and do an extended retreat after I finished at Drepung. So you see, my vision of spiritual practice at that point was one in which I kept the best of both worlds. In my mind a spiritual endeavor went along with a life free from too many problems coming my way. I had no wish to get into the stream of the important monks who were working their way up to the high *laram* geshey and from there towards important positions in the big colleges or monasteries. That path held out no attraction for me. Gen Yaro always said that sort of vision for the future was not a good one and I should avoid it. He said I should not hope to get to a special status as a monk; rather I should focus on the real meaning of spiritual life. And that is what I felt I was doing, working towards an authentic spiritual life.

ONCE DURING my year as *parsha-rawa* I was deputed to take a group of thirty monks to Gadong Monastery, where we had to recite a hundred thousand Taras and do an entire reading of the Kangyur. Nobody wanted to go because Gadong was known to be stingy towards monks—never giving very good food and making only small offerings at the end of the day. But it was a tradition that could not be avoided, so the monks had to go and I was head disciplinarian. While the monks were doing the prayers two of them fell to fighting. One of them was young, so as *parsha-rawa* I was allowed to pull him up and punish him, but the other was older and I did not have the right to criticize him openly; I would have had to report him to a higher level of the house. Hoping to take care of the problem immediately, I made an announcement to the whole group that I would be making a full report on these two monks to the house guru when we got back, and said that they had both better watch what they were doing.

Now, at Gadong there was a monk, a student of mine, working in the kitchen and I had a good relationship with him. He, in turn, was close to the Gadong Oracle so I asked him to request the oracle to come and ask me to spare the monks. I told him how my announcement had stopped the fighting, and if the oracle asked me not to make the report, then I would have a way out of getting the monks in trouble with the house guru. My cook friend passed the message on to the oracle, saying that an intervention from him would spare the two monks a very nasty punishment. The two monks themselves were quite worried about what was in store for them once they got back to Drepung.

Soon a representative of the oracle, in full formal dress, came to address the monks. He offered a scarf to the altar and said that he was very pleased that we had come to make the prayers, which were important and of great benefit. He said that from time to time small altercations would happen, that he was sorry such an altercation had arisen here amongst the monks, and that he was particularly sorry to have heard that a report was going to be made back at the monastery. He requested that the entire unfortunate incident be resolved there at Gadong, so that it need not go further.

I pretended to consult with my assistant disciplinarian and we announced that since the request had come from the Gadong Oracle himself we had no choice but to heed his wishes. I made a strong speech to this effect, and said that in view of the changed situation the two monks should make prostrations to the altar amongst the assembled monks and the entire matter then would be considered closed. They did so that day and on the remaining days of the prayers. The workers at Gadong did not know exactly what had transpired but just saw me stopping the fight and then having these fellows prostrate, apparently at my command; they thought that I must be a tremendously powerful monk and they began treating me with great respect. Of course they did not know that the monks were doing prostrations because of my behind-the-scenes arrangement with my friend in the kitchen.

When I got back to Drepung the house guru and other elders heard about how I had resolved the incident and were very happy. They said it was excellent that it had been contained and not grown into a bigger problem. The older monks must have decided from my success in this that I would be good at keeping discipline if I became house guru.

GENDUN, MY ROOM GURU, himself had a room guru called Gen Dulwa, and technically speaking he was the room guru of us all. Gen Dulwa was continually away on trade and business. He was a fine man with many relatives and students, and he treated me with special kindness. Every year he went on business to the Kongpo region east of Lhasa and when he arrived back in Lhasa he sent a message to the monastery telling us to send down someone to assist him. I often went to help him at those times.

Each year the rooms that were the common property of the house were allotted to monks for their living quarters. They were put into a common pool and there was a lottery to decide who would get which for the year to come. One time Gen Dulwa was away when the yearly lottery took place and when I went to see him on his return he asked me about the results. I had to say I did not have the slightest idea because I did not know I was supposed to take an active interest in such things. He said it was absurd that I had been in the monastery for years and still knew nothing about room allotment. "You are a fool," he said, scolding me in a friendly way for my ignorance of important matters. Then he told me to go to do any shopping I had to do and come back. When I returned he noticed that I was so poor I did not even have a proper belt to tie my robes and he began to warm to me. He said that it was good that I did not know who got which room. "You are sincerely trying to study, and I admire that," he said. "You do not poke your tea-spout in where a monk should not; you do not wander around asking about ordinary things which will come between you and your study and it seems you don't frequent the rooms of the old monks, trying to learn details about inconsequential matters. You are not one of those monks who are concerned about what the important monks have said in the house meetings. You don't even know about the room lottery."

Then he pointed to my threadbare clothes and asked, "What is going on? I thought you were the nephew of the Boss of Choo-chur. Isn't he taking care of you like we thought he is?" What could I say? That I used all the money my uncle sent me on food? Gen Dulwa then gave me an old lower robe, a belt, and a big lump of butter. "You do not have to share this with Gendun," he said. "Eat it up yourself during the retreat break," he said, "and this cheese." He told me to come down before he left again for Kongpo and I said I would. Later he again gave me butter and cheese, as well as some money and said that I did not need to give any to Gendun. "Do not get too thin," he said, "or you will find yourself falling sick."

From this time on Gen Dulwa always treated me kindly. Whenever I came to his house in Lhasa he would give me a big bowl of tsampa with good butter, cheese, and sugar, and would give me pieces of butter and money to take back to the monastery. His other students and relatives continually talked about their own petty squabbles, saying that someone had done this or taken that, and Gen Dulwa did not like it. He was pleased that I did not talk about such things and would tell them, "Choo-chur-wa sits quietly and is not always complaining about others; he should be your model for how to behave with decorum." He said this to Gendun, and said that it would be better if the others acted like I did.

Gen Dulwa also told me not to be anxious about taking on the responsibility of house guru, and said that he would help me with it. He reassured me and said I would have no difficulty with the task. At about this same time I got a letter from home saying that if I wanted to be house guru to go ahead and do so, otherwise find somebody to act as a substitute and pay them the necessary fee. "Do not worry," the letter said, "whatever the expenses involved in being house guru or paying a substitute we will meet it."

In the fourth month Gen Dulwa and his students went to Tsagu to do prayers for the villagers. When he came back he fell sick. At first he was not too bad and seemed to be on the road to recovery, but then, as time went on, his sickness worsened and I was given the job of nursing him. His other relatives and students for some reason did not offer to help. I nursed him as well as I could and he responded with trust. Sometimes I went to Lhasa twice a day, early in the morning with his urine for examination by the doctor, and then later in the day to have particular ritual prayers made.

I was so busy looking after Gen Dulwa that my study of the Middle Way began to suffer. When I went to the interclass debates, the lower-class students singled me out because I had been one of the better monks before. At first I answered their questions with clarity, but since I had not been studying I soon got tied in knots and incoherent. The abbot enjoyed my discomfort immensely. When we debated with the class above us I was again unable to answer with distinction, and was once even reduced to silence, unable to answer at all.

I was very upset at not having time to study and at my guru's relatives and students distancing themselves from him during his sickness. I thought that it was not right to abandon a sick person, that nursing him had fallen to me but that I would keep doing it even though it was affecting my study. I nursed him right through to the winter debate session. And each day I carefully set his mind at rest with an accounting of what I had spent on medicines and prayers, what I had given to his relatives, what they had purchased or arranged. Since Gen Dulwa did not show signs of recovery and the costs of medicine and prayers were escalating by the day, Gendun began to worry that his guru's money would not be enough and that he would start to go into debt because of his sickness. Most of his relatives felt that he was making too many prayers, that they were not effective and were going to bankrupt him. From my side, of course, I did whatever my guru felt was needed, without question.

Gen Dulwa's relatives wanted to separate me from him so that he would not keep giving me the money for prayers and medicine. They too were worried that he would finally die in debt and that they would have to pay back the money he owed. Gendun told me to go to the Jamyang Gun-cho, that too much of my time that year had already been spent nursing. I did as he said, but Gendun told Gen Dulwa that I was going to the debate because I was tired of nursing him. Through this double way of talking Gendun made a division between me and Gen Dulwa. So Gen Dulwa thought I was tired of him and did not feel he could ask me to stay, and I thought that he had, for some reason, taken a dislike to me. I was a fool. Since I was unsure what was going on it would have been smart to have gone right to my older guru and spoken openly with him, but I did not.

When we did finally talk briefly he said that I had looked after him for a long time so I should go to the winter debate. We decided to settle our accounts. Though he had been giving me the money for the prayers and medicines, I had also been spending my own money as we went along, without carefully separating it. When the final accounting was over I had spent much more of my own money than I realized. I was eating more than I should have been, but the final figure when all the accounts were done left me with only sixty sangs. I was shocked. You had to give forty-five sangs to the house kitchen when you arrived at the Jamyang Gun-cho, and I had to sponsor a prayer to Tara for all the Phukhang monks since I was senior *parsha-rawa* at the time. Fortunately, by taking my own supply of tsampa, eating carefully, and attending the different assemblies with different sponsors who gave out money, I was able to attend without difficulty. But when it was over I came back to the monastery penniless.

THAT YEAR the money offerings at the Jamyang Gun-cho were quite large, so some of the younger monks wanted to use their extra money to buy dried dung instead of going out to collect wood. We had already made two trips, and the monks wanted to avoid the hard work of going out a third time. This led to some friction. The *cho-togs*—the top representatives from each monastery administering the winter debate—came to ask me, as senior disciplinarian of the young monks in our house, how we felt about going out a third time. I realized that some older monks felt strongly on this matter, so even though I sympathized with my younger monks, I said that we were happy to go.

We left very early and just before arriving at the gathering grounds I led the monks in a smoke offering. Some of the monks were definitely unhappy so I told them not to lose heart, that we would change the tradition a bit and make our tea closer to where we gathered the wood. This pleased them very much. I then told the younger monks to look for dried branches, but warned them not to cut any wet ones because we were on the mountain of the god Tsirab and he would definitely be angry if he saw anyone cutting wet branches. They went up the valley in the direction of many thorn bushes and dried dung while I went down the valley to a meadow. I told the others that when they were ready to eat and drink I would be down there with the tea and food.

Unfortunately all the water was frozen solid into ice, so I had some difficulty getting water. I lit a fire and went off to cut out some blocks of ice to melt for our tea. While I was away from the fire it started to burn out of control in the dry grass around the fireplace. By the time I got back it had already spread to the thorn bushes, which were totally dry in the winter. I should have headed down the valley, since the fire was moving up, but in my fear and confusion I ran uphill and got caught by the spreading fire. It was burning out of control to the left and right of me below, driving me up the valley. I was panic-stricken. Not only was I going to die, I thought, but the others in the valley collecting fuel were all going to die as well. I am such a fool, I thought, I have somehow offended the god Tsirab and now the entire valley is on fire.

The fire made a great roaring sound and now and then I heard the sounds of explosions. I was beside myself, and not knowing what to do I prayed to the Buddha, Dharma, and Sangha. I prayed to them and to the Glorious Goddess for help. I then started prostrating into the four directions. I made three prostrations to the east, three to the west, and to the other two directions as well. The valley became totally clogged up with smoke and I could do nothing but squat down with my hands covering my eyes. Above me the younger monks could see the fire burning out of control. When they lost sight of me in the smoke they thought that I had perished and were shouting and crying as they came down to try to find me. I could not hear them at all.

After about fifteen minutes the smoke began to lift and I could see that the main blaze had burned itself out. There was just a little smoke lifting in patches and a few areas of fire left. The younger monks came running up to me, some of them still crying. They said that the fire had been roaring out of control and there had been the sound of explosions after which, for some reason, the fire suddenly died. The monks said they thought that it was me exploding in the fire, that I had been heated up so hot that I had exploded. They asked me what had happened and I said I did not know. I did not tell them that I had prostrated in the four directions out of helplessness, but I said that it was the blessing of the Three Jewels that the fire had gone out, that we should be thankful that they had come to our aid. We then put out the remaining bush fires, had tea, and relaxed.

In my heart I was still terrified. The fire, at its height, had spread over a kilometer and had raged totally out of control. I could still see it burning and I was sure that we had offended the god Tsirab, and that he would not easily forget. It was well known that he did not like anyone to cut any green branches, and he was even offended if local people came to cut dry wood. He had a soft spot for winter debaters, it was said, but still I felt in danger.

After we had eaten and drunk our fill we headed back. The monks had collected a lot of dung and branches and we marched smartly into the debate grounds in single file, carrying large loads. Outwardly it looked like all had gone well. Some older monks asked me if there had been any trouble and I said no. They said the crows had been cawing loudly all day and that they had been worried and had made a black tea offering to the gods because it was felt there was something not quite right. Then I told them about what had happened, how the fire went out of control and nearly killed us. I said I thought I had angered the god Tsirab.

Very early the next day I went to Tsirab's temple and made a black tea offering to him. I said openly that I was sorry for starting the fire. "I did not do it on purpose," I said. "It was an accident and please forgive me if I caused offense." I tried from the bottom of my heart to patch up the mistake I had made. And I retained amazement at the capacity of the Three Jewels to intervene. I had prayed to them fervently in the midst of that roaring blaze and somehow, just through the force of faith in them, with those explosions the fire had almost immediately gone out. I had always had faith in the Three Jewels, but from then on I came to have a special, unshakable faith that they would protect us.

DURING THIS PERIOD I got word that Gen Dulwa had suddenly died. The night before I heard of his death I dozed off in late evening next to a window and dreamed with great clarity of him coming from a distance to see me. I remember wondering in my dream how someone too sick to move could be coming. Then, suddenly, right next to the window a big, powerful, black man was looking in at me. The dream was so vivid it frightened me and I woke up with a shout. Some monks who had not gone to sleep asked what was wrong and when I told them my dream they said probably my guru had died and that the giant was some sort of harmful spirit.

The man who arrived with news of Gen Dulwa's death told me that Gendun wanted me to come back immediately, move out of his rooms, and find myself another guru. The essence of Gendun's message was that now that his guru was dead, he did not want to associate with me. The older monks said that it was improper to insist a person move out immediately on the death of an older guru, and told me to return in a few days after the end of the debate.

When the winter debates finished, it was the tradition for the monks from each house to return to the monastery in strict discipline, in lines. If a monk had students, as he neared the monastery they would come out to take his load and carry it the small distance back. It was an impressive ceremony. But as I arrived at Drepung, while the others were surrounded by younger monks eager to help them, I had nobody. It was very embarrassing and it was not until I was inside the walls of Drepung and had nearly arrived at my room that an acquaintance helped me with my things. Customarily, a returning monk's room guru would serve him tea the moment he arrived. I expected that I would have tea with Gendun, but he had nothing for me, just a tirade about how bad a student I was. He was extremely angry that I had not come back earlier, and said that he did not want me in his rooms at all. Finally he threw me out—pushed me out physically. I went to my own room and sat there wondering what to do. Gen Yaro knew what had happened because a short while later one of his other students came to tell me he wanted to talk to me. He gave me something to drink and eat and told me to take it easy. But inside I felt terrible. Gen Dulwa had died and I was simply thrown out as if I had been a terrible student.

THE NEXT DAY I had morning tea at a Tara prayer in the house assembly. Then I went to the house guru and got permission to go into Lhasa to talk with Chandzo Rabti about my predicament. I told the Chandzo that my room guru Gen Dulwa had just died, that his oldest surviving student Gendun disliked me, and that I did not think I was going to be able to be house guru the following year even though I had been chosen. "I feel I am now at the end of the road," I said, "and had better go home."

"Exactly what you should do!" said Chandzo Rabti. "This year both house gurus have died in the job so it is a task you would do better to pass up. It is a thankless task at the best of times so make preparations to go home. I myself will take you back," he said. "You probably have no money but do not worry about it, I will buy you a set of robes for your trip." After talking for a while I went to another part of the house, and a bit later the Chandzo again called for me. "I have been thinking about what you said and it was not right of me to tell you to leave for home so suddenly." He said it needed more preparation and thought that I should go and ask for some divinations, because if he just took me home all of a sudden like this my Red Uncle would not be happy. He would want to know why my study had suddenly been interrupted and attempts had not been made to continue. "Who should I go to?" I asked, and he said that because he knew Kanjur Rinpoche well, I should go and ask him.

I knew that no matter how many divinations Kanjur Rinpoche did, he would never say to me anything except that I should stay and study, and that it would not be good if I went home. So I did not ask for a divination but asked directly for permission to go home. "I am having a problem at the monastery," I said. "I am in line to be the house guru but my situation has turned difficult and I am not going to be able to do it. Please give me permission to go home." "No," he said. "You are talking nonsense and you should not go home, and that's that." He asked me in detail about my problems and I told him, but he said that the Glorious Goddess would not be happy at all if I left for home, and he said that he would search to see if he could find another room guru for me now that Gendun had rejected me. I then asked him to do a divination for me, which he did there and then. He turned to me with a triumphant smile and showed me the dice. "Look," he said, "it is a perfect *mo*." I had not the slightest idea whether it was good or bad, but he sat there holding out the dice for me to see with a look of triumph written on his face.

Kanjur Rinpoche then told me that Gangshingpa (the senior monk who had helped at the death of Ludrub Rinpoche) would probably take me on. "If he will not, come back and see me again and I will arrange for someone else. And do not worry about being house guru, I will guarantee that it will go well." I then told Rinpoche how I had caused the fire and appeared to have upset the god Tsirab. Rinpoche leaned back and pondered on this for some time before speaking. "No," he finally said slowly, "Tsirab is not angry. In fact he is quite pleased." Then he leaned forward and asked me if all that I had told him had really happened. "You are quite sure you made the black tea offering afterwards to Tsirab?" he asked, and when I said I had, Rinpoche said I should rest assured about the affair, that Tsirab was definitely on my side, and that he was not upset at all.

I went back to Chandzo Rabti and told him what had transpired and he said that with Kanjur Rinpoche so insistent about my staying, leaving was now out of the question. He said that he would help me with my house guru year and that I should not worry. I returned to Drepung quite late at night. I had a place to sleep but no place to cook or get anything to eat. I did not have even a spoonful of tsampa, and had to borrow some from a younger student. Then Gendun called me to his room and reminded me that I should start looking for another guru.

GENDUN'S ATTITUDE during this whole time left me with an unpleasant taste. Many of the things that should have been done following our guru's death were not done. It is a custom in Tibet that someone who has spent time nursing a sick person is remembered after the person's death with a gift or memento from the deceased person's estate. But Gendun gave me nothing at all. What was worse, the offerings which should have been made for him were left undone.

I have to confess that my relationship with Gendun was not very good. I had seen problems looming on the horizon because he was going to be guru-at-large during the same year I was going to be house guru. This could have been a mutually advantageous relation, as guru and disciple, but Gendun was not a person you could trust in a tight place; he was not reliable. So I was hoping to be able to change gurus anyway. Of course one could not voice such inner hopes, it was totally inappropriate to do so, but when Gendun said to me that he wanted me out I was not unhappy about it. It was an opportunity, as I saw it, to find a better guru for the difficult house guru year ahead. Gangshingpa, who had money of his own, was a dependable monk and a good guru. He was just the sort of person I hoped for, so I asked a young friend to be my intermediary to him.

Gangshingpa knew that he would not be totally responsible for financing my house guru year, that other people were willing to help me, so he sent back a message accepting. When I told Gendun that I had found another guru so quickly he was offended and caused me even more trouble, telling Gangshingpa that he had not asked me to leave. Gangshingpa then got very angry at me for looking for a new guru without having first received permission to leave from my earlier one. "You are a troublemaker for sure," he told me. I explained that what my earlier guru said was untrue and I spelled out the situation. He believed me and was on my side. "Still," he said, "it is going to be very difficult for me, in this situation as it is now unfolding, to be your guru. You will have to find someone else as a witness to verify your version of events." I approached my friend the intermediary and told him what Gendun had done. He was upset too because he was being made to look like a fool, so he went straight to Gendun, and told him that he had been acting totally inappropriately. After this I again approached Gangshingpa who said that he would be my guru.

OF THE TWENTY-THREE HOUSES in Drepung there is no doubt that being Phukhang house guru was worst of all. In some houses the house guru had an opportunity to make a little money, but in Phukhang it was accepted that there was a lot of work and usually a financial loss at the end of the day. The house was going through a bad period and most of the new monks were leaving as soon as their three years were over and returning to their homelands. Monks became particularly eager to leave in the year or so before their turn to be house guru came up, aware that the job would be thankless and end up leaving them in debt. That was one of the reasons why I was given the job so soon after getting to the monastery—so many of those above me had decided to return home rather than do the work.

It was possible to pay for a substitute to be house guru in one's place, but the house assembly did not agree to it easily, and it would cost the equivalent of more than fifty thousand rupees in present-day money. And anyway, I thought that if I were to take on the job and do it well I would make a lot of merit as well as purify a lot of bad karma. Also, I must admit at this point that even though I was top rank when it came to attendance at assemblies and debates, I was not top rank at putting my whole being into study. I was swayed too easily. I sometimes studied hard, but at other times I took it easy and got into long discussions about little affairs of the day. In my class I was quite good, but this was because my class was not at a very high level, not because I was particularly gifted.

In the eighth month letters arrived from home with money. The message from my Red Guru was that they were all pleased I was going to be house guru and that I could take up the job, or, if I preferred get a substitute. Gangshingpa felt that being able to stay at my study was an important consideration and he wanted to help me be able to do it. From my side I said there was a house order to these things and that I was happy to take my turn. I said I wanted to do it.

There was much to be done during the year prior to becoming house guru. You had to arrange a wood supply, memorize many rituals for offering cakes and black tea, and learn many praises to many house deities and gods. There also were many offerings to the Glorious Goddess. Once you became house guru you had to recite them all perfectly in the assemblies.

The new house guru also needed to find a guarantor, almost always his room guru. The room guru guaranteed that his student would not act contrary to laws and accepted customs, and said that if he got into financial trouble he would meet any financial obligations. Beyond the two room gurus, there were two year-long guarantors (*lo-nyer*) who stood as further guarantee. After this had been set up a monk could become a house guru. If the house guru died in office, his room guru or other guarantor was responsible for finding a replacement, not the house.

Once a monk became house guru he was responsible for accounting for every possession of the house, from the ornaments on the top of the house down to the cloth that was on the basement door. He also was responsible for the wood used in the kitchen for all listed teas and all prayers and usual assemblies. In my year as house guru I had to get in the equivalent of about three hundred dotses of wood for the year. There were two house gurus working together doing this and it meant a very large outlay of money. This responsibility for the wood supply was the main danger and difficulty for the house guru.

I had done the necessary preparations and was ready for the year as house guru when I went to see Chandzo Rabti, just before he left for Kham. "What help do you need?" he asked. I said that I had a big load of wood collected at a distance from Drepung and asked if he could help me transport it to the house. He had his own pack animals ready for the trip and was happy to oblige, transporting all my wood very quickly. He did not leave me any money, but he helped me with a number of things like this that needed to be done.

Both the house gurus from the year before me had died in office and it had been necessary to find substitutes during the course of the year. It was an unusual occurrence. People said that house gurus had never died in the middle of their duties before, for as long back as they could remember. There was a lot of talk going about, a lot of superstition in the air, and of course it rubbed off on me. I went to ask Kanjur Rinpoche, and his divination came up excellently. "No need to worry at all," he said, "I can guarantee you are going to have an excellent year." My partner (house gurus were always appointed in pairs) had a less than perfect divination, however. Kanjur Rinpoche told him that if he did one hundred thousand prostrations and many prayers his year as house guru would turn out well; for me, though, no prayers, no problems of any sort. My partner was younger than me but was a capable person experienced in business. Older monks said that I was lucky, because I had been so involved in study that I had little experience of business matters. My partner had not studied much, but was good at business. They said that we would divide up perfectly, him for the business and me for the discipline and standard of study.

I also went to the oracles of Phug-shag and goddess Tema-mo to check if there would be difficulties during my house guru year. The oracles said everything looked excellent. They set me at ease and said that the gods were on my side and would help me. There was another oracle on the outskirts of Lhasa, but I did not have much faith in it. Some people took me there and while they went in to request the god to descend into the oracle I squatted outside. After a few moments my friends came outside to say I had to come in, that the god was calling for me. I went in and the oracle in the trance came up to me and gave me a scarf. "You are a person who is going to do special work to make the teaching of Tsong-khapa spread far and wide," the oracle said, "and the gods will help you with the work of house guru. The preparations you are making are the right ones and you should have no worries at all." This god praised me right to my face in front of others.

The tenure of a house guru began in the tenth Tibetan month. Before taking office you would make a formal statement in front of the house assembly, and affix your stamp to a document to seal your commitment. In essence, you signed for the entire year's work, regardless of any circumstances or difficulties. There was even a clause covering the eventuality of your death, and you promised that if you died before the end of your tenure your room guru would finish your work for you.

I decided to have one more divination before taking office, so I went to Locho Rinpoche and asked him about the upcoming year. He said that it would go well, but that I should expect some problems. He mentioned, in particular, that I should keep in mind that I alone was the house guru and that I had to do all the work. "Do not think you have a partner in the task who will be doing this or that," he said. "Get the idea in your mind that you have to do all the work and plough on regardless." It was unusual advice, intimating that there would be problems and saying that I should think I was the only house guru, and not to expect to rely on my partner. At the time I did not take particular notice of his advice.

6

HOUSE GURU

During the ceremonial taking over of office the new house gurus are expected to dress for the part, so I bought myself a grand set of monk's robes and made many preparations to ensure that I would make an impression. As I headed down the stairs to the assembly, dressed up in my fine new robes, what should I meet coming up the stairs but a man carrying an entire yak carcass! It was a terrible beginning, a very bad sign. But what could I do? I hurried on to the Glorious Goddess temple where the monks had already begun the black tea offering to the gods.

The ceremony there was stately and very formal. We two new house gurus had to do the *nye-shin* offering and do a recitation. After this prayer we went to the main house-assembly hall where tea was offered to all the monks. As the new house gurus we went around the entire hall offering scarfs to all the deities represented there and then sat down on special seats that had been prepared for us. Just after I sat down and the auspicious ceremonial prayers began, a cat came streaking across in front of my seat and killed a mouse right there in front of me. It sat there eating the poor creature. I was shocked in my heart and felt a sense of foreboding. But I was locked into becoming the house guru, the ceremonies were underway, and inauspicious signs or not I had to go on.

Only weeks after we took up our duties as house gurus my partner came to me with a scarf and asked for my patience. This was quite unusual. Normally it would be considered inappropriate for one house guru to make an offering to another because the two were equal in all respects. It was set down in writing in the agreements signed by both house gurus that when things went well they would share the praise and when things went poorly they would share the blame. The two gurus even ate together, and did their work as one. So I wondered what was wrong. About two weeks after this my partner fell sick and he steadily got worse and worse. Soon he was so sick he could not stay in Drepung and had to go outside for treatment. This was during the new year's prayer festival, so there was a huge amount of work and I had to do it all myself. There was no provision for a substitute if a house guru got sick. My partner stayed in Lhasa for the first two months of the new year, and finally returned at the end of the mini-prayer festival. He died in his room at Phukhang just a few days after getting back.

I was beside myself. My partner had died just like the two previous house gurus, and now there was only me left. I felt that my turn was definitely next. I should have gone straight to his room where he had died, but I was so worried about my impending death that I headed straight down to Lhasa and arrived at Kanjur Rinpoche's house in a terrible state. I was so scared that I went straight in. Even as I was prostrating to the Rinpoche he was laughing at me. I was running on at the mouth: "The earlier two house gurus died...now my partner is dead...I am not worried about debt...I have friends and relatives who are my guarantors...I have a good motivation for the work...I do not want to cause trouble...I am trying my best...I do not want to die but there is a terrible hindrance out there which is about to descend on me...if I die in office it will cause great problems to my new rooms guru...." The Rinpoche was rocking with laughter as I went on and on.

"I though you were a monk studying Buddhism," he said. "Is it good logic that you are about to die just because your friend has passed away? Is it not the case," he said, "that none of us know when we will die and that that is in the nature of things? Have you not thought about such religious teachings as that? Don't you remember that you two came to me earlier and I said that you would have no problems but that your partner would have real difficulties? I told him to do a hundred thousand prostrations and promised he would be alright if he followed what I said, but did he take heed? No he did not. And didn't I promise you that you would have no trouble during your year? You have no faith," he said. "I can stand as guarantor that even if someone took a swing at your neck with an axe during this year it would not kill you, but you do not believe what I say, do you? Even a thorn could not pierce your foot during this year. Your year will not leave you in debt, and the house will praise you at the end. Your year will be a complete success so pull yourself together and stop being a childish idiot. I am the Kanjur Rinpoche," he said. "I promised you all this and you did not believe a word I said. A monk who goes to the assemblies and debates and tries to be virtuous will never have trouble." He took out his divination dice and did another divination. "Look!" he said, showing it to me. "Perfect! Can you not see it?" I can still hear him berating me, telling me that I would not die during the year even from a blow to the neck with a sharp axe.

The Rinpoche calmed me down and gave me back my confidence. I returned to Drepung faced with the reality that from then on I was alone in the work. The advice of Locho Rinpoche came back to me with a rush and I remembered vividly how he had said I should think it was me and me alone, that I should not expect help from my partner. I made up my mind I was going to pull through this difficultly and work as hard as was needed to make a success of my house guru year.

My partner's guru had also been the guru of one of the monks who had died in office the previous year. That monk had been his nephew, so he had taken on the house guru duties for the remainder of the year with all the attendant expense. Now he was faced with the same situation again, and understandably he was in a very anxious state. He could not immediately take up the responsibilities of my partner, and nobody was going to tell him he had to do so either. So for about a month I saw nothing of him and was left entirely on my own. Many of the older monks, including my guru Gangshingpa, told me that it was not possible for a single person to do the work and advised me to approach the house assembly to ask for some sort of community response to the problem. My reaction, however, was to decide that I should do all the work myself. There might be debts involved at the end of it all, I thought, but I will take them on personally and not expect anyone to help me pay them off. I did not approach the assembly, and just kept on with my duties. I did not worry myself beyond that.

A month or so after my partner died, his guru came to me as I was going about the house guru's evening work. He said that he had wanted to talk openly with me for the past month but that he had been very upset. "I am aware that over the past month you have had a very big load on your shoulders," he said, "and that you are alone doing the work designed for two people. I am also aware that you have not been directing any nasty glances my way or saying to others that I am not holding up my side of the bargain. I appreciate that and want to thank you. I am going through a difficult time," he said, "but from now on I am available for work, so do not be shy in approaching me to do it." He was an older monk than I was and I said I was heartened by his coming to me so openly. "I know you have been having a hard time," I said, "what with the death of your nephew last year, and now with another of your students dying. But I have made up my mind to absorb any losses personally. I do not want you to worry on that account, but if there is any profit at the end of the term I will divide it up with you equally. It makes me feel much more confident," I continued, "to have an older monk like you come up and speak with me so openly. If you can take on some of the work obviously I will be happy. So please keep going to the black tea offerings and the assemblies; that is a great help. I will take care of any big problems of discipline as well as time-consuming work that comes up. Do not worry about any debts I might incur because I have a lot of people who have said they will stand behind me. Up until now nobody has given me anything, but I am confident that I can get help to pay back money if it becomes necessary. Do not worry about this," I said. He was quite moved by this and from then on he was really very decent. He took on the responsibility for the black tea so I had no worry on that score at all, and he always made himself available for small tasks that needed to be done and did them with good grace. I dealt with the work that required travel, secure in the knowledge that he was looking after the house, so we made a fine pair and it worked out excellently. I found myself with a workload I could handle.

DURING MY TENURE I paid particular attention to discipline and the need to study during study-periods. In earlier years the discipline had slackened considerably in the house and I wanted to bring it back up to the higher level. I was very exacting.

One new monk was drawn into the ranks of the fighting monks soon after he arrived from his homeland and he began going to Lhasa when he should have been going to the assembly and studying. When I pulled him up for it he threatened me. After an assembly, out on the flat stones where the debate took place, I called him out and gave him a sound thrashing with a whip. Now, the code of discipline required that a house guru get permission from the guru-at-large before administering a beating with a whip. I had not done so, and the guru-at-large, remember, was my old nemesis Gendun. So he was definitely irritated by my acting out of turn and was not going to let it go by. He stirred up this fighting monk's room guru, a fool if ever there was one, who came storming into my rooms asking me what I thought I was doing beating his boy. "Has he stolen something or killed someone or what?" he asked. "You nearly beat him to death!" I confronted him head on. "Look," I said, "if I beat a young monk it is only with the intention of tightening up the discipline and standard of study, I have no other thought in the matter. It is my work, my responsibility, and I have been doing it for a time now, and I have been doing it effectively." But the silly old monk would not back down and kept saying he wanted to know what the boy had done to warrant such a beating. He began to get to me so I said, "Is your position that a whipping is warranted only when a monk has stolen or killed? Is that the position you are taking here? If it is, then get me a letter saying that this is the rule and we will continue our conversation. The power of house guru is my power during this year and I have the full right to exercise that authority. I have all the keys to the offices and storerooms. Now if you want them, take them. Let me make it clear I will be happy to see you take over. I am sick of this work, I have a pile of it and if in your concern and wisdom you do not like the way I am doing it, you do it." I worked myself up into a blaze of righteous anger, threw all the keys at him and grabbing a scarf off my altar stalked off shouting, "I am giving up this thankless task, I am going to the central authority to get this job off my back once and for all!"

As I was stalking off a number of the older monks got hold of me and told me to calm down. "Take it easy," they said, "this is getting out of hand." The silly old monk had joined the others by this time telling me to calm down. "It was my mistake," he said. "I should not have criticized your honest attempt so strongly." "No, no," I insisted, "you could not be wrong, you are the older monk here, I am just the new monk. You older monks know about proper levels of discipline." I had worked myself up into such a state that I was set on going to the central authority, and it was only when the older monk sent a representative and asked me strongly to desist that I finally decided not to go.

One of the results of this outburst was a certain fear on the part of the older monks when it came to discipline. They began to be a bit careful with me, unsure of where to draw the line. You see, there was a system of checks and balances on power in the house. During the periods when the house assembly was in session the house guru was little more than a servant of the assembly. But during the periods when the assembly was not in session, during the prayers, and during the debates and so forth, the house guru had total power over conduct and discipline. There were some odd little quirks in the way things had to be done in monastery houses, but they were not meaningless, they all linked together to make for good governance. Monks with the right to speak in the assembly normally would not listen to a house guru when it came to discipline. But since I had fought out in the open with one of the older gurus who had rights in the assembly, and gone to the line with him, from then on the assembly gurus had to be more careful when it came to discipline and study. I had shifted the balance a bit. From then on they were careful to be better behaved in the prayers even though they were older members of the assembly. And on account of this the general level of discipline in the house improved. The new monks who were humble and reserved in conduct, of course, I did not discipline. But the arrogant ones I confronted. It was rare that I thrashed them; usually I would hit them with a penalty like prostrations.

IN THOSE DAYS the Chinese were cutting down a lot of trees not far from Drepung. Soon after this began, the monastery central authority made a clear statement that it was against monastery rules for us to go to that part of the mountain to collect wood. I was careful to ensure the rule was obeyed, but a new monk from nearby Pombara house went collecting wood and was caught in the act. The central authority police monks grabbed hold of the ropes he had used to tie the wood, impounded it, and asked him which house he was from. The monk had only recently arrived in Drepung and he replied, "From the house just down from Phukhang house." The authorities mistook him to mean that he was from Phukhang.

I soon got a message from the central authorities summoning me before them. Their message to me was that they had been careful to fully advertise the new rule forbidding the collection of wood, and yet I had allowed a new monk to go collecting. I was ordered, because of being negligent in my duties as house guru, to appear outside the central governing authority along with the monk involved. I wondered what had happened.

I knew that none of the monks under my authority had gone out to collect wood, but sure enough there was the pile of wood, still tied up lying outside. So the next morning, after the offering of tea to the monastic community in general, I appeared just outside the rooms where the main officers of the central authority lived and kept court.

All affairs under the jurisdiction of the central authority were decided
here. When I presented myself, they asked me where the monk was
who had been collecting the wood. I said that I had tried to find him,
but that none of the members of my house had been collecting, and I
had been unable to find out who had done it. "Stop trying to wriggle
out of trouble," they said. "It is unacceptable that you have not brought
him before us." "I really think the offending monk is not from our
house," I replied. "I have approached everyone in our house who might
have been involved and no one was collecting wood." The central
authority said that that was enough talk and told me to appear again
the next day and make sure I had the offending monk with me when
I came. I went back to our house and made a very thorough check
with all the monks. It was none of them, so I appeared again the next
day by myself and said that I was sure it was not a Phukhang house
monk. "Stop trying to hide the fact that a monk from your house was
collecting wood," they said, "and produce him before us. Come with
him tomorrow or else there will be painful consequences."

Again I went back to the house and again, the next morning, I reappeared before the central authority alone. By now they were getting
very nasty, in particular a monk from the tantric college of Drepung.
He was very threatening, and that began to make me angry. I was always a person to speak my mind openly, and I said to him right there
and then, "There are two hundred monks in my house and I can vouch
for each and every one of them. They were not collecting wood. I am
certain and I do not even have a trace of a doubt. Since the new rule
came down I have forbidden all my monks from going out collecting,
and I am certain they followed my orders," I said. The tantric college
representative kept insisting, saying that he knew our house had been
collecting wood daily. "Yes, we did go collecting before," I replied,
"and I am not hiding that fact. But when the rule came down from the
central authority we stopped the collection totally and have done none
since that time. I know all my monks," I said, "but if you still think it
is one of them then I will line them up for you on the slabs of the
debate ground, and you can come down yourself and inspect them to
see if the offending monk is amongst them. You did not bring him to
me when he was caught, you just let him go, so I do not know who he
is, like you do, so you come down and make an inspection of them."

This incensed the tantric college representative who picked up a
whip and began to brandish it in front of me. He said I should watch
the way I talked to him, that I was beginning to act above my station.
"What am I supposed to do?" I said. Some kitchen workers came up

to me and told me to let it drop and come back the next day because it was beginning to get out of control. "This is the central authority here," they whispered to me. "Calm down and come back tomorrow and sort the matter out." They dragged me out and said that speaking roughly in the office of the central authority was very rash and that I should be careful the next day to speak respectfully because there was great power in that office and a real danger if a person was disrespectful. These kitchen workers and I were quite close; we were friends so they were worried for me. But I was totally confused and did not know what I was supposed to do. I had tried to sort it out but the authorities were obstinate and absurd. I thought that the best strategy was just to let it drop, not to go back at all to the office the next day.

Quite late that night, the Loseling college authorities sent a message summoning me. I immediately went and was told that my tone and words to the Drepung central authority had been taken badly by the abbot, that he considered it inappropriate to the dignity of the office. "Now," the Loseling representative asked me, "what did you intend to do? It was a Phukhang monk, after all, was it not?" "It was not a monk from our house," I said. "I checked thoroughly. The two representatives who caught the monk were at fault for not bringing him before me." "Mistakes are always being made," he told me, "but that is no reason for talking so strongly. It seems to me that you as house guru are in a bind, and so is the abbot from his side. It seems you are both at fault. Now, what are we going to do?" "I just do not know," I replied. The representative then told me to let the matter drop for a few days and not go to the central authorities tomorrow or the next day. "We will look into it," he said. "To discuss this now is just going to lead to further problems." I thanked the Loseling authority for trying to mediate in the problem and left for my rooms.

On the way back I went by the toilet area, and just as I was approaching I heard the sound of someone breathing. A monk came out of the shadows and when I asked him what he was doing lurking about late at night he said that he was a new monk, that he had been stopped a day or so before by the central authorities while he was carrying a load of wood, and that the authorities had said they would be sending for him. "Nobody came to summon me," he said, "and I am scared about what is going to happen. I am new and do not know what to do so I have come to get my rope back." "So it's you, is it?" I said. "Which house did you tell them you are from?" "I am from Pombara house," he said, "and I told them I was living in the common rooms building just below Phukhang. They told me to leave the load tied up right here and to come when I was summoned. But nobody came to get me so I came to see what had happened to the wood." I accused him of lying about his house, but he said he had not intended to lie. I then asked him what day he had been out collecting wood and when he told me I found that the time the central authorities said they had detained the young monk was the same. So I was sure it was him. He was very scared and obviously very new. "Big trouble has come up over this," I told him, "and you are going to have to go to the central authorities. Tell them you are very new, that you have only been in the monastery a week or two and you went to the picnic grounds near the river to wash. Do not say you went out with the intention of collecting wood. Tell them you found it lying around there and brought some back. Tell them that you said you are in the common rooms building below Phukhang, and do not on any account speak in central Tibetan dialect when you are there. Speak in your native dialect, and make yourself out to be totally ignorant of what is expected of a monk, otherwise you are going to find yourself deep in trouble. With a bit of luck they will call up your house guru who will do the talking for you."

The next day I reported this to the Loseling authorities. I told the representative that the monk was obviously new and scared of what was going to happen. "Go easy on him if you can," I said. "He did not realize what was happening, I am sure of it." "Don't worry," the Loseling representative said, "I will see what I can do. You stay away from the central authorities, do not go up there at all. They are not going to summon you and I will take care of the matter from here on."

The final outcome was that the new monk was let off without any punishment; he was given a warning and the matter was dropped. The central authority representative from the tantric college, though, did not forget what had happened between us and he gave me some very black looks, intimating that he was waiting for an opportunity to get back at me. It was a pity because the relationship between our house and the tantric college had traditionally been a close one, a relationship of reciprocal offerings and friendship, but that representative was the sort who was bound to get into trouble.

A HOUSE MAKES quite a bit of income each year and the house guru has to go to Lhasa to collect it. One time during the summer retreat period I had gone into Lhasa for this purpose. Now, theoretically monks are not allowed to leave the monastery during the retreat period, and there was a rule that a monk had to ask for permission before going and receive a special dispensation. But it was accepted that house gurus had all sorts of work to do and would have to go out occasionally even during retreat periods, so the authorities turned a blind eye to the necessary breaking of an otherwise strict rule. While I was away in Lhasa one of the sweepers employed by our house to clean the area around the main house assembly hall did not do his job very well, and the new head of the central authority noticed this while he was on his rounds. He was new to the job and he had to assert himself and demonstrate his authority, so he called for the house guru. The sweeper foolishly said I had gone to Lhasa. This was a silly thing to say to a new head of the central authority because it brought out in the open what everyone knew—that the house guru was technically breaking the rules. The tradition in the monastery was that those lower in rank than the house guru would not say such things. It compromised everyone's position and translated as an insult to the head of the central authority. So when I got back late from Lhasa I was told that the sweeper had been pulled up sharply by the new head and that I was to bring him in front of the office of the central authority the next morning to be punished. The man was going to be soundly thrashed, and not only that, I had to bring the head watchmen of the assembly hall as well, since he was at fault for the insolence of his worker.

This was a big problem. The older monks told me that I should try to head off the trouble immediately. It was too late to go directly to the Drepung central authority, but it was possible to go to the Loseling authority, so even though it was already getting dark and I had not eaten, I went straight to the new monk in that position. He said that though it was a little thing, the sweeper had been careless with his language and had offended Chagti, the new head. He told me that Chagti's assistant was a powerful Gomang monk. "Go and see him," he said. "I personally have no jurisdiction in this matter." So, late though it was, I immediately went to see him. There was a line of people waiting to see him even at that hour and it was nearly eleven o'clock before I finally convinced his assistant monk that I should see him. He ushered me into Chagti's assistant's room. "The problem," the Gomang monk said, "is that the sweeper insolently answered the new head of the central authority and the watchman was lax in responding quickly and adequately to cover his underling's mistake." "They are both new and do not know the rules," I said. He agreed, but then he said "You were in Lhasa illegally." He quickly added that he of course realized that as house guru I had a large amount of work. I told him that I really did not want to see them beaten, and he murmured something in sympathy. "Yes," he said, "you must feel sorry for them. I would like to help them too." "The older monks told me I must deal promptly with this," I continued, "so I came straight here to see you the moment I got back from Lhasa without having even a cup of tea or anything to eat." He expressed shock. "You should not have taken it so strongly. Forget about bringing them to be beaten tomorrow. They were both insolent and deserve a beating, but I will arrange that they are let off this time. Now go and have something to eat and go to bed."

When I got back the older monks were overjoyed. This watchman, an older monk, was particularly pleased because he had his sights set on a job with the Drepung central authority and a beating would have been a block to his future hopes. He was waiting anxiously and was overjoyed when I told him the news. The watchman and I were quite close friends. He had money and had a lot of respect for the monks who studied. Sometimes he was friendly and gave me tsampa and butter. He thanked me for dealing with the central authority. He knew it could have cost a lot of money to buy his way out of the punishment. After this incident the older monks began to respect me, and my status in the house went up.

ANOTHER PROBLEM soon arose with a Phukhang monk named Gyatso. He was a known troublemaker, penniless and always getting into arguments. He had been assigned to be a resident of Gonpa Ritro, a monastery on the mountain above Drepung, but he came down day after day and stood up in the house assembly, asking to be relieved of his duties.

One day Gyatso had left Gonpa Ritro without making arrangements for a substitute to take his place at their *torma* and black tea offering. As an older monk he had the responsibility to find a substitute while he was away, but he did not have to come and ask permission from me as house guru. Because he left without a substitute, there was no one in the assembly to collect his share of the money from the monastery's different benefactors. His money therefore came into my hands.

Not long after he left I was visited by an older monk who was representing the Drepung abbot at Gonpa Ritro. He came to the house and shouted out, "Where is the house guru?" This was an insult. People were supposed to come respectfully to the house guru's room. The representative yelled from outside that the house guru had to bring the absent monk up to Gonpa Ritro because a representative of the

Drepung central authority was coming to Gonpa Ritro the next day on an inspection. "In my role as representative of the Drepung abbot I am telling you that I want to see the absent Phukhang monk," he shouted. "I want to know what is happening. All the monks have to be there tomorrow for the review. This is not open to discussion, I want him there tomorrow!"

A review by the central authority could take place at any time, and when it did the full complement of monks had to be present. But this representative was being very arrogant and rude. "He is not here," I said. "He left and I cannot tell him to be there tomorrow because he left without telling me." The abbot's representative kept insisting in a pigheaded way that it was my responsibility. "You bring him tomorrow or else!" he said. I began to get irritated at this point and it was not long before we were shouting. He said that I would have to convene an assembly and appoint someone else in his place. Then I got nasty. "Whose problem is this anyway?" I said. "We sent you up a monk, you got him, and if he is not there, what does it have to do with us down here? It is your problem. Who gave him permission to leave Gonpa Ritro? Was it the disciplinarian or was it the abbot's representative? They should produce him in front of the authorities, not the house guru or others who have no concern in this matter. I gave him to you, I made the entry offerings, so what more is expected except that? If a person up there were to die that would be a different matter, we would have to supply a substitute. If he were a thief, a murderer, if he broke his root vows as a monk, you could expel him and we would properly be approached for someone else, but nothing like this has happened. What is going on here—you are given monks and you are not capable of keeping track of them?" Then he drew himself up to his full height and said that he was the representative of the abbot of Drepung in the Gonpa Ritro, not just some nobody. "You cannot talk to me in that way," he said. "I am the house guru," I replied, "and I also deserve respect, respect that I am not getting from the esteemed abbot's representative in front of me." I said that people representing the abbot of Drepung were expected to be honest in their dealings and certain representatives do not seem to be that at all." We were slinging insults back and forth at each other, and for no little time either. "Whoever gave him permission to leave," I insisted, "should bring him back for inspection. If he has been expelled from Gonpa Ritro bring us the documentation and we will find you a replacement monk. But where Gonpa Ritro monks have run off to is not our business, and do not try to make it ours to get out of your own troubles. And why did you shout at me from the street?" I asked. "I am house guru and only top officials of the central authority and the chief disciplinarian of the monastery have that right. Who do you think you are?"

This got us both worked up and I picked up a stick. He was an elderly fellow, and I would have thrashed him with no problem, but his age and the silliness of how puffed up he was held me back from it. He called out for help to the tea-maker and sputtered that he was going straight to the abbot. "Let's go," I said. "Whoever you go to I will be right behind you and let him know what really happened." There was nothing for him to say about it after that; he blustered about and then left.

Gendun and some of the older monks said that I had gone too far, that I was making problems. I just told them to shut up. "I have right on my side," I said. The old monks then called a house assembly and said that I had acted inappropriately. "The abbot's representative is going to be convening other meetings in Drepung and our house is going to get into a lot of trouble," they said. They agreed that Gyatso was the root of the problem and that it would be better if he were not in the house at all, but they were scared to bring the matter to a head. I thought that if the older monks went to the abbot of Drepung to talk about what had happened then I would do the same, because just as they had a relation with the abbot, so did I, and I was sure I could hold up my side quite well.

In fact the issue ended with that nasty altercation. Nobody came again to say that we should bring the monk for the inspection and nobody came to inquire into the matter any further. I said to the old monks that our Gonpa Ritro monk had caused us too much trouble, and made us fight amongst ourselves.

Later Gyatso came back. He was friendly to me, obviously unaware of the problems that had occurred because of him while he was away. But I knew there would be trouble. I said to him, "You left without telling me who you had deputed to take your offerings, so I have them and when I am less busy I will give you an accounting and let you have your money." "Why thank you," he said, genuinely pleased. "Thank you very much."

Then he went off to Gonpa Ritro. He must have talked with the abbot's representative because the next time he came down he was definitely angry. I could see him making his signs of displeasure and sensed he wanted to make trouble.

There was a house custom that the house guru went to the house assembly when it met, and then went to all the members of the house who had not been present and informed them of any decisions that had been made. This was called "taking the message from the assembly." One night the Gonpa Ritro monk did not attend the assembly so I dropped in on him to let him know what had happened. I also said that we would do his account very soon. He was rude and did not want to hear my summary of the meeting. He said he did not care one way or the other about his offerings, intimating that if I was going to steal his money, I should just shut up and steal it. "Watch yourself," I said. "If you want to accuse me of stealing that's fine, but be careful. You had better have some witnesses to back up what you are saying because I have stolen nothing and I will make a public issue out of your accusation." We both began to get angry and I got him by the arm and said, "We are going right now to the central authority to get a judgment on your accusation that I have been stealing your offerings. I bet you have someone to stand behind your lie, and I will be glad to see who is there. And also let me hear from you clear and out loud why you are not a house assembly member. I should beat you right here and now. I should beat you so you cannot get up off your bed, but I won't just because you are an older monk."

I began to pull him in the direction of the central authority, and a scared look came over him. Some older monks came and told me to leave him be, but I dragged him out and was heading for the authorities when a group of the old monks stopped me. Then I told that troublemaker to his face in front of all the monks the problems he had been causing us. "You are supposed to be up there in Gonpa Ritro but you went off. The abbot's representative came down here when you were away and caused us problems and then you came back in here causing trouble just like you did before you left, and you think that it is going to just go on to your liking. Let me tell you friend," I said, "your time has come. We are sick of you and your troublemaking and it is going to stop right now." The other older monks were more than pleased to see Gyatso getting his comeuppance. "If you aim to live here any longer," I said, "it is going to be according to the rules followed by decent monks and members of the house. You can come to the assembly and talk when you should say something, but otherwise just shut up and stop making problems for your house."

Gyatso apologized, and a few days later I went to his room and gave him a full accounting of the offerings that had accrued to him during the time he was away. It was a goodly amount, coming to some sixty silver sangs. From then on he was always respectful to me, using the honorific title for house guru. The matter was never again raised in the house assembly. "That Gyatso," the old Phukhang monks said, "he deserved just what he got. He needed to be pulled up, and pulled up he was by our house guru. You are dealing with affairs well, house guru—you are gentle on the ones to be gentle on, hard on the ones to be hard on, and you don't put up with troublemakers." From then on they saw me affectionately as a person who could cut through situations and resolve problems.

THE EIGHTH and ninth Tibetan months—the time of picnics and the summer offering—was also the time when traditionally our house asked the Gadong Oracle to enter a trance and give divinations. As house guru, I would get to wear a *tonka*, which is a special brocade waistcoat with shoulder straps, and I would ride into Gadong on a horse, looking very grand. The tantric college representative said that he could lend me his *tonka* for the occasion. Now, remember this representative was the one I had offended during the wood-collecting incident, so he was bearing me a grudge. When the time came, I went and said that I would appreciate it if he would lend me the *tonka* for my trip to Gadong. "No problem," he replied. He did not give it to me right then, but seemed quite happy to lend it. The next day I went to pick it up. Again he said "Oh yes—no problem, just come tomorrow evening and I will give it to you." This meant I would have to pick up the coat on the evening before I had to go to Gadong.

Later that day I was talking with Pangon Rinpoche and he said that he doubted the tantric college representative would lend it to me. "You had that trouble with him over the monk from Pombara house and he is not going to forget it easily. But do not worry," Rinpoche said, "because if he does not lend you his *tonka*, I have one that you can borrow."

The next evening when I went to borrow the waistcoat, the tantric college representative gave me a filthy old one. "I need a better one than that," I said, surprised. "Could you lend me a different one?" "I do not have a better one," he said innocently. "This is my only one." I suddenly became upset and said that if that was all he had then I did not want to borrow anything from him, and I left. I went straight to Pangon Rinpoche. "I had expected as much," he said. "The tantric college representative wanted revenge because you had spoken so strongly to him earlier. Now look," he said, "I have an excellent *tonka* but I do not let anybody know I have it. I keep it hidden, otherwise I know there would be a steady stream of people from the central authority wanting to borrow it, and I would be in a position where I would never be able to say no. So tomorrow, when people ask you where you got it, you are going to have to lie and find some way to avoid saying who lent it to you." "No problem," I said. "Nobody from the central authority will come bothering you for your waistcoat because I am going to say I borrowed it off a trader I know in Lhasa. After my trip to Gadong I will tell people that I returned it to the trader, who then went back to his own part of Kham." "Excellent," said the Rinpoche. "You are going to need a good story like that, otherwise there is no way I can escape having to lend it out after you are seen wearing it."

Then the Rinpoche comes out with an absolutely beautiful *tonka*, the likes of which had rarely been seen within the sacred walls of Drepung. It was matchless: a Reting Monastery variety made by a Nechung monk; it had a shine to it and a history of its own. And to top it off, Rinpoche lent me a whole set of expensive, high-quality robes to go with it. The next morning I walked out in a fine lower garment made of Indian wool, a thick outer shawl, and that brocade waistcoat with shoulder straps. Such a house guru had never before been seen coming down the steps of Phukhang house. I got up on my horse and had a monk lead it as my servant; we entered Gadong just as the representatives of the central authority and Loseling and Gomang colleges were arriving.

Phukang house and Gadong had a close relationship, so Gadong traditionally treated the house guru from Phukhang with a special respect. On this traditional day for consulting the Gadong Oracle, representatives of the central authority would put their seed questions to the oracle and then the oracle would call in the house guru from Phukhang even before receiving the people from Loseling and Gomang colleges. There were many questions from our house. After I had finished there was no reason for me to remain at Gadong except to show myself off in my splendor, but that was reason enough and I went to sit on one of the high seats that were set up in the temple for guests. I imagined myself as I would have looked to a visitor: as a special dignitary who had come in to consult with the oracle. I was happy to let the fiction run on, and sat there proudly without any reason at all. I caught sight of the tantric college representative eying my glorious brocade waistcoat, and when I glanced in his direction he pretended not to see me but I knew he had. I savored every precious minute of my triumph. I stayed a while longer and went outside. Immediately the tantric college representative came up to me. "That is quite a waistcoat you have on there. I cannot help wondering where the esteemed house guru might have obtained it." "I was down in Lhasa last night," I said, "with a big trader I know associated with a rinpoche's household. He lent it to me." "It really is a beauty," he said admiring it. "Any chance I could borrow it for a day or so?" "I will see if I can arrange it for you," I said expansively. "What a lower garment!" he continued. "The best Indian wool...." He was shameless. After going back on his promise, now he was drooling over my clothes and asking to borrow them off my back.

About a month later one of the two police monks from the central authority who had stopped the Pombara monk for collecting wood came to me from the tantric college representative and asked if it would be possible to borrow the brocade waistcoat for a while. I was ready with my story. "I am so sorry," I said with great conviction, "the trader returned to Kham to the rinpoche's household. This is terrible. If only you had come to me two weeks earlier I could have lent it to you. He left just two weeks ago and if I had known I could have arranged for you to borrow it. Please convey my regrets to the tantric college representative that I am unable to lend him the brocade waistcoat. If only I had known you would be coming...."

DURING MY TENURE as house guru a new monk from Phukhang house got into a fight with a new monk from Pombara house. Because of this, two gangs formed between houses and prepared for a big fight. The root of the trouble went back to Kham. Phukhang monks and Pombara monks were from areas that were relatively close together but that had a tradition of regionally-based friction.

One evening, just before debate prayers, two of the rival monks had gone off behind the area of Drepung where evening prayers were held and began fighting. I immediately went there, but by the time I arrived the fight had ended and the participants had gone. The Phukhang boy was not a particularly brave fellow, and a monk caretaker of one of the Drepung temples had grabbed him when he saw him draw a knife and had disarmed him. He gave him a slap and sent him off. When the caretaker saw me arrive so quickly, he thought that I would make sure nothing else came of it, so when he made his report to the monastery disciplinarian he played it down. He did not report that knives had been drawn and did not realize the gravity of the situation. He told the authorities that I had arrived on the scene quickly and that I had put a tight lid on the trouble.

In fact the monks had run off completely by the time I got to the scene, so I immediately went to check on what was happening at the prayer. They were already all there at the prayer except one new Phukhang monk. I waited for him and when he came running in late, I confronted him. He seemed scared, so I frisked him and found a knife the length of his forearm tucked in the back of his lower garment. I confiscated the knife and sent him on to the prayer. This was when I realized that there was real trouble.

If one new monk was carrying a long knife it was definite that a lot of the others were too. I decided I would frisk them all, but I made a tactical error. When I disarmed the first monk I boasted to him that I knew something was happening and I was going to catch the lot of them. So during the prayer he warned the other monks that I was after them, and they gave their knives to the studious monks who were staying on to recite their memorization. I had my suspicions about who the monks carrying knives would be, and after the prayers ended I told them all to stay in one group. I let the others do their memorization. When I searched them I found nothing but a single empty sheath. I knew something was wrong, so I went to check the common rooms building. The monks who were reciting had by then given the others their knives back. The first monk I came across was throwing what I suspected was a knife into his room, but I was still not sure enough to confront him.

Later that same evening I went to talk with the Pombara house guru. "There has been a fight," I said, "and probably your young monks are carrying knives. I know for sure that my monks are, but I have not been able to confiscate them yet." I told him that we would have to stay alert. "You must make sure that your monks do not fight," I said. "I am definitely going to disarm my monks, so if a knife-fight happens the fault will lie with Pombara house." The Pombara house gurus promised their monks would not cause any trouble.

Since I was very strict about discipline, and the Pombara house gurus were keeping strict control as well, we were able to prevent any fighting. But I still had not been able to confiscate the knives, and I was not happy about that. I went to ask the oracle at Phug-shag, and the oracle said that I would definitely be able to confiscate the knives, but I would have to go about it carefully.

A day or so later I learned that two of my suspects were going to ask for permission to go into Lhasa to do some work for their guru. I reasoned that they would carry their knives when they went, and I told my assistant to be prepared for them. "When they ask to go to Lhasa," I said, "give them permission immediately." Then I left, pretending that I had other pressing work. Soon the monks went to ask for permission. I watched them go back to their rooms and then immediately come back out and start off for Lhasa. I knew that they had gone back to get their knives and I confronted them just as they were starting out.

I told one studious monk who was with them to go, and took the other two up to the stone debate ground where I began frisking one of them. I could not find his knife for the life of me. Finally I found a piece of string coming off his belt and by following that down was able to find his knife, a long one, that he was holding between his thighs. After that I found the other monk's knife without difficulty. I did not punish them. "I will be dealing with this matter later," I said. "For now you have permission to go into Lhasa."

After a time I forced the monk I had found with a sheath to give me his knife so now I had a total of four. My inquiries led me to believe that there were thirteen knives that I had to confiscate. By searching here and squeezing there I came up with twelve. There was one left, and the monk who had it was a monk I entertained no suspicion about at all. He was studious, very humble, and spiritual in appearance. Now it was dangerous to go up to this monk with my suspicions without being totally sure, so I decided to go about it deviously.

One of the twelve monks from whom I had confiscated a knife was very young and easy to influence. I called him in and asked about this studious monk. "Is he hiding a knife?" I asked him. "Definitely not," he said. "Oh no! Well whose knife is this, then?" I said, bringing out one of the knives I had confiscated, acting like I had confiscated it off the studious monk and was just checking to see if this young monk was coming clean with me. I tricked him into thinking that I was testing him to see how much I should punish him. "No, house guru," he said, "that is not his knife. I know it because his is longer and is a better quality one." "Ah ha!" I said. "This is the only one he gave to me, but he has another one does he?" He said the other knife was a bit longer than the one I had, slightly better made, and with a different design.

The other house guru and I went to the studious monk, and I told him to give me his knife. "I do not have one," he insisted. I spoke gently to him. "I know you have a knife, I know what it looks like, and I know how long it is, so do not hide it any more." He still insisted he did not have one. I got nasty and told the other house guru to tie him down. "I am going to beat you until you give us the knife," I told him. When my partner got hold of him and started to tie him down he finally owned up. "I do have a knife. I am sorry, I will give it to you." He went off and a moment later returned with a paring knife. I got very angry. "Do you think I am fooling around here trying to confiscate paring knives? I will teach you, you deceitful brat," I said, and got ready to thrash him. "The punishment for carrying knives is the same for the lot of you," I said, "but for you I have a thrashing you will never forget because you have lied to me!" Then I wound up and was about to lay into him when he said "No, please don't, I am very sorry. I do have another knife." He went to get it immediately and came back with a long, wicked-looking knife, well made. "Okay," I said, "I will not punish you separately. Your punishment will be the punishment I give out to the whole group."

For a month or so I did not mete out any punishment, thinking that there might still be one or two monks left out there who I would slowly slowly find out about. The threat of punishment hanging over the group became unbearable to them. They kept coming to ask me to make a resolution of it, to tell them what the punishment was going to be and get it over with. If their brawl had happened it would have been a very serious matter, so I knew I had to make a stiff punishment. Finally I called them all in. I had ropes, my big heavy keys, and a number of canes laid out. "You are each going to get a hundred key strokes," I said. Faced with the reality of corporal punishment they paled and began to plead that, at the very least, it be reduced to fifty each. They had been talking with the other house guru who began to argue for them, saying that it might be better, since they were all making an attempt to be decent monks and were all studying well, to forgo the corporal punishment. I agreed. "If you each get some heavy flagstones from the mountain above Drepung and bring them down into the courtyard then I will consider the matter closed." I went out and measured the exact sizes of the stones they had to bring and told them that each had to bring four. I gave them the option, if it was not possible to find flat stones that big, to bring eight small ones which would cover the same area of the courtyard. "You consider yourselves a heavyweight gang," I said, "so such a load of work should cause you no problems at all. Go to it. If you can get this done it is an end to the matter." They were pleased to escape corporal punishment, and even though it was going to be hard for them, still they were happy at the final outcome. They bowed and scraped as they left, saying "thank you sir, thank you sir," relieved not to be stretched out and belittled with a thrashing. It took them ten days to finish their task. After that they went up to study in the caves.

When each of them had brought in their quota of stones I had a lovely pile stacked in an area to the side of the house assembly hall. The older monks in the house were very pleased. The government had ordered the house to improve the area around its property in Lhasa by putting down flagstones. The flagstones that I had collected met the bill perfectly. It would have been difficult, otherwise, to have found anybody to do the work.

This was the biggest crisis I faced while I was house guru, though it worked out well in the end. When I was house guru I did not terrorize members of the house. I often berated monks for one thing or the other, but I rarely physically beat anybody. I always came up with some other punishment. But I did have a sharp tongue, as I do to this day, and I was unpleasant when I got angry. People were careful when I was around.

DURING THE PERIOD that the Dalai Lama went to India to visit the sacred sites, in about 1955, during the 2500 year anniversary of the birth of the Buddha, the price of butter went through the roof. A *mar-khel*, a large measure of butter, rose to seven dotse and twenty-five silver sangs. One dotse was worth fifty sangs, so this meant that a *mar-khel* cost 375 sangs! People said that in the whole history of Tibet butter had never been so expensive. "It might be three, four, or even up to nearly five dotse, but never had it been above that," they said. The price of butter made it very difficult for house gurus to meet their responsibility of providing the set teas that had to been offered to the monks. The regular teas were paid for by interest generated by house funds, but most of the rest of the teas were paid for by outside sponsors. Phukhang house had few sponsors from the central Tibetan region—almost without exception our sponsors were people from our part of Kham who were in Lhasa on business or pilgrimage. The price of butter made it very difficult for these people to sponsor tea for house assemblies.

This was causing an additional problem for the house gurus. When sponsors offered tea, they were charged for the wood used to boil the water. The house guru was the one who provided the wood, so he would make a profit from the teas that, in turn, helped to offset the other costs of his job. If no sponsors came he was stuck with his unused wood. The older monks too were getting worked up about this situation. With the price of butter so high, they knew the house gurus would start cutting back, and they would end up with no butter in their tea.

Is it not the case, though, that the protectors and the gods work their wondrous ways when they are most needed? There are a number of districts in our part of Kham and a lot of businesspeople are always coming and going on trading expeditions. For some, sponsoring a tea was something they did when they could afford it, but for traders from other districts it was a time-honored tradition—regardless of the cost, traders from these districts would offer teas when they came to Lhasa. If sixty traders came from such a district, they would offer sixty teas. Lhasa was flooded with traders from those parts of Kham in the sixth month. They gave teas at the rate of two a day, and knowing that the house gurus were caught in a bind, they willingly paid a high rate for wood to help out.

During teas, it was the custom to offer rich butter tormas—tsampa cakes that are shaped like cones. About a dozen *khel* of ground barley flour was needed for this offering, and the house itself was expected to supply it. Until my tenure as house master, the old tormas that were removed when a fresh lot were supplied were not accounted for. Any monk who happened to be around could take some for himself. I insisted that all old tormas be returned to me as my property, which made me unpopular, as you can imagine. I was very close with those old tormas, and I was able to make some money from them. During the year, as traders and others came from Kham, they asked for some of the tormas because they considered them to be special and good to eat or to keep. I accumulated a store of these rich butter tormas and when I offered them to people they would, of course, insist on making a little offering in return—three or four Chinese dayan, and that would accrue to me. This made us both happy. In earlier years when the monks ate the tormas all up, the visitors would only get a tiny bit, but from me they got a full *dre*, the best part of a kilo.

Some traders made a hundred torma offerings. These tormas were not full of butter but I quickly retrieved them after the offering, squeezed them flat and set them out to dry. In this way they did not spoil, and there was a market for them. During this period the Chinese were putting in their motor road, which passed by not far from

Drepung. There were hundreds of workers, mainly Chinese and people from Kongpo, and they were being paid in dayan. They needed cheap but strong food, and the old tormas were perfect for them. I could sell two kilos for about two Chinese dayan. The workers lined up to buy my dried torma and I did an excellent business.

I even turned the butter shortage into good money. As traders came wanting to make offerings I sold them butter, a couple of kilos at a time, at market rates. In particular, the offering of butter for the rich butter tormas was ongoing, so I not only made money, I even had some butter left over in my store at the end of my tenure.

I was very industrious and even began a new line of business. When I had first come up to Drepung, as I said earlier, I had to go out collecting debts for Gendun. One of the borrowers was the man who had such bad tsampa to eat that I had given his family some of my own. In the intervening period he had become quite rich. He said that he did not have enough to make an out-and-out offering to the house, but that he would go into business with me selling cotton shirts and pants, which had just come onto the market from India. "If you give me some to sell," he said, "I will take them to the villages and sell them and give all the profit to the house." Now, as a house guru, I was not allowed to engage in trade so I had to be a secret partner. Whatever happened happened, I could not take any active interest. I went in with him for the equivalent of about forty shirts, and he traded them in the countryside for tsampa. I never inquired about how the trade was going, or gave any advice, or showed any anxiety. Then one day he came in with the profit that had accrued to me. It was being carried in six loads and when people asked where it came from I could not, of course, tell them the truth. I just said it was some interest that he owed and had to be repaid at this time.

The upshot of all the sponsors and my little initiatives was that the debts that had earlier seemed such a threat never materialized. Indeed, by the end of the eighth Tibetan month when I came to do the accounts (the change-over of house gurus took place in the tenth month) I found that I had ended up with a small surplus. And if you counted extra money as personal wealth, which a house guru was entitled to do, I had also made a personal profit of perhaps one hundred dotse, which was real money. I used some of this for my own clothing and my room expenses and the remaining amount I subsumed into the general funds of the house for the next house gurus, leaving them with a small surplus.

The house ate well during my tenure, and there were large stocks of all commodities on hand. That led me to think that I should make a splash with an offering of the surplus before the change-over to the new house guru. Before, there had never been much left over and often the outgoing house gurus would leave the house with a deficit. But I thought I would convene a special assembly and give away what was left, to let everyone know that I had done my job well. My partner as house guru was adamant, though, that this was inappropriate. Not only was there no tradition for such an assembly, he said, but there were still a number of responsibilities that I had to meet, and I still might find myself in debt if I was not careful.

THE LAST ASSEMBLY offering during the house guru's year was called the *tangra*. The *tangra* involved a long offering of black tea to the Glorious Goddess which lasted until late in the night. The outgoing house guru would also offer a traditional meal during this long assembly. These traditionally prescribed offerings were an excellent thing. You could neither give below a certain standard, nor could you give above it. You can easily imagine how, if one year a successful monk gave a big offering in the outgoing assembly, the next year a monk who had not been so successful would feel a strong pressure to live up to the earlier standard, even if his circumstances did not allow him to do so. Now, I had had a great year and I wanted to make sure everybody knew. But I was prevented by tradition from showing off the profits I had made. My only recourse was to load up the offering tormas by making them out of an incredible amount of butter and no tsampa at all. I also prepared as many butter lamps as I could get my hands on. I planned to make a real light show, determined to go out in a blaze of glory.

Prior to the assembly an older monk came to me and said my preparations were inappropriate and that I was breaking a tradition. "I have only made the tormas totally out of butter so they will not go to waste," I responded. "When you use tsampa, it spoils after the assembly, but butter is still butter and I can still use it. I can only sell tsampa tormas as dry tormas, but butter is butter." The old monk gave me a long look, and said, "You are a smart one for sure and you have a point. But you obviously do not care about making the best offering to the gods because you are more concerned with offerings which can be used again after the assembly. It seems to me you are not offering from the bottom of your heart." What could I say? In the end I convinced him, but he said that it was not something that should be done again in the future. "You are not doing this in the proper way," he said, shaking his head. Still, I was able to make a show on my departure, though I did not give any more money than the absolute most allowed by tradition.

After the assembly a few monks came up to me and said that it was a good show, and that I had probably gone into debt over it. They were asking in the oblique way that you use when you are probing for information. It was a topic everyone wanted to ask about but no one could ask about directly. "It was a bit difficult, of course," I opined. "There were certainly debts in such a weighty undertaking as house guruship." But I hinted that there were people, trusty people out there, to whom I could always turn when I had incurred debts for a worthy cause such as the well-being of my house, so though I had a burden to bear, still they should not worry about it; they should rest assured that before them was a man with powerful and rich friends always ready to help his fellow men. I enjoyed this moment of glory.

THE FINAL AUDIT of a house guru took four days, during which period the outgoing guru had to make a lot of offerings. One of them, on the fourth day, required making a very large offering of cooked mutton to each of the monks of the assembly. The way it worked was like this. When a house guru was installed at the beginning of his fiscal year he approached another monk and asked him if he would like to be his under-manager. This monk had more scope to engage in business activities that were either forbidden by tradition to the house guru, or which the house guru's other duties precluded. There was no particular fund set aside for this under-manager, nothing like the various amounts set aside for the house guru's responsibilities; the house guru simply staked him whatever amount he wanted, and let him go about his business as he felt best.

One of the responsibilities of the under-manager was this offering of cooked mutton on the last day of the fiscal year. But it was a responsibility that ultimately rested with the house guru. If the under-manager did not have money to buy the mutton, the house guru had to meet the expense out of his own pocket. As the time for the mutton offering came up my under-manager approached me and said I should rest easy, that he had no trouble at all in meeting the responsibility, and that he would not be approaching me for any extra funds for the feast. I was pleased about this, of course, but so was he because the tradition was that any money that he had made, over and above the amount required to pay for the mutton, was his to keep. The house guru had absolutely no right to ask for that money in an attempt to balance his books or lighten his own debt load.

On the evening of the fourth day of the audit, after the offering of cooked mutton, was the final assembly. After the house guru had offered a good meal to the assembly, a general discussion of the year and how the house guru had acquitted himself began. Monks discussed the good things that he had done and where he failed. If he had done something terribly wrong during his tenure he might be banned from attending the house assembly in the future, or stripped of all marks of authority. In the case of a small wrongdoing the tradition was to mete out some token punishment which cleared away the perceived infraction. This assembly, therefore, wasn't just a happy ending—the outgoing house guru would be in a state of anxiety, wondering what was going to be said when the senior monks stood up and let him know exactly what they thought about him.

In my case there was a mixed discussion, some saying I had done well and others saying that I had not. But nobody got up and talked about a particular event or act that I had done that was shameful. There was no humiliating confrontation, and just as water flows on over sand that remains to witness another day, my tenure as house guru passed by without any serious problem. But perhaps just because there was no strong criticism of me during the assembly, at the end the incoming house guru made an issue of the weapons I had confiscated from the thirteen fighting monks. He said that since they had not been given back to the monks, there should be some accounting for them. As the discussion of the topic got underway some monks said that it was no business of the house at all, that the swords were mine and were not items to be included in the audit. Others supported the contention of the incoming house guru that they should be accounted for. Finally the incoming house guru confronted me directly. "What have you done with them?" he asked. "Apart from the weapons of inferior quality that I have not been able to sell yet, I sold them and have plans for the money when it is all collected," I replied. I did not spell out my plan to use the money from the weapons to line the skull-cup in our protector chapel with silver. The inside of the skull-cup was not very well finished, and a trader in Lhasa told me that he would make up any extra money needed, after the sale of the weapons, to make sure the job was properly done. Some monks said "That is no good, you have to come up with the swords." I agreed and produced in the assembly the money from the swords already sold, and the remaining unsold swords. There was no fault attached to this delivering of the weapons to the assembly, and no expiatory act that the assembly said I had to do.

As the final assembly was dispersing a number of monks came up to me and said that I had done a good job. For my part, I felt slightly insulted by the affair with the swords, and I made use of the occasion to let them know that I had been preparing to line the inside of the house skull-cup, and that their insistence on making an accounting of the swords had put an end to that. "The Lhasa trader who said he would be our benefactor is a thing of the past now," I said. "You should have told us you had that in mind, then there would have been no question," they said. Some even said the swords should be returned to me so I could get the job done. "No," I said, "it is too late now, the damage has been done. That blast of self-righteousness from the assembly blew away forever the silver lining on our protector's skull-cup."

AFTER THESE ASSEMBLIES the year of the house guru was officially over and the outgoing house guru had a three-day holiday from all assemblies and work. He just rested in his rooms and people came to visit him. I had two students and I sent them out to buy provisions for a big celebration. I borrowed a beautiful carpet from our guru Gangshingpa, set up our best cups for tea, and prepared excellent food. From early morning throughout the day we sat there in splendor enjoying ourselves with our feet up. We were all having a great time, eating and drinking and living a life of ease and luxury. After a while a senior monk came by, and seeing us in such a state asked me if I was expecting a special guest. "Not at all," I said. "I am celebrating. The two house gurus before me died from the strain of it. During my own tenure my own friend died but I am lucky enough to have lived through it. Not only that, nearly every house guru ends up with a huge debt, but I have come out of it with a profit, and I was not humiliated in the assembly or accused of some terrible wrong. So many earlier house gurus were denied access to the assembly or stripped of honor, but I have arrived here today with my honor intact. So I am celebrating in style. I have just these three days and then I have to go out to work again, collecting debts, so I am going to enjoy myself in the fullest. So sit down," I said, "and have a cup of tea," which he did, and not just a few choice bits of fruit and other morsels that I laid before him as well.

He left and went off to the evening assembly where he told the other monks what was going on. "Old Choo-chur is up there living the life of a nobleman," he said. "He has out all his best carpets and crockery, is dressed up in his best clothes and is eating food you would give only to the most important guests. But he says he is not expecting anybody—just that he has got through the year without loss and is glad to be alive after the ordeal." They had a laugh about it, and after the assembly some of the monks came down to see what was going on. Most of them just congratulated me. Others said, "Choo-chur, you got off lightly in the evening assembly on the fourth day of the audit. We did not want to go hard on you so we did not bring up everything. But there are lots of things we could have brought up, you know." They joked with me and I answered them with a choice morsel or two. "Have a part of the profit I made as house master," I said, and we all had a good time of it, a nice end to a year.

IN THE SECOND MONTH of the new year our guru Gangshingpa returned from the pilgrimage to India with the rest of the Dalai Lama's retinue. For the first two weeks after his return he did not come up to Drepung; he stayed in Lhasa where I went to visit him. He was suffering from fever and said that he was anxious to get back to Loseling. When he got back, about two weeks after my visit to him in Lhasa, he had with him all the different delicacies that you could get in India, foremost amongst which, from our point of view, was sweet tea. Before that time I had not even heard of sweet tea.

On the evening of his arrival many of the older monks came by his room and my guru asked them all about how my tenure as house guru had been. They said I had been successful, and as he heard from more and more people that it had gone well, he became happier and happier. He was positively beaming when we talked later that night, and said it was excellent that at such a difficult time I had been able to do the job to the satisfaction of the members of the house. Then he said, "Look now, they are all saying that you have had a successful tenure and I am happy for you. But I know you must have gone into debt to do it, so I want you to be open with me and tell me how much you owe. If it is a huge debt you can slowly pay me back over a period of time, and if it is just a small one do not worry about it. I will take care of it myself." "I have not fallen into debt," I said. "I have come out a bit ahead." But no matter how much I insisted that I was telling the truth, he did not believe me and kept asking me how much I owed. "I am a crafty person myself when it comes to money," he said. "When

I was house guru I was no fool, but even so I ran up debts. It comes with the territory so do not be shy about it. There is no way you have not had some hardship. In my family there are some very successful traders, men with pack animals worth three hundred dotses, and if one animal died it was no big trouble. In one day, if business was going well they could easily make one hundred and fifty dotses, so your little debts are like a pin prick to them. Do not be shy about taking my help; it will be hard for you and easy for me to repay."

I could not convince him. Only later the next night when he talked to my partner and my partner told him about the remaining stock of butter and wood, did he finally believe me. Then guru Gangshingpa called me in. "It is excellent that you have not gone into debt," he said. "How much of your own money from home is left?" I told him it was all gone, that I had put it all together and that I had probably received about ninety dotses from home over the two years and that it was all gone. "But I have some goods that I acquired during this time," I said, "so I do have something in hand." "Your good fortune is because you are a decent monk," he said. "You are not haughty, and you are still learning the textual tradition. That is what helped you. I want you to move into my own personal quarters. You will not need to bring anything with you. I have all the furnishings and everything else that you will need. I want you to live there and look after the few students that I have."

Then he told me to make some sweet tea. I wanted to be a good servant but this request caused me great embarrassment. There were sweet tea sellers in Lhasa but I had never been to their places and had never made cup of it in my life. So I was unsure whether, after you put the sugar in, you added salt as well. I was on the verge of putting salt in when Gangshingpa asked me what I was up to. "Nobody puts salt in sweet tea," he said. When we were sitting down later, enjoying the cup, he began making fun of me in a friendly way. "Well, well," he said. "This really is a first for me. A Phukhang monk who has got as far as retired house guru who thinks that you have to put salt in sweet tea. Can you imagine?" He really enjoyed himself at my expense and I felt happy that he was doing so.

MY TENURE AS HOUSE GURU officially ended after the four day audit and assemblies, but the house guru is then still responsible for collecting all of the house's outstanding grain debts. This task would last through the prayer festival and well into the following year, ending with a final seed grain audit in the fourth month. When Phukhang house was at its most wealthy, it had about four thousand loads of grain. But before I was house guru, some of our seed grain capital had been sold and our supply had gone down to about two thousand loads. Of this, I had lent out more than a thousand, and it was now my task to retrieve the grain capital, along with interest, from all the farmers who had borrowed during my tenure. According to the business tradition of our house, the outgoing house guru was responsible for collecting all the outstanding debts within six months of leaving office. If he was unable to do so, it would cause big problems.

The grainkeepers were very prickly about getting all the grain. Until the final seed grain audit in the fourth month, the recently retired house guru had the right to attend the assembly, but he did not have the right to raise any issue or talk about it. After the audit was finished he would have the full right to talk about anything he wanted. So the outgoing house guru was actually in a position of servitude to the grainkeepers until that final accounting, and the three grainkeepers would always make sure that he was going out to collect the grain.

Good people, of course, repaid on time, but the few who did not pay were very problematic. One had to keep going back to try to shame them into it, a very time-consuming job. Borrowing from a college like Loseling was a dangerous affair for a farmer, because he could be whipped, though not severely, if he did not pay back. If a person did not pay back a house debt, however, one had no right to administer a corporal punishment. One could plead and could take them by the hand, but if one beat the person, the debt no longer had to be repaid. This made it rather difficult.

Just before my final audit was to take place most of the grain had come back in, but one farmer, a man named Chomo-la, was still making trouble. In addition to farming, Chomo-la worked as a petty trader; he had a certain position in his community, and was an expert tailor, so he was always well-dressed and sleek looking. He had taken fifteen loads of grain from us, so with interest he had to repay eighteen. This rate of interest was set by the Dalai Lama himself. On coming to power, His Holiness had lowered interest rates to make things easier for farmers and debtors, and had set the rate at one load of interest for every five taken, whereas before the ratio had been one to four. Another law that the Dalai Lama had instituted at that time was that lenders could not take household items off debtors who had declared themselves unable to pay.

I had gone to see Chomo-la a number of times without success. All the other farmers in the area had paid up perfectly, and we thought that if we did not collect our debt off this man, who was obviously able to pay, next year the house would not be able to recover even a handful of the grain it lent out. One day I sent out my student to see if he could bring in the grain, but again Chomo-la refused to pay. In exasperation, my student took a large ladle from him as surety until he cleared the debt. My student was pleased that he had got something off Chomo-la, but in doing so he had broken the Dalai Lama's new law. Chomo-la saw this as his chance to get out of his debt for good, and he came to our grainkeeper and began making trouble. Finally the grainkeeper lost his temper and told him to eat shit. That really got them going. "Show me how it is done, you foul mouth!" Chomo-la yelled, "Until you show me how you do it you are not going to get a single grain off me. You are not going to get anything until you bring me a bag of your shit and eat it in front of me!"

I went to see Chomo-la a couple of times after this altercation and tried to get him to take it easy, but he would not let it drop and got nasty with me too, remaining as adamant as ever that he would not pay. I knew that continuing the fight alone would be fruitless, so I took my case back to our grainkeepers.

The older grainkeeper was a capable and strong person. He called the other grainkeepers together and they decided to take the matter to court. "Go to him one last time and be gentle," they told me, "but if he persists tell him we will take him to court, and we will go after our eighteen loads even if it costs a hundred. If he does not listen, take the matter to Dungkar-dzong Courthouse, or to any other court he accepts. After you have taken him there," they said, "we will look after all the court proceedings, and your job will be finished."

When I arrived I explained to Chomo-la that this was not just a personal matter between him and me, but was actually an issue affecting our whole house. "Consider what you are getting into here," I said. "I am in a lot of trouble myself, because the house is making me come back again and again, and you are getting yourself into more and more trouble as well. We lent you grain in good faith and the time has come to repay. If we cannot resolve this now it is going to get out of hand and we will end up in court, so let's just settle it amicably." "I cannot and I will not pay," was his response. Then he said, "Look at you now, coming around here crawling on your belly trying to get the grain off me, after you have insulted me and treated me like dirt." I went back to Chomo-la twice after this, with no result, and on my final visit I told him I would come back just one more time, and on that visit, for better or for worse, the matter was going to be resolved. "Resolve it however you want," he replied, "but I am not going to pay."

Five days later I took three students with me, and set off to take him by force to the villagers' local court at Dungkar-dzong. On our arrival, we found that Chomo-la had moved temporarily to another house closer to the other villagers. I considered this a good thing. I told one student to circle around pretending he was trying to buy wood, and told another to hide in a copse of trees in a nearby field. Then I went with the third student to call him out. Chomo-la emerged from a house near the trees. "What are you doing here again?" he growled. "We decided the matter last time you were here." "Hardly," I said. "You cannot just decide not to pay a debt and then say the matter is decided." "Well, I have decided I am not paying," he repeated. "This is it then," I said to him. "It is your last chance. This is the last time you have to think about the matter, then I am taking you to Dungkar-dzong Court." "I do not need any more time to think about it," he said. "It is settled." "Then it is settled for me too," I replied.

I got a hold of one of his arms and my companion got hold of the other one. My student hidden in the trees immediately jumped out and took hold of him as well, and the monk pretending to buy wood came running up and helped us haul him off. For the first half kilometer he acted like he was more than happy to go, but soon he started to struggle and tried to turn back. "There is no going back now," I said. "Which court do you want to go to? If it is Dungkar-dzong then we will take you there; if it is Lhasa Shol-lekung Court then we will go there; if it is the Drepung Central Authority Court we will go there—you decide." He struggled to get away from us, but we held on to him tightly and kept walking, soon arriving at a farmers' community with whom Phukhang house had a close connection.

The headman of the farmers approached us and began to plead with me not to take Chomo-la to court. "I will make sure his debt is paid, I promise, but do not take him to court." "Sorry," I said, "the time for paying the debt has passed. I have asked him again and again, but he just brushed me off and said he was not going to pay. I told him that I would take him to court, and come what may that is what I intend to do." We kept pulling him along as he stubbornly tried to resist. Then some of the other farmers blocked us, asking us please to let him go. I refused to listen to them at this point, and the headman broke in again, asking us to wait a while. "At least come into my house and have some tea. Chomo-la has not had anything but a cup of tea all day, so please come in," he said, "and allow me to serve you monks some tea and offer you a good meal. Then you can go to court in plenty of time. Leave Chomo-la in my custody; I will guard him so you do not need to keep holding him. You can drink tea, have a meal, and then go off." "Okay," I said, "but let us be clear that the time for pay-ing this debt is over. The dispute has reached the rock face, and there is nowhere to go from here but court."

The head villager then served us tea, which we accepted, though my students continued to stand guard over Chomo-la who was given tea in a small room nearby, to make sure that he did not escape. The headman then took me inside and served me a fine meal, and only after I finished did he slowly broach the subject of Chomo-la. "Please, house guru," he said, "we have had a long relation, we farmers in this district and your house at Drepung. My family and I have come to your house for many years, and I will ask you to trust me. I say to you solemnly that tomorrow I will personally come and pay his debt and will be at the service of your house. The group of us elders here take it upon ourselves as a common duty to make sure that Chomo-la will come to your house tomorrow as well. It is not good for us to have you carrying him off struggling like this, so let us deliver him to your house. You can take him to court from there." I finally agreed, but reminded him that it was no longer a matter of the debt being paid. "Our only interest is in having the man incarcerated," I said. "If you pay his debt for him you will never get him to pay you back in the future. And are you sure you will be able to get him to the steps of our house tomorrow?" "Definitely," he said. "Just do not take him now." So we agreed. I thanked him for his hospitality and took my leave. "The head villager has made a personal request," I told my students, "so we will leave Chomo-la here now on his word that he will pro-duce him at the college tomorrow. It would be impolite of us to push now that he has asked this of us."

I returned to the monastery and that evening told the grainkeepers what had transpired. "Most likely tomorrow they will bring in the grain to pay off the debt," I said, "but we shouldn't be quick to take it. We should ask for Chomo-la and say we are intent on taking him to court." Sure enough, the next morning almost before sunup they all arrived with the grain that was owed and more. The headman had

twenty sacks with him and he stood there smiling sheepishly and bobbing up and down. Then the grainkeepers called a meeting and he
addressed them, asking them to please take the grain payment of the
debt. "It is too late for that," they replied. We cannot do so; we have to
have the man."

At an impasse, they all came to my room. The villagers put four or
five kilos of radish, a great pile of fruit, and some eggs on my table
and begged me to accept the grain in payment of the debt. "We have
not brought Chomo-la," they said, "but please, for the good of the
house and our village accept this repayment of the debt. We have the
grain in total and again we ask you to settle it here in a way that the
house will not be disadvantaged." I reminded them that if we accepted
the payment, they might never get their grain back from Chomo-la—
he was not the sort to pay. "It is no trouble," they said. "His land and
ours are side by side, so we will simply take it right out of his field
whether he wants us to or not! If you take him to court he will be
punished terribly. They will make it a special case because he refuses
to pay back a debt a to monastery, and he may lose all his fields. Please
consider him with love and compassion." "Well," I said, "I have to
ask the grainkeepers what they think. I certainly cannot make such a
decision on my own." "Please, house guru," they said (I was not house
guru at that point but they kept calling me house guru), "go and tell
the grainkeepers to accept our payment." I went as they asked, and in
the end they accepted. In this way all the outstanding grain that year
came back.

The head of Chomo-la's farming community was very relieved.
"That man is a pain," he said, "and he never wants to be bested in
anything. This is the first time that anyone has beaten him. You really
are tough, house guru," he said to me. "The way this has turned out is
going to be good for us all." He went away looking happy and thanking us profusely. The farmers in his district treated me with great respect and affection after that. "Oh ho! House guru!" they would say.
"I do not think anyone is going to get the better of you, now, are they?"

The final audit was on the seventh day of the fourth month. Nothing remained to be collected so the grainkeepers were delighted. On
the sixteenth was the close of the audit, when the customary offerings
are given to the house general assembly. The grainkeepers are very
powerful people in a house. It is in their power to give or not give
food and tea and to make it good or bad. During the assembly, after
the offerings had been made, they stood up and praised me to the

rafters. "The house gurus have worked on our behalf," they said, "and Lobsang Gyatso has made an effort to collect everything that the house has lent. He has stood up for the house so that in future years we will not have difficulties collecting our grain." They voted a round of thanks to me and the whole assembly agreed. "We do not have the custom of giving out white scarfs on this day," he said, "but if we did I would be giving one to our outgoing house guru."

It is true, isn't it, that how things turn out for people depends on the people themselves? Take me. I am not particularly gifted or assertive, but when there is work that is not just to do with my own personal affairs, but is for a bigger group, or has some sort of community value, I can get enthused about it and that enthusiasm works to make it turn out better. With this kind of enthusiasm you begin to feel that your job is part of a bigger picture, you feel more connected to the community, and know that your work is for the benefit of more than just one.

LET ME SAY A LITTLE in general about the Tibetan legal system. In Dre-pung, let us take as an example a monk in Phukhang house. The first station that a dispute concerning law would go to would be the house guru. If it could not be resolved at that level, it passed on to the governing officials of Loseling college, and if it was still not resolvable there it would go to the governing officials of the central authority.

Disputes that were political or financial in nature or which involved the laity came under a different jurisdiction. If there was a financial dispute in the house, the house guru would have no jurisdiction over it, and it had to go to the house assembly. If they could not find a resolution it would go to the college assembly, and finally to the general monk assembly (*lha-chi*). It would not go to the monastery's governing officials.

If there was a fight between a fighting monk and a layperson, for example, the governing authorities of the monasteries had no jurisdiction, and the issue would go to the local court (*dzong-kha*). If a fighting monk and a soldier fought it went to the government law court (*zhung-trim*). If the verdict was that the monk should be expelled from the monastery, the law court would approach the governing body of the monastery with its findings on the case and put it into their hands. Based on that the monastery authorities would expel him. Only the final expulsion was in the hands of the monastery authorities; if there were other punishments of the monk or the layperson, they were carried out by the court and court-authorized officers. The expulsion of a monk from the monastery or the order was the concern of the monastery authorities and they alone had that authority.

Disputes between monks that could not be resolved even by the general governing body of the monastery went to the government Tse Office, via an office under the jurisdiction of the Dalai Lama. It was the Dalai Lama who had the final say.

Disputes concerning lands, estates, and the like were taken to the particular court with jurisdiction over the area where the dispute took place. A property dispute that happened in Lhasa, for example, went to the Netsang Office. Its jurisdiction extended to building houses, making offerings and statues for the temples in the city, temple maintenance, and the like. When the Netsang Office could not resolve a dispute it sent it to the Kashag. Serious disputes possibly involving serious penalties and fines, however, went straight to the Kashag.

Say there was a dispute between houses in Sera and Drepung. Obviously neither of the governing authorities of either monastery could be an impartial forum, so the court with jurisdiction would be the court nearest to the place where the dispute was geographically located. Regardless of the seriousness of the dispute this was the procedure.

During the two new year's prayer festivals the jurisdiction of the Drepung general authority extended to all Lhasa and its inhabitants. During this period no other court in the Lhasa area was allowed to deal with cases. Ongoing cases were postponed, and new cases had to be taken directly to the Drepung central authority. If a fight broke out between a Sera and Drepung monk at this time the dispute fell under the jurisdiction of the Drepung central authority. It had the authority to deal fully with any dispute to do with any monk from any of the three large monasteries during this period, and the other monastic authorities were forbidden to deal with any matter of importance.

During the prayer festivals, the Drepung central authority was the highest legal authority in the land beneath the Kashag, its jurisdiction extending even to all the branches of the Tibetan government and its offices. If there was a nasty festering dispute it could be taken to the Drepung general administration during this period and the resolution of it would be binding, so the Drepung general administration was the court of choice for quick settlement. The hearings, deliberations, and penalties might all be over within twenty days, whereas if your dispute went to the courts with jurisdiction during other periods of the year the settlement was long and dragged out, with the attendant unpleasantness of more fees and payments over the more protracted period of litigation. Drepung's jurisdiction, however, never extended to important disputes concerning land and estates or to important business disputes. These had to be referred to government courts. Any criminal dispute to do with behavior, however, came within the Drepung central authority's jurisdiction and it could resolve it.

Say there was a long ongoing dispute between someone who said that someone else had embezzled money. The litigants could take the ongoing dispute to the Drepung central authority during this period and it would deal with the matter, handing down a strong and clear judgment within two or three days. If a case before the Drepung central authority was not resolved clearly and was still hanging when the court's authority lapsed, then the full report of the case was given to the government. This always led to problems, so there was a real attempt to deal swiftly and fairly with cases that came before it during this period, and everyone knew that this was one of the characteristics of the court of the Drepung central authority. All penalties were immediately assessed and carried out in the space of a few weeks. Though there were indeed stories of corruption in this court, because the cases were dealt with swiftly there was less scope for the long and ongoing bribery that was a feature of government courts. The party that paid off the court best was favored in the ruling, the other party got punished and it was all over very quickly. There was no long ongoing process in which both sides lost. It still might be expensive, no doubt, but it was over. People liked that.

The monk appointed as the judge for the Drepung central authority did not carry the authority of the office beyond the set period. There was a competition, the monk was chosen, performed the duties of the office, and then was replaced by a new monk. During the time of his tenure he was called "Sheser." It was a special rank, but when the prayer festival ended he was just one more monk. This was an additional brake on serious miscarriages of justice. During his tenure, even if the monk judge was corrupt and unjust, his decision could not be taken to another court for redress, but when he reverted to being an ordinary person it was possible to approach the new judge of the Drepung central authority with a complaint after a time had passed and get back at the earlier judge in his capacity as ordinary monk.

In the provincial monasteries a dispute to do with a monk was dealt with inside the monastery, by the disciplinarian or the assembly of monks. If a member of the laity was involved, however, it would go to the village headman or the main aristocrat of the region. Some monasteries had little authority of their own but were under the control of a regional leader or aristocrat. The reverse was also true in some cases, though, and the regional leader would be controlled by the monastery that had all effective power over a region.

If you had to go to court, you would identify the court with jurisdiction, approach it, and read out your written letter explaining your side. Then you might ask the court to reserve its judgment for a while. Particularly in the case of a representative of a house or monastery, an adjournment had to be given when he said he had to consult with the body he represented.

As for punishments, there was some leeway. If a rich man and poor man were in a dispute, the rich man could get out of a punishment by paying a large fine. The poor man, of course, would not have any money so if the judgment went against him he would have to bear the beating or whatever. This could happen only in cases of less gravity. In a grave case even a rich man would have to bear the punishment. After this the case was finished.

Offering money to judges in the court itself was forbidden—you were only allowed to offer a ritual scarf. But plaintiffs in a case could go to the private homes of the judges and give them large gifts to influence them. If they could give a large enough gift it would obviously make the judge go over to their side. Such miscarriages of justice certainly happened, but the other party could ask to withdraw the case, knowing that they could not resolve the dispute there in their favor, and go to a higher court. They could then say to the higher court that the earlier judge had not been honest and impartial, and the earlier judge might find himself being tried and punished. It was not that truth was a total casualty, but those who could argue their case well and knew the system were the ones who tended to win in the end. It seems it is the same here in India, that bribery and a slick style of talking can win a case just like in Tibet. But of course it was not that way in the majority of cases, just as it is not here.

There was also a law that the owner of a territory where a crime or dispute took place was responsible for the crime. The court asked who owned the house or place where a crime happened and would accuse the owner of not taking care of his property and allowing the crime to happen. An owner could be punished accordingly.

In general there was no capital punishment in Tibet during my days. There were very severe punishments, but when the laws and customs of Tibet were adhered to there was no death penalty. Nor was mutilation of any of the senses allowed when the law was strictly followed.

But there were times when people in power went beyond the law. Sometimes the power of an individual or group was so great that it was not possible to confront them and convict them of their lawlessness.

Beyond this, there was a further twist to Tibetan law. Let us say that a powerful and smooth-talking person took advantage of a poorer person, and the lower courts were manipulated to the disadvantage of the poorer disputant. If it was something terrible, that person could wait until the Dalai Lama was passing by on the road and then leap up and shout at the top of his voice that he had been wronged. He would be arrested immediately and following his imprisonment he would be lashed fifty times. But after that punishment he would be allowed to speak his mind in the presence of the Dalai Lama and he would be listened to carefully. Alternatively, during an audience with the Dalai Lama a person could suddenly bring up an injustice. Again the same procedure would be followed but the complaint was taken very seriously and if the person was found to have been discriminated against, the penalties against the richer party could be very severe. It was the same in the monasteries. If the managers of the college did not follow a just path in resolving disputes between estate workers, they might take a scarf to the abbot and go outside the ordinary bounds of justice. So there were final avenues where gross injustices could be righted, even by those least advantaged.

7

THE GLORIOUS GODDESS

After my year as house guru, my guru Gangshingpa said to me that I had been successful, but that from now on I should not get involved in the house assembly or its affairs. "Put all ordinary work aside," he said, "and devote yourself to study and introspection. Be sure to avoid projecting yourself forward as a man experienced in the ways of the world. Be retiring and keep your counsel to yourself. After their tenure as house guru, many monks give up the serious study of scripture and debate. This is like a disease," he said, "and it has affected too many of us ex-house gurus of Phukhang. You should not fall into this bad habit." "I have a great wish to study," I replied, "even greater than before."

I had not totally given up my studies while I was house guru, though my responsibilities certainly did interrupt them. As house guru, I was responsible for the evening prayers. Discipline was very strict as the monks sat chanting in the outer debate courtyard, wearing their heavy wool coats. The house guru was very much in charge at this time, but since he had many other responsibilities he might only remain in the debate courtyard for long enough to ensure that all was properly underway. He would return at the end of the prayers for the start of the house's formal debate session. One of the responsibilities of the house guru was to start the debate promptly and properly. While he made a slow round, all monks had to be at the debate. After the house guru's round, the older monks often went to their rooms to read and study. Monks who had been in the monastery less than three years had to stay on for the entire debate.

As the evening wore on some monks would go to their rooms for a period, leave their heavy outer coats there, and then return to debate again. During this later part of the debating session the discipline was less exacting, and there was an openness lacking during earlier exchanges. Usually house gurus did not stay on for a long time debating, but when my duties had finished I often went to the debate and stayed to the very end. Usually debaters did not like it when a house guru stayed because they had to be more careful about discipline, but I tried to make it clear that they did not have to be meticulous in their conduct at this time, that debating required everyone to be on an equal level to be successful.

Sometimes the debate would go on to one or two o'clock in the morning. Sometimes it went on so late that I went straight from the debate, at three o'clock in the morning, to the black tea offering to our house protector. This ritual had to be done very early in the morning by six monks, and the two house gurus had to be present. At the evening black tea offering all members of the house guru committee did not need to be present, so I was able to depute monks to carry out the ritual and stay at the debate.

During this time, towards the end of the 1950s, Pema Gyaltsen was the new abbot of Loseling. One evening he came to inspect the debates and knocked on the gate of our house debating ground. I was in debating and did not immediately hear him knocking. By the time it was brought to my attention, he had left. The next morning during a class he asked his students, "Who was that monk I saw from the gate last night?" When he was told that it was me, the house guru, in there debating he was very pleased. Some of his students told me later that he had asked about it. I was Pema Gyaltsen's student so of course I was very pleased. Later, when we met each other in the course of our duties, he asked me if it was true that I kept up my debating even while I was carrying out the duties of house guru. I said that I tried to go to the debates as much as I could, and often would stay on right until the end of it. "That is the way a house guru should do his work," he said.

I believe I cleaned away some obscuration by virtue of my work as house guru, and I think this was why I began to develop an understanding of Buddhism and began to be able to memorize better than I had before. When I finished my tenure, the furthest thing from my mind was to take it easy, sitting around chatting, drinking butter tea, and looking good in the assembly.

Dondup-Ling Monastery in Kongjo-rawa, Kham before its total destruction in the 1960s.

Lobsang Gyatso's elder sister and brother-in-law.

Lobsang Gyatso as a young monk.

Lobsang Gyatso's elder sister, Tsering Dolma, with Lobsang Gyatso's family home in the background above the steep gorge of the Drichu River.

The Dalai Lama debating with Lobsang Gyatso (sitting) at the Central School for Tibetans in Mussorie (mid-1960s).

Lobsang Gyatso at sports day in the Tibetan Central School, Mussorie (late 1960s).

Teacher training class graduation picture (1963). The Dalai Lama is in the center of the picture with Lobsang Gyatso almost completely hidden at the back of the second row.

Monks of the first class of the Institute of Buddhist Dialectics chanting (1970s).

The Dalai Lama visiting Lobsang Gyatso's room in the Tibetan Central School, Mussorie (1960s).

Lobsang Gyatso with Mr. & Mrs. Taring and the student cast of historical play (late 1960s).

Tibetan children at the Tibetan Central School in Mussorie acting in an historical play written by Lobsang Gyatso and other teachers (late 1960s).

Monks building an early extension of the Institute of Buddhist Dialectics (late 1970s).

Gareth Sparham with other monks and Indian workers building an early extension of the Institute of Buddhist Dialectics (late 1970s).

Delegation to Russia and Mongolia in the early 1980s. Lobsang Gyatso is at the left end of the front row.

Lobsang Gyatso addressing an assembly of Tibetan school children in South India (1980s).

Lobsang Gyatso making a donation to the members of Phukhang house assembled in a tent in South India (early 1990s).

The Dalai Lama with Lobsang Gyatso, inspecting the new campus of the Institute of Buddhist Dialectics soon after the groundbreaking (mid 1990s).

The Dalai Lama, led by Lobsang Gyatso, inspecting the new campus of the Institute of Buddhist Dialectics soon after the groundbreaking (mid 1990s).

The Dalai Lama (seated) with Lobsang Gyatso (to his right) at the new campus of the Institute of Buddhist Dialectics soon after the beginning of construction (mid-1990s).

Teachers with students from Southeast Asia assembled for a teaching in Dharamsala (early 1990s).

Visiting the wall of the temple, Jerusalem (1996).

Signing the visitors' book at the temple wall, Jerusalem (1996).

Lobsang Gyatso shortly before his death (1997).

The bodies of Lobsang Gyatso and his two students, covered with Tibetan scarves, being carried to the cremation grounds through crowds of Tibetan mourners (February 1997).

Members of the Tibetan government-in-exile assembled for the cremation of Lobsang Gyatso and his two students (February 1997).

MY CLASS WAS STUDYING VINAYA and I immediately started back in on memorizing. Something special seemed to have happened. I was able quickly to memorize about forty-five pages of the Vinaya summary. I also went to debate, and I felt confident that I would be able to study and learn. "I am going to do a good job on Vinaya and the Abhidharma, and then I am also going to increase my knowledge of the Middle Way to a higher and higher level," I thought. The older monks were behind me. My study guru Gen Yaro said to me, "Now you have finished your house work. You now have the right to speak in the assembly. But even though you have this right, do not exercise it. If you are always getting up and saying something, it will not be long before you are given some other work. Do not take an active interest in what is going on there, just keep quiet and study hard."

For three or four months I did sit quietly in the assembly. Then, in the seventh or eighth month, there was trouble. Phukhang house was made up of four main retainer groups (*mi-ser*) from four monasteries in Kham: Dondup-ling, which supplied about half of Phukhang's monks; Rongba, a house of Gye-tang Monastery that sent monks specifically to Phukhang; Kenda, another monastery near my homeland; and a big monastery called Ngang-zang. These retainer groups did not meet separately, and were indistinguishable in the general house assembly, but it was absolutely necessary, when it came time to fill any positions in the house, that two people from different retainer groups filled the positions as a pair. Where any decision needed to be ratified by our general assembly, the ratification had to be agreed upon by monks from different groups. The most important decisions required ratification by all groups, but other decisions required less.

One day I was in the assembly as a Dondup-ling representative. Besides me, there were two older monks representing Dondup-ling and another monk who was pretty much hopeless. All the rest had stepped out. These three had obviously planned their strategy in advance and brought up again a personal complaint of a Dondup-ling monk framed deviously as an issue that had implications for our whole retainer group. The talk went on and on. It got very late and as I saw it, there was nobody to say what needed saying, namely that this was a personal issue that we didn't need to deal with. I was in two minds: I felt I had to say something but it also seemed out of place for me to speak. I sat there in a quandary for a long time until I could not bear it anymore, thinking that if it went on, it was going to cause trouble later. "You three monks have been spouting on for a long time about our retainer group," I finally said. "Who gave you the authority to do that? You can bring up personal matters, but it is not the time to be talking about issues pertaining to retainer groups." I moved that we close the matter there and then. The older monks agreed and the assembly ended on that note, with everybody happy with what I had said.

But I felt very embarrassed. My study guru, Gen Yaro (who never spoke in the assembly), had come in during the discussion and had been there, sitting quietly as he always did, and now I was going back to my rooms and I was going to have to face him, having disobeyed his advice not to speak. I slowly made my way back so that by the time I arrived he had already gone to bed. The next morning I met him with some trepidation. He immediately said to me "I am happy about what you said last night. It is true that I told you not to speak in the assembly, but it is correct to speak directly about what is right and wrong. It is devious talk and posturing that I do not want you to engage in." "I wanted somebody else to speak," I told him, "but I saw that the elder monks were not present and that those who were never got involved." "Sometimes things have to be said," he replied. "When they do, then say them, it is fine by me."

MY INTENTION was still to remain silent in the assembly, but now and then the monks would ask my opinion about an issue: "Choo-chur, what do you think about this one? Come on, let us know what you think." So I would speak sometimes, but not much or for long.

The house monks were very friendly and often remarked on how well I had done in the job of house guru and how well the grainkeepers had done at that time. "We did not think that you were going to be good at it," they said, "but you were very good indeed. We are glad to see you now back at the books." It was all very amicable for a time. Then, in the ninth or tenth month, when new grainkeepers are elected, I was made a candidate without my permission. I had never considered being a grainkeeper, and had no wish to do it, but when the assembly met to talk about who was going to be the new grainkeeper the older monks schemed to keep me away. I had not even completed a year free of the duties of house guru, so I never suspected they were contemplating putting me on the list. But finally three monks were on a short list and I was there amongst them. One of the candidates was a monk who had already been grainkeeper twice, and he became very angry when he found that he had been nominated again. "Have I not done enough for this house yet?" he asked. "I have already served as grainkeeper twice and yet here you are after me again." He sat down offended so he was obviously not going to be picked again. I still thought it unlikely that I was going to be asked because I had just been the house guru, but as I considered the way the meetings were going, I could see that I was being maneuvered into having to do the job.

This put me in a terrible dilemma. "I will leave the house," I thought, "and re-enter the monastery in another house so I will be able to study." I stopped going to the house assembly. I consulted the Tema-mo and Phug-shag oracles but they avoided speaking to me. What could I do except resign from my house in which we monks had shared all good and bad? I played with this scenario in my mind and wondered what would happen if I left Phukhang but could not get back into another Drepung house after a few months. I finally decided that if the house appointed me grainkeeper I would definitely quit, but I still clung to the hope that they would not appoint me.

For a month the assembly did not make a firm decision on the new grainkeeper. They decided that the monk who had done it twice already was not going to have to do it again, but beyond that it was up in the air. Then another assembly to discuss the issue was convened and I did not go. I thought that if they sent someone down to get me I would leave the house. I fell asleep and dreamed that I was standing by the side of a big river. I felt I had to get across that river, but it seemed so far to the other side. I had this same dream when I was coming to Lhasa from Kongjo-rawa. There were eight dri (female yaks) all with beautiful, shiny, black coats coming along, just like in my earlier dream. I jumped on them, and as the eight went across I went across on their backs. When we got to the other side I realized that there was only one of them left, the other seven had disappeared. The dri that was left was huge and I had her lead rope in my hand. She wanted to go off to the right up a big path, but I wanted to lead her down into a narrow little path. As much as I tried to pull her down into the little narrow path she would pull me into the big one. We struggled in the dream with each other, her trying to pull me into the big path and me trying to pull her the way I wanted to go. Slowly I became aware of monks from my house calling me from across the river. I became aware suddenly of knocking at the door and realized that this was no longer a dream. They were from the assembly.

To run now meant to break totally with the assembly. I would literally be running away from home, with all its implications. By leaving the house I would also be breaking my connection with the Glorious

Goddess who was our protectress. I thought that was the meaning of my dream, that I was coming very close to losing my hold on that most beautiful of dri, and that were I to do so, severed of my connection with her, things would not go well for me in my future lives. If I were to cause the Goddess to be displeased, the future would not be good, but if I stayed, the work they were going to heap on me would block my chosen way. I thought I should just jump out the window, but I could not remember where I had put the money that I had set aside if I had to leave in a hurry. There was a knocking at the door. I opened it and there were the monks of my dream.

"Come on," one of them said, "you have to come to the assembly." He praised me and said the smartest things to turn my mind and make me come. "I am not going to come with you," I said, "and I am hereby resigning from this house. I do not want to be a part of Phukhang anymore." He was crafty and said, "You have done so much for the house, if you just come to the assembly they will surely give you a dispensation and find someone else for the job. You cannot just leave," he said. "You have to come and face the assembly. You can resign there if you want, but you must come. That is why I am here."

I went to the assembly and the monks there talked to me sweetly and pressured me. "You have to become grainkeeper. It is just not part of our tradition for a monk to insist that he will not do something if the group asks him to do it. Your name has come up and a group decision has been arrived at." By then I saw that I was not going to get out of it anyway, and I said okay. Everybody was very happy, and that is how I got stuck with the job of grainkeeper.

IN PHUKHANG HOUSE there were three grainkeepers (*dru-nyer*) and three treasurers (*ngul-nyer*). The grainkeepers held their office for three years, of which the first was a preparation year, the second was actual tenure, and the third was the year of accounting. During my tenure as grainkeeper we had a capital stock of about 2000 sacks of grain (*dru-ke*) of which up to 1500 were lent out each year. The interest was used to pay for daily offerings on the house altar, offerings during festivals and on special prayer days, and for tea and tsampa offered to the monks during listed and special prayers.

The total grain capital was in the hands of the grainkeeper and there was an accounting of both capital and yearly interest, neither of which came back to the grainkeeper as personal gain. There was an accounting of the expenses for the offerings, and an accounting of discretionary funds for the house (*zhung-jang*). A grainkeeper could profit tangentially from lending (in particular, the gifts he was given by prospective borrowers remained his private income), but otherwise all three grainkeepers had little to gain financially from the onerous work.

The reason there were always three grainkeepers and treasurers in Phukhang house was because of the four retainer groups (*mi-ser*). Since the treasurer and grainkeeper were particularly important, there were always representatives from three retainer groups there.

The grainkeeper was like the manager guru, or, talking in the language of today, like the chairperson of an assembly. He appointed different monks to head committees, and approached the house assembly with problems and tasks that needed to be looked after. There was no other head of the house assembly.

The treasurers, who also had three year terms of office, kept the house money in their possession. They could make loans at interest, and the interest was given to the grainkeeper. The grainkeeper used this money for teas, offerings, and to cover expenses associated with the house. So there were two accounts under the control of the grainkeeper: the one into which the interest from the grain for the use in the offerings went, and another containing the interest from the money lent by the treasurer. Money coming into the account for the house was earmarked for the improvement of the house in general. The yearly earning of interest on the grain went specifically to the listed teas and offerings.

Beyond his capital store of grain the grainkeeper could borrow money from higher levels of government. The rate on money borrowed from the central monastic authority of Drepung was seven or eight percent, noncompounded yearly. Private borrowers were considered to be risky, but lending to houses was fairly safe, and usually happened without the necessity of an external guarantor. A house could relend the equivalent of thirty or forty thousand of today's Indian rupees at ten percent, due not yearly, but every six months, so there was ample scope for profit. On top of that were the lending incentives, the gifts given by the borrower at the time of borrowing. These gifts would profit the grainkeeper personally.

When borrowers took seed grain at interest they usually accepted a few balls of tea as well, perhaps two or three kilos. The custom was for the grainkeeper to insist on this, and for the farmer to return four kilos of grain per ball when the grain ripened. Those who had a good feeling for the house would say, "Give me a few balls of tea," and they would pass them on to other villagers and farmers as gifts or barter them and then give the grainkeeper back ripened grain in consideration. Others less well disposed had to be pressed into it. It was like a tax they had to pay and it was a source of profit for the grainkeeper.

The money for offerings only came out of interest, never out of capital. The grainkeeper kept grain capital given to the house by traders for offering a particular tea each year. Wealthy traders like to endow the house with such grain capital because they received the merit from the offerings made possible year after year from the interest it generated. The grainkeeper had to invest the donated grain capital and use the profit for the particular trader's tea offering, called a listed tea. The cost of one tea offering to the house was given as seven silver sangs (and remember that in the old days seven silver sangs was a lot of money). The capital sum sufficient to generate that amount of yearly interest was all that had been given by the earlier donor. Later, with inflation, the cost had gone up and the grainkeeper had to make up the shortfall out of other sources of profit and interest. There were perhaps ninety monks with the right to attend a tea offering, not a large number, but the house had to give them the listed tea even though it cost more than the interest earned from the original endowment. The grainkeeper and other house officials had to find the difference.

Grainkeepers also bought and sold skins of butter. Skillful grainkeepers bought when the price was low and sold when the price went up, making a profit. The same held true with their grain stocks. The grainkeeper's work was there, with the smart ones coming out ahead, and the slow ones losing.

The grainkeeper also had the right to operate a small shop from his room. During the day, monks could buy goods from people who came to sell things just outside the walls of the monastery, but there were no shops inside. After these traders had gone home, monks could go to the grainkeeper's room if they needed to buy oil or tea. In this way, the monks did not have to go so far to get necessities, and the house made a profit.

LET ME SAY A LITTLE MORE about the mechanics of lending grain at interest. The grain was measured in a big, square, measuring bucket called a *bo*. There were nineteen buckets to a load (*khel*) so a bucket was about fifteen kilos worth of grain. When you were measuring the grain, specific conventions governed allowable and forbidden leveling-off techniques.

My room guru Gangshingpa had warned me not to cheat so at the start I was measuring out grain with great abandon. Soon my partner took me aside and said there would be no profit the way I was going about it, so he took over the measuring and I agreed to do the accounts, forgetting that I could hardly write at all. I did it as best I could.

In the third month farmers came to get seed grain and they harvested in the sixth to eighth month. The borrower was permitted to keep seed grain for up to a year, but even if a person borrowed for only a month he paid back the full yearly rate of interest, which was six loads for five borrowed.

From the point of view of farmers, the access to sources of credit was absolutely necessary. Without some place to lend them capital their farming would collapse. Big families had no pressing need to borrow, but they borrowed seed grain because they knew that monasteries lent widely and continually and got grain back from a number of sources. This led to the monasteries' seed grain becoming a higher and higher quality. Farmers who had a traditional borrower relationship with a particular source had to be supplied with the seed grain, because without the loan their planting would collapse. This necessity to lend only extended to the loan of seed grain; beyond that there was no traditionally ordained necessity to extend a loan. If a farmer came to a traditional source of seed grain, said that the grain was for the yearly planting and was refused the loan, that would be against the custom. The rules governing the reclamation of seed grain loans were relaxed in favor of the lender, accordingly. If a seed grain loan was called in, the loan had to be repaid and if there was delay the creditor could press very hard, harder than in other cases, to get it back. If a creditor approached the local authorities saying that a seed grain loan borrower was defaulting, the local authorities would stand behind the creditor in nearly every instance. The food economy was underpinned by this relationship.

The interest rate system on seed grain and money worked like this. At the top, the lending policy as it operated on loans of seed grain from the central government (the Ganden Potrang) was called 'taking in the wet in exchange for giving out of the dry.' What it meant in practice was that there was only a repayment of eleven loads of grain for every ten borrowed. The theory was that the extra was simply making up for the fact that new grain given back after the harvest was yet to dry out, and therefore was not as valuable as an equivalent sack filled with dry seed grain given at the outset. Only large borrowers like the central administration of a monastery or the estate offices of the lamas and aristocrats could avail themselves of these central bank type loans.

At the next level down, a lama's labrang or the ruling gentry were authorized to take in eight loads for a loan of seven. There was a particular interest policy that operated between the monastery's central administration and the different subinstitutions which were responsible for sponsoring particular events and assemblies. It was called "taking care of the root and using the leaves for offerings." The "root" was the store of capital lent by the monastery's central administration. The return on it was fixed at seven returned for six borrowed. Those who made use of the "leaves," which is to say the amount of interest accumulated on the capital lent out during the year by the houses and other branches of the monastery, were allowed to borrow at that more advantageous rate. They could then in turn charge a higher rate of interest: they could collect six on every five loads they lent out. Houses like mine were not wealthy and had to be helped to make money in this way. We were at the bottom, so to speak, with the least amount of capital and therefore we were allowed to charge the steepest interest rates. This was the interest rate for lending from monastic houses or from ordinary people to farmers.

Were the grainkeeper to take a monetary loan available from the higher levels of the monastic institution such as the central administration, it was repaid at a fixed interest rate of eight percent. He was in turn allowed to lend out that money at an interest rate of ten percent, so there was a profit margin there of two percent. On top of the two percent interest he again received the *shoten*, which was a lump payment for the kindness of lending. The grainkeeper could enter directly into financing or could invest the money in business.

THE GRAINKEEPER was not allowed to make any profit, whatsoever, from his work; he was simply expected to expected to embrace the task as meritorious. He would eat the better food given as offerings, and the like, but other than that he would keep nothing. On the other hand, if a grainkeeper was not able to meet the amount that the assembly account had determined he must pass on, then the assembly would say he had to go out and get it. He would be given a year off to earn that money, or six months, after which time he would have to give the amount owed. The capital at the start of the tenure had to be returned.

If there was a particular store of butter, of grain, or of anything at all, the keeper had to give it back so that he could say that he had not retained a penny. He would go so far as to say, "Even the old offering scarfs that I have used to blow my nose in, I have given all those back as well." Then the grainkeeper would be thanked and given a scarf. Beyond that there was no remuneration. The same was true of the treasurer as well.

There were three treasurers. They were chosen from six candidates in a lottery done in front of the Glorious Goddess, and they held the position for three years. Each of them had a locker that was kept in the house. The seal for each locker was held by the house guru, and the key to each was held by each treasurer. Before they opened the locker in the morning for business, they showed the sealed lockers to the house guru who then broke the seal and the treasurers took what they needed. In the evening after business they gave back their locker to the house guru for sealing. Treasurers were not allowed to keep the locker with the money in their own rooms, it had to be deposited in the house business-activities room. The same with collecting or lending money at interest. Such activities could not be conducted from a monk's own room, they had to take place in the business-activities room.

Besides the grain and money keepers, there were also special keepers appointed for long prayer or ritual occasions. Perhaps two keepers would be appointed if it became necessary, for example, to say one hundred thousand Tara prayers. They would then take the money necessary for this task from the general account. They would meet all expenses from this and then at the end present an account.

Again, when there was a meeting in Lhasa for business or other reasons, or if there was a special larger assembly where the interests of Phukhang had to be represented, a person would be chosen by the assembly, and his expenses would be paid by the house. Sometimes he might be invested with the power to make all decisions on behalf of the house without the need for further consultation.

PRIOR TO PRESENTING my final accounting to the house assembly I did the accounts of the year as carefully as I could myself. Then I called in someone good at arithmetic to go over them before the final presentation. When I was satisfied with them I took them up to the assembly. This was the usual procedure.

The divisions of responsibilities and the careful checks and balances designed to ensure harmony in the house community were underpinned by a transparent accounting system. There were no books with lists of figures as in the modern way of accounting, but we had a very sophisticated way of doing it with stones of different sizes. As a grainkeeper or a house guru, you had to present the record of expenses and income orally in front of the full house assembly. Stones were passed from one person to another as the accounting progressed and the others in the assembly would be watching to see if the right amount was being passed. Two sections of the assembly listened as the accounting was read slowly and in detail. The section most skilled in accounting was called "the section that sat in the dark." This section did not make its figures known but silently drew up an account based on my account as it was read out. The second section repeated the figures being read out: "That was one hundred sangs spent for rental of horses, that was one hundred bags of grain that came in," and so forth, drawing up a new set of figures right there in the assembly based on what I said. The rest of the assembly sat listening to make sure they felt the accounts were in order.

The final figures were then added up and read out to the assembly. As they were read, if there was disagreement the matter would be argued out. When everyone finally concurred on the final set of figures it was referred to the section that sat in the dark. If the section that sat in the dark was not happy about the accounting it would not say that such and such a figure was not right, it would simply reject the audit and the accounting would have to be done again.

When the section that sat in the dark was happy with the final set of figures, it asked me if the final set of figures was the same set of figures that I had arrived at in my own private accounting prior to the assembly. If I had said that my final figures did not agree with the ones presented to the assembly, then the assembly would have to go through the entire process again to see if it could get our figures to match. If there was still a discrepancy, the assembly would have to give me a few days to go over my own personal accounts to see where the discrepancy lay. If even after this there was still a discrepancy, again the assembly would meet and again I would have the opportunity to give another full account. If, after this second or even third time the accounts were not in accord, the account arrived at by the assembly would stand as the proper account. If the final account ended up with me owing money I would have had to supply it to the assembly. If, on the other hand I had ended up with the assembly finding it had more money than a strict accounting would deliver to it, still that money would not be returned to me. It would have been kept by the assembly. This was one of the reasons why a grainkeeper was extremely careful in his initial personal accounting, and why the audit was a cause of a great amount of anxiety. I had to account for everything: property, grain, butter, etc. As I consider it today, I have a great admiration for the thoroughness of that final audit.

WHEN I WAS APPOINTED junior grainkeeper, Gen Yaro had said that I had met with a terrible obstacle to study. "There is no way out of it," he said, "You have to do the house work now; you have been given the responsibility for it, and you should do the work as well as you can. But do not give up on the long-term goal of studying. The trouble is that if you focus on study then the work will not go well, and if you put the required effort into the work, study necessarily suffers. The monks had said to me, "Do not worry, it will not effect your studies. Look on yourself as appointed token representative of a certain faction of the house. Think that is why you were appointed, not because you have to do a lot of work." For a few months I allowed myself to believe that and I did not take an active part in the grainkeeper's work.

The older of the two grainkeepers who were appointed before me, though not particularly gifted, was a good man. The other was a pushy monk who wanted to do good work but was quick to get nasty in a tense situation. The two of them were not particularly good friends. Sometimes when they were at an impasse about who was going to do what, there was no choice but for me to fill the gap. It was not long before most of the work was on my shoulders. And you know how it is once you get involved in work—you start to get into it, you are always there talking about one thing or the other, and you like what is going on.

Seven months of the study of Vinaya was lost to me. My old debate partners came by again and again telling me not to give up study. But it seemed that whenever I was in a class, the house guru would send a message saying he had to talk to me and I had no choice but to go. Even now, as I think about the time I spent on that work, I feel sad. I think of the time I let slip by, caught up in the worldly affairs of being the grainkeeper, and how I relished it all so foolishly.

8

THE SADNESS OF TIBET

After nearly forty years of exile in India, as I look back at my life in Tibet, I see that I lived during a period of great tragedy for my country. But I and other Tibetans were not fully aware of the extent of the disaster befalling us; we lived our lives according to our earlier customs with only a few changes to accommodate the Chinese forces that were slowly overwhelming us. During the years when I was house guru people like myself from the border regions were aware of the Chinese military buildup and even talked of the eventual takeover of Lhasa itself, but we were caught within a complex of unhappy circumstances that made us all, as Tibetans, incapable of dealing intelligently and decisively with the threat. These circumstances, which were the karma I shared with all the Tibetan people, are as much a part of my life up to 1959 as are the personal experiences that I have so far described, even though I was not fully aware of their presence at the time. To explain how these unhappy circumstances arose I will digress a little into Tibetan history. I begin with the origin of the Tibetan government that was overthrown by the Chinese Communists.

It was called the Ganden Palace. It came into being in the seventeenth century under the Fifth Dalai Lama and was the government of Tibet until 1959. Prior to the Fifth Dalai Lama the government of Tibet did not represent the diverse population, but was under the control of particular families. The Ganden Palace was itself in its origins a government based on the early Dalai Lamas' labrang, at that time known from its geographical location in Drepung as the *zimkang-woma* (lower chambers), and it only slowly transformed into a government representative of the country. During its history (for example during the time of the Eighth and Ninth Dalai Lamas, who died young) assembly rule was sometimes usurped by powerful families or factions. The government was particularly vulnerable during times between Dalai Lamas, when power was invested in a lama regent. During those times, the lama's household wielded power like in the days when powerful families ruled Tibet. The interests of the regent's household would often take precedent over the interests of the country at large, hindering development and promoting instability. During the regencies, therefore, Tibet reverted to rule by the type of government that had flourished before the Ganden Palace period.

During the regency between the Twelfth and Thirteenth Dalai Lamas, the regent's authority had been invested in Tengye-ling Monastery. This regency was conducted with dignity and to the benefit of the country, but when the young Thirteenth Dalai Lama reached his majority, some lower officials in that monastery were loath to give up power. There were some disturbances, therefore, when he first took his traditional powers into his hands, but I will not go into more detail about what happened at that time.

The Tenth to the Twelfth Dalai Lamas had died early, and consequently the teaching and study of dharma in Drepung, Sera, and Ganden monasteries had degenerated somewhat. But a strong center was again established during the time of the Thirteenth Dalai Lama. The Thirteenth was interested in the ideas of democracy and socialism found in the west and in Russia, and his actions show he was experimenting to find models suited to Tibet. He was also interested in the modern ways of setting up an army and in modern defense systems. He seems to have been influenced by the British in his thinking about these things.

THE THIRTEENTH DALAI LAMA was an imposing presence. I was told he inspired awe, even fear. When he attended a traditional function he sat on his throne wearing robes that made him look grand and fearsome and he always appeared as though on the lookout for shortcomings. He had a short temper and would even slap a person right there and then for carelessness, particularly a government official. His attendants both feared him and loved him. He would sometimes strike out, and then a few moments later start worrying with real human concern whether his blow had hurt the person. He did not show the deep hostility that caused such action in a less noble soul.

When presented with a petition from an ordinary Tibetan complaining about an aristocrat or government official he would immediately take notice and act to punish those found guilty of excesses. If a monk or ordinary person not learned in writing presented him with a petition, he was not exacting and did not point out errors. "They have not studied; let us find the meaning and not trip up over little errors in spelling or syntax," he would say. But with officials who were supposed to know better he was unflinchingly strict. He would search out the writer of a petition if he was a government officer and punish him.

Each morning at about eight o'clock he would make a round of the offices and then go to work in his own office. He remained at work until the evening when the office was closed. No appointments or audiences with the Dalai Lama were scheduled in the evening. He ate and dressed simply, much like an ordinary person. "What they wear and eat," he said, "is what I should wear and eat." He was careful with little things, even a needle or an old picture. His actions were like the poorest of the poor who know exactly what is theirs and treat it with great importance. His everyday clothes were not designed to impress people, and in his personal quarters he was very relaxed with visitors, treating them as though they were family and expecting them to make themselves fully at home. He was just an ordinary monk there, in a totally open environment where none were afraid to ask openly for what they desired.

The Thirteenth Dalai Lama died before I arrived in Drepung. While I was in Lhasa the work that he had left unfinished was continued by the Fourteenth Dalai Lama. There is a tradition, much of it not available in the written records, that comes down from the elders about events during the time of the Thirteenth Dalai Lama. I will set down what I know of this tradition so that it becomes known to others.

DURING THE TIME of the Thirteenth Dalai Lama, the British, who were in power in India, were creating disturbances on the Indo-Tibetan border. The British caused a lot of trouble during this period, and eventually sent an expeditionary force to Lhasa. What I have to say, first, is about the time just before that expedition.

The British were interested in Tibet for trade rights, and specifically they wanted trade rights that would bring Tibet into its sphere of influence. Tibet had military installations on the borders of India, not totally insignificant ones, and at the start of the British incursions the Chinese seemed ready to help Tibet defend itself.

The Nechung Oracle advised the government that a fight would not be in the interests of Tibet, but the government officials did not heed the oracle and sent a large number of soldiers to the border. The Chinese then advised the government that stationing a large group of soldiers on the borders without a proper supply line was not helpful and that the Tibetan government should withdraw the force and try to find a peaceful resolution. The advice of the Chinese was probably prompted by discussions they had with the British, because during that period the Chinese were aware of the power of the British and were attempting to appease them.

About a year later, after it became obvious to the Tibetan government that their ill-thought-out military policy could not be pursued any further, they withdrew the army from the border, as advised by the Chinese. Since no fighting had happened, the government declared victory and scarfs were offered to all concerned. The Nechung Oracle's comment on this absurdity was, "When I first said do not send troops you sent troops. Having been sent they did nothing and were withdrawn. You then commended their work. These offering scarves and commendations when no work was done are a mistake." In his biography, the Thirteenth Dalai Lama mentions this event clearly and the older monks in Drepung talked about it during my time. They had a lot to say about how the oracle poked fun at the actions of government officials during that period.

The Nechung Oracle was frequently consulted while the Younghusband expedition was advancing on Tibet in 1904. At first, his message was that a battle would not take place, but his opinion suddenly changed, and he urged the Dalai Lama to flee. The Dalai Lama immediately fled from Lhasa towards China. Soon after, the Tibetans were wiped out in a devastating battle and the British arrived in Lhasa.

Kuno Chor-la told me that it was initially a very difficult flight for His Holiness, and he became very tired. When he arrived in Phenpo he stayed for a short time with a family who was unaware that their guest was the Dalai Lama. They felt sorry for the traveler and offered him some very fine fresh cow's milk. The Dalai Lama, who was exhausted at that point, was touched by their kindness. Later, on his return from China, he took a kindly interest in the affairs of that family, sending them the first press of fine cow butter. The family later became wealthy on that account.

When he arrived at the Sino-Tibetan border, the Dalai Lama sent a ceremonial arrow with a message to the Chinese leadership, saying that the British were invading and that he needed help. The Chinese response was to hesitate and intimate that the presence of the Dalai Lama in China at that moment would be problematic. This response appears to have angered the Dalai Lama, who sent back a message that up until then there had been a good relationship between China and Tibet, but if this was their current position then let them simply say that they were not going to help. He then began making preparations to go to Russia, via Mongolia, but before arrangements were complete he received a message from the Chinese that he was now welcome to proceed to China.

Even before the Dalai Lama arrived in China the British expeditionary force returned to India because of British doubts about the effect their incursion was having on Anglo-Russian relations. The Chinese had done nothing to help Tibet block the entry of the British. It is said that during the time the British army was in Lhasa the Tibetan government approached the Chinese envoy in Lhasa to mediate, but not only did the envoy not mediate, he bellied up to the British and tried to humor them, helping the British even at the expense of Tibetans.

After the withdrawal of the British, the Tibetan government asked the Dalai Lama to return. Their message arrived just as the Chinese leadership stopped hesitating about admitting the Dalai Lama into China so he did not immediately return. The Chinese emperor was sick during this time and decisions were being made by his wife. She had great religious respect for the Dalai Lama, and made sumptuous offerings and arranged for excellent accommodations when he finally arrived. On the political level, however, she offered no support. Before the Dalai Lama left China to return to Tibet, the wife of the emperor passed away.

There were members of the Chinese government who were not kindly disposed to Tibet. Tibetans said the one least friendly to Tibet was a fellow who had a long wispy moustache. After the empress's death he immediately got hold of the state seals, and while remaining outwardly friendly to the Dalai Lama he despatched a large military force towards the China-Tibet border. The Dalai Lama immediately left China, racing the Chinese army. He entered Tibet from the north but by the time he got back to Lhasa many columns of the Chinese army had already penetrated into parts of Kham. This was in about 1909.

It was during this period that my people in Kongjo-rawa fought the three battles with the Chinese army that I mentioned earlier in connection with my maternal grandfather. They repulsed the first incursion of the Chinese because they were able to mount a defense from a vital access point into the region. The second time they again repulsed the invasion, but the third time Chinese troops overran the region, fighting their way in and killing defenders as they came. The head of the Kongjo-rawa forces was forced to flee to a different region; Dondup-ling Monastery was taken and Chinese troops came within moments of burning it to the ground. Part of the agreement that prevented the burning of the monastery was that my homeland would pay a tax to the Chinese that would be brought down to them. Prior to that, Kongjo-rawa paid no tax to the Chinese, nor did anyone give anything else to them as a tax or tribute. From then on Kongjo-rawa was under the central Tibetan government when it came to religious matters, and under the Chinese when it came to the secular administration. It was not that we were totally tied under the Chinese, but when there was any big problem with any other region or party the Chinese had to be consulted. Our own internal problems and affairs were dealt with without reference to the Chinese. It was during this period that the Chinese burnt to the ground thirteen monasteries in Kham, including Chatreng Monastery.

The Chinese continued their advance into Tibet, reaching Lhasa about three months after the Dalai Lama had arrived back. At first the Dalai Lama remained in Lhasa with the thought that he might be able to find a resolution to the different problems. When the Chinese troops trained their guns on the Potala palace where the Dalai Lama was staying, however, he again secretly fled Lhasa, traveling to the south. He was able to cross the bridge over the Tsangpo river just before Chinese troops got there to cut off his escape. Amongst the Dalai Lama's bodyguards was a monk called Pagpa ("Porker") Chatreng, a lama from my monastery Dondup-ling, and Tsarong Dazang Damdul. They mounted a spirited defense against the Chinese, halting their pursuit long enough to allow His Holiness to make it to the Indian border. He asked for safe haven and was welcomed with great respect by the authorities of British India.

The Dalai Lama stayed in India for some time, during which period the Chinese troops in Lhasa caused great distress to the population. Their oppression of the people and statements that they had thrown out the Dalai Lama turned the Tibetan people so strongly against them that Tibetans rose up and began to fight. China was in ferment during this period so the Chinese troops in Lhasa received no reinforcements or help. They were either killed in the fighting with Tibetans or else fled back to China. The retreating Chinese troops were harried all the way back through Chamdo and the eastern regions. At this time a Tibetan military leader, a government representative at the Tsidrung level, performed with great distinction. The army united under his leadership, with many ordinary soldiers fighting bravely. There were also monks in the ranks fighting alongside the ordinary people and they expelled the remainder of the Chinese military force.

After the Chinese occupation of Lhasa ended, the Dalai Lama was repeatedly asked to return. He began his journey back and when he arrived in Pari he declared Tibet to be a fully independent country. He then returned to Lhasa and the Potala and a period of stability began.

ONE OF THE OUTCOMES of all the problems during those years was that a close watch on the inner workings of the Tibetan administration had not been possible. After the Dalai Lama's return, he began to institute reforms. He also began to clean up the administration in the big monasteries and take an active interest in the study habits of monks at Drepung, Sera, and Ganden. He called in the abbots and those in line to become Ganden Throne-Holder and had them recite and debate. Those who performed well he left in their places, and the others he replaced with more capable individuals. It is from this time that government involvement in the education process in the large monasteries began. The Dalai Lama first ensured that the abbot and high ranking gesheys were truly learned; he instituted an ordered system for monks who debated at the prayer festival and became gesheys, and insisted that they do the recitations and sit for the debates. He also instituted a financial assistance scheme that covered part of the costs incurred by gesheys sitting for the highest positions during the prayer festival. The close involvement of the government with the granting of the highest degrees to the gesheys at the prayer festival began at this time.

The educational reforms he tried to implement were far-reaching and went beyond just the monasteries. One of the policies of the Dalai Lama was to gather children from the important families of the Kham and Amdo border regions together in a new school in Lhasa. The origins of the idea lay in a policy of entrusting the defense of the border regions to the important people in those areas, with the government supplying the arms and ammunition and training for the task. This idea was opposed by the noble families who said it was too dangerous to supply guns to the border Khampas because they might turn the guns on the central government itself. That pretty much scotched that idea. It was after that plan died that he tried to open a number of new secular schools and to send a number of young Tibetans overseas for education. The main opponents to the secular schools were the abbots of the monasteries, but it seems that the instigators of the opposition were to be found amongst the noble families who feared that any change in the status quo would be a threat to the large estates that they owned. They got inside the skins of the abbots and infected them with the idea that the new schools would be a threat to study in the monasteries, and a threat to the whole monastic culture as it was then. In general, the new schools proposed by Dalai Lama had to be abandoned, though some were opened with the help of noble families who held the ideas of the Dalai Lama in high esteem, and some Tibetans were also sent overseas.

THE DALAI LAMA had many plans for far-reaching reforms but was not able to implement them because, although he faced no open opposition, when it came to implementing his policies his officials pursued a policy of noncooperation.

During a very elaborate smoke offering for the god Pelha, the god spoke through the Nechung Oracle. While rushing into the central temple the oracle picked up a water-offering bowl in front of the central image and turned to the assembled aristocrats (who were government officials) and insisted that they drink to seal an oath that they were implementing the Dalai Lama's policies. Many elders while I was at Drepung told the story of how some aristocrats drank the water offered to them by the Nechung Oracle, but how many others poured the water down their sleeves and only pretended to take the oath. The point of the story is that aristocratic government officials presented a loyal front, while harboring other thoughts in their hearts.

It was at this time also that religious problems associated with the spirit Shugden arose. The Dalai Lama wanted to stop the propitiation of this spirit, but many lamas worshipped it, and to have banned it outright would have caused a disturbance. It would have looked like the Dalai Lama was criticizing individual lamas and telling their disciples to break their commitments to them. So he was not explicit in issuing orders against the spirit, but it is clear that through various means he tried to stop it. There are many stories about how he attempted to show to Phabonkha Rinpoche that propitiation of the spirit was going to lead to trouble. Phabonkha Rinpoche did not follow the Dalai Lama's advice and got attached to the spirit, so it thereby became very famous and widely propitiated, particularly amongst government officials.

Phabongka Rinpoche was specially gifted in the Graduated Path teachings. He did not have a particularly profound understanding of classical Buddhist texts, however, so many educated monks of Tibet did not hold him in high esteem. The people of Lhasa became devoted to him because of his ability to teach the Graduated Path so well, and it became a strong basis of his support. The lack of esteem from the learned monks was a ground for some friction and a cause for Phabongka Rinpoche to feel slighted.

UNDER THE THIRTEENTH DALAI LAMA, the government decided to create a modern army. To raise funds, the finance department was directed to collect a food tax from farms that belonged to large estates. The tax appears to have been directed not so much at lower-level workers on farms and estates, but on the share of harvests or interest in the form of grain that large owners of estates, particularly the monasteries, were entitled to. The finance minister Lungshar, who was in charge of collecting this new tax, drew up a detailed plan to raise this money, but historically the relationship between him and Tashi Lungpo (the big monastery in Shigatse that is the seat of the Panchen Rinpoche) was not good. The monastery of Tashi Lungpo felt that the share of the tax it was being asked to raise was disproportionate and refused to pay. The other big monasteries also did not like a tax which threatened to lower the amount of income they were going to receive from their fields and from the grain they lent at interest.

In this dispute the monks studying in the monasteries were not really a factor; they had no say over the larger financial affairs of the institutions, but, like any ordinary person, they also did not like any plan that saw a diminution of the amount of income they were going to be getting. And as always, there was a division between those monks who understood and were influenced by Buddhism (but who were powerless in the monasteries) and those who controlled the finances and had power, but were without an understanding that would influence their behavior in a constructive fashion. As politicians, this latter group of monks were simply responding like the immediate cry of a stomach for food.

This issue of a food tax to finance a modern army caused division between Panchen Rinpoche and the central government. The Dalai Lama is said to have formed an unpublicized plan to invite Panchen Rinpoche to his summer palace. I suspect there may be truth in this because a new building in the grounds of the summer palace called the Shabten Lhakhang was built at this time. When the aristocrats in Shigatse heard about this plan, they interpreted it as a plot to incarcerate Panchen Rinpoche and convinced him it was true even though he and the Dalai Lama were relatives. They all fled Shigatse together and the plan to invite Panchen Rinpoche to live in the grounds of the summer palace collapsed.

While Panchen Rinpoche and his aristocratic retainers were running away, there were many meetings of the Lhasa administration about what to do—whether the army should be sent out to capture them and bring them back or not. At that time the later prime minister Lukhangwa was secretary. According to one version of events, he argued strongly that there was a student-disciple relation between the Dalai and Panchen lamas and that the army should not on any account be despatched. He also argued it would be inappropriate to send the army to bring Panchen Rinpoche back since he was a high religious figure. The outcome was that Panchen Rinpoche and his retinue got to China. There were many explanations about how the Dalai and Panchen lamas were not antagonistic to each other on a personal level. Some said that the external appearance of discord was simply to enable Panchen Rinpoche to get to China where his teaching of the dharma would be of great benefit to the people. This could be. But it seems that there was a rift between them.

ONE OF THE SPECIAL QUALITIES of the Thirteenth Dalai Lama was that he knew very clearly what his people were thinking. He was very concerned about the problems of the ordinary Tibetans, and when people came from far-off regions for an audience, he would often inquire in detail about their problems. He was particularly interested in how his government officials in their regions were behaving, and would frequently ask his visitors for details. There was a tradition of people speaking openly and freely, and of the Dalai Lama responding in the same vein, openly and freely with what he thought.

The Thirteenth had a small secret service of perhaps four or five trusted associates who he asked to keep their eyes on the offices, to keep their fingers on the pulse of the bazaar in Lhasa, and to keep their ears open to find out what the monks were thinking in the monasteries. They had no position in the government but were held in high esteem by the Dalai Lama, and reported directly to him. The Dalai Lama himself sometimes dressed in common clothes and went out incognito amongst the people. There are many stories about him traveling outside the Potala in ordinary clothes.

One day the Dalai Lama went to Ganden accompanied by his security agent Kumbula. They went in ordinary clothes on ordinary horses and left Lhasa traveling east. When they got to the ferries they met with an elderly man heading back home from Lhasa where he had taken a load of wood on a donkey. The Dalai Lama entered into a conversation with him. "Where are you off to?" he asked. "I am gong back home," the man replied. "I have taken a load of wood to the Norbulinka to the kitchens there." This was when a new building called the Chensel Palace was being constructed. New taxes had been introduced to pay for it and part of the tax was the requisitioning of pack animals to transport rocks. "He already has some very beautiful palaces but still he is building a new one. People have to spend a lot of their time there and use their animals for building this new palace. It is that fellow Kumbula who decided yet another palace is needed in Norbulinka even though there are a lot there already. He is not a bad fellow, this Kumbula," the old man continued, "but he really does load up the ordinary people with his taxes and requisitions. This fellow Kumbula, he always has to be starting some new project or other, he is that sort of fellow." Now Kumbula was right there with the Dalai Lama, and a bit later the old fellow started up again. "This Kumbula is definitely too quick to start up new projects, if you ask me; but you know, he is no fool either, and he is loyal to the Dalai Lama. He is useful to the Dalai Lama, no doubt about that." The gist of his remarks was that the ordinary man like himself found the taxation burdensome. The Dalai Lama was very pleased with the conversation.

"Rinpoche," the old man said, thinking the Dalai Lama was just a distinguished looking older monk, "have some tea with me." They had some tea and tsampa together and then the old fellow pulled out a bottle of barley beer and offered it to the Dalai Lama. "I am a monk, I do not drink beer," the Dalai Lama protested. "Do not be silly," he said, "a lot of the monks are drinking beer nowadays, go ahead and have a swig." "Is that so?" said the Dalai Lama. "A lot of the monks nowadays are drinking beer are they?" "Piles of them," the old fellow replied, "though I am pleased to see that you do not accept my offer." After the old man had downed his beer with some bread he was carrying, they set off in the direction of Ganden together, talking as they went. As they began to approach Ganden, at the place called Dechen, they caught sight of a large smoke offering and the monks of Ganden lined up to welcome a special guest. The old fellow said, "They are making a big welcome up there for someone today, I wonder who is coming." The Dalai Lama said, "I am not positive, but I suspect it is for me." Then the old fellow began to suspect that he was there with the Dalai Lama and he thought he had better make a run for it. As he tried to flee the Dalai Lama caught hold of him and would not let him go. He took the old man right in through the gates of Ganden Monastery and told the people there not to let him leave, but to give him a good meal and something excellent to drink. After he had been well-fed and looked after, the Dalai Lama sent word to bring him.

The old man was beside himself with fear, thinking he was going to be given a terrible punishment, but the Dalai Lama treated him as a friend and told him to sit down, right opposite to where Kumbula was sitting. "Hey, old fellow," he said, "I must introduce you to Kumbula. This is Kumbula." He was overcome with embarrassment, but the Dalai Lama said that he should not be. "You spoke your heart, you spoke what you felt was true and there is no shame in that. You described faults as faults and good qualities as good qualities. Some people only complain but you did not do that. Some, again, cover up faults and say nothing but good and that is not right either. You spoke honestly and openly, and I am very happy." He gave him fifty white silver sangs as a parting gift, a large sum of money, and said that the problems would be looked into. It was from then that the levies on the people for Norbulinka building projects stopped.

ANOTHER TIME the Dalai Lama dressed up as a Mongolian (he spoke some Mongolian) and got into a conversation with some Mongolian monks. They said that they had come to Lhasa to seek an audience with the Dalai Lama, but that aristocratic officials had not granted their request so they were going back home. The Dalai Lama said, "I see, requests to see the Dalai Lama are being refused are they?" "Indeed," they said. "We have decided to return to Mongolia now, though our wish was to see the Dalai Lama." The Dalai Lama said he was sorry to hear that, and told them not to rush off. "Where are you living?" he asked, and they gave him the address of the rooms they were staying in. When they were granted an audience the next day and found that the person on the audience throne was that same person they had been talking to on the street the day before you can imagine their amazement.

Another time the Dalai Lama went to make a smoke offering at the topmost point of Drepung. He sent his retinue and horses ahead past his palace in Drepung and went on foot straight up past Nechung Monastery, accompanied by his bodyguard Singka. As he went up past the caves where the Phukhang monks studied, he met a new monk who did not recognize the Dalai Lama for who he was. The Dalai Lama took him by the hand and asked him all about the study habits and the successes and difficulties faced by Drepung monks at that time. They walked together in conversation to just beneath Gompa Ritro Monastery. The monks above could see the two of them strolling below and recognized the Dalai Lama. They were sure the new monk was going to get into big trouble by mentioning all sorts of things to the Dalai Lama which were better left unsaid. Just above Gompa Ritro the aristocrats came down to accompany the Dalai Lama as he walked up. There he told the monk to leave. "Study hard," he said and gave him a parting present of some white silver sangs. A gift like that would have taken care of the food needs of that monk for the best part of a year.

After the smoke offering had finished, the Dalai Lama stopped at the temple of the goddess Tema-mo, and ordered his government officials to arrange that the income from a particular area be used to give each Drepung retreat monk a full *bu* of tsampa. He routed it through goddess Tema-mo's temple, which distributed it at a particular time each year. After the death of the Thirteenth a measure of tsampa was sometimes given to the retreat monks but it came from Tema-mo's temple itself. A temple official would shout to the monks in retreat, "Come and get your tsampa!" I myself went down on more than one occasion to receive tsampa from them, a tradition started by the Thirteenth Dalai Lama.

LUDRUB RINPOCHE, the lama from my hometown monastery Dondupling, had a close relationship with the Thirteenth Dalai Lama. There were a lot of different types of fruit that grew in Kham that were not available in central Tibet, and as they ripened Ludrub Rinpoche would ensure that boxes of them were sent to Lhasa for the enjoyment of His Holiness. In return, presents of gold and silver flowed from the Dalai Lama back to Ludrub Rinpoche.

On one occasion Ludrub Rinpoche collected gold from the people of Kongjo-rawa and sent it as a gift to the Dalai Lama, asking in return that the Dalai Lama bless our region with a statue of Buddha Shakyamuni. The Dalai Lama commissioned a statue just like the Lhasa Jowo but a bit smaller, which he had made by the leading craftsmen. They took great care making it because they thought that the statue was going to be kept in the Dalai Lama's own rooms. It was not the ordinary type where each part of the statue fits in another part and can be dismantled; the parts of this statue were carefully welded together, and the lower part of the statue screwed into the seat.

The Dalai Lama supervised the offering of mantras and the blessing ceremony and put it in a trunk, made to size, for its journey. Traders from our part of Kham were contacted and they were told to set out for Kham so that the statue would reach Dondup-ling on a specific date. The Dalai Lama's idea was to do the final installation ritual for the statue the day after the statue arrived in Kongjo-rawa. The traders set out with the statue, deputing one of their number to race ahead and let the people know that they were on the way and to make a large boxlike chapel for the statue to be installed in the moment it arrived. When the statue arrived and the installation rituals began in Dondup-ling, the Dalai Lama too began the installation rituals in the Norbulinka in Lhasa. The older monks said that at that time a wondrous occurrence was seen. The auspicious offerings of grain and flowers thrown in the air by the Dalai Lama in Lhasa descended miraculously on the head of the Jowo statue being installed there in my homeland. "We saw it happen," they said. It was indeed a famous statue, with a face so wonderful it was more beautiful, perhaps, than even the Jowo in the central temple in Lhasa.

THE DALAI LAMA made appointments over and above those recommended by government offices, and often added people of his own selection to committees. This was also true for the administration of the monasteries. Where persons suggested as candidates for abbot, for example, were not suitable, he would appoint somebody else. Such appointees performed a special role which had a particularly beneficial effect, and the person appointed by the Dalai Lama would often become famous for his contribution.

There was a monk from Tsawa house called Pag Gyawo who was running for a position as member of the Drepung central authority. He was from an ordinary family, was not a wealthy person, and had debts from earlier work in an administrative position. On account of this his name was not included on the first short list given to the Dalai Lama. The Dalai Lama rejected the list and said the committee should come up with further names. They submitted a revised short list and again this was rejected. At this point Pag Gyawo's name was added to the short list even though he said that he did not have enough money to work in a position as high and demanding as Drepung central authority. Pag Gyawo asked that his name be dropped but the house gurus urged him to run and assured him that if he was appointed they would help him purchase the appropriate clothes and furniture. His name was submitted and the Dalai Lama appointed him. So there he was, penniless and a high dignitary—a member of the Drepung central authority. His supporters and house members all pulled together to supply him with clothes and other necessities commensurate with such a position. He undertook the work and distinguished himself during the prayer festival when the entire power of government rested in his administration's hand. He was so successful that his name, Pag Gyawo, is famous amongst us to this day.

One of his successes was in the case of the notorious Nepalese criminal Kudum, who was operating in Lhasa. Kudum was a terrible criminal who had been charged by the government, but they were unable to arrest him since he was a Nepalese citizen. During a prayer festival he was captured and brought before the Drepung central authority, where he died while being punished. The Nepalese ambassador began to complain that the Drepung central authority had killed one of his citizens, and he wanted recompense equal to the death of a man. The ambassador said that Kudum was an important and fine citizen, and made a lot of trouble by continually insisting on recompense. Finally Drepung central authority agreed and got the recompense ready. Just before giving it to the Nepalese ambassador, Pag Gyawo said that the central authority now required recompense for the eighteen people Kudum had murdered. This, of course, caused the Nepalese ambassador a lot of difficulty and he denied that Kudum had killed anyone. The Drepung central authority, however, had a confession signed by Kudum admitting that he had killed eighteen people. They produced the confession and the Nepalese ambassador had to wriggle out of the trap by suggesting that all parties just drop the matter. He was a very famous man that Pag Gyawo, a man never bested.

SO MUCH THAT the Dalai Lama intended to do was not done, and great was the irritation that he had to put up with. Thus, it was said that though he intended to remain until his sixty-second year, he passed away suddenly at the age of fifty-nine, with the work he wished to do not yet complete.

One of the reasons the Dalai Lama passed away at that time, a few years before he was expected to, was because he saw no further benefit in remaining since he was unable to implement reforms. Some Tibetan aristocratic government officials told me this. Another possible reason was to make sure his reincarnation—the present Fourteenth Dalai Lama—was not too young when the troubles of the future invasion occurred. It could be. There are actions of the Dalai Lama that all can recognize, but he acts in ways that are inconceivable as well.

Many of the old monks told me that in the year the Dalai Lama passed away, during the new year's prayer festival the holder of the Ganden Throne—a monk from Sera-je—was approached by the Nechung Oracle while in a trance. The Nechung Oracle told him that the death of the Dalai Lama was at hand and he should offer a mandala to him to ask him to remain. This Ganden Throne-Holder, a powerful individual propelled strongly by the force of his past good deeds, immediately made preparations for a long-life-request mandala ritual for the Dalai Lama and then returned to the Nechung Oracle to ask for further instructions. Speaking through the oracle, Nechung replied that a very beautiful gift must be offered to the Dalai Lama, at which time he, Nechung, would make an appearance. He also said to invite only a few particular lamas to the ceremony and not to publicize it or let the government get deeply involved. The Ganden Throne-Holder found a beautiful gift, a pair of exquisite-sounding cymbals, which he bought from a young woman. Nechung was pleased and told him to go and fix the date with the Dalai Lama, again stressing that the government should not be involved.

The long-life ritual arranged by the Ganden Throne-Holder was not an elaborate affair, but rather a short prayer and request that the Dalai Lama remain long. As the request was being made the Nechung oracle went into a trance. The Dalai Lama did not say "I accept your request and will remain," however, but kept looking upward to the sky. Nechung then said to the Dalai Lama that though the great learned ones had requested the Dalai Lama to stay, he had not replied that he would. "Therefore," Nechung said, "if you are not staying I too am going to retire to Shambhala." The oracle immediately fell into a faint as though the god was withdrawing totally. At that point the Dalai Lama made a hand motion. "You should not withdraw totally" he said. "I am soon to die. But I will return and when I do I will reincarnate in a form that will teach the dharma even more excellently than the seventh Dalai Lama, Kalsang Gyatso, and as a person who will be even more skillful in politics than the fifth Dalai Lama, Ngawang Gyatso. None have surpassed them until now," said the Dalai Lama, "but when I return it will be in a form that embodies the twin excellences of those great Dalai Lamas. So do not worry." The Nechung Oracle then said to him, "I request you to do that."

The old monks at Drepung spoke much about this. They said that the new Dalai Lama was going to be very close to studious monks, because the Thirteenth had said he would come back in a form that was a greater scholar even than the Seventh and a greater politician than even the Fifth. When I arrived in Lhasa the new Dalai Lama was just a young boy studying his books and the older monks said again and again that the Dalai Lama was going to be close to us, and that we were very lucky. I always wondered what they were talking about, that he would be better than the Seventh as a scholar. But now, having seen what a glorious scholar the Fourteenth Dalai Lama has become, I see the point in what those old monks were trying to convey to us in those days. It was not something they made up; it was based on the prophecy of the Nechung Oracle.

Shortly before he died the Thirteenth Dalai Lama said in a new year's speech called "A Call for Unity" that he would only come back because he could not forsake the Tibetan state in its hour of need. "From a personal point of view," he said "I have no wish to return, but the intense requests of the Tibetan people prompt me to take another rebirth. But," he said, "if needed reforms are not implemented, it will surely come about that Tibetans will no longer have the right to use the property that is their own and to live in houses that are their own houses." He went on to say that if the Tibetan people did not prepare to repulse an impending invasion they would be doomed. He spoke with a prescience that in hindsight is remarkable. But of course we Tibetans did not raise the army able to stop a future invasion. We did not follow his advice.

THE DALAI LAMA DIED on the last day of the month. The Nechung Oracle was consulted on the second day of the month following, and he said that the Dalai Lama had died because his government had not implemented his reforms. The Nechung Oracle also said, "I am not able to take on responsibility for the affairs of government any longer. The future government of Tibet will be sliced with a knife. The property of Tibetans will no longer be theirs to use and power over their affairs will no longer be in their hands. The rule of birds will become the rule of Tibet." The old monks told me this, and I wondered what the rule of birds was. They said that it was the rule of the assembly; that if one in a group of birds stepped out of line the other birds immediately turned on it and killed it. "A government like that is what the Nechung prophesy is referring to," they said—a rule so despotic that the moment one person breaks rank the knife immediately descends on him to destroy him.

After that last prophecy, the Nechung Oracle fell silent and rarely spoke again until the present Dalai Lama reappeared, reached his majority, and was given the reins of power. Until that time, Nechung had nothing to say to help guide the affairs of state. When he was consulted on political matters he would simply say, "I do not know," and would only speak if he felt concern for the health of the young Dalai Lama or for the well-being of Buddhism. He suggested a number of prayers for these purposes.

Because the oracle would not advise the government during this period, some high officials tried to get around the problem by approaching the oracle through the Drepung central authority. When one abbot asked a question of a political nature, however, the oracle abruptly told him to shut up. The other abbots remarked on this, and talked about how the Nechung Oracle was no longer helping to guide the affairs of the state; they said that it did not augur well for Tibet.

MY POINT about the governing of Tibet in the period leading up to the Communist invasion is essentially this: even though the whole world was adapting to meet the challenges of modernity, the officials of the Tibetan government were stuck in old ways and did not change at all. For example, the Thirteenth Dalai Lama seems to have thought it would be a good idea to introduce the motor car to Lhasa, and to get the government aristocrats to ride in them rather than on horses. So he had some cars brought to Tibet, thinking that Tibetans would fall for them, and for a year or two the cars plied a road between the Norbulinka and the Potala. During that entire period not a single Tibetan thought, "I want to get one of these too." In the face of such a total lack of interest the Thirteenth put the cars in the garage and stopped using them. Over time, of course, the metal rusted, the fittings began to rot, and they fell into disrepair. Looking back, it is amazing how what Tibetans consider nowadays to be the special features of modernity were then considered totally irrelevant. Another example is aluminium pots: when they first came on the market in Lhasa, Tibetans said that one should not use them. "They are Lhalu's things. The ideas of Lhalu will spread if one uses those pots." This is what many people said during those days. Of course market forces were at work, and because aluminium pots are cheaper people bought them, but older people in particular would not let them in their houses for fear of contamination. They would not sell them either. They were set, like concrete, in old ideas and ways.

Consider the water supply to the Potala. It would not have been a great feat of engineering to devise a way to run pipes into the Potala, but no thought was given to the task. There was a spring behind the Potala, in Chakpori, and it was always from there that the horses and donkeys brought the water for the Dalai Lama and his entourage. The laying of pipes was always an alternative, but people stuck to the old ways.

The Dalai Lama's assistant, Kumbula, laid pipes from the Kyichu to supply water to the monks in the prayer festival, and everybody was amazed. They came to look at the pipes and admire them. They went to look at the place where the line started, fascinated by how water was made to go down the pipe. There was no electricity in those days, so the way they got the water to move down the pipe was by a water wheel powered by men who had to walk on it to keep it moving. Perhaps the pipe was not buried deep enough, because in the winter, during the prayer festival, it sometimes iced up and everybody would rush to put fires under the pipes. My feeling is that if it had been buried deeper the problem could have been overcome, because it is not that cold in Lhasa.

It would have been no problem to have piped water to Drepung, for example, because there were very good water sources above the monastery. Indeed, there is water all over the place up above Drepung. In fact it would have been no problem to have supplied water to the whole Lhasa region, but nobody had ever studied hydraulic engineering. No one was able to do it.

Not only was no attention paid to different technologies, the government paid no attention to the revolutionary events taking place in China. It went on as though nothing special was happening. Tibetans from the border regions in Amdo and Kham, of course, understood what was happening. Our people were visiting China to trade and they kept their ears open. They had more understanding of the dangers of communism and what it would mean for Tibet, but even though they made submissions to the government in Lhasa they were not heeded. The central government continually ignored requests for strong reinforcement of the borders and strong preparations for defense.

JUST BEFORE passing away, the Dalai Lama had fallen sick. After learning of his death, the Kashag said that they knew that the Dalai Lama was sick but had received no report on his condition, and they laid the blame for this at the feet of Kumbula. Kumbula was very close to the Dalai Lama, and his work on behalf of His Holiness had made him very powerful. This had led to friction with some of the older aristocratic families, who now saw a chance to get back at him. "It was a terrible mistake," they said, "not to keep the Kashag informed of the health of the Dalai Lama, and it cannot be forgotten." They used this as an excuse to incarcerate him. They also summoned the Dalai Lama's doctor—the highest in the medical institute. "What medication did you give him?" they asked. He began to equivocate and said, "I do not know exactly what he was given because the Nechung Oracle was involved." This importance given to the Nechung Oracle was also a source of displeasure. The aristocrats and government officials disliked the Nechung Oracle because his predictions and observations about them had been particularly harsh. Eventually, this group penalized the doctor, and engineered the downfall of Kumbula and the Nechung Oracle.

Within a month of the Dalai Lama's death, Kumbula, a man of great importance and power while the Dalai lama was alive, a monk to whom one lowered one's head, was jailed, reviled, and exiled. It was a political reality playing itself out, no doubt, but from another point of view it was just individuals falling out with one another.

IN THE TIBETAN GOVERNMENT there was an intelligent and capable official named Tsipa Lungshar who had served the Dalai Lama and was close to him. He knew of the reforms the Dalai Lama wanted to implement and tried to ensure a continuation of the reform process after the Dalai Lama's death. He maneuvered himself into a position where more and more branches of government were on his side, but some officials still opposed him.

When Tsipa Lungshar was forging his alliance, there was an old man, the Kundeling Dzasa, whom Lungshar wanted to attract to his party. Kundeling was a heavyweight and Lungshar sent some of his associates to meet with him to see where he stood. The conversation was very oblique and Kundeling could sense that there was a hidden agenda. "It is a great pleasure to me that you have taken the time to visit," he told them. "I sense you have a purpose, and I have heard of a great purpose afoot. It is something I am...," he intimated, "a supporter of." Kundeling gained their confidence, drew them out with great skill, and finally asked them, "What exactly is the moving force behind all this?" Lungshar's associates now found themselves revealing their ultimate hopes, which included deposing the regent, Reting Rinpoche. Kundeling was opposed to such a course of action but did not let them know, and Lungshar's envoys left the meeting convinced that he was behind them. The moment they left, Kundeling sent a man straight to the regent's office disclosing their plan. Reting immediately arrested Tsipa Lungshar's entire party, but had they not disclosed their plan prematurely, there is a good likelihood that Lungshar would have succeeded.

Once Lungshar was imprisoned, an assembly was convened to bring charges against him. There was a long discussion and it was said that Lungshar was a reincarnation of an earlier minister Tashi who, it was recollected, had the tail of a goat. "Lungshar," they opined, "is this minister Tashi come back. He is without a doubt a demon."

So they said, and I myself did not doubt the matter when I was in Tibet. When I came to India I heard that Lungshar had planned to start a democratic assembly, and the source of the friction was located there. I never heard mention of this earlier in Tibet from anybody. Anyway, some members of the assembly said they should put out his eyes, some said that he should be executed, and some said that he should be given poison. Many favored this last option. Others said that it would be wrong to kill him—that the Dalai Lama had just passed away and it would hinder the identification of his reincarnation. Finally they all agreed he should not be killed but should be blinded. The decision was sent to Reting Rinpoche for ratification, but he said that as a monk he could not assent to it, and absented himself from the decision. His deputy assistant Yabzhi Lungdul signed the order; it was immediately carried out and Lungshar was exiled to Kongpo.

In this way the progress towards democracy was blocked. It was a political fight that should not have happened. There were not many fights like this in Tibet, but those that did occur were not resolved by laws which were just. During those times our laws did not always keep us on a path that was straight or true.

IT IS HARD TO CONVEY a balanced sense of old Tibet. There were terrible episodes like the Tsipa Lungshar affair, but when one thinks of a modern country nominally at peace, our Tibet of old was a place even more peaceful. Though India is at peace it has gigantic jails full of prisoners where hangings take place at regular intervals. There are so many crimes which carry a mandatory death penalty. In Tibetan jails there were not a lot of prisoners incarcerated for long periods. Even in the big jail beneath Namsezhag court there were only two or three prisoners being held in a few cells. In other Tibetan prisons too there were no more than a few cells. This is a very good sign, is it not? Murder occasioned tremendous attention. In the monastery, for example, if monks got into a fight and one was killed, it would cause a huge stir. "How could this have happened?" people would ask. In those days we Tibetans had no conception that such a terrible type of state as the modern state, such a terrifying country, could exist. We were not dominated by a job or career. Restraint and taming the rough side of a person were valued, work was defined by reasonable human need, and gratuitously disturbing one's fellow man was avoided. And when someone got steamed up over a political event we Tibetans would often refer to the Fifth Dalai Lama's political minister Desi Sangye Gyatso and say, "Flat-head Desi will take good care of the business of the bureaucrats, just pass me another glass of barley beer." Generally speaking, in the monasteries in Tibet it was an insult to say of a person that he was taking an active interest in power politics. You could not say that sort of thing as an insult to someone's face, it was too strong, and if you talked about another monk in that way it was the worst insult, suggesting unbridled self-interest.

WHEN I ARRIVED IN DREPUNG, Reting Rinpoche had given up the regency and gone into retreat at Reting Monastery. I never had the opportunity to meet him. There are a number of opinions about why Reting Rinpoche gave up the regency. Some say that his successor, Dalung-drak, was meant to be a temporary regent, and the regency was to revert back to Reting later. The idea seems to have been that Reting had asked for temporary help with the regency, and he would repay that help by taking office again at a later date. But there was a friction between Dalung-drak's people and Reting's people, and once the power of the regency was invested in the household of Dalung-drak, it did not feel inclined to give it back. The estates and business interests of Dalung-drak were located mainly in the north, near Reting Monastery, and the estates of the two houses often bordered each other. When Reting Rinpoche was regent his estate managers caused much trouble for the stewards of the Dalung-drak estates, and now the supporters of Dalung-drak began to envision a situation where they could take all of the Reting estates. The heart of the dispute, then, as I understand it, was between the stewards of the two rinpoches, and the two labrangs became infected with enmity towards each other. Another factor was that Reting Rinpoche was attracted to Nyingmapa doctrines and some parts of the Gelugpa establishment felt uneasy on this account. Slowly but surely all this enmity between the two groups spread into the government and led to a split in government loyalties.

When I arrived in Lhasa the Reting household and its retainers were famous. Though Dalung-drak was the official regent, Reting's household was still the richest, most powerful, and the most influential in the land. Some said that Reting Rinpoche's people controlled a division of the army, the Kunkar-wang, and that this division was not favorably disposed towards the government. There were rumors that this division was going through military exercises and preparing to mount a coup d'etat. With Dalung-drak in office, those of Reting Rinpoche's faction still working in government offices and so forth were not able to wield the same authority as they had before, and this was becoming unbearable to them. They sent back a stream of reports to Reting Rinpoche painting an ever blacker picture of the government and influenced him against it.

As Dalung-drak was getting stronger Reting Rinpoche's people appear to have sent letters to the Chinese Guomindang government asking for support. The request for help had to be sent via Chamdo, on the border of Kham. The head of the Chamdo government office read the contents of the letters and revealed them to the Kashag in Lhasa. When the Kashag saw that the letter carried the full seal of Reting Rinpoche, they were enraged.

The growing split between Reting Rinpoche's household and the government had festered for the best part of two years, and now it came to a head. The cabinet sent a high army official out to ask Reting to come to Lhasa, intimating it was for important talks, but not letting on that there was trouble. The official at the head of the army detachment sent to arrest him in his labrang was Surkhang. Reting Rinpoche had some very powerful bodyguards from a part of Kham close to Kongjo-rawa, and as one of them saw Surkhang's detachment coming he told Reting Rinpoche that he thought someone was coming to hurt him and he was going to mount a defense. "Nobody is coming to harm me," Reting Rinpoche said, "let them come in." The detachment stayed downstairs and Surkhang came up and spoke politely, asking Reting to come to Lhasa. Reting Rinpoche's special horse "Yudrug" (it was an imposing mount—pictures of it are still extant) began neighing loudly and making a commotion. It made the bodyguards nervous. "There is something wrong," they said to the Rinpoche, "please let us take the matter in hand." Again the Rinpoche refused to believe them and quickly prepared himself to follow Surkhang, showing a politeness appropriate to his rank. At that point one of the bodyguards, speaking in his local dialect, said to the Rinpoche directly, "I am going to kill Surkhang on the spot." The Rinpoche gave him a withering look. After that the Rinpoche left with the detachment of soldiers for Lhasa, and one group of soldiers remained at the monastery; the bodyguard was not able to inquire again for orders.

When word of the arrest reached Sera, monks from different houses rushed to block the road. Most headed towards Mangdu near the Kyichu River, but the detachment bringing him to Lhasa went via Phenpo-go-la. Since the main contingent of Sera monks had gone to block his entrance into Lhasa from a different direction, there was no fight. The detachment continued at a trot into the Potala and immediately incarcerated the Rinpoche.

That year, 1947, we monks were at the new year's prayer festival in Lhasa when word went around that Reting Rinpoche had been arrested. Word quickly spread and the following day Sera fighting monks prepared for battle by breaking into Sadutsang's house and raiding his armory. They headed down to Lhasa and there was a standoff between them and the Tibetan army. We monks had to return directly to our houses from the prayers and were not allowed to stay in Lhasa at this time. It was particularly difficult for Phukhang house monks because we had a dharma-patron relationship with Reting Rinpoche. For this reason, during this period of tension soldiers were stationed in our house to ensure we did not band together to fight. The moment prayers ended we had to go to our rooms and were not allowed out. If we had to go out to the toilet we were not allowed to go outside the perimeter as we usually did. We had to stay within sight of the house and quickly return. When the prayer festival ended we had to immediately return to Drepung.

Dalung-drak made a commendable effort to mediate when tension was at its height. When a battle with Sera was seemingly inevitable, Dalung-drak called together an assembly of important people, agents of labrangs, and heads of monasteries. They sent a delegation to Sera to say that if they refrained from fighting they would guarantee that Reting would not be harmed and that the grievances of Sera would be looked into. The assembly said that the release of Reting Rinpoche could be negotiated, and at the very least he could be released to a place in Lhasa where Sera monks could protect him. The head of Sera wanted to accept mediation and avoid a fight, but Pu Lama was dead-set against it. "In the old days," he said, "a Sera monk walked on the ridges of the mountains with his head held high, but nowadays he has to scurry along in the deep crevices of the valleys."

Had the mediation been accepted, there is no doubt that Sera would have become extremely famous and that Reting Rinpoche would have been released without harm. The wealthy members of the assembly behind the conciliation committee had pledged huge offerings to Sera if it would back down. I know this from my own relative Chandzo Rabti, who attended the meetings. "Dalung-drak made a sincere effort," he said to me later, "but the Sera authorities would not budge."

After the mediation failed, I began hearing the sound of bombs going off in the distance as a fight raged at Sera. The story making the rounds was that the Sera monks were using their tea churners as makeshift cannons! Monks like myself in Drepung were angry because Reting Rinpoche always had a soft spot for monks from the border regions. Border monks were not just in Drepung, remember, they were in Sera too, and we saw them as brothers. As we heard the sound of fighting off in the distance it was hard to restrain ourselves. On the other hand we did not like the idea of rebellion against the Tibetan government, so we were confused and depressed about the whole affair.

The main protagonists from the Reting side, the ones who fanned the flames of conflict and felt the most animosity towards the government, were Shide Nyungnay Lama and the younger Dzasa. Another of the leaders was Katub Tulku. People said that he mounted a horse and headed into battle, but then got stuck in the mud and was plucked off his horse without difficulty. I have no idea if that is true. During the battle itself one of the main people in the fight was Tsenya Nangpa. When defeat loomed large he escaped from the government forces and came to Drepung where he hid in Ngari house for a few days. He had the option of immediately fleeing through Tolung or Chusho, both routes were wide open for him, but instead he took the route via Ratsar cave. This, of course, took him to Chusang Ritro near Sera. Some old monks in Chusang recognized him, immediately sent a report to Lhasa, and a detachment was sent up to arrest him. People said later that it was the gods and dharma protectors that drew him back because he had an open road for escape and did not take it.

The aristocrat in charge of the battery that shelled Sera was Taring, a man with whom I came to have good relations in the 1960s when I became a teacher in a refugee school in Mussoorie, north India. He was the principal there. His sectarian affiliation was Nyingma and he said to me that the government had no doubt put him in charge of the shelling thinking he would be more than happy to destroy Sera, a famous Gelugpa monastery. "Otherwise why me," he asked, "of all people to put in charge of a battery?" It seems Taring did have some knowledge of artillery, but he said that when he was put in charge he thought, "If I destroy this monastery who is going to rebuild it? It has been here now more than three hundred years and if it is destroyed it will never be rebuilt—there is nobody who could rebuild such a complex institution. How much would it cost?" But there were troublemakers, though there were not that many of them, and they had to be confronted and stopped. "I thought it would not be a difficult task to flush them out in a day or so," he said. "So I ordered shelling to the sides and in front of the monastery, not on the buildings themselves. In other words, I mounted a siege, knowing that they would get tired in a few days. I showed them our fire power." He said that later, when decorations and presents were given out at the successful close of the operation, he was given nothing because the work that he had been entrusted with—the demolition of Sera—had not been done.

The monks said Sera was not shelled because the protectors of the monastery were in full force and the government could not get its bombs through. I myself thought that was true at the time, but now I realize it had nothing to do with that at all. After four or five days the word came that Sera had fallen and the head of the insurrection arrested. There was a considerable death toll on both sides, I believe.

SEE HOW MUCH TROUBLE came from what began as a fight between just a few people? The government did not want to destroy Sera, it just wanted to arrest the leaders of the revolt. But as trouble arose, that section of the monks moved strongly into positions of power and controlled the situation. Nothing good comes of situations controlled by such people. As we say in Tibet, when the water is turbulent the fish are not at peace. Many monks from Sera were thoughtful and knew the path of right and wrong but they had no power to influence events. Those arrogant monks who did not know that path were in power, and they led Sera to unhappiness. Had those with knowledge of right and wrong influenced events—those with any eye to the future and not stuck in the immediate present—the problem would have been resolved.

Is it not always this way, though, be it the monasteries or the state? In the monasteries the ones studying and trying to live a decent life do not involve themselves in political affairs. In Drepung there were certainly monks interested in their bellies and their bankbooks who only wanted power, who wanted to control the administration and get rich. Nothing could deflect them from that aim. From the outside they were monks, but inside their minds were untamed; they were in the monastery to fill their stomachs and wield power.

This is not unique to Tibet. Throughout the world we see that as trouble arises it throws up a less noble person who grabs power and authority, causing the situation to spiral out of control to the detriment of all. In the monasteries in Tibet when such people got into power—the so-called great lamas and gesheys—people as hard as rocks, whose minds were not tamed and who were ruled by their appetites, they caused untold damage. We used to say in the monasteries that power and authority should be invested in those who had tamed their minds and who knew the path of right and wrong. "If those who see reality are our guides we will not lose our way," we said. But it was not to be. Those dominated by their appetites led us into problems and strife.

AFTER THE DEFEAT OF SERA I lost all faith in Dalung-drak. It was excellent, of course, that he had tried to arrange mediation. And that there is strife in the world is normal. But after the battle was over and Reting Rinpoche had decisively lost, his people transported all of Reting Rinpoche's belongings to Lhasa and took them to Dalung-drak. I found that repulsive. I felt enraged at what was to me a blatant robbery. The fighting was not a problem, it came with the world and the pursuit of power, but to see Dalung-drak gobbling up the belongings of Reting Rinpoche was repulsive. Even to this day, I am afraid to say, I have a disgusting feeling about Dalung-drak.

In those days I openly criticized Dalung-drak, and one day my guru Gen Yaro called me aside. "You are wrong to say bad things about Dalung-drak," he said, and he told me this story from the time of the seventh-century Tibetan dharma-king Songtsen Gampo. There were two students from the country of Liyul who came to Lhasa. In Liyul they had meditated for a long time on Manjushri but they were cynical. Manjushri said to them that he saw no connection between them and him and told them to go instead to the Land of the Snow Mountains and meet an incarnation of Avalokiteshvara who was ruling there as king. "Meet with him," Manjushri told them. "He will have something for you to do." They set out, but everyone they talked to on the road from Liyul to Tibet said that Songtsen Gampo was a barbarian murderer. When they arrived at Dampag they saw a rope stretched across the river threaded with human heads. "What is that?" they asked. "It is a garland of the heads of people put to death under the laws of Songtsen Gampo," they were told. But this was only an appearance because of the dirt in their own minds. It was not really there.

Even though Manjushri himself had sent them on this journey, because of what they had seen and heard they began to feel that they did not care if they never met Songtsen Gampo. They just wanted to go back home to Liyul, and set out immediately on the return journey. The dharma-king knew with his clairvoyance what was happening and sent a messenger to find the two novice monks and tell them to return. The messenger found the monks and brought them into the king's presence. They told the king that they had come to visit him, but did not tell him all they had seen and heard. King Songtsen Gampo took off his hat and revealed to them Amitabha, the Buddha of Infinite Light, who was seated on the top of his head. "Recognize that Manjushri was right to say that you should come to me. I am not going to hurt you, I am going to help you. Now, what do you want?" The pair just stood there silently. Even when shown a vision of Amitabha, the symbolic head of the family of the Buddha of Compassion, Avalokiteshvara, they were unmoved. The king then said to them, "It does not matter that you do not believe this vision of Amitabha. Take these cloth bags and fill them with sand. Use these bags filled with sand as your pillows, go to sleep, and when you awake you will find that you are back home in Liyul." To their amazement, when they awoke in the morning they were back home, in the very cave in which they had earlier being doing their meditation on Manjushri. "How did this happen?" they thought. The bags they had used as pillows were full of gold.

"The point of this story," said Gen Yaro, "is that they got no higher spiritual attainment for all their work than producing bags of gold from the sand. They found nothing else of greater value. The bad words they heard, the fearful things they saw, these never occurred," said Gen Yaro, "they just appeared to them because of the dirt in their minds. Even when blessed with a vision of Amitabha they had no faith. So remember, it is the dirt in our own minds that causes us to see faults in others; do not be so quick to criticize Dalung-drak." My relative Chandzo Rabti also said I was wrong to think the government or Dalung-drak was at fault. "It happened because Sera held to an un-tenable position. Dalung-drak made a sincere attempt at mediation but they refused to budge," he said. But I could not get the picture of Dalung-drak accepting those loads of Reting Rinpoche's belongings out of my mind, and I could not feel faith in him.

THE YEAR OF THE SERA UPRISING was the year the Dalai Lama was scheduled to enter the monastic colleges, but the rebellion caused it to be put off until later. The ceremony was to take place during the prayer festival, but it was put off for eight or nine months. In preparation for the Dalai Lama's entry all the monasteries had been ordered to recite a new long-life prayer called *Phuntsog Tsempo*. We young monks were ordered to memorize it, but then, after Reting Rinpoche fell into disre-pute, Dalung-drak decreed that the recitation of that prayer was for-bidden. "There is the smell of the Nyingmapa about it," it was said, "so it is forbidden to recite it." We young monks had to learn a new one called *Mishig Tagden*. When we got to India as refugees it changed again. The later prayer was consigned to silence and the older one again resurrected.

There were people in the government who had sectarian bias. It was not that the government itself was biased in favor of a sect, but officials in the government worked to implement policy reflecting their own sectarian aims. In the *Phuntsog Tsempo* the tone was nonsectarian and they did not like it. A group of people with sectarian bias were the root of the problem. There were not many, but they stirred up sectar-ian feelings largely absent from the Tibetan population at large.

The Sera uprising was one of the most serious incidents, but prior to the Chinese Communist takeover this problem of sectarianism was endemic. In monasteries in Kham, in Amdo, and in central Tibet as well there were internecine fights. It seems, looking from this angle, that it happened in those places where the followers of the spirit Shugden were more active and numerous. The problems were more frequent and intractable there. In Drepung there was a body of opinion, sometimes voiced, that the outcome of following Shugden would be problems and disturbance, but I did not take much notice of it at that time. But nowadays, with the way things have come to pass, it is clear that indeed there was a truth in what those people were trying to convey.

9

DID MAO HEAR THOSE VOICES?

Not long after the Sera uprising the Communist Chinese began their invasion of the Tibetan border region. The Tsarom region of Kham is on the border, not far from where I was born. It is located on the Tibetan side of the border imposed on us after battles with the Chinese earlier in the century. Kongjo-rawa is on the Chinese side. The Tibetan army had made a defensive position right on the new Tibetan border in the late 1940s. There was a high pass there and the Tibetan government placed a large force on this pass with cannons and other armaments to block the Communist advance. The general sent from Lhasa and the governing officials who sent him probably had in mind that the central Tibetan region started on their side of that pass, so they decided to make a defense there, and not further down the Drichu River as military tactics would have dictated. The main defending force was camped on the Tsa-shog pass and the general himself camped back in Tsa-drayur. On the path up to the pass, coming from the central Tibetan side, was a monastery called Tsa-phutug. A detachment of backup troops was billeted there, and further back again along the path to central Tibet another detachment was billeted at Tsa-drayur.

The general of the Tibetan forces was named Top (or alternatively Tong) Mapon. According to some he was the manager of Phabonkha Rinpoche's labrang. If you stop to think about it, it was absurd for the Tibetan government to entrust the work of a general to the manager of a labrang. He would not have known the first thing about fighting— he would have been a businessman. Lhalu, the regional governor at

Chamdo, was probably responsible for the appointment. Thinking, perhaps, that there might be some money in the Tsarom posting, he passed it on to a friend. Once in the position, Top Mapon began to prance about as if he knew something about military affairs, but of course he knew nothing whatsoever about such things. He had the mind of a labrang agent, not the mind of a military leader, and was ignorant of how to send out reconnaissance, how to listen to spies, how to make real preparation. He was probably saying his prayers religiously. On the other side, you can imagine the level of Communist reconnaissance and intelligence. Top Mapon probably never considered the possibility that the Communists might come by a more difficult route over the mountains. Perhaps he was a spiritual person who had not met with those who act deviously.

The Tibetan army camped there in Tsarom on full alert for a couple of years. Traders from my part of Tibet came through Lhasa at that time, and I remember asking them what was happening back home. They said that up on the Tsa-shog pass the Tibetans were dug in. "They have dug foxholes up there in preparation. The preparations look good. They are ready to put up a good fight there, but I do not know whether the Communists are going to come up that way or some other way." I remember them saying that and I remember that there was a general lack of confidence in the central government being able to handle the military side of things. And indeed, even while the Tibetan army sat in its camp with eyes peeled, waiting for the Communists to advance to the Tsa-shog pass, the Chinese were making a long detour.

When you look back it is obvious. The army was drawn up at Tsarom to stop a further advance of the Communists who had overrun my part of Tibet further down the Drichu. As they advanced, there were furious battles in the Gye-tang region of Kham. I am not sure exactly which route they followed, but one morning dear old Top Mapon woke up with his Tibetan army and found himself surrounded.

You can imagine the lot of them all sleeping soundly through the night, with the sentries, if there were any posted at all, quite oblivious to the real danger of their position. They simply surrendered. The Communists said that if they laid down their weapons they could all go home or else join the army and fight with them. The Tibetans surrendered their weapons and left.

There was a soldier from that army detachment teaching music and dance in the same refugee school where I taught in Mussoorie in the 1960s. He told me that after they had surrendered and were fleeing, the villagers abused them unmercifully. "You have surrendered and run away without a shot being fired—you should be ashamed of yourselves!" Anger was running so high that no household along the path would give the fleeing soldiers food. "When we were going through the villages armed," he said, "Tibetans did not say such things, but when we were running away without our guns the people abused us for our shameful performance and wanted nothing to do with us. 'Soldiers? Hardly! You are naked of what makes a soldier!' they said. We were turned away from doors we knocked on asking for a bowl of tsampa. 'Do you think the work expected of a soldier is just the work we expect of our pigs?' they asked. 'Do you think it is our job to make sure that you stay fat and well? What were you doing out there, giving away your guns to the Chinese without firing a shot in defense of us?' They abused us to our faces," he said, "but we had nothing to reply."

After taking Tsa-drayur, the main body of the Chinese Communist army continued their advance, but a contingent was sent to clean out the two groups of Tibetan soldiers further up the pass. At Tsa-phutug the Chinese took the Tibetans by surprise. The back of the monastery wall was quite low, so at night the Communists put up ladders and climbed up on the roof, coming down suddenly on a few Tibetan soldiers sleeping there. They gave up their guns without a shot. The Communists waited until early morning and were watching from the roof as the soldiers entered their breakfast hall. When the soldiers had gathered for their tea, the Chinese opened fire, causing total panic and confusion. The Tibetans ran helter skelter, leaving the monastery and all their provisions in the hands of the Communists. There were probably five hundred Tibetan soldiers in Tsa-phutug that morning. I heard (to laughter, because we all thought that the whole debacle was a joke) that the entire Tibetan force was routed by as few as thirty Communists.

As for the remaining soldiers up on the Tsa-shog pass, when they heard what had happened some said they should make a run for it. Others said that since they were defending the government they had to do so until the end. Many of those who chose to fight did so until their deaths. But most of the soldiers fled in panic. They had no knowledge of tactics that trained soldiers use in battle, and they scattered in fear and confusion. How absurd to sit on the main path thinking that the Communists were going to walk down into their gun sights. It is beyond belief, when you think about it, the lack of military training, the absence of the preparations that make for a viable military force.

THE GOVERNMENT'S IDEA was to make a stand at Chamdo, a large town on the border between Kham and central Tibet, and they raised a large force and put an important aristocratic official in charge there. The earlier one had been the Chamdo Sangwang Chenpo, a man named Lhalu. The Tibetans prepared for battle, merged the different forces, and defined a coordinated strategy for all the forces operating in the area. They made something approximating real preparation for war but, if you can believe it, the time period for Lhalu to stay in his post expired right then, so according to established government procedure he was supposed to return to Lhasa right at that critical moment! Of course he did not want to stay in such a dangerous place, and would have been glad to leave immediately. The person they sent to replace him was named Ngabo, but then the government asked Lhalu to stay to share the position with Ngabo.

These two aristocrats had a force of ten or twenty thousand recruits that were no match for the Communists. Still, the Tibetan government put its faith in its aristocratic little fellows and its army of new recruits and was wary of the Khampas. The careful arrangements made by Lhalu for a unified front were disregarded by Ngabo since he had a personal dislike of Lhalu and was in a competition with him. Lhalu's arrangements were thrown out and morale was destroyed. With Kham on the verge of being totally lost to the Communists, the Khampa troops were ready to mount a strong defense. They had fought many times against the Communists and lost, but they still were confident that in this defense there was a chance of winning, since in earlier battles they had killed high ranking Chinese officers before retreating. But as the Khampa troops backed up from the invading Communists, fighting and retreating, Ngabo saw the Communists coming closer, burnt the Chamdo armory and beat a hasty retreat with a column of soldiers. Lhalu headed off first, with Ngabo hot on his heels. Chamdo fell to the Communists without a fight. It took the Communists more than a year of hard fighting to make their way through Kham and Amdo. They took Chamdo in a day with no trouble at all. Ngabo, the biggest general of them all, went down in a day without a fight. What a joke! A personal dispute between top generals and an incoherent military policy led to the debacle.

After burning the armory and making a run for it, Ngabo was caught by a fast-moving Chinese army patrol. As I think about the events of that time, and reflect on the fact that Ngabo was not criticized even though he actually burnt the Tibetan armory and ran off like a frightened hare, it seems to me the inescapable conclusion is that though Dalung-drak's government was still in power (it was just before the Dalai Lama took over the reins of government), it was the Dalai Lama himself who secretly told Ngabo to do it. Knowing that it was impossible, finally, to stop the Communists, the Dalai Lama with his all-seeing benevolence saw that to fight meant in the end only killing. The final outcome was inevitable. How could we ever have stopped such a hoard of people from overrunning us? We could have stopped them for a while, no doubt, made their advance more difficult, but the sheer size of the invasion would have overwhelmed us finally.

Dalung-drak's actions, though, are to be explained by ignorance and superstition. He knew something about Buddhism but was totally ignorant of military tactics and defense policy. He had no idea how bad the Communists actually were. He thought that in a fight the many big and little gods in Tibet would line up behind the Tibetans and make a final victory possible.

The Tibetan government should have acted to defend Chamdo before it fell. But it did not and instead of facing up to the fact that the army was incapable of fighting, it took the position that the fall of Chamdo was because of a lack of discipline and unity amongst the Khampa tribes. What a nonsensical thing to say: that the Khampa tribes lacked a sense of unity and did not fight.

After the fall of Chamdo, Khampas felt the cause was hopeless. Kham had been overrun; there were Chinese behind them and in front of them, and to fight on was to fight a hopeless cause. It was at this point that the idea of a battle to defend territory changed into the idea of guerilla war against an occupying force. The Khampa guerilla movement started from that time.

IT IS MY OPINION that had the central Tibetan government made consistent efforts to forge an alliance with countries such as America or India they would have helped Tibet. A Japanese man told me that during the war in Kham there were Japanese spies in eastern Tibet. I am sure they supplied intelligence reports on the Khampas, reports that they had stopped fighting and reports that the central Tibetan government was not supporting them. They must have reported that the government had decided to surrender and that sending any help would be fruitless. These Japanese reports, filtering back to western powers who had the resources and in some cases the motive to help, dissuaded them from intervening and led them to the conclusion that it was a lost cause from the start. The central Tibetan government, by not backing up the Khampa defense of the border regions, forsook its credibility with foreign governments. Foreign governments came to know that the government of Tibet did not have the stomach for a fight, not even the stomach to support those of its people who were fighting. This perception stopped them from giving armaments and other logistical support to Tibetans. India, in particular, became certain that she was not going to help. From this the later Indian position on Tibet was formulated and hardened. I understand the continual hesitation of India to see Tibet as a frontline state that it can defend from the rear to stem from this.

Tibet was lost because the central government took the unruly border Tibetans in Amdo and Kham to be sniping at China, goading her to respond with an invasion. If everyone just took it easy the problem would go away, they thought. They did not think of the Chinese Communists as bad. "They are human beings, after all," they said with compassion.

Too much belief in Buddhism and an inflated notion of their own country: that explains how they came to have such silly ideas. "They are human beings, after all, they are not going to do such horrible things as you say." Even as they sat there, with the words of the Thirteenth Dalai Lama still fresh on his document before them, they ignored reality.

Let us leave the Dalai Lama out of this. Apart from him it is clear that religious dignitaries entrusted with leadership were at fault. When you contemplate such affairs, it is clear that though the institution of Dalai Lama is a unique one of great importance to Tibetans, nevertheless the investing of power in religious dignitaries other than him is a fundamental flaw in the way political affairs were constituted in Tibet. It caused military and other political policies to be poorly thought out and implemented. Some might rise to the occasion, but Dalung-drak, who was in charge politically, was incapable of any policy which constituted a defense of the country and backed only policies which caused internal conflict.

WHEN THE COMMUNIST ARMY arrived on the borders of Tibet, Lhasa was abuzz with descriptions of the central Tibetan government's two new army divisions: the army of the cream and the army of the monks. The first was an army of ten or twenty thousand men called the Drumdag Magmi. This army was drawn from children of upper-strata families in Tibetan society. What the Tibetan government had in mind, I suppose, was the Communist rhetoric about overthrowing the rich and supporting the poor. They thought that if they raised an army from the wealthy families they would be motivated to fight off the Communist attack because they had more to lose. This army of rich children looked splendid in their uniforms but never learned how to fight. I myself saw a division of perhaps two hundred of them, looking splendid on their horses as they trooped by. They had regal blue uniforms, and I remember thinking, "How are the kids of upper-class families going to know the gutter tactics needed to win a fight?"

There were many who said that we were in the game at last, that we now would give the Chinese Communists a real fight with these boys of ours defending the homeland. These were the soldiers that were sent as reinforcements to Chamdo. In reality they did not have a chance. They had British rifles, not even automatics, in their hands while the Communists came at us armed with the latest weaponry. Many seasoned Khampas in Lhasa at that time said that the whole exercise was a joke and that the Drumdag Magmi would just be a millstone around the neck of the soldiers. "The Communists are already here," they said, "and that silly little army is meaningless. A surrender would be a more intelligent course of action in the circumstances." These Khampas were people who knew something about modern armaments, about what the Communists had and did not have, about the training needed in order to be able to put up a fight and have a chance of winning. The people from central Tibet knew nothing about such realities. They still thought that a battle was when a brave soldier engaged in ritual warfare with an opposing brave soldier.

The other army was conscripted from the monks at the rate of one monk for every two monastic houses. It was a force of a few hundred monks called the Monk Force. They marched here and there training, a sight which brought tears to the eyes of local Tibetans who said, "Now, indeed, Buddhism is in decline, because the monks have been made into an army." I remember that I too felt sad about monks being drafted to fight and kill, and thought it was a degeneration of Buddhism.

The story doing the rounds was that the Monk Force was going to defend Chamdo; it was certain they had supernatural power on their side because at that time Tibet was filled with a sound like a dragon roaring in the sky. But before the Monk Force arrived in Chamdo it had already fallen to the Communists. It might have been reasonable to have raised that division long before and trained them, but to throw some monks out there with guns in their hands and no training was ludicrous. By the time they approached Chamdo the battle was over and they were irrelevant, but they had no clear mandate to return. They were stuck out there in the hills with no lines of supply. When the Monk Force heard that the Communist army was advancing after the fall of Chamdo, they were very scared but they had to sit out along the road just waiting. They hung about there shooting wild animals for food. What else can you do in such circumstances except enjoy yourself to the extent you can, hunting deer to have something to eat? So here we are, then, with the monk division roaming the hills shooting up the Tibetan deer, and the army of the cream of central Tibetan youth trooping up and down in their splendid uniforms. I should probably leave it there, but I cannot resist telling another story about the Drumdag Magmi.

AFTER THE FALL OF CHAMDO the retreat of the Drumdag Magmi turned into a rout. They were scared the Communists were on their tails, but the central government had them regroup. They were going to throw this magnificent fighting force at the Chinese and they had it set up a defense about three days' ride from Lhasa at Lhari-gon. You only had to come down from the pass, cross the Konbopa pass, and you were in Lhasa.

The defensive position was on a high alpine meadow sloping up to the pass. Travelers customarily left the meadow to cross the pass early in the morning. The Tibetan army of green recruits camped out on the approach to the pass. Beyond the pass was a descent to another plain. Buglers were sent up to the top of the pass with an order to sound the alert if the lookouts spied a Chinese advance from the other side. The two buglers must have been scared to death.

Now, as you know, at the top of passes in Tibet travelers leave many prayers flags. These must have been fluttering away up at the top of the pass, and the buglers, seeing these from below, took them for the military flags of the Communist army, panicked, and started blowing their bugles and running for their lives. Down below in the meadow the aristocrat general in charge of the troops leapt up and was so shocked that he came running out of his tent with his breeches on back to front and inside out. The general was probably saying his prayers at the time. Unable to walk without falling flat, the general ripped off his trousers, jumped on a horse in his underwear, and galloped off wearing a big heavy cloak. The Tibetan army never advanced up to defend the Lharungpuk pass at all. They retreated from there to the north, at least that was the story making the rounds in those days, to the amusement of all.

I DO NOT WANT anybody to think that I am saying Tibetans are cowards. They are not; it is just that they lacked any coherent defense policy or modern military training. Their officers did not know how an officer leads in a battle. When a few soldiers met head on with a few Communists they would put up a fight. Otherwise it was a joke. They had modern weapons, modern communications, a real intelligence network, and proper lines of supply while we had none of these. The rout of the Tibetans was on this account, not because of cowardice.

The Thirteenth Dalai Lama had tried to implement a new defense policy and build up a modern army capable of repelling an invading force, but he was unable to carry out that reform. I see every day, here in Dharamsala, soldiers from the Indian army base engaged in real training. Our army in Tibet never trained like that. The leaders said their prayers and our soldiers spent their time patching their shoes and grinding tsampa.

AFTER THE FALL OF CHAMDO the Communist forces advanced on Lhasa. After I arrived in India as a refugee I met a man from Kongjo-rawa— a substantial trader who knew both Chinese and Hindi quite well. He was in Kham fighting the Communists when Chamdo fell and escaped by a southern route to India, I think via Pema-gon, arriving in India shortly after the fall of Chamdo. He took his family with him. When he arrived at the Indian border the authorities detained him and then quickly sent him down to be debriefed by an officer. He became an Indian spy whose mission was to contact an Englishman and an Indian who had been captured at the fall of Chamdo. Acting as a trader, he sold tobacco and cigarettes to the Communist officers at the prison where the two foreigners were kept, and used flattery, playing on Chinese ethnic conceit, to get access to the prisoners. The Britisher, according to this Khampa, communicated a code to take back to India. In further conversations with Communist officers he learned that they were not going to central Tibet but were advancing straight to the Indian border, "even if we have to burrow through mountains to make a quick path to it." Armed with this intelligence the spy headed straight back to India to tell the Indians what he had learned.

My point is that the advancing Communists did not intend to go straight to central Tibet; they were heading for the Indian border. That is what the spy was able to ascertain. Probably the Communists thought that Tibet was no problem: it was a small, undefended piece of territory and they could pluck it when they had time. Initially the real object of their aggression was the Indian subcontinent. If the subcontinent fell to them, Tibet would fall without any trouble at all.

LHASA WAS ABUZZ with rumors that the Chinese would be arriving tomorrow or the next day. The Gadong Oracle had already said that the reins of power should immediately be taken up by the Dalai Lama, and when the Dalai Lama consulted the Nechung Oracle to cross-check this communication from Gadong, the Nechung Oracle said that he had already given the same advice. The Gadong Oracle said unequivocally that Dalung-drak must immediately deliver over the reins of power, but Dalung-drak was not going to just leap to his feet and give away such power, was he? Great lama though he may have been, people who give up power that is in their hands are indeed a rare breed. But Dalung-drak had a special relation with the Gadong Oracle and a strong communication from that oracle in particular he could not regard lightly. He immediately went to the Dalai Lama and delivered the reins of power into his hand. I was there, amongst the crowd lining the road, when Dalung-drak went up for the transfer of power at an elaborate, auspicious ritual. It was a magnificent show.

I remember after that event I went up to the winter debate session. A month after that the Communists took Drumo, the main area on the Indo-Tibetan border which traders passed through on their way down to eastern India. They had made straight for there.

It was excellent that the reins of power were delivered to the Dalai Lama at that time. Had they not been, the strain on the fabric of Tibet would have been so great that Tibet would surely have disintegrated. When the Communists heard of the transfer of power they held back a little from what would have otherwise been a totally destructive policy. Ngabo was sent to China and for the first time the Chinese opened up a line to communicate with Tibetans. I think that their initial idea was to annihilate Tibet by force of arms without any communication at all. It was only after the Dalai Lama took office that they began to talk. Just before the Communists arrived in Lhasa there was great fear amongst the people. They finally arrived about three or four days after the winter debate and the prayer festivals were over.

When they first arrived, the Communists were well-disciplined and cut a striking figure. Many of us in Lhasa were surprised and said that they did not look like people who were going to hurt us. I think that I myself had that idea when they first came.

Slowly but surely more and more soldiers arrived. But even when there was a large number of them they made no attempt to interfere in the running of the Tibetan state. Sometimes they arrived in very large columns of more than a thousand. They were billeted in places that had been arranged in consultation with the government. Other than that the government just ignored them, and they, waiting until the foundation for their larger aim had been properly laid down, bided their time without trying to influence the region they were occupying. Of course they were invading and occupying a country, but we just saw people who looked grand and acted with a fine sense of discipline. They talked very well. "Religious freedom is a non-negotiable right of all, but reforms are needed," they said. "The master and the worker must be on an equal level in society; all the earlier faults must be rectified; the religious freedom and power of the Dalai Lama to rule must not be curtailed." It sounded good to us. Reforms were needed, we all knew, but we did not want to lose our religion. We were unsure. Those coming into Lhasa from China and Kham brought many reports that the Communists said religion was poison and that they destroyed statues, books, paintings, and places of worship. The reports influenced what people thought about the occupying Chinese. But we were not against them because what they said to our faces did have a nice sound to it, did it not?

The Communists really were very skillful when they first arrived. When the soldiers bought anything they were careful to pay the full price. The translators they had were intelligent in the way they approached us. And if you went to the army camp, they offered tea, joked with us, and showed kindly feelings to us. Those with firsthand knowledge of China and the border regions said the Communists were bad. Those living in Lhasa, on the other hand, were impressed by them and thought they could live with them.

The Communist army presence in Lhasa increased daily. When Lhasa was packed with Communist soldiers there was talk that a famous general was about to arrive. We all had to go out and line the road when he came. After his arrival the army made an offering of three white dayan to each monk at the prayer festival. Soldiers even watched the monks' houses during the time they were at the prayer festival. The general also made an offering to the three main monasteries, again, if I remember correctly, three white dayan to each monk. The general was a tall, imposing man. He came personally to make the offerings to each monastery. The offerings to the monasteries did not have any letter attached, but there was a red letter with each of the offerings at the prayer festival and on it was written, "We offer to you what we consider so highly that we were just about to use it ourselves." Most realized from that that the donors were not happy with us and that trouble was coming. But it was not possible to refuse the gift, and there were, of course, some who even as they read that said that the Communists were good, that they were offering with the very deepest religious motives.

People like us, from Kham and the other border regions, knew what was happening in our homelands and never believed that things were getting better. We knew they were going to hurt us in the end, that they were elaborately deceiving us. I, for example, was interested in the reforms that they talked about but knew that they wanted to destroy Buddhism totally, and I worried about a future in which people had no belief in Buddhism. But the people of central Tibet seemed totally oblivious to the reality that was unfolding around them. I suppose there were aristocrats who knew what was happening, but ordinary people seemed happy to remain ignorant of the tragedy unfolding about them, of the nature of the Communists who were smiling and treating them so well. They believed what they saw, and what they saw was pleasant enough.

It was when the Dalai Lama was finally overthrown and driven out of Tibet that these people, in grief at what had happened, became closer to that abiding faith in him, revealing an incredible faith in him as their only hope. That all would follow the Dalai Lama to the end was in us all, immovable. All, from the regions of eastern, central, and western Tibet, without exception, carried in our hearts the understanding that it would only be through following the Dalai Lama, doing what he felt in his heart was to be done, that we would be able to succeed. And indeed, it is that belief that has foiled the Chinese in their attempts, from 1951 on, to convert us to their version of liberation from bondage. It sustains us now when the Communist Chinese have finally showed their true face and turned on us to destroy us.

This abiding belief in the Dalai Lama which all Tibetans, from beggars to lords, have in their hearts was the final barricade against the Communist onslaught on Tibetans in the years from 1951. The Communist policy of peaceful liberation of Tibet was a very important divergence from the bloody campaigns they usually waged. At the time they were using peaceful means, had we not had this intractable belief that we must follow the Dalai Lama in our hearts, Tibetans might have been swayed. So you can see how this is the single most powerful, unifying factor amongst Tibetans.

THE COMMUNISTS set up an Uyon Lhenkhang (assembly of those acquitting themselves of their responsibilities) and opened it at a huge opening ceremony with elaborate preparations. Those of us from Kham and the border regions took the opening of this office as a terrible sign marking the beginning of the end. In fact, in the central Tibetan region even after this office was opened there was no attempt to implement policies that would have provoked immediate upheaval and destruction. Instead, the Uyon Lhenkhang co-opted five people from the Dalai Lama, five from Tashi-Lungpo, five from central Tibet, five from Kham, five from Amdo, representatives from other sects, and representatives from any group which understood itself as separate, and made a council with the Dalai Lama as president, and the Panchen Rinpoche as vice-president, as it were. The talk during those days was whether or not the Dalai Lama factions in the council would be able to withstand the machinations of the Panchen Rinpoche faction, which was more favorably disposed to the Communists, and whether they would work to undermine the hold the Dalai Lama had over the country. "It is going to be bad once they get in there," many people said to me. But once the council got going all the members unified behind the Dalai Lama. The council did not give any opportunity at all to the forces trying to undermine him. Had there been a faction in the council that had openly opposed the Dalai Lama there can be no doubt that the Communists would have immediately lined up behind it and used it as their surrogate. But none emerged. It was an exemplary show of unity which greatly pleased the people. In other regions of Tibet such a unified face was not shown in the Communist-constituted councils. There was factionalism, with the Communists choosing one of the factions as their surrogates. They would line up behind the factions and, using them as camouflage, would crush and totally dominate the region. It is one of the glories of central Tibet that the Communists were not able to divide them, that they retained a unity even in the face of their deep traditional divisions.

Now, as everyone knows, there are frictions between the people of central Tibet and the easterners from Kham and Amdo. There are old grudges. The Communists tried to use these divisions as a lever to pry us apart and destroy us. They built a reception center in Lhasa for the Khampas and sent out word that the Khampa population of Lhasa should come to the center for a handout—a "help while you are abroad" scheme. This caused us a great difficulty, I remember, and it led to a discussion in our house assembly. We were caught in a bad position whether or not we accepted, because amongst us were monks who were not Khampas. In our house there were people from central Tibet, so how could we take a gift for ourselves alone? Yet how could we refuse a gift from the powerful Communists who were telling us to accept? In the assembly (I think I was house guru at the time) there was a long discussion. "What I think we should do," I said "is all go to the Communists and accept their offering with an apparent good grace, and then bring back every penny we get from them to the house, pool it all, and divide it up equally between all members of the house without regard to their region."

The Communists said that to change Tibet from its old ways meant working gently, like shaping a piece of gold with many gentle blows. "It is not a simple task that will be quickly accomplished," they said. "To smash her hard would be to destroy a tiny thing. Reforms in Tibet have to be implemented gradually." The Communist plan was to first concentrate on the revolution in India, where, they informed us, just giving people money would make them rise in revolution from the shackles of their poverty. The Communists talked a great deal about first fomenting revolution in India during the earlier stage of their invasion of Tibet. At another stage they said the Communist army did not even need to go to India, all China needed to do was launch a war of dayan on the Indians and they would fall to the inexorable Communist advance. The Communists in Lhasa always boasted like that. And they had their set stories that they told over and over again. One was about the bull from the east and the yak from the west. The story said that in a trial of strength the eastern bull always won. Another was about the tree with three branches that topples over when its root is cut. This story meant that the minds of the Tibetan proletariat would change to a revolutionary consciousness and then the Dalai Lama and his two tutors would naturally be overthrown. Another story was about millions of red bugs covering a tree. When the tree was cut down they all died. That one meant that when the Dalai Lama died all the monks would die as well. "America is just a paper tiger," they told us. "When you get near it, you see it is hollow and unable to hurt you." They told us that Tibetans had been suffering terrible oppression from the domination of foreign imperialists! Now that last one really was silly. When they said that, every Tibetan was clear in their mind that the Chinese Communists were lying. We Tibetans had never suffered beneath the oppression of foreign imperialists. If we had a fault it was that we had kept everybody out. To hear them say Tibet had been under foreign oppression was like listening to someone lie to your face.

We also got to hear more about the tall army general who had made the offering of dayan to the monks. When he was in Lhasa you could see the troops admired him, and they said to us that when the Communist forces were under his command they never lost a battle. Later the story went around that when he was in Tibet this tall general said he would not be needed, that the pacification of Tibet would be no trouble at all. He said that he was going back to Mao to help him defeat Taiwan. Mao trusted him, loaded him up with all his best armaments and sent him off with lots of money to conquer Taiwan. When he got to the coast of Taiwan he went over to the Guomindang. Whether it is true I do not know, but I remember people told this story again and again during those days in Tibet.

SOME TIME AFTER the Chinese Communists arrived in Lhasa they convened a meeting that all the cadres in Lhasa had to attend. It was reported there that the Dalai Lama had asked the Communists to delay the strong implementation of their reform policies for six years. I did not have any personal acquaintances amongst the interpreters at the meeting, but those that did relayed what was said in the meeting to me. There was a long discussion about the six-year delay and concern that the relatives of the Dalai Lama were being sent abroad. There was speculation about exactly what he and his advisors had in mind. Since the Dalai Lama had requested the six-year delay and Mao had agreed to it, the lower cadres in Lhasa had no say in the matter, but still it was the topic of intense debate. And all the while the Communists in Lhasa insisted that they provide security cover to the Dalai Lama and made sure that wherever he went Communist bodyguards were with him. During this period the Dalai Lama's power stemmed from a special relationship, through letters, with Mao, who still hoped to cultivate him for a leadership role in his new China, a role even more central than that planned for the Panchen Lama. This meant that the cadres in the Tibetan region could not interfere with him.

ANOTHER UNDERCURRENT of their talk, an implicit discourse never quite on the surface, was that the Communists were going to help us Khampas get back at central Tibetans, who had always been looking down on us and oppressing us. It was never said openly, but there was always that implication in much of what they were saying. We Khampas though, had already experienced the reality of Communist rule firsthand, so we never trusted them. And the troubles between central and eastern Tibet had faded once the Dalai Lama took over the reins of power, so we were not much influenced. There were individuals who felt strong regional pulls and voiced their animosity, but amongst the population at large the regional animosity was not there in the measure the Chinese would have liked it to be, so that they were unable to exploit it to much advantage.

The Communists went into the villages and took aside the poor and asked them their main grievances, saying that they would try as hard as they could to help them. One section of the people said that whatever their problems they wanted to listen to the Dalai Lama and to follow his path to solve them. They asked the Communists to work in accord with the Dalai Lama's leadership. They said that they, themselves, did not know much about it. The Communists even gave money to villagers and tried to set them apart as poor peasants who would benefit specifically from the new regime, but they did not succeed in dividing the people at large, either in the towns or in the villages.

I had a long conversation with one villager who used to bring us dried dung for fuel, and he spoke about what had passed between him and one of the Communists. He told me that the Communists had told him he was being oppressed by the monks. "Your poverty and the hardship you face is because the monks oppress people like you." He said that he had replied that he had little relation with the monks. He said they are up there in the monasteries and he does his work in the fields. The years go by like that. "Every now and then," he said, "I take up a load of dung or firewood to sell to the monks and they pay me for it. Apart from that we live separate lives and there is no oppression that I have to report." He told me the Communists had also talked to him about Buddhism, telling him that there was no cause and effect across the barrier of death; no Buddha, no Dharma, and no Community. "If the Three Jewels exist, then where are they?" they asked. "Have you ever seen them?" The farmer replied that he had never seen them but they were there anyway. The Communists then asked him if he had ever seen anything accepting the offerings he made to the Three Jewels. He replied that he had not, but that was no different than the Communists in the army who got up every morning and shouted out the praises of Mao: "Did Mao hear those voices?"

THE LAST ATTEMPT to forge unity amongst Tibetans was the call for offerings of gold to make a special seat for the Dalai Lama. The Chinese were trying to drive a wedge into the Tibetan's unity by promoting the Panchen Rinpoche as an equal of the Dalai Lama. They insisted that the seats the two lamas sat on at functions should be the same height. The organization that was to become the Four Rivers and Six Mountains Resistance spread the word throughout all three regions of Tibet that gold was needed for a special throne, and donations poured in. Some people associated with the Dalai Lama said the idea should be shelved, but it was clear that they were not conveying the Dalai Lama's own words, just nervously saying what they thought he would say. The intention behind constructing the throne was the protection of the Dalai Lama and the budding organization behind it had approached the Nechung and Gadong Oracles, both of whom had given their blessing. The Four Rivers and Six Mountains Resistance suggested a focus for a real movement towards unity based on this attempt to build a new throne. It was a unity which was impossible to forge around the offices and officials of the government.

THE COMMUNISTS no doubt intended, from the very start, to conquer and colonize Tibet by force of arms, but as their first columns entered Lhasa we did not see their long-term aim. First they set up an army camp (Silimpu) not far from the Potala and stationed another detachment in Lhasa itself. They took over forty or more acres, and slowly expanded their camp, making it over time into a very big base. They put up secure iron fencing in front and had the protection of the river at their backs. From the start they were making preparations. Near their camp had been a small bridge and from then on nobody could use it.

They soon began another base near Dip-tsechog-ling. This was the biggest encampment to the south. To the east they had a smaller encampment at Lhasa Dronto-ling, and another, bigger, encampment near the Tibetan military installation at Trachu. They quietly set up the infrastructure to take over Lhasa. They also had a camp at Paru-khu and another near Drepung, not far from the Norbulinka. There had been a lot of trees there but they cut them down and stationed troops there too. They had forces placed strategically all around Lhasa, and at Tse-guntang they set up another encampment in support of their position at Dip-tsechog-ling. On the road towards Chang-tang they set up a big camp with offices and an assembly hall. They had a small military office around the back of the Ramoche temple and they built a big hospital off to the east of the Potala. The main military leadership was billeted at the Paru-khu encampment. In the end they had installations near every place that could possibly, in a battle, constitute a military threat. So it is clear that the idea from the start was to conquer Lhasa by force of arms when the preparations had been properly made.

Some did take notice of the implications of the Communist encampments and said that one day the Communists would take over Lhasa without any trouble, but the Tibetan government was blissfully ignorant of the real import of the military preparations being made in their capital city. They should, of course, have been very interested in what was going on, but they were not.

The Communists wove a perfect web around Lhasa and more experienced Khampas and Amdo-was said Lhasa was finished. "The government has let the Chinese make preparations so now they are unstoppable," they said. But the central Tibetan leadership could not see the reality in military terms. They thought since there had been no war for generations, military intervention was an impossibility. They lived happily in that silly belief even as military preparations were being made in front of their eyes. The Communists prepared to fight and the Tibetan government did not get ready, and even if they had it was already too late.

THE DALAI LAMA was scheduled to sit for his geshey degree at the prayer festival on the 13th of the first Tibetan month, in 1959. All Tibetans were happy at the thought, and indeed it was an auspicious occasion. There was nothing special scheduled for the 14th, after the Dalai Lama's examination was over, but on the 15th he was scheduled to come to the prayer festival assembly and gave his traditional religious discourse.

On the evening of the 14th we had no suspicions. We went to see how the arrangements had progressed and found that the table in front of the throne the Dalai Lama would sit on to give his traditional religious discourse was a silver one with beautiful decorations but that the seat was not the beautiful new one given by the Four Rivers and Six Mountains Resistance. But at that time on the 14th we just felt that the government was being petty. Later that evening the Dalai Lama's throne was taken away and another throne set up in its place for the Holder of the Throne of Ganden, who, we heard, would be giving the discourse in the place of the Dalai Lama. It was then that we began to suspect a Chinese plot. After talks in the houses at the monasteries, five monks from each house were sent to the central temple in Lhasa as guards for the Dalai Lama. The Dalai Lama did not come to the prayer festival on the 15th. On the 16th the Dalai Lama came to the temple for a short time but we were not allowed there. We noticed that the Communists were fortifying their positions with sandbags. They were getting ready for something, but we Tibetans just shouted and did not get ready at all.

Then the Communists invited the Dalai Lama to a performance in the main army camp. They first sent an invitation that was not quite proper, but a second invitation was issued later and was very carefully framed; it said that he should come but bring no guards, or anybody with guns. It was an unusual request and it alerted us all to danger. The Dalai Lama did not go around in those days like he does now. In those days he always had an armed guard of at least twenty officers, so Tibetans streamed to the Norbulinka in a frenzy to stop him from going. Some aristocrats, Surkhang and others, apologized to the Communist army leaders Tanh-wen and Tang-chow and said that the Tibetans were blocking the Dalai Lama from coming. The Chinese abused them, but the aristocrats said that the ceremony could go on after the Tibetans calmed down. Surkhang spoke very nicely, otherwise it is certain that he would have been arrested.

Later in India, Sharko Khen Rinpoche, an honorary abbot of Drepung who became my guru, told me that he had gone with another abbot to check arrangements at the army camp. He told me that there was nothing prepared there: no chairs, nothing at all. "It is certain that they were going to arrest the Dalai Lama and take him immediately to China. If they had not been able to do that they would have killed him," he said. Remember that the Dalai Lama's address was scheduled for the 15th of the first month. I think that part of the overall Communist plan was to start the battle then, when all the monks were assembled, and to kill the lot of them, the Dalai Lama included. We would have been an easy target and they could have wiped out the lot of us. But the Nechung Oracle said that the Dalai lama must not give his traditional discourse at the prayer festival on the 15th.

Pema Gyaltsen, the abbot of Drepung, told me this. He was there when the oracle spoke. Even though the oracle had said this before and the Dalai Lama must have known, it was the special descent of the oracle on that evening that dissuaded the Dalai Lama from going. That was why the throne was changed at the last minute.

Hemming in the venue where the Dalai Lama was scheduled to give his traditional discourse was the Samdup Potrang house and Pomdatsang house. They were both full of Chinese troops ready, according to rumors, with their guns. They could have killed us all. The path the Dalai Lama was to use to arrive was very narrow and he could not have escaped.

You should not think this is just unfounded fear. I was in Mongolia some years ago, and the Buddhists who invited me took me to a place where, they said, the Communists had convened a meeting of monks and dignitaries. The Communists opened fire on them there, at a huge prayer gathering as they were seated receiving offerings. Later this became a place of pilgrimage. I think the Communist troops in Lhasa intended to murder thousands of us in the same way. When I visited this site in Mongolia I remembered the preparations made for the 15th of that first Tibetan month, and I thought about how the Nechung Oracle had strived so hard to prevent it. I remembered that the Communists only began to ask the Dalai Lama to the ceremony in the army camp after his traditional discourse on the 15th had been aborted, and that surely it was their plan to arrest him and take him to China (the airport was just hours away and there were no soldiers to stop them) or to kill him once they had lured him there.

FROM 1951 TO 1959 the Chinese Communists quietly but purposefully laid down the military infrastructure for a toal takeover of Tibet. When these military preparations were complete there was no longer any value to them in maintaining the fiction of kindly intentions towards us. They wanted Tibet to themselves and were prepared to kill to get it. When the final battle for Tibet began, the Communists brought the troops manning smaller posts and encampments in central Lhasa and at Ramoche into the bigger camps. They had all their soldiers in their heavily fortified enclosures. The Tibetan government had one or two canons on the top of the Chakpori hill near the Potala, and there was also talk of canons in the Potala itself and in the Norbulinka, but I am not sure if there were any there.

His Holiness left for exile on the 8th of the 2nd Tibetan month, if I remember correctly. The Communist shelling began on the 11th. The bombardment began early, at about two in the morning. The Communists sent up flares and I could hear the sound of the shells landing. When I got up in the morning there was just one gun shelling us, from an emplacement a long way off. But we were told that the Communists had moved many canons to a place not far off from Drepung and had trained their barrels on us. They must have thought that we were going to start to fight. None of the canons were shelling Norbulinka. One of the guns was a big one mounted on a truck frame, and could lob shells for a long distance. As for the Tibetan battery on Chakpori, it got off a few rounds before it was blown away with a burst of artillery fire from the Communist compound at Dip-tsechog-ling. Immediately the Communist forces attacked the hill from the rear and took it. They had a perfect shot at the Norbulinka from there. In fact, the main shelling of the Norbulinka was from the Dip-tsechog-ling camp; the Silimpu camp did not have a good line of fire. Once they took the Chakpori hill, though, they poured in shells from there.

That morning I went out to make a smoke offering above Drepung. At first we could see only one gun, a long way off, shelling the Norbulinka, but we watched as the Communists slowly advanced. Before long they set up guns in the space between the two streams and started an incredible barrage. There were a hundred or more Communists with a large battery set up there. A truck came up bringing shells. Then, when the Norbulinka was badly damaged, the soldiers waiting in the encampment at Chang-tang road were sent into the battle and took over the whole of Lhasa. The Norbulinka had fallen and Lhasa was gone by about three o'clock in the afternoon. Tibetans were fleeing the city. The Communists had a spotter high up on the mountain above Drepung who was signalling to the batteries where to fire so they were able to direct their shells with great accuracy and cause havoc amongst the Tibetans.

The Communists shelled the Norbulinka because they thought that the Dalai Lama was there. Tibetans went to the Norbulinka to try to protect him. The Tibetan government did not order this, and the Tibetan troops were irrelevant in the fight. The Tibetan armory was in the hands of Samdup Potrang who had sold his house and many possessions to the Communists. Though not a real sympathizer in his heart, he must have felt that a policy of appeasement was the best way to deal with a difficult situation. He did not give out guns until the bombardment started. I saw Tibetans running about with boxes of ammunition and guns. Samdup Potrang gave only a hundred guns to the whole of Drepung. The houses got five or ten guns each plus about a hundred rounds of ammunition. Our house, which with two or three hundred monks was bigger, got eight guns, but some only got five guns for over a hundred people. It was absurd. The people trying to defend the Norbulinka (and do not forget that those were the really brave ones, the ones who had left Lhasa to mount the defense) were not given guns until the bombardment began.

There were a few soldiers in the Potala where there was also an armory. Perhaps a thousand Sera monks arrived there to try to arm themselves. That occasioned the barrage of the Potala that started in the early afternoon—that was why the Potala was shelled so badly. In the shelling of the Norbulinka the buildings were not flattened, though very badly damaged, but the trees were blown to smithereens. Many Tibetans died there.

By early evening the occupation of the Norbulinka was complete. When the Communists found that the Dalai Lama was not there they began looking for him. They hauled out all the monks and took a good look into their faces, even the dead ones. After that they realized he had fled, and informed their officials. A day or so later, planes arrived trying to spot him on his escape. So you can see how close it all was.

We said amongst ourselves that it would have taken a month of hard fighting for a Communist division to take a valley in Kham where people fought to the death, but all of Lhasa fell in less than a day.

When the Communists found that they had won so quickly they radioed the news, out and two army columns advancing towards Lhasa from the Chang-tang road side and from the road coming in through Kongpo quickly converged on Lhasa. While the battle began on the morning of the 11th day of the Tibetan month, it appears from these troop movements that the Communists were in fact planning to attack Lhasa on the 15th. The troops in Lhasa must have wanted to show that they could do the job themselves and so, without waiting for the divisions to arrive, opened up early. I was told that on the 16th a huge troop reinforcement arrived in Lhasa—so many trucks that the road was filled all the way from Drepung to the army camp. This was the division coming in from the Chang-tang road.

The division coming in through Kongpo was held up by the Four Rivers and Six Mountains Resistance forces led by the Amdowa Angdrub Gonpo Tashi and was not able to come in as fast as they planned. That division, coming in on the road from Kham, was finally able to get through to Lhasa on about the 20th. The Chang-tang division had itself broken into two: one part going straight on to Shigatse and the other coming down through Lhasa. They killed many scared and confused Tibetans who were running away from Lhasa and attempting to flee towards Lhoka. It was those soldiers of the Chang-tang division who killed the refugees. That the battle happened before the arrival of these troops was a stroke of luck (if you can call it that in the middle of such a disaster), because otherwise I think none of us would have been able to escape. And had the Dalai Lama not fled when he did there would have been no way out. Because the battle started a few days too early many of us were able to flee. Since the Chinese soldiers were all bunched up near the Norbulinka fighting, we all escaped as we wanted, something which would have been impossible if the big troop divisions had already arrived. Tibetans fled via Gyalrutang and Tilung. You could go up quite close to the battle, hear it raging, without a problem because all the Chinese troops were tied up there.

LIKE LHASA, Shigatse too quickly fell to the Chinese. Tibetans there were angry that some people in Panchen Rinpoche's labrang had been consorting with the Communists, because they were clear in their hearts that the Panchen Rinpoche himself was a Tibetan patriot. When the news came that Lhasa had fallen, the Communists said that the Dalai Lama had been captured. The people of Shigatse, led by the Panchen Rinpoche, were crestfallen. A monk fleeing Shigatse said to me that when the Panchen Rinpoche heard that the Dalai Lama had escaped he said, "Excellent. Now I will stay. I will remain and I will bear the horrors. It is good that the Dalai Lama has escaped." There was never a division between them, no matter how much the Communists try to make out that there was.

The Panchen Rinpoche was soon brought to Lhasa where he gave a talk in the central temple. "There is the body, speech and mind," he said. "Two are now in chains, but the third one is free and must be kept that way." He was using the Buddha as an analogy for the relationship between himself and the Dalai Lama. "The body, speech and mind of the Buddha are one. The Chinese have captured me—fettering my movements and ability to talk to you," he was saying, "but His Holiness the Dalai Lama, the mind and motivating force behind us is free in exile in India." When he said that the people realized that he was one with the Dalai Lama, and the people's faith became firm.

The Communists tried to make him sit on the Dalai Lama's throne and take his position but he refused, and that made a rift between them from the beginning. He was always behind the Tibetan people. How fine that there was always an indivisible unity between the Dalai Lama and the Panchen Rinpoche. The problem was between their labrangs. How fine that the Communists plucked him out from the stultifying shell of his household where his own views were hidden, and allowed him to be himself to the great benefit and joy of the Tibetan people.

10

LAST PILGRIMAGE AND EXILE

After making the morning smoke offerings on the mountain above Drepung, I remained there watching the Chinese troop movements until early in the afternoon. When I got back to Phukhang house I told the monks that defeat was inevitable, that we had no army to talk of and that those who were fighting were in a state of total confusion. "You should leave the monastery until the fighting stops," I said. "I have to remain to establish a presence in the house otherwise we will have no control at all over what happens, but you should leave."

At that point my intention was still to remain right in Phukhang house. When they all insisted that they were going to stay with me I told them to prepare themselves to leave on short notice. I had personal responsibility for a group of five and I was looking after the young Tagbar and Janglung Rinpoches. Later in the afternoon we heard that the Dalai Lama had already fled.

After that there was confusion. I decided that it would be safer to leave Drepung until the fighting stopped. Some young Phukhang monks said they were not going to leave; some said that they were; some had on lay clothes; some had on their monk's clothes. "Come if you want to come. If not, stay," I said. But none of us thought at that point that we were going to India, we just thought we were going to a place of safety for a while.

My group of students and I went up on Gadong Hill, where we were told that Sera monks were waiting out the shelling on the other side of the mountain behind Drepung. We decided we would go there too, and thought that we could come down in the night to get tsampa.

On the way we found the region full of monks, many just squatting down in their heavy outer garments. "You will be killed by artillery fire if you go down," they said.

We stayed the night in the area above Drepung and the next morning moved to Chushu. The sound of the shelling was still clear, as it had been during the night, and even before we could finish a quick meal of tea and tsampa we saw a truck coming towards us full of Chinese soldiers. We fled in confusion in the direction of Nyetang Norbugo. There one of my students, Yaro-wa Changchub Chophel, said he was going no further. "I am going back," he said. "Fine," I replied, "we will probably go on a pilgrimage to India. But be sure to pick up our portion of the offerings at Drepung. Keep them safe for us." After Yaro-wa left I asked the others in my party what they wanted to do and they said they wanted to stay with me. Since there was now somebody to look after our affairs at Drepung we felt easier about leaving.

In the middle of that night, Chinese soldiers arrived again and I said to my students that the two young rinpoches and I would have to flee. We packed up the few things we had and made our escape in the night through Nyetang, making it as far as Chedeshu, where we stayed in the temple of the earlier Dalai Lama, Thubten Gyatso. From there we made our way to the Yarlung valley.

THE YOUNGER OF THE RINPOCHES had a bundle of large-denomination notes that he planned to use on the path to buy provisions. He first put the bundle in his prayer book, which he wrapped in cloth, but as many people approached the rinpoche for blessings and offered scarfs to him on the path, he transferred the money from the book to the scarfs and then he gave the scarves to me to carry. When we arrived at Riwoche, we went to pay homage in the Maitreya chapel that is two or three stories high and threw up our scarfs to greet the great Maitreya.

A day or so later the rinpoche was looking for his money. "Have you got that bundle of big notes?" he asked me. "Where did you put them?" I asked. "I wrapped them in the scarfs," he said. I soon realized what had happened, that all the money had fallen on the floor of the chapel and I had lost it all. There was no way to go back since the Maitreya statue was nearly a day's ride back towards Lhasa. I was devastated. There were already seven of us in our party, students and teachers, and now we had no money to pay for our provisions on the path. That whole night I was so upset I could not sleep.

FROM RIWOCHE, halfway up the mountain to the pass was a monastery with a profound statue of the Indian saint Jowo-je Atisha that had been made at the time of Atisha himself. There are many legends associated with this statue, and I remember how still and silent it was and how we cried. There was nothing we could do.

We went on from there, up and down ridges, until we came to Yarlung Castle where the Four Rivers and Six Mountains Resistance had its main headquarters. For a while we stayed in a protector chapel in a village across from the castle. We needed to get a pass from the Resistance so we would be able to get to the border unhindered, but they did not want to give it to us. "You have a lot of students with you," they said. "They should come into the Resistance and fight." "I cannot order my students to do that," I replied. "If they wanted to I would be happy enough, but I have talked to them about it, and they do not want to join."

One day when I went back to the Resistance office to try to get a pass, an important looking lama or geshey was deep in conversation with the leaders. I was outside the office but I could see they were nodding respectfully to him and agreeing with all he said. I wondered what he was talking about and thought he must be an elder, distinguished monk. Then I caught the drift of his conversation. He was saying that the resistance movement was a movement for the protection of Buddhism and that if a soldier was able to kill one Communist it would be a great virtue; no nonvirtue was attached to such acts. "The more Communists you kill the better," he was saying. "It is your responsibility to slaughter as many as them as possible." I was shocked. Here was a noble religious figure saying such things, and he was not just talking as an ordinary man; he was talking with the authority of a religious figure, someone that was listened to and respected in our society.

I wondered who this was and waited until he came outside. He was wearing a chuba and looking very grand with his two servants. I was told he was Ganden Phara Rinpoche, a monk known for his knowledge of Buddhism and skill in debate. He was famous for having stood up and conducted a very skillful debate with the Dalai Lama when the Dalai Lama was sitting for his examination at the main temple in Lhasa. How could it be, I thought, that one with such knowledge of the Buddhist texts would say such things—that there is no bad karma from killing a Communist?

I did not go to pay my respects to him because to say that there is no wrong in killing another being is a shocking statement, particularly when it is made from a Buddhist teacher to a faithful listener, by one famous for his knowledge of Buddhism. That lama looked so fine as he walked away, but I remember thinking these lamas are not worthy of our faith if they say such gross things to the people. It was a revolting thing to say and I returned from the office with a sad feeling in my heart.

WHILE WE WAITED for our passes we decided to go on a pilgrimage to the statues, books, and stupas around Tsedang. We then continued our pilgrimage up the Yarlung valley to see the Tagchen Bumba. On our way back down we visited the Rechung and Miri caves, and a *shedra* (a monastic place of learning) near Tsedang. There were many caves there and a special place where the hat of Padma-sambhava was still to be seen. While we were there on our pilgrimage, looking down into the valley, we saw the Communist planes arrive. We had intended to go on to Tradrug and the statue of Tara that could speak to the faithful, but the planes were circling the area dropping bombs.

The Communist troops had advanced as far as Tsona Gompo-ri and been surrounded there by the Tibetan resistance. On the other side of the pass from where we were, the Communists had bombed a nunnery and it was in flames. The smoke was rising up into the sky. The Communist soldiers trapped on Tsona Gompo-ri were fighting fiercely. You could hear the sound of the guns: the Communist guns had a staccato sound and the guns of the resistance were like little bombs going off at intervals. After the plane had dropped its load of bombs we watched the Communists making a break through the resistance lines, but even though there was fierce fighting we did not feel particularly scared.

As we descended from the *shedra*, a crow suddenly landed in front of us and gave a loud call. I thought this was strange. We went down a little further and again the crow landed in front of us and again gave a loud "caw." We threw some blessed seeds to the crow and it ate a few, but again landed and started cawing, making a terrible noise and leading us to think that it was a sign. "We must take note where it lands," I said, "and where it flies off to because it is probably trying to help us." Even as we watched it, without going to the left or the right, it flew from us in an unwavering line straight towards the Indian border. It was then we all knew we had to flee to India as quickly as possible.

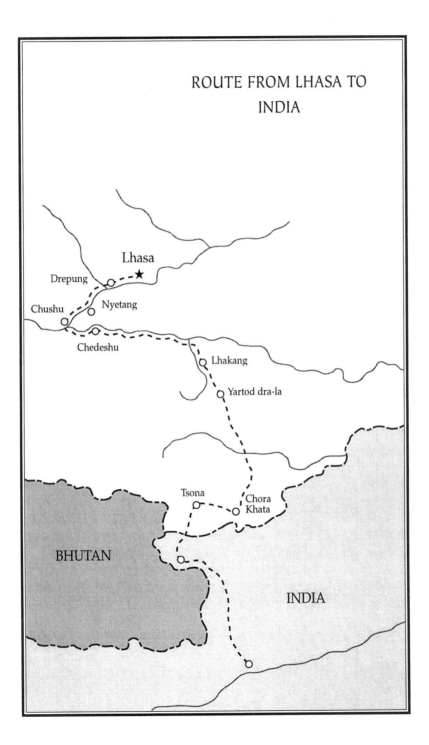

ROUTE FROM LHASA TO
INDIA

Lhasa

Drepung

Chushu   Nyetang

Chedeshu

Lhakang

Yartod dra-la

Tsona   Chora
            Khata

BHUTAN

INDIA

AS WE HURRIED BACK across the plain, Resistance soldiers appeared out of nowhere. "Where have you come from?" we asked them. "We have just come from Tsona," they said, "where we were dug in. Let us come with you. We will go wherever you are going." "Don't be absurd," I replied, "how can we tell soldiers where to go? You are going to have to find your own way. This area is deserted so you can chose your direction and go where you want."

Samlu house of Drepung Gomang had an estate near Tsedang where we stayed for a while. When we went down to the manager's office we found he had already fled, and his belongings were strewn all over. The people there said that we should leave immediately because the Communists were just about to arrive. We left in such a great rush we were unable to see the Tara statue or visit any of the other monasteries. All the Resistance fighters were in full retreat back to their headquarters near the Yarlung Castle and we went with them, heading back as fast as we could go.

Two studious monks had arrived at our camp after us and did not accompany us on our pilgrimage to the holy places of the Tsedang region. When we arrived back they had already left for India and left us a message saying that the fighting between the Resistance and the advancing Communists had heated up, and they advised us to get out as quickly as we could while we still had the opportunity.

On our way back to Yarlung Castle I met a squinty man from our part of Kham carrying a rifle. "Where are you going?" I asked him. "I am going down to fight the Communists and stop their advance," he replied. I told him there was not a chance in the world but he headed off anyway. A bit later I met a Phukhang monk who had joined the Resistance and been wounded. I saw him being taken away from the field of action strapped to a horse; I wanted to help him but could do nothing except say "take care of yourself." Before leaving Drepung I had thought those who left before us to fight would be able to help us when we came through, but I saw that they could not help us and I could do nothing for them either. I had placed great hope in the Khampa soldiers, but I remember thinking that they were not being particularly intelligent.

At the Yarlung Castle, the Resistance had dismantled their office and were carrying everything off in full retreat. We packed up in haste and headed off as well, traveling into the night until we reached the head of the Yarlung valley where we stayed with a family. It was very cold and we did not have any proper bedding, so in the dark I put on whatever was at hand, trying to keep warm. When I woke up early in the morning and lit a lamp I found that I had wrapped myself up in women's underwear. This caused a chuckle amongst us. Before dawn we had to set off again and I headed straight out of the house towards a wide opening I saw stretching out in the darkness. Thinking it was the path, I went straight out and walked right into a freezing stream of water and was soaked to the skin. Can you believe it? There was no time to rest or change my clothes, I just backed out and headed off into the night, feeling absurd and with my teeth chattering. It was cold and after a while ice formed on my clothes, but I kept going in fear of the advancing Communists. When the sun came up we stopped to rest and have tea and let our horses and pack animals graze. People were rushing by us—some people on foot, the Resistance fighters riding on their horses—we were all rushing off in a mass together, in full retreat.

THE OLDEST MEMBER of our party—Tagbar Rinpoche's teacher, Gen Puching—had a horse but he walking beside it because he had never learned to ride and was scared of horses. Gen Puching told his student (an older monk than me) that he was so tired he did not want to go on any further so this monk came to me and asked me to talk to Gen Puching and try to dissuade him from his plan of finding a little retreat in the mountains and staying there. I agreed and dropped back to walk along beside Gen Puching, at the back of the group. At first he did not say anything, but after a while he said he did not feel he could go on. I pretended not to hear. He was insistent so I allowed myself to get a bit angry. "You are a big geshey," I said, "so you should have gone into retreat earlier, when there was peace, not now when the Communists are chasing us with guns. You are talking nonsense about finding a retreat when there are Communists running all over the place shooting people. Now get on the horse and stop acting like a baby." He was very hesitant but finally climbed up on his horse and I got one of his students to lead it by the reins. When we had surmounted the pass and got down to the plain I did something wicked. I told the student to pass the reins up to the geshey and then I gave the horse a mighty slap on its rear and sent it galloping off across the ground with the geshey crouched down on its back, his hands around its neck, crying out in fear! It was not long, though, before the geshey found out that if you got up on a horse you did not necessarily fall off. He became confident and soon rode along quite nicely indeed. "Thanks,

Gen-la," he said to me, "this definitely beats walking." "Yes," I said, "and strange is it not that people do not fall off like they thought they might...?" "Hmm...," he said. By the time we got up onto higher ground (it was midday by then if I remember) he was bobbing along with a certain look about him, getting into his new role as a horseman.

We stayed for a day in a village a short distance from Yarlung Dargayling. In the evening I went to investigate the monastery and found it full of people. Many Resistance officers were there and a lama was distributing fried bread to people. One of the people helping was Chomo-la—the man I had nearly taken to court over the unpaid debt while I was house guru—but we did not show we recognized each other. He gave me a pile of food which I accepted with grace and then went back to our camp and said to Puching, "Next morning we are heading out of camp early and we are riding horses. No more getting tired because of walking and saying that we are going to give up the escape." "Hmm...," he said.

We started out early and took the path going up to the Yartodrag pass. Above the monastery at a fork in the path, where one path went to Nye and the other to Tsedang, we met an older monk named Gato from Tsokang house. He was in Resistance uniform and carrying a gun, and was officiously stopping people from proceeding further. "Nobody allowed to go further on the path!" he was saying. "No entrance above this point—everyone has to stay here!" His job was to protect high Resistance leaders. I had a knitted hat which I pulled down over my face and went up to him as though I did know who he was. "No entrance beyond this point—everyone has to stay put here...," he was shouting. He was the real policeman, totally into his new power. When I got up next to him I pulled off my hat and said, with feigned surprise, "My god! It's Gen Gato!" He was a few classes above me and was terribly embarrassed by my presence. There he was, a soldier carrying a gun, and yet an older monk. He was so embarrassed he shut up immediately and turned his face away. Our party then went past him as he said, "Be sure to go towards the east because the Communists are already at Tsona. It is very dangerous there."

FROM THE PASS AT YARTODRAG, we went down a path with many many switchbacks. We could see, not far off in the distance, a man on horseback with many mounted soldiers. These were the government troops that had escorted the Dalai Lama when he had fled, now returning from the border. There were thirty or forty of them and in front of us and off to the east we saw another group of eight or nine people with a grand looking man—probably a lama, I thought—riding horses as well. When the groups met, the soldiers got down from their horses, prostrated, and went up to this grand-looking man for a blessing. I remember thinking that he must be a very high lama. One of the monks in our party, Gen Punde, went over and I saw him prostrating and going for a blessing. When he came back he said, "Are you not going to go?" "Who is it?" I asked. "It's Song Rinpoche," he said, so I immediately set off to get his blessing. As I got closer and could see the imposing figure of the Rinpoche more clearly, I found that he had exchanged his monk's clothes for a fine chuba with the fleece turned inside. He looked exactly like an army leader or a big trader, and had a pistol in a holster tied onto his belt, a rifle slung over his shoulder, and a bandolier of bullets alongside his reliquary box. Four or five of his students traveling alongside him were carrying guns as well. I stopped. "Why would a rinpoche dress up and act like that?" I thought. It was a dangerous moment, no doubt, but there was no reason for him to be dressed like that and to be carrying a gun as well. I went back to our party and when I was asked if I had got a blessing, I said no. "Why not?" they asked. "Why should I go for a blessing to a man who has his reliquary box on a gun belt? The Dalai Lama dressed up in lay clothes so that he would not be recognized while he was escaping," I said, "but what is the need for this lama to be traveling in that sumptuous chuba?" "You have a horrible view," they said, "and you should not think that way. There are times when extreme strategies are necessary and you should not think in such a negative way about the lamas." "That may well be," I replied, "but I am not going to get his blessing." It was from that time that my admiration for Song Rinpoche shrivelled. I never much cared what he did from then on.

WE DESCENDED from the pass onto a meadow where we found a few walls for shelter, made tea, and camped for the night. The dried out droppings of the sheep and goats that grazed there had made a flat carpet all around. We all felt toasty warm and were sleeping very well, not noticing that our campfire had spread underground, into the dry dung. I remember feeling wonderfully warm and then slowly beginning to think that somehow it was getting uncomfortably hot. I wondered what it was and when I roused myself to see what was happening, I found that my pillow and boots were burning! I leapt up and moved away very quickly, but the next morning I found that half of one of my boots had been totally burned away and my hat and some other things had been burned as well. The others had not lost anything. What was I going to do? I did not have any other shoes to wear so I set out with my one good shoe and the other flapping, having a terrible time. Halfway up to the next pass I met a villager who asked me why I was walking without proper shoes, and gave me a pair of very comfortable leather-soled boots when he found out what had happened.

ON THE OTHER SIDE of the pass in the valley was Chenye Monastery, which earlier had been the seat of some of the great gurus of the Kadampa sect. Chenye means "Right Eye," and in that monastery was said to be found the right eye of a Buddha. In the chapels were beautifully made statues of Maitreya, lovingly cared for through the centuries, and there were twenty or so Kadampa stupas, each the size of a human being, and a very special library. We did not stay there long, but I remember that the old monks in Chenye had robes like the monks who looked after the chapels and statues in Drepung—so coated with butter fat as to be unwashable—the robes of those in the monastery who drifted into the ranks of the fighting monks. "Have you heard anything about Dedrub Rinpoche?" they asked me. "What has happened to him?" "I do not know," I said. "Has he run away?" "I do not think he has yet," I replied. "In his three previous incarnations, Dedrub Rinpoche came to our monastery and worked hard for us," they said, "gracing our assembly with large offerings which showed he liked us, and making big offerings to all the monks here. We have worked ourselves to the bone for this present incarnation. The whole monastery has worked with the hope that Dedrub Rinpoche will come. We worked so hard," they said, echoing Communist propaganda, "that we skinned ourselves alive to be able to see him, but he has not come." They did not offer us any tea, we had to brew our own, and I felt sad thinking that here the Communists had found a field for the plants they wanted to sow, here in the amazing beauty and transcendent symbols of the Kadampa sect, in the minds of these bitter monks. My mind was overcome with sadness as I listened to them and reflected on the fact that these were people ready to rise up and denounce their rinpoche in a public meeting, to humiliate him and spit on him. They would have been ready to distinguish themselves at such a task I was sure. Whether they did humiliate Dedrub Rinpoche in a public meeting I do not know, but they were ready and prepared to do so. Recently here in India I inquired of some people who visited Tibet whether Chenye Monastery was still standing, but I have not been able to find out.

AFTER OUR CONVERSATION with the old monks we decided not to spend the night there, but to immediately move on. We were invited to stay in the private chapel in the house of a wealthy family not far off who gave us tea and fried bread and said that we were welcome to stay as long as we wished—"Two, three days, we will be honored to have you," they said. "All we have we have given to the Four Rivers and Six Mountains Resistance movement. We too are about to flee. The country is finished; the Four Rivers and Six Mountains Resistance movement has mounted as much of a rear-guard action as they can, but now it is over." "You are right," I said sadly, "you should escape now while you still can."

We stayed with them for a day and then went on to a village in the valley opposite Nye-grio Monastery. A group from the Resistance was camped there and we had to get another pass from them to continue. They kept telling us to come back the next day. When I got back from the office on the fourth day, again unable to get a clearance, my students were in a very anxious state. A message had come from Ludrub Rinpoche. He was staying in a monastery further up the valley and he said that the Communists had taken Tsona. There was a statue of Mahakala in the monastery where Ludrub Rinpoche was staying and he had made a divination in front of it to decide on the best course of action. "We are leaving immediately for lower Nye," the message said, "and you should come with us." Everybody was very agitated: some were saying to go down to lower Nye, others were saying that we should go off in another direction. Changma Rinpoche had already left. I still had Tagbar and Janglung Rinpoches with me and I asked them to do divinations as well but one said to go in one direction and the other in the other. At that point the father of one of my students who was in the Resistance arrived at our camp and said it was excellent that we had come. He gave us some tsampa and butter and said that Angdrub Gompo Tashi, the leader and financier of the Resistance, was camped a little lower down and was getting ready to move the next morning. He was at Nye-tiley Monastery. "Stay with him and go wherever he goes," he told us. "The Resistance is fanned out around to make sure that he knows what the Communists are doing and to make sure he is safe. If you go anywhere else you will get caught. We Resistance fighters are heading down to Tsona. Stay with Angdrub because the Communists are all over the place." We felt reassured by this and went along the upper path over the pass to the camp of Angdrub. There were four or five hundred people there; we could see the encampment of the Resistance down below us as we crossed the pass.

I went ahead of the rinpoches and my other students to try to find a house for the night when I met a man I knew. "Do not stay right here," he said. "Retrace your steps a little and find a place to stay a bit closer to Tsona. Angdrub is probably going to be heading back in this direction when he breaks camp. If Tsona is blocked, there is a way through at a place called Jyura-kata; from there you will be able to cross a high pass over to Indian territory. The Namseling group went that way a few days ago and have made a trail up there through the deep snow. You will escape if you go that way. If you do not want to leave, then a bit further down there is a large stream near a hermitage; it is hidden so if you do stay there even when the Communists come they probably will not find you and you can wait it out until they go." He gave me excellent information and he said it was up to me to decide the best course of action. There was no way we were going to the hermitage, the Communists would eventually find us, so I looked for a house to stay in while we discussed our options. Some wealthy people wanted us to stay in their house because of the two rinpoches in our party. They knew that Angdrub was coming (his people could already be seen coming up by horse) and they knew that if we stayed, the army would not have the opportunity to requisition their house and food. They positively begged us to stay, ushering us into their lovely shrine room and urging us to stay as long as we wanted. They fed us very well, but early the next morning as the Resistance was moving up on the opposite side of the valley we moved on with them as well.

Groups of Resistance fighters were in front of us and groups of them behind, and we were already quite high up when some of them started returning back down the valley the way we had come. They rushed past us looking anxious, the ones who spoke saying that the Communists were already in Tsona so we must go back. We began rushing back down and stopped briefly to make tea near Jyura Monastery, in an area full of Resistance fighters. They were distributing fried bread, but we left immediately for the pass where we met six monks and lay people who had come straight from Kongjo-rawa, without even visiting Lhasa, to join the Resistance. They cried uncontrollably when they met with the rinpoches in our party and we too broke down and cried as we met them. What could we do? Each immediately offered us a dayan—they gave me five or six between them—and I said that we were going on ahead and that they should slowly follow on after us.

The village of Chora Khata was off by itself. There were no fields and the family houses, though attractive, were not the houses of the wealthy, but of small businesspeople. A trader invited us into his small house and we found a place to stay in the area in between his rooms, in a large hallway. We made the black tea offering there, we felt we had to at least do that much, and the husband and wife plied us with as much food and drink as we could eat. They put a veritable hill of dried meat in front of us. "Please eat," they said. "Eat as much as you will." We took them up on their offer and remained there until noon the next day.

Nearby was the estate of the Samdup Potrang. The owners had surrendered and gone over to the Communists so the Resistance fighters had looted the place. When we passed through it, the property was totally bare except for a few saucepans and cups lying here and there and some grain and tea. We took a saucepan, a nice Indian one for boiling tea, and perhaps two loads of grain; we loaded these on our pack animal and headed off. After a short while I got to thinking about what we had done. Nobody gave these things to us, I thought, so it was a perfect case of stealing. The others had been looting, true, but that was no reason for us to take them. "I just do not want to carry the saucepan any further," I said, "and I am not going to do so. If others want it, fine, let them take it, but I am not going to carry stolen goods any further." Another member of our extended party immediately said he would be happy to take it, and thanking me effusively he carried it away.

This part of the journey was the most dangerous; we were near death and were unsure whether the next day would be our last, but there we were having a last little steal before our final exit. I was shocked at myself and disturbed by the implications of such behavior. True the owners had fled, the belongings were strewn all over and would probably be ruined, but stealing, taking without permission what belonged to others, was there so clearly. That evening when I went to sleep, I remember that for some reason I felt very well; I felt happy and my mind experienced a very pleasant, relaxed feeling.

We were leisurely making the evening black tea offering when a man rushed in to say that the Communists were very close by. We did not believe him at first, but one of our party went off with him a ways and came running back to say it was true, that the sound of shooting was distinct, and that the Communists were now very close to us. I said that we must leave immediately. "We are very close to the Indian border. From here it is a quick one-day horse ride at the most," I said, "so we must make a run for it even if it seems impossible to get out." The man who had told us the Communists were near said there was a path coming up from Tsona and that if we followed it up we would be able to cross over a steep pass and into India. "To be so close and yet not to escape is silly," I said. "Let us make a run for it right now. If there is no means of escape, then we could properly think of our plight as karma, but to have the means of escape and yet not use it, that would just be silliness." We quickly packed up everything we had, loaded it up, and set off. Our informant had been given in marriage to a woman in Kham and had to wait for his wife and other family members to catch up with him, but he accompanied us until we were properly on the path up to the high pass and then went back. We continued on up the path through the night. He had told us that there were two different paths higher and said not to go to the right—it led to Tsona. The path to the left was the one to India.

After a while my leg began to hurt terribly. We were all scared, but I was finding it harder and harder to go on. Finally I could no longer bear it. One of my companions came and I used him as a crutch until we arrived higher up in a valley with nettle bushes, but then I just could not keep going any longer. "I have to stop," I said. "I will sleep for a while under some bushes." I told the others to keep going on ahead, thinking that if the Communists did come after us in the night they would keep to the path and not find me under the nettle bushes. I could then continue on later, when I felt able to do so. "You go on ahead," I told the others, but one student stayed close by me, hiding under some other bushes, and no matter how much I told him to go on he stayed. I lay there, not quite sleeping, for two or three hours and slowly felt my leg begin to get better. When it did not hurt anymore I got up, went over to my student and asked him, "Why did you not go on?" "I was waiting for you," he said. "It would not be right for you to be left alone, you should have someone to accompany you. Are you alright now?" he asked me. "Yes, I feel better now," I said. "Thank you." We both got ourselves staffs to feel the path in the dark and set off.

The rest of our party were camped in a cave near a goat and sheep enclosure further up towards the head of the valley. We ate and then slept so soundly there that we were still asleep even when the sun came up. When I awoke I lay there thinking how if my leg had stayed as it had been the night before, I would have been unable to escape from the Communists. I reflected on how I had prayed to the Three Jewels and how my leg had improved and I had been able to go on, and now, even as the sun was already climbing into the sky on a new day, I had a chance to escape. I felt peace and happiness.

We continued up the valley after breakfast. At about nine or ten in the morning as we were coming down from a ridge on the approach to the pass, we heard the whirring sound of a plane engine. The mounted Resistance fighters ahead of us on the path shouted out to us not to bunch up, to spread out along the path, because the plane had a gun. Luckily we were in the clouds at that height and the pilot could not see us, but we could hear the sound of the bullets. Tsona was very close, and there was intense fighting there; probably the plane was involved in that battle.

After we had gone down a short distance from the ridge, our path met with another path coming up from below. This was the path from Tsona to India via the very high Margo Pass—a pass open in summer and usually closed in winter that marked the border between India and Tibet. In earlier times both sides of the pass were Tibetan territory. Now the caves high up on the pass were used by Indian army patrols during the summer. In the winter the Indians went down to lower regions. The first Tibetan refugees to escape this way—the Namseling group—had cut a path through the winter snow and ice. The path was so narrow that they had walked through single file, and we had no choice except to follow the way they had gone. "On the other side nobody can get us," we said.

We were a motley collection. Most of our group did not stop and just kept on walking to the pass, but I was so tired I had to stop with a few of the others for a rest. Further up towards the pass, the Namseling party had dumped large amounts of their baggage: tea, tsampa, and all sorts of food, because they had had to throw away all but the absolute necessities in order to get over. Those who went ahead of us without stopping picked up the provisions, and by the time we got there, the next morning after a leisurely night's sleep, there was nothing left apart from empty dishes and the harnesses of pack animals.

The path cut through the high snow and ice banks was so narrow that the horses and our pack animal were in a single file, and we could not pass either on the left or right. The line of pack animals was moving slowly, sometimes stopping, and in the distance was the sound of a plane engine and the sound of bullets. With no place to run we could have been slaughtered like pigs, but the pilot could not see us because of the clouds and mist. We were lucky.

Just before the pass, the path widened out and we zigzagged past the pack animals to get ahead of them, only to be confronted with what seemed to be a sheer drop down. It was terrifyingly steep: if you slipped you fell until you landed in the valley far below. Most of the refugees were from villages and in front of us people inexperienced in handling pack animals and frightened by the height of the path were frozen with fear. An elderly lady was trying to lead her animal by a rope instead of letting it find its own way and as she held the rope up high the animal was not able to look down at the path in front and refused to budge. I had a staff with which I was able to cut out a solid footing near the stalled animal and said to her that she should just put the rope around the animal's neck and let it find its own way. I cut out a little place for us to stand to let the animals pass by. "The horse will slip if I do not lead it," she said. "It will slip if you keep holding it," I replied. Finally she let it go and the animals started off again, slowly finding their footing down the path. The yaks, of course, had no problem, they walked down with ease, but the horses and mules were scared. A tall man in a long, red chuba with four or five pack animals loaded with tsampa and other provisions was in trouble and I also helped him to get moving again. He was effusive in his thanks. "I will feed you all well when we get down to the valley," he said.

IT WAS A VERY STEEP DESCENT, made even more dangerous by the heavy snow, but we got down safely. Further down the trees began, the snow thinned out, and the path improved. When we arrived our food was nearly all gone but we had to stay there for about a week, in the upper reaches of the valley in a forested area where others were already camped waiting for papers to get into India.

The edible vegetables and leaves were soon all collected. I found some leaves off trees during this time so we were able to survive, but later arrivals faced great difficulty and had nothing to eat except the bark of the trees. Some tried to barter the precious things from their shrine rooms for tsampa, but there was no tsampa to be had, even for the price of a silver offering bowl. Many died: some from the strain of the escape, some from the difficulty of the high pass, and some from the hunger when they could find nothing at all to eat. Finally the papers came through and we were allowed to continue.

Further down we stayed for a night in an empty, run-down, wooden hut used by herders during the summer. We lit a fire and set out the pack animals to graze. Some were so famished they ate the leaves of the rhododendron bushes that grew in abundance in that area and immediately swelled up and died. I put the money I was carrying in a gap between the wooden logs of the wall of the hut to keep it safe, intending to take it with me the next day. The next morning we set out to cross a ridge and halfway to the top that I remembered I had forgotten to bring the money. Other refugees went inside the moment we left. I was not sure it was recoverable and it was a very long walk back so I just considered it gone. Earlier, if I had lost a hundred sangs I would have been so upset I could not sleep for a whole night, but I did not feel very upset at the loss of this pile of money. I had begun to think it was our karma—all the work we had put in to amass money and food, and the good fortune to be able to enjoy the fruits of our work, all this was now in the possession of the Communists, so there was no longer any purpose in struggling against the inevitability of it all.

Halfway up to the high pass we stopped and made tea. Not far from where we stopped we came across a man who had stopped for a rest and died. His head was on a small chest containing a bag full of dayan. There were bodies of people who had died from exhaustion and lack of food, bodies of dead pack animals, and other animals that were still alive but with terrible wounds on their backs, just standing there along the path with their heads bowed, worn out and ready to die. We did not stop and look carefully when we saw dead bodies on the path; even if we had wanted to, we did not have time.

There was not enough food to go around, so to move faster I left the pack animals with others and led a small advance party to get down to a place where there might be something to eat. The rinpoches also stayed behind with the remaining food. We had to go high up to cross the pass and soon we were again walking on snow, using the protection strips from around our necks to protect our eyes from the blinding sun. On the other side it was extremely steep but the gradient was even, there were no cliffs to fall over, and we were able to run and jump our way down on the fresh snow as if on a scree slope. We were in good shape and made good time.

This border region of India, called Mon, is inhabited by Monpas, a people similar to Tibetans who share our religion. We arrived at a big house owned by a Monpa. Many refugees were there already: some were brewing tea but others had nothing, and were simply drinking hot water. I had a special half-ball of tea left from the Dalai Lama's general new year's offering to the monks and I gave it to the owner of the house and told him what it was. He was very happy to receive it and would have liked to have given us something to eat but the number of refugees made it impossible. He said we should stay the night because the path was dangerous, but we were starving and decided to keep going down until we got some food. Night fell when we were in a forest and we lost our way. From the sound of rushing water close by we knew that we were near the side of a steep gorge and realized that we could step over to our deaths at any moment. I headed the line down and my students behind me shouted out in fear to stop, thinking it was too dangerous to go on. We were very scared but continued, picking our way down in the dark, listening to the water below, sometimes losing the path, sometimes picking it up again. Thoughts raced through my mind: "We are on the edge of slipping and falling into the gorge...there are animals lurking in the jungle...if we meet with a wild animal we are finished...there are two people with us carrying guns...it does not make much difference at this point whether anyone is carrying a gun or not...." We all went down on our bellies and on our hands and knees, scratching for finger holds and toe holds for more than three hours until the gorge flattened out and we found a narrow path. Still the light of the moon could not penetrate the forest, and we felt frightened.

Finally the trees thinned out and we came to a mountain meadow where by moonlight we saw some wood stacked near a few stones that had been arranged for a fire. We put down our packs and I sent some of the party to get water. We cooked up a watery soup and then fell into a deep sleep until quite late in the morning, when we immediately set off again.

That day we had nothing to eat and only hot water to drink, so when we came across a flock of sheep and goats one of the new members of our party—a Phukhang monk who had gone into the Resistance and was carrying a gun—said that he was going to shoot an animal for food. "Gen-la," he said, "I am going to kill a sheep; we are starving." I said that I did not like the idea. He had his gun up and ready and was on the verge of killing one but I kept going at a trot, starving though we were, and passed by without giving him time to shoot.

By this time my eyes were red and sore with snowblindness. We came to the upper part of a river and by following its winding course we began to pass through small settlements. My eyes were in such a terrible state I had to cover them and be led along. Since I was not able to go myself, I told my two youngest students to beg from the villagers. They came back with bananas, plantains, quite a bit of dried meat, some roasted corn, and corn tsampa.

After eating we set off again and came across some Tibetans who had killed a yak and were eating it. The monk who had wanted to kill the sheep pointed out to me that I had been a fool and should have let him kill the sheep. "Look," he said, "they killed a yak and are eating it." "We have full stomachs," I said. "We did not need to kill anything so you should not be sorry that you did not shoot the sheep. If you are going to shoot something at least shoot a Chinese Communist. The sheep have done nothing to us to deserve to be shot." He was younger than me and could not argue back.

We stayed the night in a forest a bit further down where we boiled up a soup full of all the provisions the villagers had given us. This soup was no watery fare, it was real food. Near our fire were a few Chinese from the pre-communist Chinese community in Lhasa. They had surrendered to the Resistance and fled from the Communists, taking the Buddhist dharma as their ornament, their deep Buddhist faith ennobling their actions. They were starving and destitute and they came and squatted near our fire. We gave them the remainder of our soup and some tea.

We did not get up very early the next morning (after all, we were no longer scared of a Communist attack and for the first time in a while had eaten a good supper) but we could not linger either, because we had been told that the river became impassable with the melting snow towards the beginning of spring.

The path down through the forest was deserted and we met nobody until we finally got to the river crossing quite late at night. We ran out of food again and the next day walked on empty stomachs. We came to a village house full of refugees who had arrived before us. Again, we had nothing but hot water to drink. As I was boiling it an old Monpa man came and watched us for a while. "Do you have anything to eat?" he asked. "No," we said, "we have nothing. We would like to buy anything you have to eat." "Just wait, I will come soon," he said. He came back hiding something in the folds of his clothes, scared that if anybody saw what he was carrying he would be attacked by starving refugees. He gave us some tea, salt, and a smidgen of butter. "Come on," he said, "brew yourselves up a bit of tea. I will come back later." And he did, with a friend carrying a bit of tsampa. "We would like to invite you to our house," he said, "but we feel it would invite a stampede amongst the refugees, so please just eat this in secret and do not let anyone know we are giving you anything." After we had eaten he told us to leave. "It is not far now," he said, "just a bit further down is a big town with temples where you can stay."

WE SET OUT in much better spirits with our stomachs, if not full, at least not totally empty, and soon we arrived at a town with a number of temples full of Tibetans. We went hungry when we first arrived. Even though it was quite a big town, there were so many refugees milling about that if someone was seen giving food to one he was besieged with requests from many others. A number of people secretly passed us food, which we hid in the folds of our clothes. When we pooled it we had the makings of a feast. A man told us there was a retreat place not far away and said he would be happy to look after us while we rested there. The older monks in our party, myself amongst them, were attracted by the idea, but I was told that a refugee relief center was set up at Mon Tawang Monastery and they were giving refugees a small sum to live on, so we went and camped in the village below there the next day. We met up with some other people from Kongjo-rawa who were amazed to see us because they were sure we had been caught by the Chinese.

I went up to the monastery looking for the refugee reception center but did not arrive until late at night. Pangon Rinpoche was there and when I shouted and gave some sharp raps on the door, he was up off his bed immediately and opened up. "So you made it! You made it, did you?" he said. He was happy to see me, and invited me inside and gave me something to eat. "I heard that you had gone on a pilgrimage to Yarlung Potrang," he said. "Everyone told me you had gone and we thought you had been captured by the Communists. We had given up on you, so it is excellent that you have been able to escape and are here." I stayed with him that night and the next day while others went looking to find rooms for us.

An elderly Mon Tawang monk very generously made his own room available to us. A grand fellow, he was very hospitable and made us feel right at home. "It is great that you have come," he said. "I feel so fortunate that fine learned monks like you have come to grace my unsuitable rooms. Stay as long as you want. I will leave you here, but the wood is yours to use, and please consider the place your own. I know that a lot of learned monks say 'no thank you' when people come to give them offerings. Make sure that you are not that sort of learned monk. If people come to give you food you be sure to take it now, do you hear me? The people want to give it to you and you must be sure to take it and eat it." With those kindly words he left to sleep elsewhere. The manager of Mon Tawang Monastery came and gave us a *loma* (a big bowl that holds about eight or nine kilos) of *kunsang* tsampa—a grain that looks like a little pyramid and gives a dark-colored flour. He measured out the amount with a scoop and he gave us about three kilos of oil besides. "This will keep you going," he said. So we were well set up, with food and a splendid room.

Now, we were famished, the lot of us. We had not eaten properly for days, so the moment he had gone we set about making a meal with the tsampa. In our part of the world there was a tsampa called *drahor* and I thought it was the same as that. We cooked up a thick porridge, heated up the oil separately and poured it in. This way of cooking makes for an excellent meal with *drahor*, but unfortunately with the *kunsang* tsampa we only succeeded in burning the outside and leaving the inside totally uncooked. We were so ready for a meal though, that we picked at the burned outside crust and ate it, going back again and again, convincing ourselves that this or that portion was cooked and edible. What with our recurring pangs of hunger, the four or five of us succeeded in finishing off the whole eight or nine kilos, though most of it was uncooked and had a very nasty aftertaste as it went down. When you are famished you can get down just about anything, even a sticky mess of burned porridge.

The owner of our room was an administrator of a nunnery close by and he told the nuns that there were learned monks staying in his rooms for a while and, if they wanted, they could go and make offerings. The nuns came, some with a little wood, some with a bit of tsampa, some with handfuls of black grapes, some with a few onions; each brought a bit and over the week that we stayed there we had no problems with food.

When we went to get registered as refugees and collect our aid money, there was a Kinnaur monk there from Drepung Guge house who recognized me, though I did not recognize him. He was acting as the interpreter, and said that he would give me the rations and that I did not have to line up. He gave me a full ration, the best available, and after a day or so said, "You do not have to come in person, you can send a student to pick it up." Some people from my part of Kham were having a lot of trouble and I asked him if he could let me have some old sacks for them to sleep on. He immediately passed some on to them. He was really very kind to us. But we soon passed on from there, so I was not able to go to him and properly express my appreciation for his kindness.

In Mon Tawang Monastery, during the short time we stayed there, we had no problems with food or lodging. Other Tibetans said we had good merit because they had a much harder time than we did. We passed on some of our food to people from our part of Tibet who came by to visit us and see how we were. One said he had come straight down an easy path from the border to Mon Tawang and that it was only a two day walk. "The Chinese could get here easily," he said. That started us worrying. Our rations were being dropped by plane and there were no Indian troops where we were staying. I had a dread of waking up in the morning in a field of the green uniforms of Chinese Communist soldiers, and I wanted to move on as quickly as possible. A local told us that a day or so walk along the path was a place where people would receive us warmly. "The lamas and older monks can do the prayers for the people, and the younger monks will be able to find work there. It is a nice little valley, off by itself in the mountains," he said. "Go and live there for a time. You will not need to fear the Chinese, the mountains are very high along the border and there is only a single path into that valley." He urged us strongly to go there, but we were sure that the Chinese Communists were coming, after our experience in Kham, and we thought that if there was only the one path in and out we would be easy targets. We decided not to go. "We have been told that lamas and gesheys should proceed down to Musalmari, in Assam," we said. "His Holiness has already gone down to the plains of India, and we are going to follow." "If it is too hot be sure to come back up," he said. "The valley is safe and you will be happy there."

Just before we left I told the younger students to beg in the village below the monastery. They went to nine or ten households and came back with tea, butter, tsampa, dried meat, and all sorts of things. The people were very generous.

The little rinpoche did not have any proper shoes so before setting out for Musalmari from Mon Tawang I bought him a pair of Tibetan boots. Unfortunately they were too tight and he was in agony by the time we reached the top of the pass. The Indian officials had marked out the distances we were expected to travel each day but the lama refused to go on. He kept stopping and bursting into tears and throwing temper tantrums. I had to make him go on, but it was like trying to move a stubborn mule. Before long we were left alone in a wooded area. The rest of the group had gone on ahead and the little rinpoche was very upset. "I am going to jump into the river...or throw myself off the cliff!" he said. Nearby was a little drop, perhaps half a story in height and down below was some soft earth, so even if he did jump he would not hurt himself badly. He stepped up to the lip and announced, "I am going to jump!" He refused to move on any further and I finally lost my patience. "Jump if you want to, it is of no concern to me." It was getting late and I went off to a nearby tumbled-down nomad hut. Through a chink in the wall I could see the young fellow getting his courage up for the jump. Two or three times he rocked himself back and forth, trying to make himself jump—you could see him thinking to himself about the injustice of it all—and two or three times he shied off from it. I lost all my anger and started to find the whole scene funny. Finally I went out to him. "We've got to go," I said. He did not reply, and kept his head down, shaking it. But he followed me, and we arrived at the camp well after the others had got there and were already drinking tea. The name of this camp was Lion's Lake, and the little rinpoche did not become upset at all during the time we were there, or over the next days when we camped at Daram and went over a very high pass to reach Bomdila.

In Bomdila we were given rations of flour. I had seen flour in Tibet, but this was the first time I had made a proper meal of it, because in Tibet, of course, we always ate tsampa.

There was a monk with us, Thubten Tashi, and a man from the army. We camped outside because they had not given us rooms to stay in. Late the first evening we began to brew our tea and had it on the boil when Thubten Tashi went out looking for more wood. He came running back to where we were camped shouting, "Don't drink it, don't drink it—it is the water from the toilet!" He said there was a really stinking toilet close by and the water was running down from there. I said I did not believe him (I really wanted that cup of tea) but he insisted. We found some other water and finally had our tea.

The next evening was the fifteenth day of the special month when the Buddha was enlightened. We made a light offering and a good puja with some tsampa, cheese, and our few other provisions there in the field at Bomdila.

THE NEXT DAY we set off down to the plains. When we were quite close to the outskirts of Musalmari we passed by a large army camp with trucks lined up to take us the rest of the way. They had brewed up tea for us and served it to us in metal mugs. Of course I had never drunk tea from a metal mug in my life before, and what with them hurrying us up, the splendid taste of the sweet tea, and my unfamiliarity with the heat of a metal cup, I burned my mouth quite badly trying to get it down. It was going to be a different life from the one I knew, I thought.

In Musalmari we were put in makeshift bamboo houses. We could see out through the walls and people could see us inside. We were about one hundred refugees in each of the houses and there were lots of people that I knew. It was so boiling hot I was hearing sounds in my ears, and we were all perspiring so much that we broke out in rashes on our underarms. Everyone was trying to get to the small river to cool down.

The Indian relief workers brought us cotton shirts and trousers and told us we were not allowed to wear our monk's robes and Tibetan chubas. Our Tibetan clothes were very heavy, of course, but I felt very upset about giving them up. I had worn my monk's robes during the whole of the flight from Tibet, but now it had come to this. One day I met with the saintly ex-abbot of Drepung Loseling from Gyerong. I was still wearing my monk's clothes and he told me to put them aside. "You will die in this heat wearing clothes like that," he said. "Not wearing monk's clothes breaks a monk's vows when he does it with the thought that they are not attractive, or when he despises them. Now is a special time, our robes are much too hot, and we have to put them aside to look after our lives. But in doing so we do not look down on the clothes. There is a great difference between the insistence of the Chinese that we not wear the clothes of the monk and the insistence here today that we take off our robes and wear the cotton clothes. The Chinese talk comes from their despising Buddhism, the Indian talk comes because they know we will die from heat if we wear our own clothes. They are saving us from death, and helping the dharma," he said. As I had seen him walking towards me in his shirt and trousers, I had felt a sadness inside me, thinking that even a person like the ex-abbot had taken off his robes. But after his stern lecture I reflected on the meaning of what he was saying and felt better. I put on the Indian cotton clothes.

We monks were a motley bunch when we had our confession ceremony on the fifteenth of that lunar month. Apart from the abbot and a few other monks, we all attended in our government-issue shirts and pants. Afterwards we had a debate period. We went at it in our new outfits, but sometimes the heat was so unbearable we could not stand it.

As for what was left of my money, it did not give us any help at all. A trader who was a relative of one of the lamas I was looking after arrived, and I gave it to him to change into rupees. When he gave me back Indian money he only gave me the equivalent of half the money that I had given to him. The rest disappeared.

AT THAT TIME some of us were resettled in camps, some wandered off to look after themselves, and some made their way to Kalimpong and other towns known to Tibetans. I had the two young monks and the young rinpoche with me. I could not set them all to work, and since I had to look after them I could not go off to work either. The Indians had forbidden us to beg, and I began to get depressed thinking about the hopelessness of our situation. I entered into a downward spiral of negative thoughts, seeing no hope, and it affected me badly. I withdrew into myself and immediately got angry when anyone talked to me—I sat down if someone said to go; I abruptly walked off if anyone came to talk. I began to skirt the edge of madness. A friend came up to me and spoke sharply. "You are brooding over things too much," he said. "Just forget it, whatever you are thinking, and take it easy. You are going to drive yourself mad if you are not careful."

His talk made me think more positively for a while, but I was still in the grip of a deep depression. "I have been able to escape," I thought, "but my homeland is in the grip of the Chinese and my family no longer has a say in its own destiny. My monastery in Tibet is destroyed, my spiritual friends and teachers have been killed and are no more. Even now, many of my friends are under the heel of the Chinese, facing terrible hardship. I did not even have time to approach my most important teacher, Gen Yaro, to ask permission to leave Tibet." As I thought of that I felt the darkness of the time—that I had not even gone to my own most precious gurus to ask them for permission to leave. For days I hardly ate or drank anything, hardly talked, just sat there buried in my own thoughts, irritable and unable to do anything except sink into the dark sleep of depression.

Then one day, as I was walking down the long bamboo shelter, I came across a Pombara monk reading the *Lamrim Chenmo*, Tsongkhapa's *Great Exposition of the Path*. I knew he was not a particularly gifted monk intellectually, but that he was a spiritually-minded person. I saw him there, quietly reading that wonderful book and I thought of my false pride in my ability to take care of myself. I had not brought a single book from Tibet, I did not even have a prayer book to read, but this monk, even though it would have seemed rather silly, had the foresight to bring something so valuable with him as this book. I felt a tremendous admiration for him, thinking that he had hidden talents to have seen the future so well as to have left the monastery taking with him a book like the *Lamrim Chenmo*. I went up to him and expressed my admiration for his foresight and excellent dedication. "This book is the only thing I brought with me," he said "but if truth be told I really cannot understand it. I am sitting here reading the words but the meaning does not make itself evident in my mind. If you want to borrow it you are more than welcome. Just be sure to return it to me before you leave."

So I took his book and with a feeling of great pleasure I sat down to read. As a divination I opened the book to see which passage would turn up, and there in front of my eyes was the section on cause and effect where a quotation from a sutra reads, "There is no place, wherever you may go—the results of your earlier actions will follow you." "How true," I thought, "how very true." Then I opened it again, to the Jataka Tale that says, "Further than the distance between the near and farther shore of the ocean, further than the distance between the different directions of the sky, is the distance between my thoughts and the thoughts of the dharma." I wondered for a while about the meaning of the distance between my thoughts and the thoughts of the dharma. It hit me strongly that I was just the same as I had always been—a person with intractable thoughts, with a mindstream still totally unaffected by the dharma even though I had studied for so long. And with that I realized that I had to pull myself up, to again align my thoughts with the positive thoughts of the dharma. With that I turned with a prayer to reading the *Lamrim Chenmo*. I felt happiness come over me, saw the silliness of depression, the childishness of my irritability, and the value in a happy and free mind. "What is the use in worrying about something that worry will not change?" I thought. "If I am in trouble why make it worse by worrying about it? It just drains me of the energy to work to improve the situation, and when I am depressed everyone around gets into a depression too." I realized how destructive depression is, how it hurts everyone, and how valueless it is.

I cannot describe how greatly I benefited from being able to keep the *Lamrim Chenmo* during that time—how much happiness it brought to my mind, how much strength it gave to me personally and to my ability to cheer up others. Later I was cheerful when I was in Dalhousie, and again, when I went to teach in Mussoorie I felt excellent, as I do to this day here in Dharamsala. That I was able to retain my sanity in that terrible time and place is because of the excellence of the Buddhist teaching in the *Lamrim Chenmo*. That experience made me see that people have a say in the way they think, in the way they look at things. I also saw how putting the words of a spiritual book into practice in one's own life is very much a variable of a particular time. At a certain moment just a few words of advice can hit the heart. Then they transform what a person thinks and does. If the words do not confront one as a direct advice about one's immediate situation, one's personal difficulties, then even if one reads a whole text from the start to finish the words will not come across with the force and clarity that is needed to transform one's perspective. If they do, they are so relevant that one's personal practice becomes almost self-motivated in its force. It is amazing, if the time is right, how a single line of a spiritual book can have the force to motivate a practice for an eternity. Sitting there reading, I felt strongly the value of following the spiritual life until my death.

ONE DAY I WENT to visit Pangon Rinpoche, but a Trehor Khampa named Sinja Rinpoche, a graduate of Tashi Lungpo Monastery (the skin on whose cheekbones, I remember, was black) told me Pangon Rinpoche had stepped out for a while. Then he told me not to worry. "The Dalai Lama and the other high lamas have escaped with us to India so we need not worry. We will be taken care of and you will be placed somewhere in the not distant future. When the opportunity comes to leave this temporary refugee camp, be it to go to Darjeeling or wherever, you should take it immediately, no matter where you have to go. All will work out well, but whatever you do, you should think of yourself as a monk and always be careful to keep your vows and the dharma in your heart."

A short while later twenty-five learned monks from each of the large Gelugpa monasteries in Lhasa were chosen to proceed to Dalhousie. Rinpoche and I were amongst them. Since I was unable to get my other students enrolled as scholars, one of them went off with his father who was living nearby. Another had already attached himself to a Khampa trader, but my remaining student was still with me. He was not very bright and I told him not to worry. "Even though you cannot come with us now it will not be long before you will be allowed to join us. I have been promised that," I told him. "Now take this woolen chuba and these other things of mine and keep them or sell them and use the money." I gave him five rupees as well, and then had only twenty rupees left to use on our journey.

When the time came to leave I was going to cook up our remaining flour into fried bread to take with us, but a know-all monk named Tsultrim Tashi who had been on pilgrimage in India said we would not need food, that it was readily available everywhere. Off we went—there must have been two hundred of us in total—and when we got to Alipore the Indians took us to a restaurant to have something to eat. Now, I had never seen a lime in my life, so when the waiters brought one along with my meal I thought it was a sort of plum, and popped it straight in my mouth and then I did not know what to do—it was so bitter I could not swallow!

A rumor went around that we must not eat much otherwise the Indians would think we were greedy. This was a stupid worry because the Indians were giving us a good meal before a long journey, but some monks were very nervous about looking bad in front of them. I thought they knew something I did not know, and so even though the Indians gave me a large plate of very good food, I just ate a little bit of it and left the rest. We were so stupid, because immediately afterwards we were taken to the station and put on a train. And then of course there was nowhere we could get food. Some of the others were sleeping but I was so hungry I got down at a station in the middle of nowhere and found a man selling milk. I drank a glass of that. The others got nothing and were talking about employing some very extreme strategies to get something to eat. We were very strange when we first arrived from Tibet. It was not such a terrible suffering as all that, but before long we were so hungry that we were talking about committing mass suicide by jumping off the train. We were cramped up in the compartments nursing our hunger and at a loss as to what to do about it. A great talk started up. Tsultrim Tashi, our great leader and maker of the pilgrimage came in for a real earful. "Where is all the food?" we asked him. "We thought you said it would be available everywhere." On the bigger stations we all trooped out and stood in line to get food off the vendors, but it always ran out before I got any. Again a line would form up, but I did not have the personality to dig in at the front, and again the vendors would run out. The train kept pulling out of the station before we could eat and we had to pile back on. At Lucknow someone remembered that it was the fourth day of the sixth Tibetan month. "Today is the festival of offerings to the gods of the world," he said. "We should make a puja." We did the Guru Puja and recited the Perfect Wisdom and Middle Way root texts.

At Pathankot, the railhead for Dalhousie, I finally got something to eat. To my surprise the food was served up to me on a great big leaf. I was so hungry I ate it all, but it did give me pause. That was all I got, a single leaf-full of lentils, during the whole journey. Some got two or three platefuls during the time, but they were the ones who knew how to push in at the head of a line.

To top this all off, there was the bus ride up to Dalhousie. I had never been in a bus and the pain in my rear end from having to sit on that seat for so long was excruciating.

ONCE IN DALHOUSIE it was not so bad. We were billeted in a place called Oga, where buildings had been set aside for us. But it was a free-for-all as to who got what room so we venerable monks all ran for it. I got in with some other Khampas in a very nice room with a wooden floor. I staked my claim to this room, and let it be known to everybody. Then I stepped out for a moment. When I got back a claim-jumper had moved in—an elderly monk, quite a distinguished look-ing man—and a debate was underway about whether he should be evicted. Some of them recognized him slightly as a learned monk, but some of us, and I was at the head of them, were of the opinion he should be thrown out unceremoniously. In the end we let him stay and it turned out he was from the excellent Nyari house, and was the extremely learned Ngawang Phuntsog. I did not know him at all be-fore, but I found him to be a most learned and fine man. It was an embarrassment to me to remember how rude I had been at the start, trying to defend my new territory with its nice wood floor against the learned interloper.

Dalhousie is a beautiful place, the mountains around there are like a mandala, building up to a central magnificence. And the hills are wooded, giving a secluded, quiet feel to the place. Below us was a big army camp. The bazaar was small but when we first arrived there we felt totally lost. Tibet seemed to have disappeared. Sometime later a monk said that the mountains off in the distance were the mountains of the Chamba region and that the Communist Chinese had arrived on the other side of them. This started us worrying again. We huddled around the radio listening to reports of Communist Chinese military movements and threats to advance and worried about them sneaking up on us unawares. We had no sense of Indian geography, and we did not know the roads or paths, so if they came again we thought we would not know where to run. We felt very vulnerable, wondering if we would wake up one morning to find ourselves surrounded by the Chinese.

The food at Oga was excellent. A cup of tea was only five paise in those days, and a kilo of flour was about forty paise. In the first months we were so well looked after we did not even have to go and get our food—it was delivered right to us. Some monks were not quite sure what was going on. When food was left outside their room if they were not in, they were not quite sure why it was there or what they were supposed to do with it. Though we had excellent food, inside, thinking about our country, we felt sadness.

Some monks were studying, but the people I was with just hung about talking and passing the time of the day, worrying about nothing in particular. I used the time to memorize the *Root Text on Wisdom* by Nagarjuna. Later I forgot it. There were no books there so I could not read as I would have liked to. Then the two tantric colleges were given a set of the collected works of the three founders of the Gelugpa sect and I was able to read some of the work of Kedrup-je. The rest of the monks just wandered about chatting and wasting time.

The Indians set up a school for us. It was very well run and the teacher was excellent. I began to study Hindi and the teacher was inspiring. I worked very hard for a couple of weeks and made excellent progress. I was thinking to make a go of it, but then the teacher changed, and an old man was put in there to teach us instead. He just sat on his rear the whole time doing nothing, so I soon lost interest and stopped going.

WE HEARD THAT THE DALAI LAMA was going to move from Mussoorie to Dharamsala. Of course we had no idea were Mussoorie was, but felt that it was excellent that he was moving to Dharamsala because it was quite close to us. We asked if we could go to meet him when he came through Pathankot. The manager of our compound said we could go, but that there was no bus. We had just arrived from Tibet and were used to walking everywhere, so this presented no problem to us and we set out. Since it was hot we walked at night, resting under the trees during the day, and the whole journey only took us three days. What amazed us, though, when we arrived, was that the manager was there before us with our tents pitched and food ready. We had no real knowledge of roads and transport, and since we traveled in the night we did not know he had taken a truck down before us.

After a day or so we were told to go to the railway station where we all sat in a line. When His Holiness came we were so moved we began crying. We could not stand up, but it obviously meant a lot to us and this set off the Indian police, who also started crying. I think they were confused by what had motivated us to walk all that way just for a few minutes with His Holiness. He moved swiftly past us, but then when he was about to leave he turned around and came back. We got up and he gave a talk to us. I was so emotional I could not understand a word of what he said.

After he left we were told that we should make our way back home. Some of us by then understood about paying money and going on the bus. It was only four or five rupees, so most of us could have found the money, but many of us, myself included, did not know anything about public transport, so we just set out on foot again back the way we came, traveling at night and resting during the day. We were back in three days.

I THINK IT MUST HAVE BEEN because of the faith we demonstrated in His Holiness that a wealthy factory owner came to us and asked us if we would like him to invite His Holiness for a visit. You can imagine the response. He was drowned out in the clapping and thumbs-up signs. About four months later His Holiness came to Dalhousie and gave the Guhyasamaja Tantra empowerment. On the first day of preparation he ran through the ritual quickly and then launched into a long talk on the faults of the old society we had left behind. He said the old government, dominated by myopic, self-serving aristocrats had let us down; the households of the high lamas had let us down; the different monastic colleges had not risen to the occasion. He was so strong in his descriptions of the shortcomings of our old way of life that we just cried and cried. Again this set off the Indians around us. His Holiness was extremely wrathful at that time, and we could not even lift our faces to look at him. What he said, of course, was right, and we knew that we had not lived up to our responsibilities. He told us, in essence, that the Chinese Communist invasion was our karma because we had not lived up to the responsibilities that a Buddhist way of life entailed.

On the day of the empowerment itself a great rain and wind sprang up. The canopy set up for His Holiness was blowing here and there and the rain was lashing everything. It struck me that the canopy was going to blow down, so I rushed to the back and got a hold of the line to one of the pegs. Another monk came and got ahold of another one. His Holiness quickly finished the ritual. After he left we let go of the pegs and the canopy came crashing down. Our clothes were as full of water as sponges. We were totally drenched. His Holiness left just a day or so later, but before he did he came to the debate ground that we had set up near the school. It was in the forest, and we had little more than sacks to put there as a seat for him. Again he began to lecture us, but again, before he could speak much, or we could do the debates we wished to do, a great rain and wind sprang up. I wanted just to get near to His Holiness but the push was too great. I could not even see him as he left. And in my rush I left my shoes behind and lost them.

His Holiness's lecture was made into a small book. It showed a new path and I began to see the terrible invasion and loss of our country as the outcome of faults in our own earlier Tibetan ways, and I saw a need for change and work on my own part. But we Tibetans, as a people, are a happy-go-lucky sort, not the sort to buckle down easily to new and hard realities. Practically speaking, our situation in India meant we had little in the way of facilities for a new start, but in my heart, and in the hearts of many Tibetans, a new light had been lit, a light that was to guide us to a new future by looking more realistically at the faults of the past.

A GROUP OF FIFTY MONKS was sent to work on road building near Chamba. They used dynamite and back in Dalhousie we heard sounds like the bombs in Lhasa when the Chinese shelled the Norbulinka. Fear came flooding back. The border was far beyond the mountains we could see from Dalhousie, but we thought the Chinese were just over on the other side. In 1963 the Chinese Communists invaded Ladakh and Assam and we were terrified. Our fears were compounded by the thought that when the Chinese arrived the Indians would rise up and support them. The Indian manager of our compound was a Communist and he said that India needed a good invasion by the Chinese.

"India has many poor people and the Chinese will liberate them all," he said. Where would we go? We would be finished. It might sound silly when you know the geography and political realities of those times, but back then we were very scared.

Late one night some elderly monks arrived from the lama camp in Buxador and there was a lot of talking. Our old guru Sharko Khen Rinpoche, Gen Nyima, was in rooms quite near me. He woke up because of the talking, thought that the Chinese had arrived, and immediately took off into the forest wearing nothing but his underclothes. A few others also thought that the Chinese had arrived and ran off as well. The next morning the monks with Gen Nyima wondered where he had gone and when they found him some distance off from the camp under a tree it was quite a joke and he was kidded about it for some time. But it shows just how on edge we were in those days. I often spent a sleepless night planning what I would do if the Chinese invaded Dalhousie. There was no place to run, I thought, but there were forests. I decided that I would run into the forest where I would be able to survive by eating wild berries and vegetables.

GEN TREHOR CHOPON RINPOCHE and the two tutors of the Dalai Lama came and taught us and brought happiness into our lives. The office of the Dalai Lama sent a long, handwritten copy of the *Vinaya Soti* commentary and told us to copy it out by hand. The office also sent the three main Perfect Wisdom Sutras with instructions to read them many times. We were many monks so we only got a page or two each. We copied out and recited our bits the number of times we were asked. I got about a page and a half which I copied out and recited. You had to circulate the part to others after you had finished with it. Similarly with the *Soti* commentary, I copied out about fifteen pages. Trichang Rinpoche asked us "Have you been able to read the sutras?" We told him what we had done. "You have done well," he said. I think one benefit of all this was that I learned how to write the *u-chen* script.

They also started a school to teach writing and Tibetan grammar. Everyone under forty had to go but I did not want to. I might die tomorrow, I thought, and the time spent learning how to write would be time wasted. Some monk teachers came from the class and said that I should be there. I told them what was in my mind, but they said that I was being silly. "It is easy," they said, "and if you do not want to come to the classroom one of us will come to your room and teach you." One monk came for a few days and that started me off. Like many others I began to work day and night at it (perhaps the sorrow of losing our country made us work so hard) and we learned in a few months what usually took more than a year to learn. Samdong Rinpoche was also there to teach poetry but I, for one, was unable to learn anything from him.

WHEN THE MANAGER of the rinpoche I was looking after decided to join the Four Rivers and Six Mountains Resistance he brought the horses and other belongings of his labrang to Gangtok in Sikkim. Many Khampas from Kongjo-rawa were doing road work there and they sent three hundred rupees for me and a helper to come. In those days many Tibetans went on pilgrimage without buying a ticket, they just got on the train, but we bought tickets and got reservations. The rinpoche's manager was waiting for us in Kalimpong. Since I had no traveling papers for that sensitive part of eastern India he sent me with his friend by a path parallel to the road to avoid the police. As we were going along this path a policeman stopped us and asked to see our papers. The manager's friend, who was a road worker and had papers, said that I had left mine in Kalimpong but the policeman did not believe him. "You are not from here," he said to me in a kindly voice. "I am not going to arrest you, but at the top of the pass there is a police post that you will have to be careful to avoid. And if you are caught do not say that you have already been stopped by the police." Later an officer drove up in an army jeep while we were resting at an eating place not far from a road. He was from the army but he looked like a policeman to us, so I hid in the dark for hours while my partner chatted with him. I doubt he would have cared even if he knew that I was there. The next morning we set off early and arrived in Gangtok without further problems.

The manager had left the horses in the care of his helper at Lachin Lachun, two or three days from Gangtok. When this helper arrived in Gangtok with the animals and goods he said, "It is excellent that you have arrived. I have brought everything except for one pack horse." All that he handed over, however, was the five bare pack animals. He was shameless. "I have been given nothing for my help," he said, intimating that he wanted the other horse as a gift even though he had stolen the harnesses and the manager had already paid him. "Then take the horse," I said, "and thank you very much for all you have done." I sold the five pack animals for five hundred rupees each, which in those days was a lot of money.

When I was in Gangtok, the ex-abbot of Loseling from Geyrong was there and I went to visit him one day. The moment I walked in he began abusing monks in general and me in particular. "The lot of you are a bunch of thieves," he said. "Monks take vows not to steal and monks should not steal." I could not get a word in edgewise. I began to understand that he was displeased with monks who went on pilgrimage without paying for their train tickets. When he calmed down he asked me, "Did you come from Dalhousie by train?" "Yes," I answered carefully, "I paid for my ticket and reservation and then came by train." He immediately softened and became more kindly. "It is shocking that some monks go about without paying for their tickets. It is different if a monk is totally destitute and has to get somewhere," he said. "But if he has any money left in his pocket he should spend that on the ticket, otherwise he is just a common thief."

The Loseling Abbot Pema Gyaltsen was in Kalimpong when I arrived there on the way back from Gangtok to Dalhousie. I took about a thousand rupees of the money and divided it up to give to him and the other monks and lamas. Then I bought a few clothes and a mandala offering plate.

When I got back to Dalhousie, Gen Trehor Chopon Rinpoche was there teaching. The community had improved greatly from the presence of the Rinpoche. He had instituted a proper confession ceremony, some monks were doing retreats, and though there were no mandala offering plates and so forth, monks were using flat slates to do their spiritual exercises.

SOMEBODY APPROACHED the Dalai Lama with the idea to send Tibetans to learn Sanskrit in Nalanda, Bihar. Sharko Khen Rinpoche, Gen Nyima said to me that if I felt like going it might be a good idea. I had decided to do it when a monk from Dema called Kedrup Junior said to me, "Don't go; just stay put here. It is as hot as fire down there." He was so negative he turned me against the idea so I dropped my plan to go.

Then I got the idea that I was going to go off and do a retreat in the forest. There were leaves and nuts growing wild—the sort we fed to our pigs back home—and I decided to live on them and do a retreat. Just as I was about to set off I read a work called the *Guide to the Authoritative Path*, by Khedup-je, the disciple of Tsong-khapa. The book was a detailed guide, focusing on practice, to exactly what a person did in retreat. In that work I came across a passage from Dharmakirti's

Commentary on Valid Cognition, which said, "Somebody upset at an immediate problem in a present situation who goes off into a retreat is not entering a retreat. They are just going to a place to have more trouble." It struck me, after thinking about it, that the only reason that I wanted to go into a retreat was because I was feeling sorry about my present situation and imagined another situation—the forest—was going to be better for me. My renunciation was, as Dharmakirti pointed out, a renunciation full of frustration and anger. I was unhappy with one particular part of the world, but if one thinks about it with a more spiritual attitude, all of the world is difficult in its nature. To go to the forest motivated by the pervasiveness of suffering would make the life of the retreatant very meaningful. But I could see none of that in myself. I felt dislike—a frustration with the immediate situation in the world that was confronting me, and I hoped that by running away to the forest I would find a better situation. That did not, I reflected, run in the true direction of the dharma so I dropped the idea. How unpleasant, I thought, to have a motive tied up with frustration and dislike.

THERE WERE A NUMBER of old Phukhang monks in Dalhousie. My student and I were the only younger ones, so the work of looking after them fell pretty much on my shoulders. "All the work in my life up to now," I thought, "has come to naught. All my attempts to position myself well in the world have come to naught. All my hopes to study the dharma have come to naught. So I am going to throw myself heart and soul into being a servant of the older monks and try to live totally in accord with the monk's discipline. I will not behave badly. I will try to cultivate faith in the Buddhist refuge and I will be a servant to the monks. If I am lucky this will give me the opportunity in a future life to meet with the dharma." I did work hard, from the bottom of my heart, all the while retaining strongly that drive to study and be a monk renounced from worldly activity that had been the ideal in the monasteries in Tibet.

TWO MINISTERS of the Dalai Lama came to Dalhousie to say that a school was going to be opened near Dharamsala to train teachers and that examinations were to be held to chose which Dalhousie monks would attend. I did not want to become a school teacher, such activity was tied up in my mind with non-monk activity, and I did not have a high estimation of my own abilities when it came to learning the different subjects involved, but I had to sit the examination. I came in forty-fifth and the cutoff point was twenty-five. But when the selection committee was discussing my bad writing and generally poor exam result, one of the two teachers in Dalhousie, Gen Namgyal, said I was promising material, a learned monk, a hard worker, and that when I put my mind to something I was capable. On his recommendation they included me on the short list submitted to the Dalai Lama.

A monk from Sera-me told me how I had got on the list and I felt quite put out by Gen Namgyal's action. He was butting his nose in business that was none of his concern, I thought. When the meeting was over he came to see me. "I tried as hard as I could to keep your name off the list," he said, "but the examiners insisted on including you. I made sure your name was at the bottom of the list of candidates, even though it was earlier at the top, to ensure that they passed over you as unsuitable material. I described you again and again as a hopeless case with bad writing, not cut out for the course, but they insisted on including you. If His Holiness says you have to attend the course you are going to have to go." As I listened to him lying, I felt my anger disappear. He did not know that I knew what had happened and I was tickled to hear him being so skillful with me.

Fifteen days later news came that His Holiness had included me in the final list. I asked Sharko Khen Rinpoche about it. "I do not want to go and am thinking of backing out," I said. "Once the Dalai Lama has given his word on a matter there is no question of backing out, you have to go," he instructed me. Then I went to the ex-abbot from Gyerong and he gave me a long look and in his slow and measured way said, "The stupid owl with pleasure flies up to the beckoning cage. You are so conceited about your new-found skill in writing, showing off to us old men what you think is such an excellent skill. They played you perfectly my little one! You are finished and now you have to go to the course. You studied writing and now they got you just like you deserved; you have to go!"

As the time came for leaving I felt more and more unhappy and the monks I was serving began to worry about who would look after them when I was gone. They accompanied me down from our camp to the bus station. We were all very upset, and once I got on the bus I could not stop crying. They were out there on the bus stand crying and I was in the bus crying like a baby. I felt devastated inside for some reason. Tsering Tashi tried to comfort me. "Cheer up," he said. "We have to go, and who knows, we may end up as important teachers."

We traveled to Dharamsala and had an audience with the Dalai Lama in his old residence, above the village of McLeod Ganj. I was sure he would have something to say to people like me—monks who had spent our lives studying Buddhist scriptures—that we should now feel free to go back to our old lives, that he was making an exception in our cases, but he did not say a word. He just said that we all should go to the course and study hard.

The course took place below Dharamsala in a quiet setting near Kangra. Feeling terrible inside I began the first year of study. There were many different subjects and we all pushed ourselves to the limit, never taking a break from study, not even on Sundays. One day a doctor was sent from the administration in Dharamsala because they were worried that we were driving ourselves mad. The catalyst had been dear old Gen Chodrak. The teachers insisted he express himself in poetry, poor fellow, and he had not been able to do so. They pushed him and he broke, went totally mad and refused to stop. He was rushing all over the place spouting off poetry, so they sent down the doctor to make sure the whole group of us were not going to go over the edge with him. The doctor examined us and reported back that we were all sick with the life-force winds from trying too hard. Kundeling, the minister for religious affairs, quickly came out and he had a long meeting with the principal, Zemey Rinpoche. After the meeting there was an assembly and he addressed the lot of us. "I should be coming down here to say that you should be working," he said, "but I am coming here to ask you to take it easier. There is talk that you are pushing too hard, so I want you to take a holiday every Sunday. It is compulsory. Otherwise I have been told that you might all go mad." After that we had to take a holiday on Sunday. It began at about nine in the morning and went until four. They sent down some inner tubes and we all went to swim and float about in the river. Even the Rinpoche would be there with us frolicking about.

We studied hard and I think I kept up with the work, but inside I got more and more upset. I felt that I was getting further and further away from the familiar life of a monk. I started to plan an escape. One monk had already run for it, just disappearing in the middle of the night, and I thought that I was going to do the same. I felt incapable. In a school I was going to have to teach writing, grammar, and poetry, and never mind teaching others, I was no good at those subjects myself. "I will never be a successful school teacher," I thought. "I am going to have to make a run for it."

At this time a letter came for me from Pangon Rinpoche in Dalhousie. He was my teacher from Drepung and I respected him deeply. The letter read, "Stop thinking about other things, and just set yourself one-pointedly on the work of training to be a teacher. Have confidence in your ability, work solidly at your lessons, and do not get depressed about how things will turn out. I know you are a worker and that you are studying, but I am saying to you that you must keep at it without letting yourself get depressed. Do not let your mind wander, and never let yourself entertain the notion of running away."

I felt strange as I read the letter. It was as if from a distance Rinpoche knew what was in my mind and had written a letter just when it was needed to help me. I showed it to some friends who said that I should take his advice to heart. I did and I stayed at the course.

NOT LONG AFTER THAT the Dalai Lama came to visit and gave us a tremendous talk. We were so shy we sat in our seats without raising our heads. How terrible to be so shy that one does not even escort the Dalai Lama properly and serve him well. "You are monks who have spent your lives learning Buddhism in the way we have learned it for centuries," he said, "and now you are in a teacher training course. I have felt, as I am sure many of you have, that tinge of sadness as I think of monks in your situation, but times have changed. Now the need of the hour is teachers for the young of Tibet, and if our Tibetan teachers do not know their intellectual and spiritual heritage we will not be able to pass on to our youth the necessary spirit that will keep them and our country living and well. You are studying writing and the minor subjects, it is true, but those are not the deeper subjects that you are involved in. You will teach the minor subjects to children, but at the same time you will be contacting the minds and spirits of Tibetan children, and through that your influence will be great. I have been reading through some of your exam papers. I feel that you have gone through ten years of study in a single year and know how you must have pushed to do that. So I want to say to those of you who see the time you would have spent in spiritual exercises and study of spiritual books as slipping away—know that the times have changed. The need now is the education of our youth. It is possible," he continued, "that some of you have lost your great enthusiasm for studying Buddhism. This break, this change to the study of quite different subjects in a different way, may, when it is over, rekindle your interest to study Buddhism even more. It is like a watch," His Holiness said. "Sometimes the watch stops going. But if you take it apart and then put it back together again it will go as well as before. So this stop in your study of Buddhism will be a break that will cause you to understand even better in the future. It is only now that you cannot study Buddhism, not forever. You will be teachers in schools, but if you cannot both by your teaching and your actions demonstrate the reality and truth of cause and effect—the law of karma—then the doctrine of the enlightened ones will be lost to Tibet and Tibetans, and our work will all have been in vain. If you cannot give advice to our children that is rooted in the truth then you will not have done what I hoped you would be able to do. This is the need of the hour."

That talk by His Holiness filled me with inspiration and removed all my doubts. I felt at ease and dedicated myself to this new vision of life that His Holiness had set before us. Whatever I might say, think, or do would be in line with his vision. I would put all my effort into learning how to be a school teacher and into teaching the children of Tibet. From now on I would serve the Dalai Lama's government by becoming a teacher, and unless I was incapable and was asked to step down, I would dedicate myself to this task. I felt this deeply, and since then I have not worried about what was going to happen to me personally. When I taught in Mussoorie my own personal life was filled with an inspiration to teach the children. The monthly salary I received as a teacher I spent on the children, on their needs and on little treats for them. I have never felt that it was an onerous task, and it has always been work that caused a happiness ever present within.

Afterword

THE LAST TWENTY-FIVE YEARS OF LOBSANG GYATSO'S LIFE

Lobsang Gyatso was murdered in his home in Dharamsala in February 1997, before completing work on his memoirs. This final chapter was written by his student and translator Gareth Sparham.

After graduating from the teacher training course in 1963, Gen-la (those who knew Lobsang Gyatso in his later years almost without exception called him by this title, which means "teacher") was sent to Mussoorie to teach grade three at Baristan Elementary School. When it became clear that the Chinese occupation of Tibet was going to last a long time, the Dalai Lama and the Indian prime minister Jawaharlal Nehru discussed the long-term needs of Tibetan refugees. At this time they designed policies that would attempt to protect Tibetan Buddhist culture and provide modern education for the new generation of Tibetan children growing up in exile. This led in 1962 to the creation of a separate residential school system for Tibetan children, the Central Tibetan Schools Administration, which was funded by the Indian government. One of these new schools was in Mussoorie, and Baristan was a small elementary school connected with it. It was housed in a single, big bungalow and Gen-la lived right there with the children.

When Gen-la first arrived in Baristan he was still so weak in Tibetan grammar and writing that he was unable to correct his students' exercises without consulting the Tibetan books he had brought with him from the teacher training course. He found to his embarrassment that some of the older students in the elementary school had better handwriting than his own, but he was inspired to teach the children and found himself gradually improving as time went by.

The medium of instruction in the schools was Tibetan, but most of the teachers of non-Tibetan subjects were Indian, and Hindi and English were widely spoken. Since Gen-la knew neither of these languages he had much trouble communicating. An Indian teacher volunteered to teach him English but after a few sessions he dropped the attempt and never tried to learn English again. The same man then suggested he should try to learn Hindi. Gen-la again dropped the attempt after a few lessons though he later did pick up enough words to communicate with local people. "I am already having a big struggle just keeping up with my responsibility as Tibetan teacher for the children," he said to a friend. "I do not need any additional burden of trying to learn another foreign language, so rather than learning English or Hindi I am going to put all my efforts into improving my Tibetan."

This decision to focus solely on Tibetan enabled Gen-la to surpass most other exiled Tibetans, including his old classmates, in writing and teaching Tibetan. He wrote over twenty books, many in verse, during the later years of his life and was quite at home writing in Tibetan and talking about the finer points of Tibetan grammar and poetry. He used to joke with his old classmates and say that he felt he had achieved what he set out to do in the teacher training class, but he wondered if they could say the same.

Gen-la came to like the children in the elementary school very much. He changed from seeing his teaching position as a hindrance to spiritual life to feeling lonely without children around. "I felt empty when there were no children," he wrote in later years, "and they responded to the affection that I felt for them by coming to my room and even laying down on my bed with me. They were seeking love and affection from me because most of our young Tibetan children in that school were orphans, their parents killed or left behind in Tibet. I loved them very much. I never kept any of my salary but rather used it to buy them books, pencils, ink and little things to eat. I used up all that I earned, as I got it, buying things as the children had the need, and during the four years that I was at Baristan Elementary School I tried as hard as I could to improve the academic standard."

It was not long before Gen-la's dedication and ability came to the notice of the principal of the Mussoorie senior school, Mr. Taring. Faced with an intractable discipline problem in the senior girls' hostel, he approached Gen-la and asked him to be in charge there. At first Gen-la refused, saying that as a monk teacher it was not appropriate, but Mr. Taring insisted. Since nobody else would accept the job of running the hostel, and Gen-la was by nature a man who responded to a challenge, he finally accepted. He moved right into a room at the end of the second floor of the hostel, located in a big house in Mussoorie, and stayed for about eight years until he finally left to become principal of the Institute of Buddhist Dialectics in Dharamsala in 1973.

Gen-la employed a number of novel ways to bring the girls into line: sometimes fining them, sometimes making them sit in a sack for a period of time, and always holding them to the higher standard of which they were capable. "When Gen-la got worked up and angry at a girl she would run into the toilet," recalls Pema Dawa, a former student in the girls' hostel. "He would come running after her. She would wait until one of the girls would come and say, 'He has gone now,' and she would come out. Oh! he would beat us if he caught hold of us then. But then he would go to his room in confusion and cover his head with his monk's shawl and his heavy monk's coat and start crying." Gen-la never held a grudge against any of the girls and they came to like and respect him. "He was a very good monk," recalls Pema Dawa. "He never treated any of the girls differently. And because he gave all his money to us he did not have good monk's clothes. A relative of Mrs. Taring, I think an aristocrat from Bhutan, would buy his monk's clothes for him each year." Gen-la continually encouraged the girls in their study. "We were supposed to go to sleep at nine o'clock, but during the exam periods we would stay up until eleven or so. He would come by when it was late with tea and pounded rice for us and say that we would all be falling asleep tomorrow if we did not go off to bed."

It was while he was teaching in Mussoorie that Gen-la first came to the notice of the Dalai Lama. In an interview with the Indian journalist and writer Sonia Jabber shortly after Gen-la was murdered, the Dalai Lama recalled, "The first time that I began to know him individually was when he became a school teacher in Mussoorie. In those early days in exile all the children—boys and girls—were introduced to debate in their senior religious education classes. I had been invited to Mussoorie and after a day of ceremonies, in the evening assembly the children were given an opportunity to debate in front of me. Then I had two monks sit down to answer questions. During one debate the late geshey-la [this is honorific Tibetan for a monk of long standing] was answering the questions and I stood up to debate with him, stimulated by the course of the argument. I successfully put forward a line of argument in that debate that was a true Middle Way. It was memorable. I stood up at that time because I wanted to give encouragement to the young students by providing myself as a model for them to emulate."

For Gen-la, the debate with the Dalai Lama was a turning point in his intellectual life. Having only briefly studied the Middle Way in Tibet, and sceptical of the beliefs of the learned gesheys and lamas whose behavior was often self-serving, Gen-la had taken the Mind Only system, with its strong theoretical basis for cause and effect, as the final Buddhist truth. During the debate, the Dalai Lama's arguments in favor of the Middle Way presentation of dependent origination caused Gen-la to fundamentally question his earlier Mind Only view, and led him to accept the Dalai Lama's position.

IN 1973 GEN-LA LEFT MUSSOORIE and became the head of the Institute of Buddhist Dialectics in Dharamsala. He was asked to do so by the Dalai Lama, who opened the new educational institution in response to the requests of young monks graduating from the Central Tibetan School System. In October 1972, at a meeting of the Council for Tibetan Education held in Dharamsala under the chairmanship of the Dalai Lama, there was a discussion about this state of affairs. The Dalai Lama asked Gen-la to ascertain whether or not there really were interested students and, if so, to start collecting names. Gen-la submitted a list of the names of twenty-three monk students in grades ten and eleven. These were to become the Institute's first class.

"There were a number of reasons why I decided to start the Institute of Buddhist Dialectics here in Dharamsala," the Dalai Lama recalled. "First was the extremely difficult circumstances in those early years before the revival of the monasteries in South India. Many monks were unable to study Buddhism at that time. Second was the system of education in the new secular Tibetan school system. It differed from the traditional monastic system and it was increasingly evident that a place for monk students who wanted to continue studying Buddhism, but who were reluctant to join one of the old monasteries, would be necessary. When I looked for a person suitable to be its director I decided on geshey-la."

The Institute was formally opened in 1973 on the Dalai Lama's birthday, July 6, and was housed in a single two-story building next door to the Dalai Lama's own compound. The Dalai Lama donated seventy-five rupees a month for living expenses to twenty-three of the students. Another six students financed their own studies.

When first asked by the Dalai Lama to come to Dharamsala to be in charge of the Institute, Gen-la told Mr. Taring that he did not want to go. There were more highly educated Tibetan monks capable of teaching Buddhism and Gen-la was greatly enjoying the company of the school children. He also felt he was doing a good job educating them now that he had gained experience as a teacher, but Mr. Taring's response was that when it was the order of the Dalai Lama one had to go without question.

In 1976, pleased with the hard work of the students, the Dalai Lama decided to constitute the Institute on a permanent basis. "Most of you students in this Institute have received an up-to-date education in foreign subjects and in modern literature," he said during a visit to the Institute at that time. "You could have gone on in those subjects if you wanted to, yet you have instead delighted in the study of the dharma which benefits this life and future lives as well. This is excellent." His Holiness then stated that he hoped graduates of the Institute would stay in meditation on the essence of what they had learned, or else serve in Tibetan society. "If after completing your training in this Institute you do not fulfill either of these two aims," he said, "and are just content with reciting the verses on refuge and wearing religious robes, then undoubtedly the new Tibet will be full of parasite monks."

Once established, under the guidance of Gen-la and the Dalai Lama the Institute began to expand rapidly. In the late 1970s the students, now in many ways better educated than their teachers, began to feel uneasy about the lack of a coherent and practical vision of the future. The conservative monk in Gen-la felt that the students' request for formal examinations and a degree system would undercut the spiritual basis of the school, but the students had the strength of their convictions and helped to steer the Institute along a path less fearful of modernity.

At the end of the 1970s, after the death of Mao and the partial liberalization in China, Tibetans from Tibet began to visit Dharamsala, mainly from the Lhasa region at first, but then from Amdo and Kham as well. As the stream of new visitors and refugees began to increase, the Dalai Lama suggested that Gen-la establish a day school at the Institute to give new arrivals some access to education. A teacher was appointed from amongst the students, and by the mid 1980s more than a hundred newcomers had received some education there. As the number of new arrivals from Tibet increased, the government-in-exile opened a big school in Bir and the Institute's small day school was closed.

IT WAS AT THIS SAME TIME, at the end of the 1970s, that Gen-la suddenly received a letter and a picture from his sister in Kongjo-rawa. For twenty years he had heard nothing from her or from anyone who knew his family and he had not known if she was dead or alive. He sent back a letter to Kongjo-rawa with a member of the Dalai Lama's second fact-finding mission to Tibet. Lobsang Yeshey, the grand nephew of Lobsang Gyatso, now a monk studying in the Institute of Buddhist Dialectics, was there in Choo-chur when his great-uncle's letter arrived. "I first heard about my Red Great-Uncle when the members of the second fact-finding mission came through our town in about 1979 or 1980," he said. "There were six or seven cars and jeeps coming up along the road while we were having a break from field work, and we children were very excited. We all lined up along the road. I could not understand the central Tibetan accent, so I was told to run and get our distant relative Cheting Benser. The members of the fact-finding mission told us there was a Choo-churwa in India who was asking about his relatives. I remember them saying that. There was a great pile of us children milling around and of course we were very excited. I was about thirteen or fourteen at the time. All I knew at first was that there was a lot of talk about someone who had sent a message. When I was told that it was a message from my Red Great-Uncle I was ecstatic. My granny had always been saying that I had an Anyi-me, a Red Great-Uncle. She used to give me her beads to do the bead-divination and ask, 'When is he coming?' I would do a divination, even though I was not qualified to do it. We did not know if he was in Lhasa, in India, or dead. We knew nothing about him for the whole of my childhood, but since my granny often used to wonder out loud about him, I grew up in his presence. When I gave my granny the message she threw up her hands in the air and I could not stop her crying. She just cried and cried and cried. When I later said I wanted to become a monk my granny said that I should go to India to be his servant. She died just before I came to India in 1988."

AS THE INSTITUTE became more established, philosophers, scientists, and religious groups began to visit. They were interested in dialogue and exchange and Gen-la was quick to organize assemblies where they gave lectures, but in the absence of proper translation and commitment the assemblies were at first little more than a forum for Gen-la to pontificate about the superiority of all things Tibetan.

Gen-la was initially very hesitant about other systems of knowledge. In New York, during a discussion with young educated Tibetans about their intellectual heritage, he remarked that just as foreign students will never be as familiar with Tibetan language and culture as Tibetans themselves, so westernized Tibetans would never be at home in Western culture unless they are solid in their own culture. "If Tibetans do not value and master their own intellectual heritage first, but try to learn the Western one," he said, "they are doomed to second-rate status forever."

Sherab Gyatso, an English monk who served as a translator for Gen-la for many years, observed that Gen-la's attitude to Western thought began to change at about the time Professor Jay Garfield set up a Tibetan Buddhist Studies program in India for Western college students. Professor Garfield, who believed that Western academics were responsible for the education of not just Westerners but Tibetans too, recalls that at their first meeting in Varanasi, India, Gen-la stated baldly that Tibetans had nothing to learn from the Western philosophical tradition. Jay Garfield said he had replied to his face that he sounded exactly like a Western philosopher, who, without studying a word of Tibetan Buddhist philosophy, rejected it as unworthy of investigation. Gen-la, who always liked a good fight, asked Jay to name his best text (his choice was Kant's *Critique of Pure Reason*) and then invited him to come to Dharamsala to teach it at the Institute. "Later he asked me to teach a complete History of Western Philosophy course for the students of the Institute," Professor Garfield recalls, "which I did over parts of the next four years."

GEN-LA'S RELATIONSHIPS with Westerners were defined by his intense commitment to educating Tibetans. The first Westerner that Gen-la met was Judy Tethong, or "Miss Judy" as he called her, a young Canadian volunteer who taught classroom skills and modern subjects in his teacher training course in the early 1960s; he respected her as his teacher. He loved to recount how on the last day of the course a monk student of Miss Judy broke into her room and took some of her clothes, squeezed himself into her tight mini skirt, put socks in her blouse, and arranged some straw under a hat to look like long, blond hair. He was imitating her teaching manner perfectly, wiggling about in her tight skirt tapping on the blackboard with chalk, when Judy Tethong walked in to gales of laughter. "When I entered the assembly and saw that monk," Mrs. Tethong said some twenty-five years later, as she and Gen-la sat together reminiscing in a beautiful apartment over-looking the Pacific Ocean in Vancouver, "I began to laugh so much that I felt that I might burst my stomach. We had all worked so hard together, and there was a special bond that had formed between us, the bond of trust and togetherness. When I look back on that time I consider it the most special time of my life."

Since Gen-la insisted all entrants to the Institute speak Tibetan, the number of foreigners studying there was initially very small. He did not encourage Westerners to join but never stood in their way if they pushed. "When I went to his office with my few words of Tibetan he was really nasty, and as far as I could make out, with my limited Tibetan, he said he was not there for the likes of me," recalls Sherab Gyatso. "That was when I first met him. After spending a year in Nepal improving my Tibetan I came back and asked if I could join the school. Gen-la was very positive and beaming, exactly the opposite of what he had been the first time, and a month later he arranged a room for me in the Institute itself." Of his foreign students only one, George Dreyfus, successfully completed the whole course; he now teaches at Williams College in the United States. Many other foreigners studied for a time in the Institute and then went on to other universities and careers.

GEN-LA'S FIRST FOREIGN TRIP was towards the end of the 1970s when the Tibetan government's Department of Religious Affairs sent him as its representative to a conference in Japan with the Nyingma scholar Khetsun Zangpo. Not long after this, the Russians, during the Brezhnev era, began taking an interest in the affairs of the Tibetan exile commu-nity and Gen-la was asked by the Department of Religious Affairs to go to conferences in Russia and Mongolia. In Mongolia he found only a few monasteries and hardly any monks who knew anything about Buddhism. The Communists and Stalin in particular had destroyed nearly everything. But he found many people with great faith and some monks still chanting their traditional tantric rituals in Tibetan.

Gen-la had a strong connection with Mongolians. Close by the In-stitute there was a lawn of green grass with apricot trees and a gravel path. During the afternoons the students of the Institute debated there. One day in the late 1970s a very old Mongolian man in brocade robes appeared, supported by two assistants as he walked along the gravel path from the temple towards the Dalai Lama's private quarters. As he approached he stopped and with great difficulty began to make prostrations. He picked up little pieces of the gravel, which were relics to him just because the Dalai Lama had walked there. He did not know Gen-la, and could speak no Tibetan, but as he passed Gen-la who was standing by the path supervising the debate, he put into his hand, without saying a word, a red coral necklace. His offering was a spontaneous one, out of faith in the Buddhism that had been nearly totally destroyed in his own country and in Tibet. It was a very expensive necklace that realized more than 15,000 rupees, a huge sum in those days, when Gen-la later sold it to help meet the Institute's expenses.

In 1996 a Russian delegation came to Dharamsala and one of the members, a lady from Buryatia, had been working as a protocol officer for the Buddhist delegations when Gen-la visited Russia in the 1970s. Gen-la recognized her, found out which room she was staying in, and sent up two monks to her room with a gift. Gen-la often expressed his wish to visit Mongolia again and was making arrangements to travel there at his own expense when he was murdered.

In the late 1980s, Gen-la began traveling more often throughout Southeast Asia, North America, and Europe at the invitation of his foreign students. He used to joke that since he only spoke Tibetan he traveled like a cardboard box: somebody put a label on him at one airport and somebody picked him up at the next airport and delivered him where he was supposed to go.

His interest was always in teaching. He never taught tantra, though in Israel, after launching into a long traditional discourse on the first day of a course he quickly realized it was not what the people wanted. "He was a practical man who could listen to advice," recalled his translator. "He asked what he should do and I told him they liked tantra. He taught them Vajrasattva, but I remember he was laughing because he had forgotten to bring his prayer book and was a little unsure about how the Vajrasattva recitation went. He made up a great meditation over a period of five days, with the sutra teaching on the clear light nature of mind, the four immeasurables, and emptiness there in the meditation. On the plane on the way back to India he suddenly remembered that he had omitted to say anything about a mantra. I chuckled to myself thinking how angry I could make him by saying that he was a finder of treasure texts in the sky-like nature of his mind. But there is no doubt he was a very fine teacher indeed, and a very fine and simple monk."

THE LAST MAJOR PROJECT Gen-la embarked on before his death was an expansion of the Institute. His plan called for the construction of a residential college for about two hundred students, and though he had not worked out the full estimate when he started, it was to cost many millions of Indian rupees by the time the construction was completed. He presented the idea to the Dalai Lama in 1992 who agreed in principle. Since the infrastructure costs involved in the expansion were huge, and the Institute itself had no money at all beyond yearly sponsorships and a small income to cover running costs, Gen-la first had to convince the principal financial secretary of the Dalai Lama, Kuno Tara, to lend the Institute enough money for a down-payment on four acres of land ten kilometers from McLeod Ganj near the airport in the Kangra Valley. Kuno Tara, an extremely reserved and upright man, was a close friend of Gen-la, but he would later remark to the Dalai Lama that Gen-la really was pushy and sure of himself—a common complaint of those who had to work with him.

Once he had his piece of land, Gen-la set about looking for benefactors for the cost of the buildings. One of Gen-la's students was an elderly Chinese monk, Tenzin Jamchen, who had moved to America in the 1950s after the Communist takeover. Deeply committed to Chinese cultural values, and believing that a deeper understanding of Buddhism would be of value to Chinese society, he first came to Dharamsala alone during the mid 1980s, staying at the Institute each year for a few months. Not a wealthy man in those years, with few students of his own, he lived in a simple room as an ordinary member of the Institute. Gen-la taught him Tsong-khapa's *Great Exposition of the Path* privately each evening. Gen-la's lectures, carefully recorded and translated into Chinese, became the basis for the program that Tenzin Jamchen developed to teach Buddhism. During the 1990s this teaching program became very popular in Taiwan and throughout Southeast Asia, and Tenzin Jamchen opened a large number of study centers in Taiwan, as well as a monastery incorporating some of the features of the Institute of Buddhist Dialectics.

"A group of my Chinese students came to Dharamsala not long after the new year and I set my new project before them," Gen-la wrote later. "They expressed their belief that it was beneficial both for Buddhism and for the Tibetan people and said that they would help. With their financial help, and the smaller donations of a number of other foreign aid organizations, the new campus is now nearly finished. Sometimes over the last five years when I have gone to teach my

Chinese students I have joked with them, saying, 'I am coming to get money for my new campus.' They always very respectfully say to me they are happy I am coming. 'We have a lot of money nowadays,' they say, 'it is no problem. But in return we want all the Buddhism you can teach us.'"

Though invited by his overseas students to teach many times, Gen-la never became involved in the administration or ownership of foreign centers. When his students separated to develop new groups they invariably remained on friendly terms with each other and he continued to teach them all. Both Tenzin Jamchen and Mr. Gene Lin, a retired Chinese businessman and scholar living in Los Angeles, have remained committed supporters and benefactors of the Institute and the Dalai Lama even after Gen-la's death.

Gen-la's relations with his Chinese students were always scrupulously honest and correct. "I have been invited to Taiwan many times but I never went because our Tibetan government says we should not go," he said shortly before his death, and before the Dalai Lama's government had set up a liason office in Taipei. "My students there say again and again that I should come because many of the Tibetan teachers who go there do not teach, they just do rituals for money and Tibetan Buddhism is getting a bad reputation. Because I cannot go there my Chinese students come to Dharamsala for teachings, sometimes more than a hundred of them at a time. And for the last few years I have gone to Hong Kong during the annual winter break, and have met my Chinese students and taught."

GEN-LA WAS BRUTALLY MURDERED along with two of his students on the evening of February 4, 1997, four days after returning from a month in Hong Kong. There he had taught Nagarjuna's *Jewel Garland* and Tsong-khapa's *Praise of Dependent Origination*, and he told me that his trip had gone well. "I taught three times a day," he said, "and only went out once, on a trip with the students to release fish in Hong Kong harbor."

The murder was widely reported both in the Indian and foreign press because Gen-la was seen as a surrogate for an attack on the Dalai Lama by a lunatic fringe of the Dorje Shugden group, a fanatical Tibetan religious sect. Little more needs to be said about Gen-la's attitude to the spirit Shugden. The later parts of these memoirs, set down only a few months before his death, show how outspoken he was in his belief that the spirit was harmful to Tibet. But what singled out Gen-la for attack was not the intensity of his opposition to Shugden but his ability and willingness to write down clearly in Tibetan what he thought. In particular, a number of articles that he wrote about Shugden in the summer and autumn of 1996 responded to attacks on the integrity of the Dalai Lama by groups of Indian and foreign-based Shugden supporters; these appear to have been the catalyst for his murder. As the Dalai Lama remarked to Sonia Jabber, "Geshey-la was always sceptical about this controversial spirit Shugden and it was natural, when I introduced restrictions, that he extended his full support to me and published a number of articles in support of my position. These articles were the cause of his death." These later articles have been reprinted in a short book entitled *An Honest Statement* (*Bden pa'i tshang thig*). In one article he wrote, "...The worship and propitiation of Dolgyal Dorje Shugden, by promoting a rabid form of sectarianism, has caused great trouble to the fabric of Tibetan society and hindered greatly the ability of the government to govern effectively. It harms Buddhism and the teaching of Tsong-khapa in particular by promoting a rabid form of Gelukpa sectarianism."

And in response to a Ms. Eileen Dickenson, the director of the Freedom Foundation, he wrote, "In her letter Ms. Dickenson refers to thousands of Tibetan people within the refugee communities in India who are being denied religious freedom. We Tibetans in exile, and there are more than one hundred thousand of us, do enjoy real religious freedom. The complaint against the Dalai Lama's government is baseless, therefore, and embodies a lie. What the Tibetan Government-in-Exile is saying is that the propitiation of Shugden harms the general cause of Tibet and hurts the Dalai Lama. The Dalai Lama has said this openly in the East and in the West. He has said so not once but again and again since 1978. The Shugden worshippers in the Tibetan settlement attacked the information officers of the Tibetan Government-in-Exile because they were saying this and because it was not something they wanted to hear. It is exactly like your letter Ms. Dickenson. It hurts me, it is not something I want to hear. But I do not come to attack you on that account."

It is noteworthy that although Gen-la felt very strongly about Shugden and wrote a great deal about the issue he never talked about it in the Institute or with his students. I was his student and translator for twenty years and he never mentioned the subject to me until some six months before he was murdered when I told him I had written an article about Shugden in reponse to reports in the foreign press that the Dalai Lama was being accused of religious intolerance.

Some British students in the Institute were also students of Kelsang Gyatso, who later became the main proponent of Shugden and the focus of the opposition to the Dalai Lama. They retain their respect for Kelsang Gyatso as a teacher, while deploring sectarianism. One of them, reflecting on sectarianism amongst Western disciples of Kelsang Gyatso, remarked, "I think the trouble in the foreign centers is because of the struggle the students have there to find a direction. Even if something is wrong the students embrace it fanatically because it seems to offer direction to the directionless. That is the big difference for a foreigner here at the Institute in Dharamsala. All know which direction they are going in here. You fit in with it and continue your study without making waves. In the foreign centers the people are seeking for ways to impress on others that they are sincere, and to convince themselves that what they are doing is worthwhile. There is much confusion on that account, a confusion which is totally absent in such a diverse Tibetan environment as Dharamsala. There are so many conflicting traditions and opinions here but everyone is still sure of themselves and not trying to prove anything to others.

"In all the years I lived in the school and was his interpreter, Gen-la never said one thing to me about different traditions or about Shugden. Since his death I have never set foot in his room and I know I will never set foot in his room again. Some people deal with it by talking about it but I know I will be too upset, it will bring back all the memories and I cannot deal with them. It is not denial. It is just a realization that while some can talk about it, with me the facade will evaporate and when the memories come back I will not be able to deal with my sorrow."

Even Gen-la's grandnephew Lobsang Yeshey recalls that he never mentioned Shugden or sectarianism. "When I first came from Tibet I had only intended that I would be a good servant to my Red Great-Uncle. Instead, he set me to studying. 'There would be nothing wrong in you being my servant,' he said. 'But if that is all you ever were to do, then when I am gone you will have nothing. So you must study.' He never said anything to me about Shugden. When he was murdered I had no thought. My mind went totally blank and I could only hear, as if far off, a faint dull noise.

THEY CAME IN THE EVENING just before dark and stabbed him. They stabbed him through the eye, cut his throat, and unkindest of all, stabbed him through his heart. It would be better if this were the ending to a story book, not a description of the end of the life of the outspoken

Tibetan monk who recorded these memoirs. But that is not to be. The entire Tibetan community was shocked. Tibet was a rough, even violent place but elderly, unarmed monks living alone were never the victims of murderous attacks.

When Sherab Gyatso came suddenly to the door of my room just before eight o'clock in the evening of the fourth of February and told me something terrible had happened, the thought flashed through my mind that it was the Chinese Communists sending a warning to the Dalai Lama not to go to Taiwan. But when I went out onto the street and one monk said that Gen-la had been murdered, I knew, as did everyone else, that it was to do with Gen-la's writing about Shugden.

In hindsight it was foolish to have moved Gen-la after he had been discovered dead. It would have been better to have left him in the room to help the police detect clues. But when you walk into the unlocked room of the abbot of a monastery next door to the Dalai Lama, you do not expect to find him stabbed to death, so the reaction of the monks, to somehow get him back to life even when it was obvious he was dead, is understandable. His two students were alive when they were found; they were peripheral in the attack, and in the end it was their bad luck to have been in the way. They were both gifted young Tibetan monks fluent in Chinese. One of the students was still groaning his life out in puddles of blood when I arrived at the hospital some twenty minutes or so after they had been found. The other had already died.

When you see a dear friend and guru dead, what you should or should not think is irrelevant, thoughts just come without any sense of shame. The thought came to me that my guru had tried every way possible to teach me the most basic Buddhist truth—that hatred and prejudiced opinions are the cause of great suffering. He was taking a rest from his hard work now, sure that he had conveyed at last what he had tried so hard to teach.

I did not see the wound to his heart until a policeman began to write out his report. I had left the hospital after about ten minutes to go down to the police station. I came back to the hospital immediately, and by the time the policeman began to write his report I had been standing beside his body for nearly two hours. Lobsang Yeshey pulled up his Red Great-Uncle's saffron sweater, quite reddened with blood. "*Thi bombo*" (butcher knife), he said when the wound became clearly visible. It was a terrible wound, into the kindness of a person, the place where Gen-la finally lived, a wound to make sure there was no retreat from which to return, and it sucked the mind, like a vortex, back down the path it had traveled. The point was needle sharp, the final peak of a tapering blade that got broader and broader towards the handle. The assassin had pushed it so deep inside I wondered if the knife had actually come out of Gen-la's back. The wound to his heart gaped; it and the cut to his throat, which the policeman measured and wrote down in his report, suggested long knifes, sharpened to a razor-like sharpness. Great sadness, those unfortunate and misguided young men who did those things. Great sadness, those who motivated them to do it. May all the good we do be theirs wherever they may be.

The people who killed Gen-la came upon an unarmed man, but they also came upon an extremely brave man. It is characteristic of Gen-la that in the seconds before he was murdered he grabbed a bag off one of his killers and grasped it so tightly to himself that they could not pry it loose. It is one of the main pieces of evidence in the case against the murderers, who now live in China and against whom the Indian police have initiated extradition procedures.

GEN-LA WAS INTENSELY LOYAL to the Dalai Lama, even while he was scathing in his criticism of other members of the Tibetan religious establishment. In the late 1970s Gen-la wrote a book in which he criticized the Dalai Lama's teacher Trichang Rinpoche for his propagation of the Shugden cult. Even though tame by Western standards, the Tibetan religious establishment—the gesheys and the lamas—were outraged. How could a nobody like Lobsang Gyatso, who was neither from an aristocratic family nor the head of a Tibetan region, indeed, not even a full graduate of a religious university, dare to criticize in print an important establishment figure? George Dreyfus at that time remarked that in pre-1959 Tibet Gen-la would have been killed outright for his temerity. Many in the Tibetan community ostracized Gen-la, even though the Dalai Lama had already by that time begun speaking publicly against the Shugden cult. Even the Dalai Lama appeared to distance himself from Gen-la. "He is headstrong and his lack of sensitivity is making trouble," seemed to be his attitude towards Gen-la at that time.

Gen-la's views differed slightly from the Dalai Lama's. Gen-la had a clear and pragmatic approach to the world, but I think he would agree that the Dalai Lama's views have always been superior to his own. The Dalai Lama has always been unwaveringly true to the principle of nonviolence. In Israel, when Gen-la was teaching his students there, he said that Israelis should not be stupid like Tibetans and mix up the duties of politicians with the duties of religious people. He said Tibet was lost to the Chinese because her religious people did not do what religious people should have been doing and her secular leaders were too involved in religion.

The Dalai Lama's views differ. He cannot, caught as he is in the role of secular and religious leader, separate out violent action and give it to the secular arm of the state. He has said, and I have no doubt that he means it, that he would like to get out of the role of Dalai Lama, and he has on more than one occasion suggested that Tibetans would do well to find a different institution for the supreme leadership of their country. But he cannot run away from the responsibility that fate, karma, or kindness has thrust upon him. He is the only leader Tibetans have and he therefore preaches an almost absolute form of nonviolence.

This explains, for me, the relationship he had with Lobsang Gyatso. The Dalai Lama's only personal public act after the death of Lobsang Gyatso was to publish a small booklet containing the three most profound prayers of Tsong-khapa in the name of his Institute of Buddhist Dialectics, and distribute it free to all who came to his New Year's teaching. During the afternoon break in his teaching he led everyone in recitation of the prayers. Only a small line at the end of the booklet said it was printed in memory of Gen-la. "This is what I did and my life has gone well," said the refrain to each verse of one prayer of Tsong-khapa, "thanks to you Lord, wellspring of understandings."

I was deeply moved by the Dalai Lama's tribute, not to a teacher or a student, but from one simple Buddhist monk to another. Not to descend into the gutter of the world, to stay true to one's ideals even when those most precious and defenseless are killed without mercy, is a true way to honor a departed friend. And the true way as well to reaffirm the values of the Gelugpa sect, to not allow it to be hijacked by fanatics, and to stay true to the sublime vision of its founder.

Sources used in the afterword:

Garfield, Jay L. Three page written remembrance of Lobsang Gyatso. Hobart, Tasmania, 1997.

Jabber, Sonia. Twenty-five minute interview with the Dalai Lama, with the Dalai Lama answering questions about his relationship with Lobsang Gyatso and his death. No date.

Lobsang Gyatso. *History of the Institute of Buddhist Dialectics.* Dharamsala, 1978.

——. Typewritten, 18 page memoir in English, no place or date.

——. *Bden pa'i tshang thig.* Institute of Buddhist Dialectics, Dharamsala, 1997.

Personal remembrances supplied orally by Claire Issit, Dondup Dorje, Elena Pakhoutov, Geleg (Max Redlich), Pema Dawa, Purushotam Ram, Sherab Gyatso, Pema Rinzing, Gelek, Kalsang Damdul, Kusang Chodron, Lobsang Yeshey, Mochog Rinpoche and Tenzin Tsepak.